LIGHT FROM ANCIENT LETTERS

LIGHT FROM ANCIENT LETTERS

JOHN L. WHITE

Fortress Press

Philadelphia

Library of Congress Cataloging in Publication Data

White, John Lee.
  Light from Ancient Letters.

  Bibliography: p.
  Includes indexes.
  1. Greek letters. 2. Letter-writing, Greek.
3. Bible. N.T. Epistles. 4. Fathers of the church.
5. Manuscripts, Greek (Papyri)—Egypt. I. Title.
PA3487.E43W49 1986   886'.01'08   85–16300
ISBN 0–8006–2110–7

TYPESET ON AN IBYCUS SYSTEM AT POLEBRIDGE PRESS

2094G86   Printed in the United States of America   1–2110

They say three is a perfect number and a holy one too.
So, this dedication is threefold.

To my parents, Frank W. and Clarice Mistler White

To my mother-in-law, Sophia Schalk Wacker

They are good tillers of the soil, patient cultivators of the spirit. May the harvest, offspring as well as produce, prove worthy of the labor.

To my academic father, Robert W. Funk

This book's publication coincides with his sixtieth birthday. Happy birthday, Bob.

Contents

Contents

Contents

Contents

Foundations & Facets: New Testament has two major divisions as indicated by the title.

Much of the more creative biblical scholarship on the contemporary scene is devoted to *Facets* of biblical texts: to units of the text smaller than canonical books, or to aspects of the New Testament that ignore the boundaries of books and canon. In one sense, *Facets* refers to any textual unit or group of units that does not coincide with the boundaries of canonical books. In another sense, *Facets* refers to aspects of the biblical materials that are being addressed by newly emerging biblical disciplines: literary criticism and its partner, narratology, and the social sciences in various guises. These two senses of *Facets* produce the second major division of the series with its two subdivisions: Literary Facets and Social Facets.

The creative and innovative impulses in current scholarship are also linked to emerging new methods in biblical criticism or to the reconception of old ones. In addition, the collections of primary comparative material made early in this century cry out to be replaced by new collections, at once more comprehensive and more scientifically structured. These two needs have shaped the first division of the series: *Foundations*. And *Foundations* are of two types: Reference works and Texts for Comparison.

Together, the two divisions of *Foundations & Facets* will form the basis for the next phase of biblical scholarship.

Polebridge Press
Riverbend 1986

Robert W. Funk, editor

First of all, I want to express my appreciation to Loyola University of Chicago from whom I received a paid research leave to begin writing this book in the fall of 1983. Special thanks is offered to J. Patout Burns and John Nilson, my former and present chairman respectively in the Theology Department.

My family has been patient for a long time and, though more recognition is called for than this written thanks can convey, I want to offer some words of appreciation. Thanks, Myrna, for continuing to be supportive when the project grew aggravating. And, to John Barak, Karis and Kristen, who are old enough to know about the birds and the bees but not old enough to understand the slow results of a father's research, thanks for loving me anyway.

Associates at Loyola rendered the following kinds of assistance. Margaret Watzek, my graduate assistant, compiled the indices for the book and, when we received page proofs, "Meg" helped me read the Greek in a painstaking manner. Carole Myscofski, a former colleague at Loyola University, collaborated on the translation and commentary of the Serapeum Correspondence (letters 34–42). She prepared an early translation and an early form of the commentary. James G. Keenan, Professor of Classical Studies at Loyola University, and a papyrologist, provided useful information on two or three technical matters in the book, including advice that caused me to exclude one letter from the collection.

Finally, the responsibility of turning the manuscript into an aesthetically pleasing and readable book became the task primarily of Stephanie A. Funk and Tami Haaland of Polebridge Press. Stephanie Funk supervised both the general design of the book and the arrangement of the individual parts. Tami Haaland is to be credited with turning my comments on technical subjects, occasionally expressed in a confusing manner, into engaging prose. The value of their collective work may be recognized in the finished product, but the reader would be even more impressed if the doors of the workshop were open to view.

Loyola University
June 1986

John L. White

Spelling of Names

The general practice in this book, following the precedent of Naphtali Lewis (*Life in Egypt*, p. ix) and several modern authors, is to transliterate rather than latinize Greek personal names and places: Philadelphos instead of Philadelphus, Kallikles and not Callicles. There are three exceptions. First, certain personal names are so familiar in an anglicized or latinized form that they are retained in that form: Ptolemy rather than Ptolemaios (except in letter headings), Cleopatra and not Kleopatra. Second, Latin personal names that appear in Greek letters from the Roman period are rendered in a latinized form: Caesar rather than Kaisar, Lucius Bellenus Gemellus rather than Loukios Bellenos Gemellos. Third, latinized forms introduced by the Roman government are used for certain place names: Hermopolis and not Hermoupolis, Coptus and not Koptos.

Method of Publication and Editorial Signs

Lines of Greek text correspond to the lines of Greek in the original letters. The lines are numbered sequentially, except for Greek lines on the verso. Since verso material is on the reverse side of the papyrus sheet and contains information that we place on the envelope (the outside address), it is treated as an independent entity and its lines are not numbered. When Greek letters are cited, from another collection or from this volume, the letter number is followed by line numbers. For example, 96.1–3 refers to letter 96, lines 1–3.

Accent and punctuation marks are added in conformity to modern usage. Where feasible, symbols in the original are rendered by an equivalent symbol. Iota adscript is generally printed if it appears in the original. Otherwise, iota subscript is used. The following editorial signs are used in the Greek texts.

[ ]   Square brackets indicate a lacuna in the original.
( )   Parentheses indicate the resolution of a symbol or abbreviation.
⟨ ⟩   Angle brackets indicate the enclosed letters were mistakenly omitted in the original.
[[ ]]   Double square brackets indicate the enclosed letters were deleted in the original.
{ }   Curly brackets indicate the enclosed letters are superfluous.
       Dots within brackets (. . . .) represent the approximate number of letters lost or deleted.
       Dots outside brackets indicate mutilated or otherwise illegible letters.
       A bar above a letter means the letter is used as a numeral.

Abbreviations

The abbreviations used to designate the published series or collections of papyri represented in this volume conform to those advocated by J. F. Oates, R. S. Bagnall and W. H. Willis in their *Checklist of Editions of Greek Papyri and Ostraca*. I do not always use the original edition as the primary basis for the Greek text. The edition which is followed most closely is identified first and the original or additional editions of the text follow in parentheses. For example, letter 4 in this book is identified as PYale 33 and another edition (the original) is identified in parentheses as (=PHib I 44).

The abbreviations of the twenty-one collections of papyri identified as the primary sources in this book are listed below.

BGU   *Aegyptische Urkunden aus den Königlichen* (later *Staatlichen*) *Museen zu Berlin, Griechische Urkunden*, vol. 1 (1895), nos. 1–361, edited by U. Wilcken, Fr. Krebs and Paul Viereck; vol. 2 (1898), nos. 362–696, edited by U. Wilcken, Fr. Krebs and Paul Viereck; vol. 4 (1912), nos. 1013–1209, edited by W. Schubart and others. Berlin: Weidmann.

CPJud   *Corpus Papyrorum Judaicarum*, vol. 1 (1957), nos. 1–141, edited by V. A. Tcherikover; vol. 2 (1960), nos. 142–450, edited by V. A. Tcherikover and A. Fuks. Cambridge, MA: Harvard University Press.

PAmh   *The Amherst Papyri. Being an Account of the Greek Papyri in the Collection of the Right Hon. Lord Amherst of Hackney, F.S.A. at Didlington Hall, Norfolk*, vol. 2: *Classical Fragments and Documents of the Ptolemaic, Roman and Byzantine Periods*, edited by B. P. Grenfell and A. S. Hunt. London: Oxford University Press, 1901.

PBour   *Les Papyrus Bouriant*, edited by P. Collart. Paris: Librairie Ancienne Honoré Champion, 1926.

PCairZen   *Zenon Papyri. Catalogue général des antiquités égyptiennes du Musée du Caire*, vol. 1 (1925), nos. 59001–139, edited by C. C. Edgar; vol. 2 (1926), nos. 59140–297, edited by C. C. Edgar; vol. 3 (1928), nos. 59298–531, edited by C. C. Edgar; vol. 5 (1940), nos. 59801–53, edited by O. Guéraud and P. Jouguet from Edgar's materials. Cairo: Service des antiquités de l'Egypte.

PCol   *Columbia Papyri, Greek Series*, vol. 3 (1934): *Zenon Papyri: Business Papers of The Third Century B.C. dealing with Palestine and Egypt*, nos. 2–59 edited by W. L Westermann and E. S. Hasenoehrl; vol 4 (1940), nos. 60–122, edited by W. L. Westermann, C. W. Keyes, and H. Liebesny. New York: Columbia University Press.

PFay   *Fayum Towns and their Papyri,* edited by B. P. Grenfell, A. S. Hunt and D. G. Hogarth. London: Egypt Exploration Fund, 1900.

PHib   *The Hibeh Papyri,* vol. 1, nos. 1–171, edited by B. P. Grenfell and A. S. Hunt. London: Egypt Exploration Society, 1906.

PLond   *Greek Papyri in the British Museum,* vol. 3, nos. 485–1331, edited by F. G. Kenyon and H. I. Bell. London: Oxford University Press, 1907.

PMert   *A Descriptive Catalogue of the Greek Papyri in the Collection of Wilfred Merton,* vol. 1, nos. 1–50, edited by H. I. Bell and C. H. Roberts. London: E. Walker, 1948. Vol. 2, nos. 51–100, edited by B. R. Rees, H. I. Bell, J. W. B. Barns. Dublin: Hodges Figgis, 1959.

PMich   *Michigan Papyri,* vol. 1 (1931): *Zenon Papyri,* nos. 1–120, edited by C. C. Edgar; vol. 3 (1936): *Miscellaneous Papyri,* nos. 131–221, edited by J. G. Winter and others; vol. 8 (1951): *Papyri and Ostraca from Karanis,* Second Series, nos. 464–521, edited by H. C. Youtie and J. G. Winter. Ann Arbor: University of Michigan Press.

PMilligan   *Selections from the Greek Papyri,* edited by G. Milligan. Cambridge: Cambridge University Press, 1910.

POslo Inv   "Three Private Letters from the Oslo Collection" (Oslo Papyri, nos. 1460, 1475), edited by S. Eitrem and L. Amundsen. *Aegyptus* 31 (1951): 177–83.

POxy   *The Oxyrhynchos Papyri,* vol. 1 (1898), nos. 1–207, edited by B. P. Grenfell and A. S. Hunt; vol. 2 (1899), nos. 208–400, edited by B. P. Grenfell and A. S. Hunt; vol. 4 (1904), nos. 654–839, edited by B. P. Grenfell and A. S. Hunt; vol. 7 (1910), nos. 1007–72, edited by A. S. Hunt; vol. 8 (1911), nos. 1073–1165, edited by A. S. Hunt; vol. 12 (1916), nos. 1405–1593, edited by B. P. Grenfell and A. S. Hunt; vol. 41 (1972), nos. 2943–98, edited by G. M. Browne, R. A. Coles, J. R. Rea, J. C. Shelton, E. G. Turner and others. London: Egypt Exploration Society.

PPrinc   *Papyri in the Princeton University Collections,* vol. 3, nos. 108–91, edited by A. C. Johnson and S. P. Goodrich. *Princeton University Studies in Papyrology 4.* Princeton: Princeton University Press, 1942.

PRyl   *Catalogue of the Greek Papyri in the John Rylands Library, Manchester,* vol. 2 (1915): *Documents of the Ptolemaic and Roman Periods,* nos. 62–456, edited by J. de M. Johnson, V. Martin and A. S. Hunt; vol. 4 (1952): *Documents of the Ptolemaic, Roman and Byzantine Periods,* nos. 552–717, edited by C. H. Roberts and E. G. Turner. Manchester: at the University Press.

PSI   *Papiri greci e latini (Pubblicazioni della Società Italiana per la ricerca dei papiri greci e Latini in Egitto),* vol. 4 (1917), nos. 280–445, edited by G. Vitelli, M. Norsa and others; vol. 5 (1917), nos. 446–550, edited by G. Vitelli, M. Norsa and others. Florence: Pubblicazioni della Società Italiana.

PTebt   *The Tebtunis Papyri,* vol. 1 (1902), nos. 1–264, edited by B. P. Grenfell, A. S. Hunt and J. G. Smyly; vol. 2 (1907), nos. 265–689, edited by B. P. Grenfell and A. S. Hunt; vol. 4 (1976), nos. 1094–1150, edited by J. G. Keenan and J. C. Shelton. London: Egypt Exploration Society.

PYale   *Yale Papyri in the Beinecke Rare Book and Manuscript Library,* vol. 1, nos. 1–85, edited by J. F. Oates, A. E. Samuel and C. B. Welles (*Am. Stud. Pap. II*) New Haven: Yale University Press, 1967.

SelPap   *Select Papyri,* vol. 1 (1932): *Private Affairs,* nos. 1–200, edited by A. S. Hunt and C. C. Edgar; vol. 2 (1934): *Official Documents,* nos. 201–434, edited by A. S. Hunt and C. C. Edgar. Loeb Classical Library. Cambridge, MA: Harvard University Press.

UPZ   *Urkunden der Ptolemäerzeit (ältere Funde),* vol. 1: *Papyri aus Unterägypten,* nos. 1–150, edited by U. Wilcken. Berlin-Leipzig: Walter de Gruyter, 1927. Vol. 2: *Papyri aus Oberägypten,* nos. 151–229, edited by U. Wilcken. Berlin: Walter de Gruyter, 1935–57.

The reader should consult the *Checklist of Editions of Greek Papyri and Ostraca,* compiled by Oates, Bagnall, and Willis, for other abbreviations of papyrus collections cited within the book.

Short titles used within this book may be identified by referring to the Bibliography (pp. 221–24). Standard biblical abbreviations have been used with the exception of GThom (Gospel of Thomas).

Opposite: Michigan Papyrus I 29
Senchons' letter to Zenon (letter 20). Written by a native Egyptian scribe with a brush rather than a pen. See the introduction to letter 20, p. 46, and see p. 214 for a more detailed description of writing methods in Graeco-Roman Egypt. The photograph is reproduced with the permission of the Department of Rare Books and Special Collections, The University of Michigan Library.

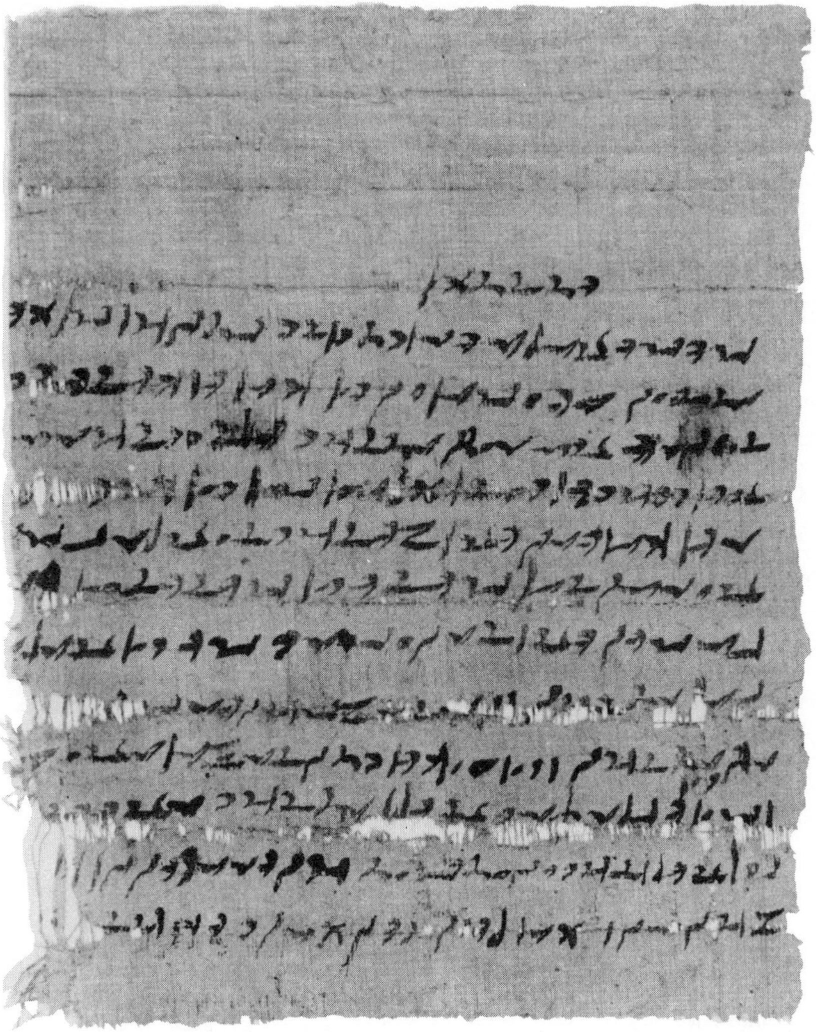

INTRODUCTION

1. PURPOSE

The primary purpose of this collection of letters, written on papyrus and discovered in Egypt, is to provide a comparative body of texts for assessing the epistolary character of the early Christian letter tradition found in the New Testament and the Early Church Fathers. There are at least two subsidiary purposes, however, which I intend for these sources to serve: (1) they may be used to illuminate broad environmental factors or conditions that aid in understanding Judaism and Christianity in the Graeco-Roman period; and (2) they contribute, in particular, to an understanding of socio-political and economic factors within Egypt itself during the same period. I will comment on these latter ideas eventually but first I want to explain how the letters in this volume were selected.

(a) Selection of Letters

In the course of working with two Society of Biblical Literature research groups for a decade on ancient letter writing, the larger lineaments of the present letter collection became clear to me. One of the most important lessons which I learned was that one should not study "secular" letters merely in order to find parallels to one or another feature in the Christian letter tradition. One needs an overview of Greek letter writing to properly assess the special character, if any, of Christian letters. Once it became evident that a working familiarity with the broader tradition was required, the means for accomplishing that end came gradually into view. It became clear, for example, that one could track the development of the stereotyped language, which was used to express the more common epistolary functions, by examining letters by period. Consequently, the present collection is arranged in chronological sequence, from the third century BCE to the third century CE, to illustrate the evolution of epistolary conventions.

These chronological limits were determined by the following considerations. The earliest extant Greek letters from Hellenistic Egypt, in any quantity, date from about 270–260 BCE. To properly map the evolution of Greek letter writing in Egypt, it seemed important to start at this earliest point. On the other hand, the number of letters would have been too great, if I had continued the collection up to the the Arab conquest in the seventh century CE. In any case, a letter collection which continues into the second or third century CE is broad enough to serve as a comparative body of sources for examining the early Christian letter tradition.

Allied with an understanding of chronological development and breadth, I realized, was a working familiarity with, and representation of, epistolary categories or types. However, considerably more flexibility in classification is required in this case than in chronological arrangement. So far as I can tell, the only discrete letter types which are identifiable according to stereotyped language and structural features are letters of recommendation, petitions, invitations, family letters and, perhaps, memoranda (these letter types are explained more fully in Part Two of this work). To properly represent something of the breadth of Greek letter writing, other means of classification were added. It seemed important, for example, to include letters from various societal levels, from both sexes, from different ethnic groups, and so on. As a result, the following are included in the present collection: letters from inferiors to superiors, from superiors to inferiors, and correspondence between social peers and family members; letters to and from women; correspondence from Greeks, Romans, native Egyptians and Jews; Ptolemaic and Roman administrative correspondence from various levels in the bureaucratic system; government and private business letters; friendly and family letters; and letters that reflect religious practice and belief. For the most part, I did not use these factors as an organizing principle within the letter collection. Two major exceptions are the Serapeum correspondence (letters 34–42) and the letters concerning Jewish troubles in Alexandria (letters 86–88).

Having made a case for inclusiveness, I must now admit that the breadth of this collection is limited to the documentary letter tradition, more commonly known as non-literary letters. Apart from the Emperor Claudius' letter to the Alexandrians (letter 88), neither literary letters nor Hellenistic royal (diplomatic) letters are included. Unlike the documentary letter tradition, the stylistic features of these categories of letters suggest that they were written with an eye to posterity as well as to the present. They contain primarily what the individual or the government wanted to be preserved. This distinction does not mean that literary letters and the diplomatic inscriptions are non-real letters. Nor is their exclusion intended to suggest that they are irrelevant to the study of early Christian letters. The use of rhetorical techniques, especially in the theological body of St. Paul's letters, indicates that a knowledge of these traditions is quite relevant to the study of early Christian letters.

The principal reason that they are excluded from the present collection is that their inclusion would have resulted either in an unwieldly volume or in a superficial representation of each of the three corpora of letters. The documentary letter tradition alone is both so large and so diverse that it warrants the 117 entries of this volume. A comparable collection and analysis of literary letters needs to be made, but there is less necessity for a volume of diplomatic inscriptions, since a number of Hellenistic royal letters were examined extensively by C. B. Welles several years ago.[1]

One sizeable segment of the documentary letter tradition was largely excluded from illustration. Apart from two texts in Eirene's archive, letters 30 and 33, I did not include legal contracts of various kinds (e.g., wills, marriage contracts, bills of sale), which, for one or another reason, happened to be written in the form of a letter. While working with one of the aforementioned research groups on ancient letter writing, Chan-Hie Kim and I edited a collection of documentary letters that included a number of these legal documents in letter form. But, since these documents have an identity independent of their epistolary form, and since their inclusion contributes little to distinctly epistolary considerations and limits the number of other letters that could be included, it seemed justifiable to limit their number in the present volume.

One other factor aided the selection and arrangement of this volume of letters. In order better to assess the relative status of any set of correspondents, and to understand better the details within any piece of correspondence, it was important to study multiple letters to or from the same correspondent(s). Though chronological constraints dictated that a representative number of letters be selected from each period, I attempted to include letters within each period which belonged to an individual's or a family's archive. Consequently, two-thirds of this collection are arranged according to archive, as well as by period. Most documentary letter archives are addressed to the same recipient, though a few are united by having the same sender. In the latter case, the letters are almost always first drafts that the sender kept for his own records. There are no examples of this latter type of archive, in which several letters have the same sender, in the present letter collection. However, the phenomenon is illustrated by a text within the Zenon archive (number 6) which contains five first drafts.

(b) Purpose and Scope of this Volume

The primary purpose of this letter collection, as indicated at the start, is to provide a comparative body of material for determining the early Christian letter tradition's dependence upon, or relation to, ordinary letter writing. To facilitate this end, the Greek documentary letter tradition is analyzed extensively in Part Two of the present volume. The actual comparison of Christian letters with ordinary letter writing lies outside the scope of the present study. That task will probably occupy a number of us for several years.

In this volume, however, I will defend the choice of ordi-

nary Greek letters as a comparative body of sources for studying the Christian letter tradition, and in the sixth and final section of this introduction, I will discuss some features of Christian letters with reference to the documentary letter tradition. The following subjects are treated in sections two through five of the Introduction to provide a proper background to the collection of documents in Part One: (2) the discovery and classification of papyrus documents; (3) the geography and climate in Egypt; (4) Greek and Roman administrative structure in Egypt; and (5) Hellenistic and Roman rule.[2] In addition to commenting upon political and economic factors in this last section, the relative status of each social class in Egypt, including Egyptian Jewry, is examined. Moreover, broad environmental forces are identified in section five, which are used to illustrate biblical details that are relevant to the understanding of Palestinian Judaism and primitive Christianity.

2. DISCOVERY AND CLASSIFICATION

(a) Sources of Papyri

The three principal sources of papyrus documents have been town and village rubbish heaps, some as high as thirty feet, ancient collapsed buildings and, finally, tombs and cemeteries.

The preservation of papyri in ancient ruins, the first two sources, coincides with the abandonment of villages, especially in the geographical depression known as the Fayum. The villages became ghost towns and their adjoining lands unproductive when, for various reasons, the government failed to maintain the irrigation system. Dry climatic conditions in the Fayum saved the documents from disintegration.

The papyri found in cemeteries, the third source of papyrus texts, unlike hieroglyphic and hieratic papyri that were discovered in tombs, were rarely placed in the tomb as part of the departed person's grave furnishings. Rather, the discovery of papyri in Fayum cemeteries arose as a result of a burial custom which was in vogue during the Ptolemaic period. Instead of the traditional linen, mummies were wrapped in cartonnage made of layers of discarded papyri, glued together like papier-mâché. The cartonnage, molded to the shape of the body, was covered with plaster and embellished with paint. These papyri have been recovered by breaking up the cartonnage coverings, by separating the layers and, finally, by removing the paint and plaster.

In addition to the human mummies, mummified crocodiles have been discovered at Tebtunis (the crocodile god Sobk was especially revered in the Fayum), wrapped in papy-

---

[1] *Royal Correspondence.*

[2] This last subject is presented in a broader survey than the subjects that precede it.

rus and sometimes with a roll or two inserted in the throat or other body cavities. These latter papyri (PTebt I) are, with few exceptions, from the second and early first centuries BCE.

(b) Discovery

European visitors of Egypt had begun returning home with ancient papyrus documents as early as the 1770s. It was in the late 1870s, however, before there were massive finds. These were accompanied by variously funded archaeological expeditions, which were organized deliberately for the purpose of excavating papyri.

The history of the major discoveries is an exciting subject. But it would take too much space to report even the main lineaments and to identify the most famous papyrologists. An interesting, and relatively thorough account of the story is told in E. G. Turner's *Greek Papyri*.[3] The comments by Grenfell, Hunt, and Hogarth in *Fayum Towns and their Papyri*[4] are also illuminating and a shorter, more recent, description is given by Naphtali Lewis in his book, *Life in Egypt under Roman Rule*[5] Lewis estimated in 1981 that some 25,000 papyri of Roman date alone had already been published and that twice that number from the same period probably still remained to be edited and published.[6]

(c) Classification

The papyri have been classified, in general, according to two main categories: literary and documentary (non-literary). It is of little consequence that timeless literary texts are written on papyrus rather than on some other writing material. The documentary papyri, by contrast, are of considerable moment for illuminating the political, economic, and social conditions of the time when they were written. Large quantities of Graeco-Roman ostraca have also been discovered and, because of the nature of the writing which they contain, they have become a valuable supplementary resource for information gleaned from documentary papyri. In fact, they have been included traditionally in the science of papyrology. Physical characteristics of the ostraca, notably their limited space and the nature of the writing surface,

result necessarily in briefer information than what is found on the papyri. They contain lists, short letters or notes, school exercises and, above all, tax receipts.

The documentary papyri are, of course, the subject of the present collection of texts. They have sometimes been subdivided into two classes of texts, official and private. Since there is some ambiguity in the use of these terms, it will prove helpful, at least in reference to letters, to provide a fuller explanation of these categories.

When F. X. J. Exler applied the designation "official" to Greek letters, he was referring to the administrative correspondence of Hellenistic and Roman Egypt which emanated from the various levels of the administrative system.[7] There is some warrant, it seems to me, in identifying administrative correspondence explicitly as official. On the other hand, benefactions and similar messages from Hellenistic kings and Roman emperors should probably be classified more specifically as "diplomatic" or "royal" correspondence, in the manner of C. B. Welles' study of such correspondence.[8] The designation "private" needs to be extensive enough to include all correspondence in the personal domain, whether it concerns business or family.

(d) Dating Documentary Letters

Some extant papyri from Graeco-Roman Egypt were written either in Latin or in the native Egyptian language, called Demotic in its late form of writing. The vast majority were written in Greek, however, even during the Roman rule of Egypt. Since most documents were written in Greek for several centuries, it is sometimes not easy to date a text.

Fortunately, documents of an official or contractual/legal nature were usually dated. Under Roman rule, and apparently also under the later Ptolemies, it was customary to give the regnal year of the present ruler, followed by the month and day. Greater difficulty arises in dating early Ptolemaic documents and in converting dates to the Roman (Julian) calendar. This is the case, in part, because of differences between the Macedonian and the native Egyptian year (which was essentially equivalent to the Roman year)[9] and partly be-

---

[3] *Greek Papyri*, pp. 17–41.
[4] *Fayum Towns*, pp. 17–74.
[5] *Life in Egypt*, pp. 1–8.
[6] *Life in Egypt*. p. 6.
[7] *Ancient Greek Letter*, p. 23.
[8] *Royal Correspondence*.
[9] Whereas the Egyptian year consisted of twelve months of thirty days, plus five intercalary days, Macedonian months were lunar, with an average length of twenty-nine and one-half days. In dating papyrus documents, the ordinary practice was to count six Macedonian months full (thirty days each) and six short months (twenty-nine days each), with the full and short months alternating from year to

year. Though Macedonian months were lunar, the year was professedly solar and was assimilated to the solar year by the occasional insertion of an extra month. The following studies are helpful in converting early Ptolemaic dates into the Egyptian and Roman calendar: C. C. Edgar, "The Problem of Dating"; T. C. Skeat, *The Reign of the Ptolemies*; and Alan Samuel, *Ptolemaic Chronology*.

Before the end of the second century BCE, the Macedonian calendar was adapted to the Egyptian year and lost its lunar character. Edgar and Hunt (SelPap I, p. xvf) set out in tabular form the correspondences from that time forward between the Macedonian, Egyptian and Roman months.

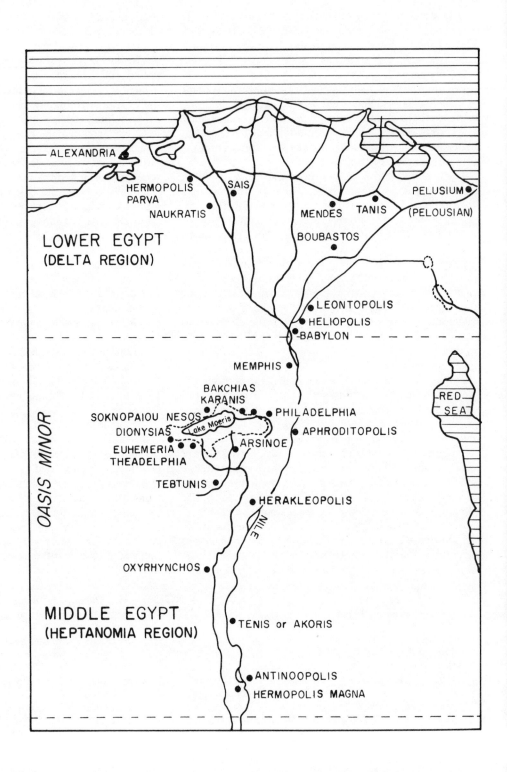

ALEXANDRIA

HERMOPOLIS
PARVA

SAIS

PELUSIUM

NAUKRATIS

MENDES   TANIS

(PELOUSIAN)

BOUBASTOS

LOWER EGYPT
(DELTA REGION)

LEONTOPOLIS

HELIOPOLIS

BABYLON

MEMPHIS

BAKCHIAS
KARANIS

SOKNOPAIOU NESOS   PHILADELPHIA

DIONYSIAS   Lake Moeris   APHRODITOPOLIS

EUHEMERIA   ARSINOE
THEADELPHIA

OASIS MINOR

TEBTUNIS

HERAKLEOPOLIS

RED
SEA

NILE

OXYRHYNCHOS

MIDDLE EGYPT
(HEPTANOMIA REGION)

TENIS or AKORIS

ANTINOOPOLIS

HERMOPOLIS MAGNA

*This page and
opposite:*
Maps of the three
major geographical
and administrative
divisions of Graeco-
Roman Egypt.

6

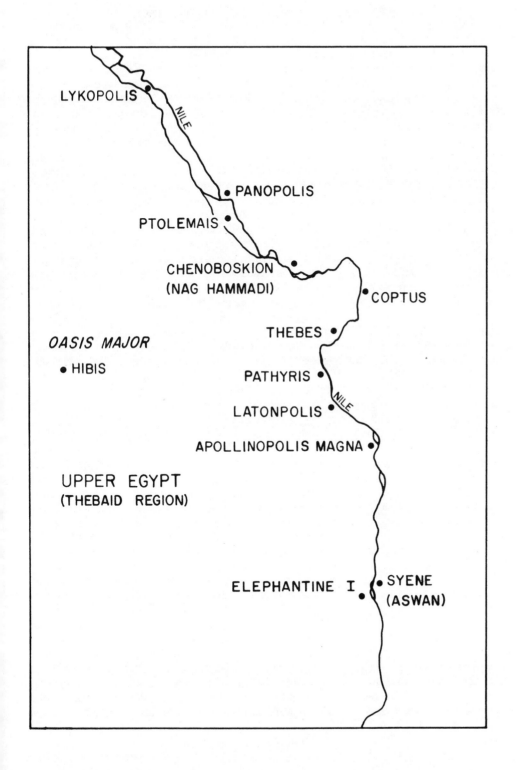

cause documents were dated to the financial year as well as to the regnal year.

Private documents are frequently not dated. But, if the papyrus either is found with, or turns out to belong to, a body of documents which are dated, its approximate date may also be established. However, when this type of control is missing, other more flexible guidelines may be employed. For example, a broad index is provided by the well-known fact that earlier papyri were superior in quality to the later writing material. An Egyptian Ramesside papyrus was extremely well made, light, and of fine, even texture. By comparison, a good quality sheet manufactured in the Ptolemaic period, a thousand years later, was both heavier and thicker, though still of good quality. Sheets from the Roman period tended to be still heavier and coarser and, from the third century CE onward, the quality of ordinary papyrus deteriorated markedly so that, as E. G. Turner describes it, papyrus came to resemble cardboard.[10]

Admittedly, this means of dating papyrus texts is relatively imprecise. There are at least two other means of determining approximate date which, though not adequate to establish a hard-and-fast chronology, are somewhat more precise.

The one is a working knowledge of the evolution of handwriting patterns from one age to another. It is nearly axiomatic that whereas early Ptolemaic documents tended to separate letters and to form them in a manner reminiscent of Greek inscriptions, letters became increasingly ligatured or cursive with the passage of time. Fortunately, the thousands of dated papyri comprise a sufficient body of palaeographical data of handwriting patterns that a document's date may often be determined within a few decades.

Comparable dating may be accomplished through a knowledge of the evolutionary stages through which formulaic phraseology passed in the various kinds of documents. Though the essential structure of certain types of writings remained constant, the stereotyped language which was employed to express these customary features underwent certain modifications. Several of these patterns are illustrated concretely in connection with epistolary writing in Part Two of this work.

3. GEOGRAPHY AND CLIMATE

(a) The Nile and Agriculture

The single most important physical feature of ancient Egypt was the Nile River. Habitable areas were defined by its course and without it the entire region would have been desert wasteland. H. I. Bell aptly compared this arable area to a tadpole with a very long tail.[11] The head of the tadpole, of course, was the fertile delta of Lower Egypt—an equilateral triangle of roughly 120 miles on a side—where the Nile fanned out into seven branches enroute to emptying into the Mediterranean Sea. The tail was the Nile River Valley proper of Middle and Upper Egypt, which ranged from six to twelve miles in width. The only other arable area of any size (and it constitutes an exception to our tadpole's anatomy) was the natural depression of the Fayum (named from a Coptic word for lake), about sixty miles southwest of Cairo. It was an area of about 640 square miles that was fed by a branch of the Nile which fed, in turn, an elaborate network of irrigation canals before it formed a "dead" sea. The only other habitable parts of Egypt were the oases, watered by subterranean wells or springs.

Despite the limited amount of arable land in Egypt, agriculture was, and is, the primary economic base. In the eyes of the Greeks and Romans, Egypt was legendary for its productivity. This productivity was directly dependent on the annual flooding of the Nile which provided not only the means of irrigating the arable areas but which also fertilized the fields by leaving large quantities of rich silt behind after the river had returned to its bed. According to Naphtali Lewis, the ancient inhabitants were aware that crop size was proportionate to the height of the Nile flood: a twelve cubit rise was too little, and near drought resulted; an eighteen cubit rise was too much, since the waters did not recede quickly enough for farmers to get into the fields for planting; sixteen cubits was just right.[12]

There were various ancient theories which tried to account for the annual inundation. We now know that melting snows from mountains in Ethiopia swelled tributaries of the Nile, and that the Nile began overflowing its banks when it entered Egypt at Elephantine in early June. It was roughly a month later that it reached the area of the Fayum (the Arsinoite nome). For the first month or so the flood waters' penetration of cultivable areas was slow, but shortly thereafter its level rose sharply and it continued to rise for nearly two more months, so that the entire flood plain took on the appearance of a broad lake. By mid-September the flood had begun to recede in the Arsinoite nome (by mid-August at Elephantine) and by the end of October the river had returned to its bed and the planting of cereal crops was begun.

The effectiveness of the annual inundation was enhanced by an irrigation system, particularly elaborate in the broad basin of the Fayum, which was first engineered by the Pharaohs and was expanded under the Ptolemies. Parts of the system were allowed to fall into disrepair under the last

---

[10] *Greek Papyri*, p. 2.
[11] *Egypt*, pp. 1f.

[12] *Life in Egypt*, pp. 109–10.

Ptolemies, but when Augustus annexed Egypt to Rome his soldiers and compulsory work gangs rebuilt crumbling dikes and cleaned out cluttered channels. Thereafter, regular maintenance was ensured through a dike tax and by requiring every able-bodied male to work a certain quota of unpaid days each year on the dikes and canals. Flood waters were directed onto the grain fields by means of the irrigation canals. After a few days, the fields were drained off. Then, sheep or other small livestock were frequently turned in to graze upon the fields, for the purpose of fertilizing them prior to planting.[13]

(b) Other Resources
In addition to the agricultural productivity assured to Egypt by means of the annual inundation of the Nile, physical conditions were significant in at least one other positive respect: Egypt's relative inaccesibility. Desert borders, both to the East and the West, and the Mediterranean Sea on the North, made the kingdom of the Ptolemies the longest lasting of all the Hellenistic states.

In the settlement at Babylon in the summer of 323 BCE, Ptolemy, who had the first choice of states, wisely chose Egypt as his satrapy. Despite Egypt's great wealth and easily defended borders, however, there were certain negative aspects of the physical setting. For example, timber was scarce and trees were so small in diameter that heavy construction lumber had to be imported. Though not so scarce as timber, stones constituted another kind of problem as a building material. All mineral deposits, including rocks, had to be dug from quarries or mines that lay mostly in Upper and Middle Egypt between the Nile and the Red Sea. The isolated location of most mines, the difficult labor required to dig the rocks, and the adverse weather conditions of the desert made mining rock and ore very unpleasant work. All mineral deposits were state property and N. Lewis notes that, because of the severe working conditions, manpower was obtained by one of two principal means. Either the government leased the mine or quarry to a private contractor, who attracted workers by offering premium wages, or the state compelled lower-class criminals and slaves to work the mines and quarries.[14] In the frontier provinces of the Roman Empire, lower military ranks might also be required to quarry stone for the construction of roads, cisterns, aquaducts, fortifications, and so on.[15] Unfortunately, after rock in Egypt was quarried, it still had to be transported overland to the Nile and, then, it had to be loaded onto specially built barges to be carried up or downstream as needed. From there, it had, once again, to be transported overland to worksites. It is little wonder that ordinary construction was of sun-dried brick, made everywhere in Egypt from mud provided by the Nile. Stones and kiln-fired brick were reserved for special needs, e.g., to provide wells with an impermeable lining and to face public buildings.

4. GREEK AND ROMAN ADMINSTRATIVE STRUCTURE

(a) Greek Administrative Structure
1) *The crown.* The absolute source of authority in Egypt throughout the Ptolemaic period was the crown, represented by the king and queen who, from about the mid-third century BCE, were accorded the status of divinity during their own lifetimes. All departments of state, finance, justice, public works, and the military were ultimately under their control. During the reign of Ptolemy II Philadelphos in particular (285–246 BCE), who established the lineaments of the central administrative system, the crown closely supervised these departments. Needless to say, a considerable amount of paper work was generated at this topmost level through the promulgation of financial and legal ordinances, by means of decrees on a number of subjects, and at least in the earlier period, because demands for redress were frequently addressed to the king and queen. Whether the rulers or their representatives dictated the communiques, the royal chancellery was always busy. The offices of *epistolographos* ("letter writer") and *hypomnematographos* ("memoranda writer") are identified as types of chancellery secretaries.

2) *The dioiketes.* The second most influential figure in the administrative system was the *dioiketes*. As the king's minister of finance, he was responsible for elaborating all details of taxation and for collecting all revenues. His office was responsible for drafting and revising the regulations governing royal monopolies. He supervised agricultural production on crown lands and the collection of rent on crops through periodic tours on which he inspected his subordinates' records in each of the administrative districts of Egypt. In addition to inspecting the operation of various phases of state work, the dioiketes decided certain kinds of judicial cases during these tours. The concerns with which he had to deal during such tours, both legal and agricultural in nature, are illustrated in the correspondence which the dioiketes Apollonios received in letters 9–19 of this collection. Apollonios was the minister of finance under Philadelphos (Ptolemy II Philadelphos). Zenon, who was Apollonios' private secretary during the tours illustrated in letters 9–19, docketed all the correspondence as it came in, recording where it was received and the date of receipt.

3) *Other offices.* The country was divided into some thirty

---

[13] See the comments on letter 95.
[14] Lewis, *Life in Egypt*, pp. 137f.

[15] See letter 105, written by a soldier in Arabia to his family in Egypt.

administrative districts called *nomoi*, a Greek word anglicized as "nomes." The governor of each nome was an official with the military title of *strategos*. His chief assistant had the title of "royal secretary" (*basiliko-grammateus*) and, whenever the office of strategos was temporarily vacant, he filled in as his replacement. The chief financial officer of the nome was the *oikonomos* who, at the district level, had responsibilities comparable to the dioiketes. The oikonomos worked closely, as we might expect, with the district bank, whose chief officer was the *trapedzites*. The accounts of the oikonomos and the trapedzites, respectively, were examined and verified by officials with the titles of *antigrapheus* and *dokimastes*. Because of their similar function, the titles of both these latter officials may be rendered in English as "controller."[16] By the second century BCE, the office of oikonomos seems to have been largely overshadowed by the strategos. Other subordinate officials were the nomarch, the toparch, and "district secretary" (*topogrammateus*). Each nome had an administrative capital or center, the *metropolis*. Following the precedent of Naphtali Lewis,[17] we may call these metropoleis "towns," as a means of differentiating them from the three cities in Ptolemaic times and the four cities in Roman times which had the status of Greek "cities" (*poleis*).

Six metropolitan offices are mentioned in extant sources (i.e., *gymnasiarch, kosmetes, exegetes, eutheniarch, agoranomos,* and *archiereus*), in addition to the ones we have already identified. These latter offices are honorary designations, however, governing responsibilities related to social functions within the towns themselves, rather than governmental offices. At the village level we find the following administrative offices: the komarch, the "village secretary" (*komogrammateus*), and the chief of police (*epistates*).[18]

There are certain other offices and functions identified in the available evidence, but this is sufficient to indicate the main lineaments of Ptolemaic administrative structure.

(b) Roman Adminstrative Structure

1) *The emperor and the prefect.* Following the defeat of Antony and Cleopatra in 30 BCE by Octavian, afterwards known as Augustus, Egypt was ruled by Rome. Augustus' policies made it clear that he regarded Egypt, like the Pharaohs and Ptolemies had, as his own preserve. While certain other Roman provinces were governed by Romans with the rank of proconsul, in Egypt the emperor appointed a lower ranking prefect to govern. Thus, Augustus was assured that the post would always be filled by a member of the equestrian order, his own class of origin and an order habitually loyal to Augustus.

The senate possessed no authority in Egypt and no one of

senatorial rank was even allowed to visit Egypt without the express consent of the emperor. Though all important policies were decided by the absent emperor in Rome, the prefect normally functioned in the capacity of the Ptolemaic king. He commanded the army, administered civil affairs and exercized judicial authority. Like the Ptolemaic dioiketes, the prefect made periodic inspection tours of the various administrative districts and, during these tours, also held assizes.

Though we are not certain of the respective judicial functions of the following, the prefect was assisted by officials with the titles of *iuridicus, archidikastes, exegetes, idios logos,* and *dioiketes*. One or more of these figures accompanied him on his inspection tours.

2) *Other offices.* Augustus retained the traditional division of the country into nomes. These nomes were grouped into three large divisions, each of which was governed by a Roman of equestrian rank with the title of *epistrategos*. These three divisions were, from north to south, the Delta, Heptanomia and Arsinoite nome, and Thebaid. As in the Ptolemaic period, the strategos presided at the nome level, assisted by the royal secretary, nomarchs, and other subordinates. The most active functionaries in the villages were still the village secretaries, until they were superseded by the komarchs in the third century CE. The three cities of Alexandria, Naukratis, and Ptolemais continued to enjoy certain privileges as Greek cities (poleis). The emperor Hadrian founded a fourth city of similar standing in 130 CE, Antinoopolis, to commemorate his handsome young companion Antinous, who had drowned during a trip on the Nile.

(c) Roman Changes in Greek Adminstration

The administrative structure appeared to remain essentially the same under Roman rule, apart from the use of Roman personnel to fill the higher offices and the use of Roman nomenclature to identify the top positions. But in fact, substantive changes were effected in the actual implementation of Roman rule. Much of the original authority of the Ptolemaic dioiketes was now vested in a distinctly Roman official, the prefect. Certain other financial responsibilities were divided with a subordinate, but important official, who was given jurisdiction over the emperor's private purse.

Regarding this private account, Augustus set out a number of regulations governing the various means whereby financial penalties and private property could be exacted by the state. These regulations which had the technical title, *The Gnomon of the Idios Logos* (literally, "the rule of the private account"), were administered by a Roman appointed by

---

[16] See the introductory comments on letters 1–4.
[17] *Life in Egypt.*

[18] Cf. letter 48.

The Agricultural Schedule in the Fayum (Arsinoite nome)

Roman Calendar	Egyptian Calendar	Agricultural Schedule
June	Payni	The rise of the Nile begins. The harvest of cereal crops ends. Threshing continues.
July	Epeiph	The Nile accelerates its rise and enters flood stage. Threshing ends.
August	Mesore	The Nile approaches full inundation. The season of gathering grapes begins.
September	Thoth	The inundation peaks and begins to fall. The grape season is completed. The date harvest begins.
October	Phaophi	The Nile flood is past and the sowing of cereal crops begins. The date harvest reaches its peak. Olive gathering begins.
November	Hathyr	Sowing of cereal crops continues. Cultivation begins. Olives continue to be gathered and the date harvest ends.
December	Choiach	Cultivation continues. Olive gathering continues.
January	Tybi	The olive harvest ends. The new season for vines and olives begins.
February	Mecheir	Preparations begin for the harvest of cereal (grain) crops.
March	Phamenoth	Preparations for the grain harvest continue.
April	Pharmouthi	The grain harvest begins.
May	Pachon	The grain harvest continues. Threshing begins.

Adapted from Naphtali Lewis, *Life in Egypt*, pp. 115–16.

the emperor himself. It is clear from the stringent nature of the regulations that they were intended to impede social advancement from one social strata to another.[19]

All administrative posts, other than the higher level offices, were filled with descendants of the Macedonians and Greeks. Since administrative affairs were still conducted in the Greek language, the central chancellery office in Alexandria included bilingual staff members who translated Latin communications from the emperor and prefect into Greek before distribution to the general populace.

But, even in these examples, there is more change than is apparent at first glance. In particular, we may note the manner in which Ptolemaic titles at the nome level were redefined under Roman rule. For example, though the governor of the nome was still styled strategos, he no longer retained the military authority which he had under the Ptolemies. He now had only civil authority. The only military officials in Roman Egypt were those of the Roman armed forces. Comparable changes had been effected in certain other posts. We have already referred to the manner in which the authority of the Ptolemaic dioiketes was replaced by the authority of the prefect and the administrator of the idios logos. Though the office of dioiketes still appears in documents, it is obvious that the post had diminished in authority.

As a result of these and other changes, the social, political, and economic structures of Roman Egypt, though ostensibly a continuation of the Ptolemaic patterns, resulted, in fact, in a more impersonal and harsh set of living conditions.

5. HELLENISTIC AND ROMAN RULE IN EGYPT

(a) Evaluation of Hellenistic Rule

There are two broadly divergent assessments of the Ptolemies' disposition toward their native subjects. One group maintains that throughout the long period of Ptolemaic rule, Egyptian natives were bitterly oppressed and that the Ptolemaic god-king, who conceived of Egypt as his private estate, had no interest in the native people other than to see that they filled the royal granaries and the banks of the royal *oikos*. Moreover, according to this viewpoint, whereas the Macedonians and other Greeks who streamed into Egypt were accorded privileged positions of authority over the indigenous inhabitants, little legislation, if any, was enacted by the Ptolemies for the welfare of their Egyptian subjects. The second perspective, by contrast, while agreeing in the fundamentals, arrives at a positive estimation of the dynasty's aims and concludes, furthermore, that Ptolemaic administrative

enactments and decrees were constructive in their effects upon the native element.

This latter perspective is the one which I find confirmed by the evidence, some of which will be illustrated shortly. Even this second perspective, however, is not excessive in its praise of the Ptolemies. By and large, Ptolemaic rule is regarded as an expression of benevolent paternalism or, stated in slightly different terms, as an enlightened self-interest that was guided by practical considerations. Notwithstanding, according to W. L. Westermann, there was an attractive directness in the honest justification of actions offered by the Ptolemaic king and his bureaucrats. Instead of appealing to right for right's sake, Ptolemaic administrators frankly advised their subordinates to act in a certain manner because it was advantageous to the crown.[20]

1) *The early Ptolemies*. Any adequate evaluation of Ptolemaic rule must take into account the amount of political, economic, and social innovation that was actually feasible in Egypt. Certain political and economic factors were so entrenched in Egypt that, in order for the Ptolemies successfully to continue in the land, Ptolemaic policy had to work within these limits. For example, the paternalistic conception that the country was the king's private, "feudal" estate, and that the king and queen were gods of the land, were certainly Oriental absolutist ideas and not ideas native to Greek thinking. Similarly, eastern bureaucratic absolutism was incompatible with the autonomous organization of the Greek city state. It is to the Ptolemies' credit that they were able to graft Hellenic culture onto a centralized administrative structure that was geared to the socialization of production.

The Ptolemies' ability to work within an Oriental system was aided by certain fortunate congruences between Ptolemaic rule and Egyptian culture. Diodorus and Curtius report that the Egyptians hated the Persians because they had committed impieties against the temples and, in general, because they had governed harshly.[21] Not only did the Macedonians have the advantage, initially, of being welcomed as liberators from the Persians, there was less intrinsic occasion, subsequently, for the kind of hatred which the Persians had generated. Egyptian polytheism, so offensive to Persian culture, was acceptable to, and compatible with, Greek religiosity.

Correspondingly, the Persian king had been an absent god, remote from the rule of his Egyptian habitat and, moreover, precisely because of his distance, he had tried to dismantle the centralized, administrative structure of Egypt. Initially, administrative arrangments under Alexander were also unworkable. Absent from Egypt, and trusting no one very much, Alexander divided the rule of Egypt to commanders with equal status. When Soter became ruler, however,

[19] See Lewis, *Life in Egypt*, pp. 32–35.
[20] Westermann, "The Ptolemies," p. 284.
[21] Geer, *Diodorus of Sicily*, 17.49.2; Rolfe, *Quintus Curtius*, 4.7.1.

he made use of the traditional bureaucratic system, including the use of natives to fill certain offices, both because he had taken up residence in Egypt and because this system was easier to implement in the early years of his reign than any other alternative. Though Soter preferred Greeks for his administrative offices and army, he was in no position initially to reject Egyptian support. Papyri from the reign of Soter are limited, but Diodorus indicates that Soter secured considerable military support at Gaza[22] and texts from Elephantine show that Greek officials and institutions were not common during this early period of Ptolemaic rule.[23] Eventually, Soter was able to replace, or at least balance, the higher bureaucratic ranks with Greeks.[24]

During the reign of Philadelphos, Greeks and other aliens streamed into Egypt and Philadelphos engaged them both as administrative overseers of the native cultivators and as the resource for his regular army. The extent to which the status of the native soldiers was devalued under Philadelphos, and perhaps already by the end of Soter's reign, is indicated by letter 4 in the collection. Consequently, though the rule of the early Ptolemies represents an accommodation to Egyptian political and economic structures, the first three Ptolemies—who ruled roughly during the first one hundred years—were also strongly Macedonian and Hellenic in significant respects. In addition to the diminution of the native soldiers' status, the native element generally was treated as a conquered people and the power of the Egyptian priesthood, the principal rallying-point of national sentiment, was severely curtailed.

2) *The later Ptolemies.* Despite the strength of the early Ptolemies, the process of "de-Hellenization" was almost inevitable because of the aforementioned constraints, and that process was hastened by policies of the feeble rulers who followed.

One policy of considerable consequence was precipitated by an event early in the reign of Ptolemy IV Philopater (221–203 BCE). The young Seleucid king, Antiochos III, had decided to reconquer Palestine. Since the regular Egyptian army had not been properly maintained, Philopater abandoned the traditional policy of the two immediately preceding Ptolemies and enlisted a large body of native Egyptians which he armed and trained in the Macedonian manner. Philopater met Antiochos at Raphia in 217 BCE and the Egyptian army was victorious. Rendered confident by their share in the triumph, the native element began to offer a bolder front and, according to H. I. Bell, they become more prone to revolt, so that Philopator and his successors had to

grant more and more concessions. Bell illustrates the process by showing how Ptolemy VIII Euergetes II was driven to grant a number of concessions to the peasant masses following the revolt of the Thebaid in 131–118 BCE.[25]

I agree with Bell that, under the later Ptolemies, certain Egyptian elements (most notably, the native soldiers and the native priesthood) regained some of their former status. But unfortunately Bell interprets Egyptian revolts too narrowly as nationalistic uprisings. For example, the revolt of 131–118 BCE was occasioned by the interdynastic struggle between Cleopatra II and her crown brother, Euergetes II, rather than by native unrest. The violence erupted along party lines, both among the Greeks and the Egyptians; one side was loyal to the queen and the other supportive of Euergetes. The joint decrees issued in 118 BCE, which reflect the reconciliation of Cleopatra and Euergetes, were occasioned by the fact that the rival governments had each made land grants to their own constituencies, which went unrecognized by the opposition party. The decrees acknowledged that present ownership was valid, regardless of whether the land had been granted by Cleopatra or Euergetes.[26]

In short, it is inaccurate both to interpret the violence of 131–118 BCE as a nationalistic revolt and to explain the concessions which followed upon that confusion as the appeasement of the native element. It is true that latent nationalistic sentiment seems to have been awakened in the revolt of Dionysius Petosiris in 165 BCE[27] and that nativisitic revolution erupted early in the first century BCE in the Thebaid, following upon the rebellion of native leaders in the ancient city of Thebes (see letters 56–58). Nonetheless, the amount of nationalistic rebellion is exaggerated. In the case of the revolt of the Thebaid, interdynastic tension and weakness of the central government was once again a contributing factor. Moreover, native revolt was more endemic to the Thebaid, both because of physical distance from Alexandria and because of the status of Thebes as a center of ancient nationalistic sentiment.

Similarly, the second century BCE prophecies of a messianic deliverer reflect the interests of the native priesthood much more than the feeling of the masses. Eventually, the prophecies would be appropriated by the masses, but that state of affairs seems not to have emerged until rule by Rome began. In general, the rebellion and confusion of the last two centuries BCE appear to result more from internal weakness and division within Ptolemaic rule than from anything else.

3) *Egypt's Welfare.* Having referred generally to the manner in which the utilitarian and economic interests of the

---

[22] Geer, *Diodorus of Sicily,* 19.80.4.

[23] For example, there are no references in Rubensohn, *Aegyptische Urkunden* (*PEleph* 1–4) to governmental officials.

[24] See C. B. Welles, "The Role of the Egyptians," p. 508.

[25] "Hellenic Culture in Egypt," p. 147.

[26] See the introductory comments to letter 43.

[27] See the introductory comments to letters 34–42.

Ptolemaic dynasty contributed to the welfare of the Egyptian subjects, I want now to illustrate the dynasty's contribution by means of specific examples. In particular, two measures of Ptolemy II Philadelphos, though clearly introduced to serve the aims of the crown, contributed nonetheless to the welfare of the country. They were: (1) his vast land reclamation project in the Fayum, and (2) his issue of Revenue Laws and the creation of an oil monopoly.

One of the major problems of the new Hellenistic kingdoms was the tendency of their mercenary troops to defect under adverse battle conditions. Philadelphos devised the plan of binding his soldiers more tightly to the land of Egypt by granting them land allotments or *kleroi*, varying in size according to their rank and extent of service.

A practical difficulty in the implementation of Philadelphos' project was the possibility that any redistribution of arable land could disturb both the production of food and the stability of village life. Egypt's former stability and its strong central government had been achieved by binding Egyptian peasants to the hereditary cultivation of crown lands that bordered on their villages. Artisans were similarly limited in choice of occupation and movement. Consequently, lest he alter an effective system, Philadelphos began his land reclamation in the Fayum where, under Persian rule and during the later Pharaohs, the irrigation system had been allowed to deteriorate and the amount of arable land had dwindled steadily. By granting land allotments to his administrative staff and soldiers, and by limiting taxes on the land until it became productive, Philadelphos secured greater continuity of service from the Greek and alien elements.

Improvement on the personal land grants enhanced the general stability of the Fayum and contributed thereby to the greater productivity of crown land, which was the greater proportion of arable land in the area. Moreover, even gift lands were granted with the intention of serving state interests, e.g., the state worked closely with private landowners in determining the types and percentage of crops or orchards that were to be planted. Ultimately, the Ptolemaic project embodied the Egyptian idea that the king was the sole proprietor of the land. And yet, in its total effect, the land reclamation project was quite humanitarian.

The second policy from Philadelphos' reign which contributed to the crown's control of agricultural production, while simultaneously securing the stability of the masses, is the Revenue Laws. The Revenue Laws dealt with the establishment of a state controlled oil monopoly. The foodstuffs most essential to the native diet were the cereal and oil crops. Sesame oil was used for cooking and human consumption generally, castor oil was used mainly for lamps. Olive oil is not mentioned in the Revenue Laws, apparently because, at the date of their issue, it was not yet being manufactured in Egypt. An extant copy of the Laws shows that the crown strictly controlled every stage of oil production, from the sowing of the crops to retailing the final product.[28] The only element of the population to which certain privileges of private oil production and consumption were granted were the temples.

The Revenue Laws were designed to serve state aims. Though modern westerners would probably regard them as oppressive in their thoroughness, the strict control of oil production, like state control of most other essential crops, served the positive end of guaranteeing an adequate level of food production. Moreover, while this elaborate system of checks and balances did not wholly eliminate individual acts of injustice against the native element, it did limit the amount of administrative corruption that the state would tolerate. If corruption became too great, the crown itself suffered.

The spirit which infused the governmental machinery was, at least in certain respects, explicitly humanitarian and personal. Though I think one could argue that Philadelphos' land reclamation and his revenue laws were conceived with the welfare of the country in mind, the following policies probably evidence more deliberate consideration for the governed.

Three concessions, though paternalistic, limited the theoretical absolutism of the Ptolemaic state. They were: the right of asylum, the assurance of freedom from arrest and molestation under certain conditions, and the Egyptians' right of access to native law.

During Ptolemaic rule, unified groups of peasants, usually cultivators, had the right to walk out on their work to "go up" to certain temples (those granting the right of asylum), as a protest against the threatened or actual injustices of administrative officials.[29] The available evidence indicates that their "strikes" attained the desired result more often than not.

Another concession granted chiefly to agricultural peasants was the assurance of freedom from molestation and arrest for a period of either thirty or sixty days, granted in the form of a letter of safe-conduct. It is true that the purpose of the concession was utilitarian, since it insured freedom of activity to crown cultivators or to other state workers who were engaged in activities during critical periods of production.

The third concession granted to Egyptians was the right to

---

[28] See SelPap 203, which contains cols. 38–56 of the Revenue Laws.

[29] See letters 18, 22, 46 and possibly 34–35. In particular, see the note to line 11 in letter 22 and the introductory comments to letter 46.

settle private legal issues before a native tribunal. Proceedings were conducted in the Egyptian language and according to native custom. A separate court system was established for the Greeks and was administered by "circuit judges," who traveled at certain intervals to the Greek settlements. This bipartite legal system continued in effect throughout the Ptolemaic period. This does not mean that the two systems were mutually exclusive in principle. Though disputes between Egyptians gravitated to the native tribunal and those between Greeks to the circuit court, any litigant could choose either court. Many of the barriers between Greek and Egyptian law fell down over the centuries, as the two populations mixed. But they were never merged into one unified legal system until the Roman rule of Egypt. H. J. Wolff suggests that the early Ptolemies did not attempt to impose a unified system of private law on their subjects because their own conception of law, shaped by the Greek polis, differed radically from the traditionalism that characterized Egyptian law.[30] It was to the early Ptolemies' credit that they acknowledged the plurality of different traditions.

Finally, in addition to the preceding, we may take Ptolemaic letters of petition as an instance of the legal means of redress open to the Egyptian population. In the early Ptolemaic period, many of the petitions are addressed to the king himself. The stereotyped reference to justice at the close of petitions does not in itself demonstrate that Ptolemaic officials were concerned with fair treatment. Occasionally, however, an economic or physical handicap, or some other extenuating circumstance, is cited as a case which requires special consideration. The implied expectation is that the official's investigation will take the disability into account, as well as the legal aspects of the case.[31]

The fact that the petitioners' expectations of personal consideration were not totally unfounded is attested in the instructions of a higher official, probably the dioiketes, to his subordinate, an oikonomos, regarding his responsibility toward crown cultivators: "On your inspection tours try to encourage the peasants by word of mouth and by investigation of their complaints against village scribes or komarchs regarding agricultural matters, and, as far as possible, put an end to such things."[32]

(b) Evaluation of Roman Rule

By comparison with the paternalistic concern of the Ptolemies, Roman rule of Egypt proved to be impersonal and inflexible. Lest this suggestion sound unduly harsh, I must add that this result was probably not by conscious desire or intent but, like Ptolemaic rule, issued from necessity. Whereas the Ptolemaic god-king had been near, and the internal socialization of food production required at least a minimal consideration for peasant laborers, the Roman emperor was a remote god who was detached from the day-to-day conditions of the land. Be he man or god, the absentee owner has seldom distinguished himself as a considerate landlord.

W. L. Westermann illustrates the difference between the two rules with reference to Egyptian grain surplus.[33] After the quota of grain had been filled for feeding the population of the capital, Alexandria, the Ptolemies sold the surplus in Mediterranean markets. The resultant revenue from this and other Egyptian sources went into the royal treasury. The treasury served the purposes of the centralized rule, to be sure, but the natives regarded these as national purposes. By contrast, Augustus had decided that Egypt would supply one-third of the annual grain required for Rome. Consequently, any surplus grain, over and above the needs of Egypt and Alexandria, was regularly shipped to Rome. Needless to say, the treasury of Egypt did not benefit from this transaction.

1) *The military.* The distant and detached character of Roman rule was enhanced, unfortunately, by Rome's strong military forces. We noted above, in the description of Roman administrative structure in Egypt, that though each of the administrative districts or "nomes" continued to be governed by a strategos, the strategoi were stripped of their military authority and all military functions were performed by Roman armed forces. Moreover, the soldiers were concentrated in fortified camps and garrisons according to the Roman system, not living with families on lands alloted to them by the king in the Ptolemaic pattern of soldier-farmers. As a consequence, soldiers constituted a separate, largely alien element of the society; they had little, if any, commitment to the land and were not compelled to work constructively with the masses.

We hear of soldiers abusing their privileges during Ptolemaic times[34] but, since the peace of the Roman Empire was dependent upon its military prowess, the Roman army seems especially to have been indulged. As usual, the people were taxed for the maintenance of the Roman army. But the military could also requisition additional supplies and services from the people as deemed necessary. Common abuses in Roman Egypt were demands for temporary quarters and for means of transport. Matt 5:41 refers, apparently, to compulsory transportation duty. Similar abuses resulted from the

---

[30] "Political Background" pp. 313ff.

[31] See the examples cited in Westermann, "The Ptolemies," p. 283, n. 44. See John White, *Form and Function,* pp. 76–83, letters 4–8.

[32] PTebt III 703.40–49 (III BCE). See A. E. Samuel's comments on PTebt 703.

[33] "The Ptolemies," pp. 286f.

[34] E.g., see SelPap 207 (III BCE).

requisition of special food supplies to support the emperor's foreign wars or to entertain important Roman visitors and their relatives.[35]

2) *Taxes and tax collecting.* One may add to the immediately preceding example the corruption which resulted from the system of farming out tax collection to the highest bidder. The state required a fixed amount of revenue, usually in kind but sometimes in currency, from agricultural plots and from the various Egyptian industries. The overriding intent of the tax-farmer, beyond the payment of the contracted tax to the government, was to show a profit. Since Rome was dependent upon the success of its collectors, tax-farmers were sometimes accompanied by armed guards, ostensibly for protection. Strong arm tactics were employed more often, in fact, for the purpose of gouging taxpayers. We know from ample attestation in the gospels that tax collectors or "publicans" had an equally notorious reputation in first century Palestine.

Though one might protest that the same system was in effect under the Ptolemies, the complicated interdependence of Ptolemaic ruler and subject resulted, in practice, in less abuse. The difference in spirit may be illustrated by the difference between group walkout or "strike" in the Ptolemaic period and the individual act of flight under Roman rule. Whereas the theoretical absolutism of the Ptolemies was limited by the right of group asylum (i.e., a native protest against injustice), under Roman rule the act of flight became an individualized effort to escape fiscal oppression. The group walkout was relatively successful in gaining its ends during Ptolemaic rule. But no matter how many people fled from a Roman village, little if any attention was paid to the extenuating circumstances which occasioned the flight. The tax deficiencies, resulting from these acts of flight, were shifted to the shoulders of the remaining villagers. Consequently, the original spirit of resilience and resistance that had infused the traditional Egyptian system was destroyed. Westermann identifies the cause in graphic language: "Rome was distant and detached in its interest. So far as Egypt was concerned its hand was a grasping and heavy one, deadening in its effects."[36]

Social status in Roman Egypt, or the lack thereof, was affected by the introduction of one type of tax. Few New Testament stories are better known than the account of the nativity in Luke 2:1ff., which begins with a reference to the census which brought Joseph from Nazareth to Bethlehem. Nonetheless, it is only in Egypt, as Naphtali Lewis rightly suggests,[37] that we have sufficient data to explain the separate steps involved in the enrollment of the populace for taxation which this story assumes.

The type of enrollment in question, broadly enacted through the eastern half of the Roman Empire, was the poll tax, technically designated the *laographia* ("populace registration"). Only the most privileged classes in Egypt were exempt from this general tax. All other male inhabitants from the age of fourteen to sixty were subject to enrollment and were lumped together under the appellation, "Egyptians."

The populace had been required to register annually under the Ptolemies, but Augustus initiated a system of registering the population at intervals of fourteen years. The length of interval was determined by the fact that Egyptian males were enrolled as taxable adults at the age of fourteen. Each head of a household was required to list each person residing in the residence by name, relationship, and age.

In addition to the obvious financial burden of the tax, enrollment carried a social stigma, which the Roman government deliberately used as a means of impeding social advancement. The tax was analogous, in this effect, to the account of the emperor's private purse, referred to in our earlier survey of Roman administrative structure. N. Lewis describes the political structure as an oppressive social pyramid, which consisted, at its tip, of a small number of Roman citizens who lived in the province. Below them, but still near the top, were citizens of the four Greek poleis (hereafter described as "urban Greeks") and, until their fall from favor, urban Jews. Beneath these two upper strata was the remainder of the population. Within the bottom mass, only the townspeople of Greek descent who lived in the district capitals (the metropoleis), hereafter called metropolites or town gentry, were taxed at a reduced rate and were allowed certain privileges.[38]

What was the effect of this pyramidal social structure? We have already noted that exclusion from the two upper strata resulted in the necessity of paying an annual poll tax. Along with this tax, "Egyptian" males were required to pay six and two-thirds drachma per year for a dike tax, which was used, presumably, to pay for materials required for upkeep of the irrigation system. The dike tax was in addition to five or more days of manual labor which were required of each male Egyptian per year. More importantly, in the first century CE, only the two top strata of the pyramid were eligible to purchase public lands that were put up for sale and, when these same two strata owned parcels of distant farmland, their lands were exempt from taxation. Nor were they and their

---

[35] E.g., see SelPap 2ll (19 CE); see letter 51 in the present collection.

[36] W. L. Westermann, "The Ptolemies," p. 287.

[37] *Life in Egypt*, pp. 156ff.

[38] Naphtali Lewis, *Life in Egypt,* pp. 18–35, 169–70.

families subject to the various compulsory services, which were required of other local residents and land owners. Finally, urban Greeks, like Roman citizens, were eligible to serve in Roman legions in which, already upon enlistment, they automatically received Roman citizenship. By contrast, though town gentry were eligible to join Roman auxiliary units, they received Roman citizenship only upon honorable discharge, after a quarter century of military service. Till late in the second century, the mass of the population was barred from enlistment even in auxiliary units.

3) *Egypt's Welfare.* Roman rule seems to have been somewhat more oppressive in Egypt than in most provinces. Though Rome may have had no intrinsic hatred of Egypt, personal factors appear to have played some part in the mutual antagonism of Augustus (Octavian) and the Alexandrians. The resentment of the subjugated shows up even in the next to the top stratum, in the attitude of urban Greeks of Alexandria and in the urban Jews.

A very early cause of antagonism, at least between Alexandrian Greeks and Octavian, was the war between Octavian and Antony. It should be recalled that the last member of the Ptolemaic dynasty, Cleopatra, was consort to Octavian's enemy. And one should not forget that Antony was married to Octavian's sister.

The story of the grievances of the Greeks and Jews of Alexandria is narrated more fully in letters 86–88 of the present collection. For the present, a brief explanation will suffice. We begin with the Jews of Alexandria. Following the Ptolemaic precedent, the Roman emperor allowed urban Jews the right of self-rule, which included the election of their own council of elders. As a result, they initially had a status equivalent to the urban Greeks. However, when Augustus initiated the poll tax, the only elements of the populace to be excluded from registration were Roman citizens and urban Greeks. Consequently, Jews were degraded, in effect, to the status of "Egyptians." They attempted unsuccessfully to remove the stigma of the poll tax, but all chance of repeal ended in 41 CE, when Claudius refused to grant citizenship to the Jews (see letter 88 below).

The Roman Empire's subsequent attitude toward Judaism in general, and toward Palestinian Judaism in particular, was colored by the "Jewish troubles" in Alexandria. Claudius' letter implies, indeed, that a Palestinian element had cooperated in the Jewish reprisal against Alexandrian Greeks.

The resentment of Alexandrian Greeks was kindled by Augustus' refusal to confirm their right to their own elected council (*boule*) and to local autonomy, a right granted to the two remaining Greek cities of Naukratis and Ptolemais. Octavian's decision was prompted by the Alexandrian

Greeks' negative attitude, first toward Caesar and then toward himself, even after he had defeated Antony and Cleopatra. This precedent was upheld for over two hundred years by Augustus' successors.

The jealousy both of Greeks and Jews in Alexandria—the Jews, because of the stigma occasioned by the poll tax, and the Greeks, because they lacked the right of self-rule granted to the Jews—resulted in mutual recriminations that broke out in the civil war described in letters 86–88.

More emphatic and persistent than the Greeks' anti-Semitism, was their continuing resentment toward the Roman government, which gave rise to a body of "underground" literature that has been titled *The Acts of the Pagan Martyrs*.[39] The martyrdoms purport to give verbatim accounts of the hearing of an individual or of a small group of Alexandrians before the emperor, from Augustus to Commodus or possibly to Caracalla. Without exception, the Greek heros justify their position over against the immorality, tyranny, and injustice of Roman emperors and Egyptian prefects.

An analogous kind of resentment rankled the town gentry (metropolites) who, as scions of Greek culture, also regarded themselves as entitled to greater status. Though they were granted certain concessions and privileges, which were denied to the peasant class, they were nonetheless classified as "Egyptians."

Far worse than the lot of any of the preceding, was the plight of the Egyptian peasantry. Though the vast majority remained in their villages of origin, enduring all kinds of harsh imposts, the embers of resentment and hatred among the peasants smouldered with greater intensity and potential effect than with any of the preceding groups. Whereas the more literate and affluent element articulated its frustrations in the irreverent kind of words expressed in the "martyr" literature, the peasants' hatred was revolutionary and, from time to time, broke forth into violent action.

The difference in the peasants' resentment is reflected in their apocalyptic writings (e.g., *The Narrative of the Potter*), which predicted the cataclysmic downfall of their inhuman and contemptuous masters. Though most villagers stayed put regardless of excessive taxation and contemptuous treatment, a small element became fugitives when their situation seemed to become hopeless. Their flight took one of two principal forms: (1) they either made their way to a city, especially Alexandria, where they could disappear into the "melting pot," or (2) they sought desert hideouts, where they formed or joined robber bands.[40]

The major trade routes which traversed the desert between the Nile and the Red Sea, principally in Upper and Middle Egypt, were especially vulnerable to the raids of

---

[39] See Musirillo, *Acts of the Pagan Martyrs.*
[40] See N. Lewis, *Life in Egypt,* pp. 183–84, 202–5.

these fugitives ,and those arteries regularly had to be patrolled by desert police.[41] The biblical account of the man who was beaten and robbed, while traveling from Jerusalem to Jericho sounds remarkably like the situation just described here.[42]

6. DOCUMENTARY GREEK LETTERS AND THE CHRISTIAN LETTER TRADITION

(a) Relevance of Papyri for Interpreting the New Testament

Most biblical scholars seem reticent to work with the vast body of documentary sources from Graeco-Roman Egypt. Perhaps the sheer bulk and the diversity of information are deterrents to use. Or, it may be that, with the exception of discoveries like the Amarna Correspondence or the Nag Hammadi Codices, documents from Egypt are thought either largely to be lacking in theological relevance or, so far as social environment is concerned, to be an inappropriate model for understanding the biblical setting.

It is certainly the case that, apart from considerable sifting, these sources are lacking the immediate religious relevance of the Nag Hammadi find or, in the case of Palestinian data, the Dead Sea Scrolls. But, so far as social setting is concerned, Greek and Roman political structures were similar enough in Egypt and Palestine that the lot of the inhabitants was analogous. If the present flurry of interest in the social world of late Judaism and early Christianity is serious, the papyri, ostraca, and inscriptions from Graeco-Roman Egypt certainly should be added to the body of primary source materials. The previous examples of Roman policy, though not numerous, illustrate the supplementary usefulness of Egyptian documentary sources, especially for clarifying data in the New Testament.

Documentary papyri may also be used directly to interpret the New Testament. A few examples will illustrate this point. A number of parables, which we find preserved in the synoptic gospels, describe agricultural activities or other aspects of ordinary life that often come to expression in documents from Egypt. Sometimes the activities described in the parables are quite realistic in comparison with the evidence from Egypt. Other times details or actions are exaggerated. In the latter case, the hyperbole appears to be intentional and, consequently, the comparative data underscores the exaggeration.

Let us take the parable of the Sower as an example (see Mark 4:3–8; Matt 13:3–8; Luke 8:5–8; GThom 9) and let us look, in particular, at the description of the harvest. The yield is described as returning thirty, sixty, a hundredfold. By comparison, we know that agriculture averaged a five or sixfold return in Italy and Sicily; especially fertile areas yielded as much as ten and fifteenfold. A cultivated area of the Negev produced seven and eightfold of wheat and barley, respectively, in the sixth century BCE. In Egypt, average yields varied from nine to twenty-seven times the amount of seed planted.[43] Since the productivity of Egypt was almost legendary in the eyes of the Greeks and Romans, it is clear, by comparison, that the yield in the parable of the Sower was abnormally high—we might say, more accurately, an impossibility.

Another detail of agricultural life in the parables, this time the payment of day laborers hired to harvest a vineyard (Matt 20:1–16), may be illustrated by a second century list of wages (POxy 1049). Slave labor was almost non-existent in the agricultural work of Egypt and Palestine. This state of affairs resulted in part from the fact that free peasantry afforded a cheaper source of seasonal labor than slaves, who required year-round maintenance. But during the periods in which seasonal crops were being harvested, the competition for seasonal laborers was brisk and good seasonal laborers could command wages nearly equal to skilled artisans.

In the aforementioned source, a man lists the wages paid to various categories of seasonal workers during one four-day period. Sheavers were each paid a daily wage of three and one-half drachmas; two drachmas per animal were paid for the use of donkeys per day; and donkey drivers, who required little special skill, received an obol less than two drachmas. By comparison, day laborers in the parable each received a denarius. Since the Roman denarius was equivalent to a tetradrachm, the vineyard laborers received slightly more per day than the sheavers in the document to which we just referred. If the difference in inflation between the first and second century were added to our bank of data, the wages in the parable may appear even a little greater. Nonetheless, the wages do not seem to be particularly excessive. Perhaps the most striking element in the story is the vineyard owner's generosity toward the laborers who worked only a portion of the day.

The parable of the Wicked Tenants (cf. Mark 12:1–11; Matt 21:33–44; Luke 20:9–18; GThom 65–66) is often interpreted as a construction of the early church, and not as an authentic saying of Jesus himself. Nonetheless, the relationship of the tenants toward the absentee landlord and, conversely, certain aspects of the landlord's relationship with the tenants, would have been feasible both in Roman Egypt and in Palestine. One can well imagine the hatred of peasant

---

[41] See the following examples of tolls collected on overland traffic, some of which are specified as paying for desert police services: SelPap 382, 383 and OGIS 701.

[42] See Luke 10:29–37.

[43] See the documentation cited in Naphtali Lewis, *Life in Egypt*, pp. 121ff. and 223, n. 19.

tenants, especially toward certain kinds of absentee landowners. If Jesus told some version of the story, one can equally well imagine the antagonism of the landed gentry in his audience. Unfortunately, much of the plot rings all too true.

(b) The Letters

One might argue that studying Greek literary letters rather than documentary letters is more advantageous for understanding the Christian letter tradition. But that position, which certainly has adherents, is not the most essential issue. The greater problem is one which Paul Schubert diagnosed many decades ago,[44] and unfortunately, it is still with us to an appreciable extent, namely, the general reticence to study Christian letters as letters. Consequently, I do not intend to disparage the use of any epistolary corpus which might illuminate Christian letter writing. In particular, and as I stated at the beginning, I do not want to justify the value of the documentary letter tradition at the expense of literary letters. However, ordinary Greek letter writing has much to teach us about Christian letters. A comparable body of literary letters probably would be equally useful.

1) *The Christian letter tradition.* Before making any further observations, it will prove helpful to explain generally what is intended by the designation, "Christian letter tradition." We are not referring indiscriminately to all letters written by Christians in the early centuries of the Roman Empire. Indeed, one should not expect evidence of Christianity even to show up in ordinary correspondence written by Christians. The earliest papyrus letter which clearly was written by a Christian in Egypt, for example, is from the first half of the third century.

The Christian letter tradition to which I refer is that in which a Christian leader wrote a letter of instruction to a Christian community under his leadership. Apparently, St. Paul created the tradition when he wrote in his capacity as a Christian apostle to Christian communities which he had founded. The influence of his precedent is evident in the fact that almost all of the twenty-one New Testament letters purport to be written by an apostle. And, when a letter like *1 Clement* or the correspondence of Ignatius did not claim to be written by an apostle, the author of such correspondence laid claim, nonetheless, to some type of status which gave him the authority to instruct a Christian community on certain issues.

2) *The comparative value of documentary letters.* Now, what kinds of things may be learned by studying documentary letters? In addition to the more obvious recognition that Greek letters usually have a tripartite structure of opening, body and closing, we learn that set epistolary phrases are employed within each of these three epistolary parts. The

particular form of an individual phrase, or a certain combination of epistolary conventions, frequently signals the basic intention or occasion of the letter. For example, when the wish for health is expressed in the letter opening, a degree of intimacy or familiarity is assumed. Or, when the recipient's name is written prior to the sender's in the opening address formula, the letter is a petition or some similar type of document in which the sender is the inferior in the epistolary situation.

Generally speaking, if the opening and closing are full, the letter is a family letter or a letter between friends in which the ongoing maintenance of friendship is an important consideration. By contrast, if the opening and closing are minimal, the letter is probably a business letter, a legal transaction in epistolary form, or a piece of administrative correspondence. When the above information is applied to the Christian letter tradition, it is evident that the preservation of friendly or "family" ties was an important aspect of the correspondence. But a proportionately large letter body indicates that something more specific than the maintenance of contact actually occasioned these Christian letters. An even more important characteristic of Christian letters, than the evidence of friendliness in the opening and closing and the presence of a discrete body of information, is the total length of each piece of correspondence. Even a superficial comparison shows that, with few exceptions, Christian letters are considerably longer than ordinary Greek letters. Their length appears to be directly related to their function as letters of instruction.

Comparison also makes evident, and almost as quickly, that conventional elements of Christian worship and belief come to expression in a more pervasive manner than in Greek documentary letters, even when the latter are concerned with religious subjects. The Apostle Paul appears to be the Christian leader who was responsible for first introducing Christian elements into the epistolary genre and for adapting existing epistolary conventions to express the special interests of the Christian community. These alterations are more readily comprehended when one recognizes that the letter was a substitute for Paul's apostolic presence with his Christian communities. His use of Christian formulas shows, more exactly, that the setting for which the letter served as a surrogate was the Christian congregation at worship. Namely, it was in his capacity as God's representative that Paul addressed his congregations. Given the Jewish conception of the evocative power of the spoken word of God, one may understand Paul's reticence in using the letter as a surrogate medium for that message. On the other hand, the religious and cultic nuances of the letter, as well as Paul's use of rhetorical techniques that are reminiscent of oral argumentation, all make sense in this light. The comparative

---

[44] "Pauline Letters," pp. 372–77.

value of ordinary Greek letters might appear to be minimal at this point, since Christian letters differ from them in such major respects. My immediate rejoinder is that the characteristic features of the Christian letter tradition would be ill defined, if not undetected, without a working knowledge of ordinary letter writing. But a positive and studied estimation of the comparative use of Greek documentary letters causes me to add that Christian letters function as actual letters only to the extent that they serve conventional epistolary purposes.

This means that even a creative letter writer like Paul had to express himself by means of recognizable conventions. He may have altered epistolary formulas in a creative fashion but he certainly did not ignore them. We will not appreciate his use of these conventions, consequently, until they are identified. I am convinced that the documentary letter tradition enables us to identify many stereotyped features of Paul's letters and it provides a basis for understanding the epistolary function of these conventions.

To illustrate, though Paul never uses the most commonly expressed form of the wish of health in the letter opening, he nonetheless retains its function, and gives it a distinctly Christian nuance by two means. First, Paul replaces the typical word of salutation, *chairein* (i.e, "the sender to the recipient, 'greeting.'"), with a fuller, separate, phrase, "Grace to you and peace from God our Father and the Lord Jesus Christ." Some scholars attribute this substitution to Paul's dependence upon an oriental (Jewish) form of epistolary salutation. Even if this is the case, he gives the Jewish prayer for grace and peace a Christian cast which, moreover, conveys the sender's concern about the recipient's welfare in a manner analogous to the wish for health. Secondly, the opening grace prayer is followed, customarily, by Paul's prayer of thanksgiving to God, which has been occasioned by news of some virtuous, spiritual activity of his recipients. Thereupon, he prays that the same cause for which he gives thanks will abound to even greater effect, with the result that his recipients will be spiritually mature and blameless by the time the Lord comes to complete the new spiritual age.

In summary, though Paul never cites the conventional wish for health, he does express his concern for his recipients' welfare; his concern is not with ordinary well-being, but with his recipients' spiritual conformity to the standards of a new spiritual age.

(c) Conclusion

It would take entirely too long to continue in this manner, comparing Christian epistolary conventions with corresponding phrases in the documentary letter tradition. An extensive examination of the documentary letter tradition is taken up in Part Two of this work. The identification of major epistolary functions there, along with the formulas which express these functions, should prove useful to anyone who wants to engage in a comparative study of the two bodies of data.

Opposite: Statue of Harmhab
An Egyptian scribe seated in the customary writing position with a papyrus roll stretched across his lap. Harmhab was also the commander-in-chief of the armies of Tutankhamen. The photograph is reproduced with the permission of the Metropolitan Museum of Art.

TEXTS & TRANSLATIONS

I

These four letters are all addressed to Harimouthes, who was first the nomarch and later the toparch of the Oxyrhynchite nome (cf. the introduction by Grenfell and Hunt in PHib I 40). Though not included here, PHib I 42 belongs to the same archives. The entire correspondence concerns the activities of government officials and illustrates the blanketing Ptolemaic bureaucracy introduced by Ptolemy Philadelphos (283–245 BCE).

The first and second letters are from Polemon who, while his office is unspecified, was probably Harimouthes' superior. The first seems concerned primarily with the sale of state barley (for planting?) and Harimouthes is informed that his price for supplying barley is too expensive. Polemon notifies Harimouthes in the second letter that the *dokimastes* (the "controller"), a certain Mnason, has been sent under guard to collect arrears (of oil?). Harimouthes is directed both to obtain security for Mnason while he is present and to assist him in performing his duties.

It appears from lines 21ff. of the second letter that the arrears were connected with the government oil industry (e.g., the crown monopoly governing the production and sale of sesame oil) and, owing to the precaution taken against his absconding, Mnason himself must have been personally liable for the arrears. The Revenue Laws issued by Philadelphos specify that manufactured oil is to be sold to retail traders by the *oikonomos* and the *antigrapheus* (PRev column 48), while the dokimastes is not mentioned. But the Revenue Laws probably had not been issued when this letter to Harimouthes was written, and some special circumstance may have resulted in the present activity of the dokimastes.

Elsewhere, the Hibeh papyri indicate that the dokimastes was an official closely associated with the state bank and, more particularly, that he functioned as a check on the activities of the state banker, the *trapedzites,* in the same way that the antigrapheus functioned as a "controller" over the office of the oikonomos. In PHib I 106–7 and in 136–42 the dokimastes and the trapedzites issue receipts for the payment of taxes on the profits derived from the sale of beer, the customary alcoholic drink of native Egyptians.

The third letter is from Kallikles, another superior whose title is not identified in the letter. Though not included in this collection, Kallikles wrote another letter to Harimouthes, PHib I 42, about grain which Harimouthes had failed to deliver. The same Kallikles is mentioned in the first letter of this collection.

In the fourth letter, Deinon instructs Harimouthes to send a detachment of native soldiers, *machamoi*, with their commander. He intensifies the order by referring to Apollonios' instructions on the matter. Apollonios was the *dioiketes*, an officer under the early Ptolemies who seems to have been second only to the king himself. In effect, the dioiketes was both the king's executive secretary and minister of finance. (The extensive activity and authority of Apollonios will be illustrated in the Zenon archives which will be discussed immediately after the Harimouthes correspondence. The status of the native soldiers under early Ptolemaic rule will be discussed in a separate introduction to letter 4.)

1 POLEMŌN TO HARIMOUTHĒS
PHib I 40

Πολέμων Ἁριμούθηι
χαίρειν. περὶ τῶν
συμβόλων γεγράφαμεν
Κρίτωνι καὶ Καλλικλεῖ
5 ἵνα γένηται ὡς ἐπέ-
σταλκας. ἐπίστασο
μέντον ἀκριβῶς
ὅτι τῆς κριθῆς
ἧς συγγέγραψαι
10 τιμῆς δώσειν
δραχμὴν μίαν οὐθεὶς
σοι μὴ πλη⟨ρώσ⟩ηι· καὶ γὰρ
οἱ παρὰ Κερκίωνος
ἔχουσιν ἤδη ἐμ παρα-
15 γραφῆι ἐκ τοῦ λογι-
στηρίου.
ἔρρωσο. (ἔτους) κδ, Ἐπεὶφ κα.

Verso: Ἁριμούθηι.

Polemon to Harimouthes greeting. Concerning the receipts, we have written to Kriton and Kallikles that the matter be handled as you instructed. But understand clearly that so far as the barley is concerned no one will pay even one drachma for the price which you have written that you will supply it; since the agents of Kerkion already have (a lower price?) in a statement from the audit office. Good-bye. (Year) 24, Epeiph 21.

Outside address: To Harimouthes.

---

12 The use of μὴ πλήρηι for μὴ πληρώσηι seems unlikely but the reading μή is supported by the subjunctive ending of the verb. Μέντον (for μέντοι) in line 7 shows that the writer could make grammatical errors.

14-15 It seems clear that Harimouthes' intention had been thwarted in some way by Kerkion's agents, but the exact meaning of ἔχουσιν ἐμ παραγραφῆι is not clear.

2 POLEMŌN TO HARIMOUTHĒS
PHib I 41

Πολέμων Ἁ[ριμο]ύθηι χαί-
ρειν. ἀπεστ[άλκ]αμεν πρὸς
σὲ Μνάσωνα [τὸ]ν δοκιμασ-
τὴν μετὰ φυ[λα]κῆς. διεγ-
5 γυήσας οὖ[ν] αὐτὸν παραμονῆς (δραχμῶν?) Ἀ ἄφ[ε]ς αὐτὸν
εἰσαγαγεῖν τὰ ὀφειλή-
ματα κα[θ]ὰ σύγκειται
πρὸς ἡμᾶ[ς], τ̣ὸ πρόστιμον
10 αὐτῶι συμβαλὼν παρὰ σαυτοῦ οσου.μ. ἐπιτρέψει
ἀποβιάζεσθαι αὐτὸν καὶ
. . . . σε[. .]μ. ., καὶ συνεπι-
λαμβάνου αὐτῶι πρὸς τὸ
15 εἰσαχθῆναι πάντα, καὶ
ἡμῖν ἐπίστειλον ὅτι
παρείληφας αὐτὸν παρὰ
τῶν παρ᾽ ἡμῶν μαχίμων
καὶ ὅτι διεγγυήσεις αὐτὸν

Polemon to Harimouthes greeting. We have sent Mnason the dokimastes (the controller) to you under guard. Therefore, after you obtain a security of one thousand drachmas for his stay, let him pay in (collect) the arrears according to what we agreed upon; you yourself contributing to his penalty from your funds. . . . Support him also so that everything be paid in, and write us whether you have received him from our soldiers and whether you will obtain the security of one thousand drachmas for him; taking care in addition that the existing store of oil be sold at this time and when the price of it is collected that it be paid into the royal bank. . . .

Outside address: To Harimouthes.

4-6 διεγγυήσας . . . παραμονῆς: PHib I 92 and 93 are actual contracts of sureties for the appearance of accused people. Μετὰ φυλακῆς ("under guard") is a technical phrase (e.g., see PHib I 59.4).

20 τῶν Ἀ (δραχμῶν), ἐπιμέλειαν δὲ
    ποιήσαι ὅπως καὶ τὸ ὑπάρ-
    χον ἔλαιον δι' αὐτοῦ ἤδη
    πραθῆι καὶ ἡ τιμὴ ἀνα-
    κομισθεῖσα πέσηι ἐπὶ τὴν
25 [βασιλικὴν] τράπεζαν.
    . . . . . .

Verso: Ἁ]ριμούθηι.

3 KALLIKLĒS TO HARIMOUTHĒS
PHib I 43

261–260 BCE

Καλλικλῆς Ἁριμούθηι
χαίρειν. σύνταξον μετρῆσ[αι
τὸ σήσαμον τὸ ἐμ Πέλαι
Πρωτομάχωι καὶ τῶι σιτολόγ[ωι,] οὐ γὰρ ἔστιν
5 ἐν τῆι πόλει σήσαμον. ἵνα οὖν
μηθὲν ὑστερῆι τὰ ἐ[λ]αιουργία
φρόντισον ἵνα μὴ αἰτίας ἔχῃς
καὶ τοὺ[ς] ἐ[λ]αιουργοὺς ἀπόστειλόν μοι.
10   ἔρρωσο. (ἔτους) κδ, Ἐπεὶφ κ.

Verso
1st hand: Ἁριμούθηι.
2nd hand: (ἔτους) κδ, Ἐφεὶφ κ, παρὰ
Καλλικλέους περὶ ση-
σάμου ὥστε Πρωτομάχωι.

Kallikles to Harimouthes greeting. Command that the sesame which is at Pela be measured out to Protomarchos and to the *sitologos* ("grain/seed officer"), because there is no sesame in the city (i.e., Oxyrhynchos). Take care therefore that the oil manufacture not fall behind, lest you be blamed; and send the oilmakers to me. Good-bye. (Year) 24, Epeiph 20.

Outside address: To Harimouthes.
Docket of receipt: (Year) 24, Epeiph 20, from Kallikles about sesame for Protomachos.

4 DEINŌN TO HARIMOUTHĒS
PYale 33 (=PHib I 44)

5 April 253 BCE

In this letter, Deinon orders the toparch Harimouthes to send a detachment of native soldiers (machimoi) under their commander, Bithelmeinis. The name Bithelmeinis, probably Semitic and likely Aramaean, is explained by Oates, Samuel and Welles, the editors of PYale 33, in connection with the place name BT'LMYN, "house of God." If this assumption is correct, a native of the Levant, or at least a Semite by race, could rise to the military rank of *hegemon*. Commanders of this rank in the regular army were apparently Greek in the third century BCE, whereas the equivalent commanders of native troops (machimoi) were, as intimated here, bilingual Asiatics or Egyptians.

We stated in the general introduction to this work that Philadelphos both increased the agricultural productivity in Egypt and insured the support of his army by a vast reclamation of land in the Fayum: he granted an allotment of land (a *kleros*), differing in size according to status and service, to soldiers as a means of wedding their loyalty to Egypt. The lowly status of the machimoi under Philadelphos is indicated by their small klerouchic grant of only five *aroura* (about three and one-half acres) recorded in PPetr III 100b. Moreover, in PPetr III 59a (a census listing professions), these native soldiers are listed with menial occupations (potters, shopkeepers, fishermen). This suggests that the earliest Ptolemies, Soter and Philadelphos, devalued the prestige of the machimoi who, formerly, were second in rank only to the priesthood under the king.

In the period of Philopater (221–203 BCE) and later, after the Ptolemies were well established in Egypt, the machimoi were gradually restored to a position approximating their former glory (see introduction to PYale 33). At the time of this letter, however, they were neither regular army nor police. (A Zenon letter distinguishes regular police and machimoi: PSI IV 353.) They received fewer traveling expenses than vinedressers (PColZen II 77) and they could be transferred in groups as common workmen, as this letter indicates, much like farm laborers hired for state land.

Δείνων Ἁριμούθηι χαίρειν. ἐγράψαμέν σοι πρότερον περὶ
τῶν μαχίμων
τῶν ὄντων ἐν τοῖς ὑπὸ σὲ τόποις ὅπως ἀποσταλῶσιν μετὰ
Βιθελμείνιος τοῦ ἡγε-
μόνος καθότι γράφει Ἀπολλώνιος ὁ διοικητής, ὡσαύτως
δὲ ‘[[σε]]’ καὶ τοὺς ἐπιγεγραμ-
μένους θεριστὰς κατὰ τὴν δοθεῖσάν σοι γραφήν, ὁρῶντες
δέ ‘σε’ καταραθυμοῦντα
5 ᾤμην δεῖν καὶ νῦν ἐπιστεῖλαί σ[οι]. ὡς [ἂ]ν οὖν λάβηις
τὴν ἐπιστολὴν πάντα π[ά]ρεργα
ποιησάμενος ἀπόστειλον πρὸς ἡμᾶς τοὺς μαχίμους ἤδη,
τοὺς δ[ὲ θερισ]τὰς ὡς ἂν
ἑτοίμους ποιήσηις ἐπίστειλον ἡμῖν. οὐ γὰρ ὡς ἔτυχεν περὶ
τούτων τὴν σπουδὴν
ποιεῖται ὁ διοικητής.   ἔρρωσο. (ἔτους) λβ, Μεχεὶρ ιγ̄.

Verso
1st hand: τοπάρχηι   Ἁριμούθηι
τῆς κάτω   *Mecheir* 14 (in demotic)
2nd hand: Μεχὶρ ιδ,
περὶ μαχίμων
καὶ θεριστῶν.

Deinon to Harimouthes greeting. We wrote to you before about the machimoi who are in the places under you, that they be sent with Bithelmeinis the hegemon, just as Apollonios the dioiketes writes and similarly that the reapers be enrolled in conformity with the list given to you; but seeing that you are remiss I thought it necessary to instruct you now again. Therefore, as soon as you receive this letter, lay everything else aside and send the machimoi to us immediately and, as for the reapers, write to us as soon as you get them ready. For in no ordinary manner is the dioiketes making haste about these things. Good-bye. (Year) 32, Mecheir 13.

Outside address: To Harimouthes, toparch of the lower (toparchy).
Docket of receipt: Mecheir 14, about native soldiers and reapers.

The Zenon papers are the largest, best preserved archive of Hellenistic papyrus documents. A representative sampling of the stages of Zenon's correspondence, drawn from the several hundred items already published, is included here. The main find was discovered by peasants in the winter of 1914–15 at the site of the ancient village of Philadelphia in the Fayum. The lot was acquired by dealers, who divided it into parts and sold it to various purchasers. Though the largest part was slowly acquired by the Cairo Museum (PCairZen I–V), a large segment was purchased by the Società Italiana per la ricerca dei papiri (PSI IV–IX), a representative collection by the British Museum (PLond VII), the Rylands Library (PRyl IV), the universities of Michigan (PMich I) and Columbia (PCol III–IV=PColZen I–II); smaller portions went to France and Germany and the supply may not yet be exhausted.

The two central figures of the correspondence are Apollonios, the dioiketes ("minister of finance") during the last fifteen years of the reign of Philadelphos, and Zenon, the personal agent of Apollonios. When we first meet Zenon, he is Apollonios' agent in Syria and elsewhere, transacting business for his master and himself (letters 5–8). Later, he accompanies the dioiketes on the long tours which the latter made in the interior of Egypt (letters 9–19). Finally, in 256 BCE, Zenon settled down in Philadelphia as manager of Apollonios' private estate, the *dorea*, which was a large land "grant" allotted to individuals especially favored by the king (letters 20–25).

The correspondence falls within the two decades which begin about 260 BCE and continues into the first years of Euergetes' (Ptolemy III) reign. Because Zenon worked for such an important official, his activities often impinged upon the regular bureaucracy, and he functioned in a quasi-official capacity on Apollonios' behalf. Nonetheless, his own position seems to have been essentially private, both as an agent for Apollonios and as the manager of Apollonios' estate at Philadelphia.

Two excellent English analyses of the Zenon correspondence are: Rostovtzeff, *A Large Estate* and Edgar, Introduction to PMich I, pp. 1–60. Regarding the history of Egypt during this period, see Bevan, *History of Egypt,* pp. 56ff.

5 DĒMĒTRIOS TO ZĒNŌN

PCairZen I 59016 — 30 December 259 BCE

This letter belongs to the earliest extant phase of Zenon's work for Apollonios, when Zenon was probably both an official envoy for Apollonios in Syria and Palestine as well as his private agent. Demetrios, a *grammateus* stationed in Cyprus, had traveled to Phoenicia on business and, at the time of writing, had expended his traveling allowance on purchases in Tyre. Zenon himself must have been moving about, since Demetrios inquires where he must send money to Zenon. The Charmos, referred to in line 4, was one of Apollonios' ubiquitous commercial agents. For the itinerary of Zenon's travels in Palestine, see map 177 in Aharoni and Avi-Yonah, *Bible Atlas,* p. 113.

Δημήτριος Ζήνωνι χαίρειν. ἐν τῆι Τύρωι ἀγοράσματά τινα λαβὼν ἀνήλωκα τὸ ἐφόδιον. καλῶς ἂν οὖν ποιήσαις δοὺς Νικάδαι τῶι τὰ γράμματά σοι ἀποδεδωκότι ⊢ ρν. ἔφθασεν δέ με προαπελθὼν Χάρμος, ἐπεὶ μετ᾽ ἐκείνου ἂν αὐτὸν ἀπέστειλα. φρόντισον δὲ ἵνα καὶ τὸν Νικάδαν ἀποστείλῃς εἰς Βηρυτὸν μετ᾽ ἀσφαλείας.
καὶ
γράφον δέ μοι ὅπου δεήσει τὸ κερμάτιον ἀποστεῖλαι.
ἔρρωσο. Lκζ, Ἀπελλαίου ιγ.

Verso

1st hand: Ζήνωνι.

2nd hand: παρὰ Δημητρίου τοῦ ἐν Κύπρωι γραμματέως ἀργυρίου ⊢ ρν.

Demetrios to Zenon greeting. I have spent my travel allowance because of some purchases in Tyre. Therefore, you would do well to give 150 drachmas to Nikadas who has brought the letter to you. Charmos finished before me and went ahead, otherwise I would have sent him along (with Nikadas). Make certain too that you send Nikadas to Beirut safely. Also, write to me where the money must be sent. Good-bye. (Year) 27, Apellaios 13.

Outside address: To Zenon.

Docket of receipt: From Demetrios the scribe in Cyprus, (regarding) 150 drachmas.

6 DRAFTS OF FIVE LETTERS BY ZĒNŌN

PCairZen I 59015 (verso) — 259–258 BCE

These first drafts were written in Alexandria on the verso of an oil account (PCairZen I 59015 recto), either in the summer of 259 BCE or at least before the following summer. The entire correspondence concerns three runaway slaves, recently bought in Idumea from a certain Zaidelos and his brother, Kollochoutos. Straton, one of Zenon's employees, is the intermediary both in this and in the following letter (letter 7). Zenon writes to Pasikles and to Epikrates, in the first and second letters respectively, requesting that they assist Straton, who carries the correspondence. The slaves are apparently being held at the home of one of the brothers who sold the slaves to Zenon. Moreover, a ransom of one hundred drachmas is being claimed for their return, though there is some ambiguity concerning the identity of the claimant(s). One cannot tell whether the original owners are themselves demanding the money or if someone else has returned the slaves to the brothers and is claiming the recovery fee.

In the third letter, Zenon asks Peisistratos to remind Pasikles (recipient of the first letter) of his duty in assisting Straton to recover the slaves. In the fourth and fifth letters, Zenon requests Epainetos and Ammon (Ptolemaic officials?), respectively, to see that Straton's recovery of the slaves is not hindered by any compulsory government service.

Πασικλεῖ. εἰ ἔρρωσαι, καλῶς ἂν ἔχοι· ὑγιαίνομεν δὲ
καὶ αὐτοί. ἀνήγγελλέν μοι Κρότος γεγραφέναι σε αὐτῶι
ὅτι οἱ παῖδες οἱ ἀποδράντες μηνυτρίζοιντο

                   οὕτω καὶ   ωι τῶι

εἶναι παρὰ τῶι Κολλοχ [[. . ι]] τῶι Ζαιδήλ [[ου]] ἀδελφῶι
5   καὶ αἰτοίησαν [[μνᾶν]], ἐφ᾽ ὧι ἀνάξουσιν, ἀργυρίου Ⱶρ.
καλῶς ἂν οὖν ποιήσαις τὴμ πᾶσαν σπουδὴν
ποιησάμενος τοῦ συλληφθῆναι αὐτοὺς
[[ἵνα καὶ οια . . οι]] καὶ παραδοὺς Στράτωνι
τῶι κομίζοντί σοι τὸ ἐπιστόλιον. τοῦτο γὰρ

                   δ

10   ποιήσας εὐχαριστήσ[εις ἡμῖν. [[. .]] . . . .]] δ᾽ ἂν
    ἀνηλώσηις
[δώσ]ομεν. πεπραμέ[νη δ᾽ ἐστὶν ἀλ]αβαστροθήκη

                  ἐπίστειλον

[. . . . .]σαι· εἰ δὲ μὴ [βούλει, [[γρ]άψον]]
[ὁ δὲ πρ]ι[ά]μενος ἀποδώσει. [καὶ σὺ δὲ ἐάν τινος]
[χ]ρείαν ἔχη[ις] τῶν ἐν τ[ῆι χώραι, γράφε ἡ]μῖν·
15   ποιήσομεν γὰρ φιλικῶ[ς.   ἔρρ[ω]σο.

᾽Επικράτει. ἐπιδημήσαντες ἐμ Μαρίσηι ἐπρ[ιάμεθα]
ἐκ τῶν Ζαιδήλου σώματα, [[ὧν ἀποδεδρά[κασιν]]]

               δ᾽

[[ἀδελ]] ἡμῶν εἰς Αἴγυπτον εἰσπορευομέ[νων
        [α]ὐτῶν παῖδες γ, τούτων
ἀπέδρασαν ἀδελφοὶ δύο, [[οἱ ὄνομα]] ὧν [τὰ ὀνόματα]
20   καὶ τὰς εἰκόνας ὑπογέγραφά σοι. προσήγγ[ελται δὲ]
ἡμῖν εἶναι τ[ούτους παρ]ὰ Κολλοχούτωι τ . . [
καλ[ῶς ἂν οὖν ποιήσαις τὴμ π]ᾶσαν σπουδὴν
π[οιησάμενος

                 υς

[τοῦ συλληφθῆναι αὐτο]ὺς καὶ παραδο[[θῆναι]]
    Στράτωνι]
[ὃ δ᾽ ἂν ἀνηλώσηις τοῖς ἀ]ναγαγοῦσιν α . . [
25   ]υ . . ιαι τουτ[

Πεσιστράτωι. εἰ ἔρρωσαι, καλῶς ἂν ἔχοι· ὑγιαίνομεν δὲ
καὶ αὐτοί. ἀνήγγελλεν ἡμῖν Κρότος γεγραφέναι
Πασικλῆν μηνυτρίζεσθαι τοὺς ἀποδράντας
παῖδας [[τ]] ὧν ἐπριάμεθα [[παρὰ]] ἐμ Μαρίζηι
30   τῶν Ζαιδήλου. γεγράφαμεν οὖ⟨ν⟩ ἀξιοῦντες
τὴμ πᾶσαν ἐπιμέλειαν ποιήσασθαι

To Pasikles. If you are well, it would be excellent; we too are well. Krotos informed us that you had written to him that the runaway slaves are with Kollochoutos and Zaidelos his brother and that the ones who claim a reward demand one hundred drachmas, over which they will set the terms. Therefore, you would do well, making due haste that they be recovered, to hand them over to Straton who carries this note to you. For by doing this you would grant me a favor. And whatever you spend I will repay. The alabaster case is sold . . . ; but if you do not want (to sell it?), the one who is buying it will return it. Moreover, if you ever have need of anything in the country, write to us, for we will gladly do it. Good-bye.

To Epikrates. When we were in Marisa, we bought slaves out of Zaidelos' stock but, while we were making for Egypt, three of the same slaves ran away and I have appended for you the names and descriptions of two of these who are brothers. We were informed that they are at Kollochoutos' place . . . Therefore, you would do well, making due haste that they be recovered, to hand them over to Straton. And whatever you pay to those who . . .

To Peisistratos. If you are well, it would be excellent; we too are well. Krotos informed us that Pasikles had written that the runaway slaves, which we bought in Marisa from Zaidelos' stock, are being held for reward. Therefore we wrote requesting that all effort be made that they be recovered and that they be handed over to Straton who is carrying these letters to you. Therefore, you too would do well both by reminding him and by eagerly cooperating, lest they make good their escape. Moreover, you would favor us by writing, if ever you desire anything from the country; for we would gladly do it for you. Good-bye.

To Epainetos. Some of our slaves, who happened to run away, are reported to be in Idumea, and we have sent Straton for the same reason. Therefore, you would do well to order your son not

ὅπως ἂν συλληφθῶσιν καὶ παραδῶι αὐτοὺς
  ἃς
Στράτωνι τῶι τ[[ὴν]] ἐπιστολ[[η]] ἃς ὑμῖν
κομίζοντι. διὸ καὶ σὺ καλῶς ἂν ποιοῖς
35 ὑπομιμνήσκων τε αὐτὸν καὶ συνσπουδάσ ⟨ας⟩
ὅπως μὴ διαφύγωσιν [[οἱ παῖδες]]. καὶ σὺ δὲ εὐχαριστήσεις ἡμῖν γράφων, [[τίνων.]] ἐάν τι βούληι τῶν
ἀπὸ τῆς χώρας· φιλικῶς γάρ σοι ποιήσομεν.
  ἔρρωσο.

40 Ἐπαινέτωι. παῖδές [[ἡμῖν]] τινες τ[υγχά]νουσιν
ἀποκεχωρηκότες ἡμῶν, οἳ προσηγγελμένοι εἰσὶν
ἐν τῆι Ἰδ[ο]υμαίαι, ἀπεστάλκαμεν δὲ ἐπ᾽ αὐτὸ
Στράτωνα. καλῶς ἂν οὖν ποιήσαις σ[υ]ντάξας τῶι υἱ⟨ῶι⟩
μὴ ἐνοχλεῖν αὐτὸν τὰ κατὰ τὰς λειτουργίας, ὅπως
  συνλάβηι τοὺς παῖδας.

45 Ἄμμωνι. τὴν αὐτήν.
[[ὅπως Δωροθέωι καὶ Δημαινέτωι]]
καλῶς ἂν οὖν ποιήσαις γράψας Δωρ[ο]θέωι καὶ
  Δημαινέτωι
ὅπως μὴ ἐνοχλῆται τὰ κατὰ τὰς λειτουργίας.

to trouble him with compulsory service, in order that he may recover the slaves.

To Ammon. The same (letter). Therefore, you would do well to write Dorotheos and Demainetos lest he (Straton) be troubled with compulsory service.

7 ALEXANDROS TO ORYAS
CPJud I 6 (=PCairZen I 59018)   258 BCE

We learn in the present letter that Zenon's man Straton has tried unsuccessfully to recover money loaned to Jeddous, who was probably a native Jewish sheikh. Since Straton was forcefully ejected from the village, we may assume that Jeddous was a man of importance, probably a larger landowner in Judea or Idumea. Regarding the relation of the Ptolemaic government to Palestinian landowners, see Tcherikover, "Palestine under the Ptolemies," pp. 9ff.

[Ἀλέξαν]δρος Ὀρύαι χαίρειν. ἐκομισάμην τὸ παρὰ σ[οῦ
  ἐ]πιστόλι[ον],
[ἐν ὧι ὑ]π ἔγρ[α]ψάς μοι τήν τε παρὰ Ζήνωνος πρὸς
  Ἰεδδοῦν γεγρ[αμμένην],
[ὅπως ἄν], ἐὰμ μὴ ἀποδιδῶι τἀργ[ύ]ριον Στράτωνι τῶι
  παρὰ Ζήνωνος [πα]-
[ραγενο]μένωι, ἐνέχυρα αὐτοῦ π[αραδ]είξωμεν αὐτῶι. ἐγὼ
  μὲν [ο]ὖν
5 [ἄρρωστ]ος ἐτύγχανον ἐκ φαρμακείας ὤν, συναπέστειλα
  [δὲ Στ]ράτωνι
[παρ᾽ ἡ]μῶν νεανίσκον καὶ ἐπιστολὴν ἔγρ[α]ψα πρὸς
  Ἰεδδοῦν. παραγενόμενοι
[οὖν εἶπ]όν μοι μηθένα λόγον πεποιῆσθαι τῶι ἐπιστολ[ίωι
  μου], αὐτοῖς δὲ

[Alexan]dros to Oryas greeting. I received your note, to which you appended a copy of what was written to Jeddous by Zenon, who said that unless he (Jeddous) gave back the money to Straton, Zenon's man, we were to hand over his (Jeddous') pledge to Straton. Since I myself happened to be sick because of some medicine, I sent a lad, a servant, to Straton and wrote a letter to Jeddous. When they returned they told me that he had taken no account of my letter, but had attacked them and thrown them out of the village. Therefore, I wrote to you (that you might know). Good-bye. (Year) 27, Peritios intercalary 20.

Outside address: To Oryas.

[χεῖρας] προσενεγκεῖν καὶ ἐγβαλ[εῖ]ν ἐκ τῆς κώμης.
γέγραφα οὖν σοι.
ἔρρωσο. (ἔτους) κζ, Περιτίου ἐμβολίμου κ.

Verso: Ὀρύαι.

8 MEMORANDUM TO ZĒNŌN FROM KYDIPPOS
PSI IV 413

259–257 BCE

Ὑπόμνημα Ζήνωνι
παρὰ Κυδίππου.
εἰ μὲν ἦν τι τῶν ὑπο-
γεγραμμένων πράσι-
5   μον λαβεῖν ἐκ τοῦ ἐμ-
πορίου, καθάπερ οἱ ἰα[τ]ροὶ
συντάσσουσιν, οὐκ ἂν
ἐνωχλοῦμεν ὑμᾶς·
νυνεὶ δὲ γεγράφαμέν σοι
10   ὧν χρείαν ἔχομεν, καθάπερ Ἀπολλώνιος ὤιετο
δεῖν. εἰ οὖν παράκειταί σοι,
ἀπόστειλον ἡμῖν ο[ἶνο]υ τε
ἢ Λεσβίου ἢ Χίου κεράμιον
15   ὡς ἡδίστου, καὶ μέλιτος
μάλιστα μὲν χοῦν,
εἰ δὲ μή, ὅσον ἂν ἐνδέ-
χηται· καὶ ταρίχου τὸ
σταμνίον σύνταξ[ο]ν ἡμῖν
20   ἐμπλῆσαι. τούτων γὰρ ἀμφοτέρων πλείστην χρείαν
νομίζουσιν εἶναι. ἐὰγ γὰρ
ὑγιάνωμεν καὶ εἰς
Βυζάντιον ἀποδημή-
25   σωμεν, ἄξομεν ὑμῖν
πάλιν σπουδαῖον
τάριχον.

Verso: ὑπόμνημα Κυδίππου.

Memorandum to Zenon from Kydippos. If I were able to purchase any of the things written below, which (just as) the physicians prescribe, we (I) would not trouble you; but as it is we have written to you about what we need, since Apollonios considered it necessary. Therefore, if you have it in stock, send us a jar of the very sweetest Lesbian or Chian wine and, if at all possible, a chous of honey or, if not that much, as much as you can; and command that the jar be filled with salt fish. For both of these things are considered necessary. And if our (my) health improves and we go abroad to Byzantium, we will bring you back some excellent salt fish.

Outside docket of receipt: Memorandum from Kydippos.

9 PHILŌTAS TO ZĒNŌN
PCairZen V 59804

7 September 258 BCE

Dated Zenon documents indicate that Zenon returned to Egypt about the end of year 27 of Philadelphos' reign (spring 258 BCE) and, though we cannot follow his movements exactly at this point, by the beginning of year 28, we find him functioning as Apollonios' executive secretary on a long inland tour. Edgar suggests (see PMich I, Introduction) that Zenon may have returned to Egypt because of a change in the political situation (e.g., Philadelphos' stepson seems to have instigated a rebellion about this time, and the second Syrian War broke out), but he prefers to interpret the return as Apollonios' need for Zenon on his lengthy tour. This marks a new stage in Zenon's career because, though he might have traveled with Apollonios earlier in an inspection of the outer provinces, it is only during this period (years 28 and 29) that we find dated letters addressed to Apollonios among Zenon's papers.

In the summer of year 28 (258 BCE), Apollonios sailed away from Alexandria on his inspection tour, accompanied by many accountants, scribes and servants (see PCorn 1); he moved up the Kanopic branch of the Nile and stopped for several days at Naukratis and Nikiou. By October, he was at Krokodilopolis in the Fayum and here, we may presume, Zenon first visited Apollonios' estate at Philadelphia. Returning down river at the beginning of winter, Apollonios spent a month at Memphis, where he owned a second estate. After sailing down the eastern branch of the Nile to such places as Leontopolis and Mendes, the party returned to Memphis before the end of April. Then, sailing down the western (Kanopic) branch of the Nile, stopping briefly at Naukratis and Hermopolis, Apollonios arrived at Alexandria in late May 257 BCE, after an absence of eleven months.

Apollonios apparently visited the nome capitals and other centers to inspect the operation of the various phases of state work and to hear cases that came under the dioiketes' jurisdiction. Moreover, several documents show Apollonios checked on his own estates and discussed their operation with the managers, Panakestor at Philadelphia and Addaios at Memphis (e.g., see letters 18 and 19; PCairZen V 59814, 59815, and III 59387). During the tour, Zenon handled Apollonios' correspondence and screened his potential visitors and applicants. Since Apollonios was often busy and not always accommodating, Zenon's authority to grant an audience gave him a good deal of influence. By the same token, his position required discretion. That some of Apollonios' mail was sent directly to Zenon indicates Zenon's standing: the letter writers wanted Zenon's personal influence on their behalf, as he delivered their messages to Apollonios.

Zenon's activities and the activities of the clerical staff, indicate that Apollonios did not strictly separate public and private business. But Zenon, more than other members of the retinue, seems to have been occupied with Apollonios' private affairs; he gave the orders regarding domestic staff salaries and he received staff complaints and requests.

The present letter concerns runaway slaves. Though these could be the same slaves about whom Zenon writes in the letters of number 6 above (since Marisa, where those slaves were bought, is not far inland from the harbor at Gaza), the several months interval between these two pieces of correspondence favors a separate situation.

Φιλώτας Ζήνωνι χαίρειν. ἠξ[ί]ωσεν ἡμᾶς Κρότος γράψαι
  πρὸς σὲ περὶ τῶν
σωματίων τῶν ἀποχωρησάντων ἐκ το[ῦ Γα]ζαίων λιμένος.
  ἐτύγ[χ]ανον γὰρ παρειλημ-
μένος ὑπό τε Ἀπολλοφάνους καὶ αὐτοῦ [ὅπως] ἂν αὐ[τοῖς
  τὰ π]ερὶ τοὺς τελώνας
συνοικονομήσω καὶ τὸ τάχος ἀπο . . . .
  α[. . . . . αὐ]τοῖς [ἀποστ]εί[λ]ω. πορευθεὶς οὖν
5 πρὸς Ἡρώιδην τὸν τελώνην κατελάμβανον
  Ἀπολλοφάνην συγχώρησιν πεποιημένον

Philotas to Zenon greeting. Krotos requested us to write to you concerning the slaves who ran away from the harbor of Gaza. For I happened to be called in by Apollophanes and him (i.e., Krotos) in order to work with them on matters with the tax collectors and (to recover and send the slaves?) quickly to them. Therefore, having proceeded to Herodes the tax collector, I found that Apollophanes had made an agreement with him for a tax of eighty drachmas in the name of Apollonios.

πρὸς αὐτὸν τέλους ⊦π εἰς τὸ Ἀπολλωνίου ὄνομα. ταύτην
μ[ὲ]ν οὖν τὴν ὠνὴν ἠρά-
μην, ἄλλην δὲ ποιοῦμαι εἰς τὸ Ἀπολλοφάνους ὄνομα καὶ
ἀπὸ τ[ο]ῦ συγκεχωρημένου
τέλους ἀφεῖλον ⊦μ καὶ συγκατέστησα τὰ σώματα ἐπὶ τὸν
λ[ι]μένα καὶ εἰσηγάγαμεν
τὰ σώματα πρὸς Ἡρακλείδην καὶ παρεδώκαμεν
Ἀπολλοφάνει καὶ [ἔ]φη αὐτὸς φυλάξειν,
10 ἡμᾶς δὲ οὐκ εἴα πράγματα ἔχειν βουλομένων ἡμῶν
συνδιατ[ηρ]εῖν. γέγραφα οὖν σοι
ὅπως ἂν εἰδῆις. χαρίζοιο δ᾽ ἄμ μοι περὶ ὧν σοι τὸ
ὑπόμνημα ἔδωκα ἀγοράσας καὶ ἀποστείλας μοι.
καὶ σὺ δὲ γράφε πρὸς ἡμᾶς περὶ ὧν ἂν βούληι· ποιήσομεν
γὰρ αὐτό σ[οι] προθύμως.
ἔρρωσ[ο]. Λκη, Πανήμου κζ.

Verso
1st hand: Ζήνωνι.
2nd hand: Φιλώτου.

Whereupon I annulled that (contract?) and made another in the name of Apollophanes and decreased the tax agreed upon by forty drachmas and I brought the slaves back to the harbor and we brought them in to Herakleides (the boat captain in whose ship the slaves were to be carried to Egypt) and handed them over to Apollophanes and he said that he himself would guard (them) and he did not let us concern ourselves with it although we were willing to assist in watching (the slaves). Therefore, I wrote to you that you would know. You would favor me by buying and sending to me the things about which I gave you the memorandum. And write to us concerning whatever you want; for we will eagerly do it for you. Good-bye. (Year) 28, Panemos 27.

Outside address: To Zenon.
Docket of receipt: From Philotas.

10 SIMALĒ TO ZĒNŌN
PCol III 6

early March 257 BCE

This letter was docketed by Zenon at Berenikes Hormos, the place where Apollonios' retinue remained for about two weeks in early March of 257 BCE. The letter's form is largely that of a petition or complaint. It is unusual however, given this format, that the addressor's name is written before the recipient's in the opening address. This is probably to be explained by the social class of the addressor, Simale. Moreover, the fact that her son's regular allotment of castor oil (*kiki*, used for illumination), while on tour with Apollonios, had been changed to the higher grade olive oil (see PCorn 1.66–69, 137–38) also suggests the status of the family. This letter illustrates Zenon's personal influence with Apollonios, since the letter is addressed to Zenon himself even though the request could only have been granted by Apollonios.

Σιμάλη Ἡροφάντου μήτηρ Ζήνωνι χαίρειν. ἀκούσασα
ἠνωχλῆσθαι μοῦ τ[ὸ παι-
δάριον καὶ σφοδρότερον, παρεγενόμην πρὸς ὑμᾶς καὶ
ἐλθοῦσα ἤθελον ἐντυχεῖν σοι ὑ[πὲρ τῶν
αὐτῶν τούτων. ἐπεὶ δέ με Ὀλύμπιχ[ο]ς ἐκώλυσεν τοῦ μὴ
ἴδειν σε, ε[ἰ]σεκομίσθην πρὸ[ς τὸ
παιδίον ὡς ποτ᾽ ἠδυνάμην, καὶ εὗρον αὐτὸν καὶ μάλα
γελοιώσα[ς]α κείμενον καὶ ἤ[δη ἱ-
5 κανόμ μοι ἦν ὁρῶσαν ἐκεῖνον λύπεισθαι. ἀλλ᾽
ἐπιπαραγενόμενος Ὀλύμπιχος ἔφη αὐτὸ[ν
τύπτων σαπρὸν ποιή[σε]ιν ἢ πεπο[ί]ηκεν ὃς ἤδη σχεδὸ[ν]
ἦν. εὐπρεπῶς δέομαι οὖν σου

Simale, mother of Herophantos, to Zenon greeting. When I heard that my son was exceedingly distressed, I came to you and when I arrived I intended to complain to you about these same things. And when Olympichos hindered me from seeing you, I gained entry to the boy as well as possible and, though I laughed heartily, I found him lying (ill) and that was already enough to grieve me when I saw him. But when Olympichos arrived he said that he would beat him (until) he made him useless—or he had done so, since he already was nearly that. Accordingly, therefore, I

καὶ ἱκετεύω ἐπιστρόφην ποιήσασθαι περὶ τούτων καὶ
ἀνάγγειλαι Ἀπολλωνίωι ὅν [τινα
τρόπον μοῦ ὑβριζόμενον τὸ παιδίον διατετέληκεν
ὑπ᾽ ᾽Ολυμπίχου ὡς καὶ τῆς νόσου τ[οῦ-
τον μεταίτιον γεγένησθαι. ἐγὼ γὰρ πρὸς τῶι μηδ᾽
εἰλήφεναι μηθὲν ἐνιαυτοῦ ἤδ[η
10 ἀλλ᾽ ἢ τὴν μνᾶν καὶ τρεῖς ἀρτάβας σίτου τοῦ Δύστρου
μηνὸς οὗ εἰσπορεύεται Ἡρόφα[ντος
πρὸς ὑμᾶς. τὴν μὲν οὖν Ἀπολλωνίου εὔνοιαν καὶ τὴν σὴν
ἀναγγέλλει μοι αὐτὸ τὸ παι[δά-
ριον ἣν ἔχοντες διατέλειτε εἰς αὐτόν. ἀξίω οὖν σε ἄμα δὲ
καὶ δέομαί εἰ τι συντέ[λειν τέ-
ταχε Ἀπολλώνιος αὐτῶι ὀψώνιον ἀποδόθηναί μοι.
γ[[.]]ίνωσκε δὲ, ὡς ἂν τάχιστα αὐτὸν
ὁ θεὸς ἄφη, καταστήσω αὐτὸν πρὸς ὑμᾶς ἵνα καὶ σε ἴδω
ὑπὲρ τῶν λοιπῶν. τὰ δὲ λοιπὰ
15 πυνθάνου τοῦ φέροντός σοι τὰ γράμματα. οὐ γὰρ
ἀλλότριος ἡμῖν ἔστιν.
εὐτύχει.

Verso
1st hand: Ζήνωνι.
2nd hand: Σ]ιμάλ[η]ς τῆς Ἡ[ρ[ο]φ[άντου μητρός].
(ἔτους) κη Περιτίου ϛ.
ἐν τῶι Βερενίκης Ὅρμωι.

request and entreat you to bring about a correction of these things and to report to Apollonios in what manner my boy has been so thoroughly mistreated by Olympichos that he has become the cause of (accessory to) the illness. Moreover, I also have received nothing now for a year except the mina and three artabs of grain since the month Dystros, when Herophantos came to you. Indeed, the boy informs me of the good will of Apollonios and of yourself which you always have for him. Therefore, I request and entreat you in this light that, if Apollonios has ordered that he be paid anything else (still outstanding), his wages be paid to me. Be aware ("Know") that as soon as the god releases him (of sickness), I will bring him back to you in order that I may also see you about other matters. The rest (i.e., anything else that remains) learn from the one who carries the letter to you. For he is no stranger to us. Farewell.

Outside address: To Zenon.
Docket of receipt: From Simale, mother of Herophantos. (Year) 28, Peritios 6. In Berenikes Hormos.

6 Westermann, the original editor of this letter, suggests that Simale's motherly affections have made her somewhat incoherent at this point. It is evident that Olympichos did not think highly of Herophantos' work.

11 SŌSTRATOS TO ZĒNŌN
PMich I 6   24 March 257 BCE

This is a somewhat literary letter of recommendation on behalf of Aischylos. The addressor is probably the Sostratos of PMich I 70, not the Sostratos who, subsequently, was a friend of Zenon at Philadelphia. Zenon received the letter at Boubastos in the delta, the next stop after Berenikes Hormos (see letter 10). Several other letters of introduction were received as well during the brief stay at Boubastos, recommending Greeks either to Zenon or to Apollonios (see PCol III 7; PCairZen I 59045, 59046).

Σώστρατος Ζήνωνι χαίρειν. οὐκ οἶμαι μέν σε ἀγνοεῖν περὶ
Αἰσχύλου ὅτι οὐκ ἔστιν
ἡμῖ̣ν ἀλλότριος, ἀναπέπλευκεν δὲ πρὸς ὑμᾶς ἵνα
συσταθῆι Κλεονίκωι. καλῶς ἂν οὖ[ν]
ποιήσαις φιλοτιμηθεὶς ὅπως ἂν συστήσηις αὐτὸν
Κλεονίκωι. ἐὰν δ᾽ ἄρα μὴ κατα-

Sostratos to Zenon greeting. I do not think you are ignorant regarding Aischylos, that he is no stranger to us. He has now sailed up river to your company in order to be introduced to Kleonikos. Therefore, please make a sincere effort to introduce him to Kleonikos; and if he does not [come

[λάβηι ἐκεῖνον παρ᾽ ὑμῖν, ἐπιστολὰς πα]ρὰ τῶν φίλων
λαβὲ πρὸς αὐτόν. τοῦτο δὲ
5 π[οιήσ]ας ε[ὐχαρι]στήσεις ἡμῖν· σπεύδω γὰρ περὶ αὐτοῦ.
γράφε δὲ καὶ σὺ ἡμῖν τί ἄν σοι
[ποιοῦ]ντ[ες χαρ]ιζοίμεθα.
ἔρρωσο. ⌐κη, Περιτίου κ̄.

Verso
1st hand: Ζήνωνι.
2nd hand: Traces of line.
⌐κη, Περιτίου ..
ἐμ Βουβάστωι.

upon the latter in your company,] get [letters of introduction] to him (i.e., Kleonikos) from his friends. By doing this you will do us a favor; for I am interested in him. You also must write to us regarding whatever we could do to favor you. Good-bye. (Year) 28, Peritios 20.

Outside address: To Zenon.
Docket of receipt: (Year) 28, Peritios . . . In Boubastos.

12 ANTIMENĒS TO ZĒNŌN
PMich I 10
1 April 257 BCE

Antimenes, an acquaintance of Zenon in Alexandria, sends a copy of a letter received from Sosipatros concerning the arrival of a lady named Doris at Arsinoe in Cilicia. Four months earlier, Antimenes had reported sending the same woman off on a voyage (PCairZen I 59029), after having extended certain courtesies to her. Though Antimenes' own letter is somewhat fragmented, the enclosed (appended) correspondence of Sosipatros is nearly complete and it speaks of the arrival of two people, Ariston and "the sister." "The sister" is the lady named Doris in Zenon's docket. Both she and Ariston may have been Zenon's relatives.

Though references to family affairs are rare in the Zenon correspondence, we know that Zenon was a native of Kaunos, on the coast of Caria (brought under Philadelphos' rule ca. 280 BCE), that his father was named Agreophon and that other sons were still living in Kaunos in the year 28 (see PCairZen I 59056). Zenon belonged apparently to a respectable, though not particularly distinguished or wealthy Carian family (see Edgar's Introduction to PMich I, sect. 9, pp. 43ff.).

Ἀντιμένης Ζήνωνι χαίρειν. εἰ ἔρρωσαι, εὖ ἂν [ἔχοι·
ὑγίαινον δὲ καὶ ἐγώ].
ὑπογέγραφά σοι τῆς παρὰ Σωσιπάτρου ἐλθούσης μ[οι
ἐπιστολῆς τὸ ἀντίγρα]-
φον, ὅπως εἰδὼς ἀναφέρηις ἐν λόγωι Ἀπολλωνίωι ἐ[
οὐθὲν αὐτοῖς συνετέθη ἐφόδιον οὐδ᾽ ακ.ρ..ν..[
5 ὑπὸ τοῦ χειμῶνος κατηνέγχθησαν εἰς Ἀρσινόην[
[ἔρρωσο. ⌐]κη, Περιτίου κ̄η.
Σωσίπατρος Ἀντιμένει χαίρειν. εἰ τῶι τε σώματ[ι
ἔρρωσαι καὶ] τὰ γοιπά σοί ἐστιν
κατὰ γνώμην, ἔχοι ἂν καλῶς· ἐρρώμεθα δὲ καὶ αὐτοί.
π[αραγενόμε]νοι πρὸς ἡμᾶς
Ἀρίστων καὶ ἡ ἀδελφὴ ἀνήγγελλον πεπολυωρῆσθαι
ὑ[πὸ σοῦ κατὰ] πάντα. καλῶς οὖν

Antimenes to Zenon greeting. If you are well, it would be excellent; I too am well. I have appended below for you a copy of the letter which came to me from Sosipatros in order that, by being made aware, you could enter to the account of Apollonios . . . no traveling allowance was delivered to them . . . were driven in by the stormy weather . . . to Arsinoe. [Good-bye]. (Year) 28, Peritios 28.

Sosipatros to Antimenes greeting. If you are well in body and everything else is to your satisfaction, it would be excellent; we too are well. Upon arriving here, Ariston and the sister reported that they had been treated very well by you in every respect. You do well then by not acting like a stranger

10 ποεῖς πρὸς ἡμᾶς οὐκ ἀλλοτρίως ἔχων· πειρασόμεθα γὰρ
   [καὶ αὐτοὶ π]ερὶ ὧν ἂν σὺ σπου-
δάζηις καὶ γράφηις πρὸς ἡμᾶς τὴν πᾶσαν ἐπιμέλεια[ν
   ποεῖσθαι. γί]νωσκε δὲ ὑπὸ
τῶν χειμώνων κατενεγχθέντας εἰς Πάταρα, κεῖθε[ν δὲ
   μισθωσά]μενοι πλοῖον
παρέπλευσαν πρὸς ἡμᾶς εἰς Ἀρσινόην. τὸ δὲ ναῦλον
   διωρθ[. . . . .]νων ⊦γε. γέγραφα οὖν σοι ὅπως εἰδῆις.

15   [ἔρρωσο. Lκη], Ἀπελλαίου κϛ.

Verso
1st hand: Ζήνωνι.
2nd hand: Ἀντιμένης περὶ Δωρίδος
             καὶ τῆς παρὰ Ἀντιπάτρου
             ἐπιστολῆς ἀντίγραφον. Lκα, Δύστρου
             ιζ, ἐν Μένδ[ητι].

toward us; for we ourselves will make an all-out effort to do whatever you would be concerned about and whatever you should write to us about. Know that they were driven in to Patara by the storms; from whence they hired a boat and sailed here to Arsinoe. The fare has been paid . . . amounting to thirty-five drachmas. I have written therefore to you in order that you may know. [Good-bye. (Year) 28], Apellaios 26.

Outside address: To Zenon.
Docket of receipt: Antimenes about Doris, and a copy of the letter from Antipatros. (Year) 28, Dystros 17. In Mendes.

---

17   Ἀντιπάτρου: apparently a slip for Ζωσιπάτρου.

13 ALEXANDROS TO ZĒNŌN
PCol III 9   received 27 April 257 BCE

This letter is from Alexandros, a cavalry commander, to whom a certain amount of back pay was outstanding. Menetos, a superior connected with the army, who was probably the official administrator of the revenues from soldiers' agricultural holdings, had promised to pay the money, but had died before fulfilling the obligation. Subsequently, Alexandros had consulted with Mys, an assistant to Artemidoros who, at that time, held Menetos' office. Since Mys was about to meet Apollonios and Zenon, Mys and Alexandros agreed that a memorandum to Apollonios should be carried along. Alexandros requests Zenon's support in connection with the memorandum to Apollonios.

Ἀλέξανδρος Ζήνωνι χαίρειν. εἰ ἔρρωσαί τε καὶ ἐν τοῖς
   λοιποῖς [κατὰ νοῦν
ἀπαλλάσεις, εἴη ἂν ὡς ἡμεῖς βουλόμεθα. ἐρρώμεθα δὲ καὶ
   αὐτοί. παραγ[ινομένου
πρὸς ὑμας Μυὸς ἔδοξεν ἡμῖν βελτίον εἶναι αὐτῶι τε τῶι
   Μῦι ὑπόμνημα ἀ[πόστειλαι ἐν ὧι
μνησθῆι Ἀπολλωνίωι περὶ τῆς συντάξεως ἧς ἔταξεν ἡμῖμ
   Μένετ[ος ἀ]ποτ[αχθηναι ἕως τὴν
5 ὀφειλομένην κεκομίσμεθα. οὔτε ἀφ᾽ οὗ χρόνου κεῖνος
   τετελεύτηκε [τὴν σύνταξιν
ἀποδίδωσιν. καλῶς δ᾽ ἔχειν ὑπέλαβον καὶ σοὶ γράψαι
   ὅπως ἐὰν τινὰ σὸ χρεί[αν τὰ πάρον-
τα ἔχηι συναντιλάβηι φιλοτίμως καὶ ἡμῶν ἕνεκεν καὶ
   Μενέτου. ὅια ἂν α[ἰτήσωμεν σοῦ
βουληθέντος πάντα ἡμῖν τὰ φιλάνθρωπα ἔσται παρ᾽
   Ἀπολλωνίου, καὶ ἡμεῖς δ[ιαγνωσόμεθα
διὰ σὲ σεσῶισθαι καὶ ἀνέσταναι. περὶ ὧν σπουδάσομεν καὶ
   αὐτοὶ καθ᾽ ὅσον [ἡμῖ]ν κ[

Alexandros to Zenon greeting. If you are well and [your mind] is at rest about other things, it would be as we desire. We ourselves are also well. Since Mys was coming to you, it seemed better to us (me) and to Mys himself to [send] a memorandum in which he would remind Apollonios about the allowance which Menetos had ordered to be assigned to us (me) until we had received what was owed. Not from the time of his (Menetos') death has he (Apollonios) paid [the allowance]. I have thought it advisable to write to you also in order that, if the matter requires your assistance, you may cooperate zealously both on our account and that of Menetos. Whatever we should ask, if you desired it, will result in generosity (extended) to us from Apollonios and we [will be cognizant] that it was on account of you that we were saved and restored. Regarding these (favors) we ourselves

10 τὰς χάριτας ἀποδίδοναι σοί.
    εὐτύχει.

will try, as zealously as possible, to repay the favor to you. Farewell.

Verso

1st hand: Ζήνωνι.

2nd hand: Ἀλέξανδρος περὶ τῆς γινομένης
αὐτῶι συντάξεως. (ἔτους) κη Δύστρου κδ.
ἐμ Μέμφει.

Outside address: To Zenon.
Docket of receipt: Alexandros, about the pay coming to him. (Year) 28, Dystros 24. In Memphis.

14 MNASISTRATOS TO ZĒNŌN
PCol III 10   30 April 257 BCE

The Mnasistratos of this letter (identified as Mnasistratos in Zenon's docket of receipt) is the same person as the Mnasistratos of PCairZen I 59041, namely, an assistant of Zoilos, the oikonomos of the Arsinoite nome. Mnasistratos informs Zenon that he has been very ill and, because of this, requests Zenon's consideration.

Μνασίστπατος Ζ]ήνωνι χαίρειν. καλῶς ἂν ἔχοι εἰ ἔρρωσαι
    καὶ ὑγιαί-
νεις τῶι σώματι. ἐ]γὼ εἰς μεγάλην δὲ ἀρρωστίαν ἐνέπεσον
    καὶ εἰς ἀπο-
ρίαν. σὺ δὲ ἐπιμέλ]ειαν ἔχε ἡμῶν καὶ ἐπίστελλέ μοι ἄν τι
    σοὶ βούλη γίνε-
    σθαι.]
5   ἔρρωσο. (ἔτους) κη, Φαμενὼθ ζ.

Verso

1st hand: Ζήνωνι.

2nd hand: Μνασίστρατος.
(ἔτους) κθ, Ξανδικοῦ β.
ἐμ Μέμφει.

Manistratos to Zenon greeting. It would be excellent if you are (feeling?) well and if you are physically sound. I have fallen into a grave illness and into a difficult strait. [Be considerate] of us (me) and send to me regarding whatever you should want. Good-bye. (Year) 28, Phamenoth 7.

Outside address: To Zenon.
Docket of receipt: Mnasistratos. (Year) 29, Xandikos 2. In Memphis.

---

5   Mnasistratos writes "year 28, Phamenoth 7," but the regnal year 29 had already begun two days earlier on Phamenoth 5. The original editor of this letter, Westermann, suggests that Mnasistratos' illness may account for his failure to recognize the change of year.

15 HIEROKLĒS TO ZĒNŌN
PCairZen I 59060   ca. 5 May 257 BCE

Two of Zenon's favorite pastimes were the public games and the religious festivals. He had a personal interest in the various competitions, since some of the contestants had been trained in the gymnasium at his expense. One musical protégé, Herakleotes, complains about his treatment (PLond VII 2017), and a certain youth called Kleon addresses Zenon as father, though he too was probably only another recipient of Zenon's sponsorship.

The present letter from Hierokles comes in response to Zenon's letter about the athletic training of a boy named Pyrrhos. Zenon had written that Pyrrhos, who was being educated in Alexandria, should be trained only if he could win a prize. Otherwise, the effort would only distract from his studies. Hierokles replies that Ptolemy, the master of the palaestra, which was probably attached to the palace of Apollonios in Alexandria, is pleased with the boy's progress.

PLond VII 1941 and PCairZen I 59061 arrived a day earlier and they appear to almost duplicate the first and second part, respectively, of the present letter. Edgar attributes the dispatch of these similar letters to some mistake (PCairZen I 59060, introductory comments) and, since they arrived on different days, they were probably delivered by different messengers.

Ἱεροκλῆς Ζήνων[ι χ]αίρειν. [εἰ ἔ]ρρωσαι, ἔχοι ἂν καλῶς·
ὑγιαίνομεν δὲ καὶ ἡμεῖς. ἔ[γραψάς]
μοι περὶ Πύρρου, εἰ [μὲ]ν ἀκρει [βῶ]s ἐπιστάμεθα, ἀλείφειν
αὐτόν, εἰ δὲ μέ, μὴ συνβῇ[ι ἀνήλω]-
τε
μά μάταιον προσπεσεῖν καὶ [ἀ]πὸ τῶν γραμμάτων
ἀποσ{σ}παθῆναι. π[ερ]ὶ μὲν οὖ[ν τοῦ με]
ἐπίσ{σ}τασθαι οἱ θεοὶ μάλιστ᾽ ἂν εἰδέησαν, Πτολεμαίωι
δὲ φαίνεται, ὅσα κατ᾽ ἄ[νθρωπον],
5 ὅτι τῶν νῦν ἀλιφομένων, οἳ προειλήφασιν χρόνον
πολύν, πολὺ κρείττων Πύ[ρρος?]
καὶ σφόδρα ὀλίγου χρόνου πολὺ ὑπερέξει αὐτῶν·
προσπορεύεται δὲ καὶ πρὸς [ταῦτα]
καὶ πρὸς τὰ λοιπὰ μαθήματα· σὺν δὲ θεοῖς εἰπεῖν ἐλπίζω
σε στεφανωθήσεσθαι. ἀπ[όστειλον]
δὲ αὐτῶι ἐγλουστρίδα ὅτι τάχος, καὶ μάλιστα μὲν ἔστω
τὸ δέρμα αἴγειον, εἰ δὲ μέ, [μόσχειον]
λεπτόν, καὶ χιτῶνα καὶ ἱμάτιον καὶ τὸ στρωμάτιον καὶ
περίστρωμα καὶ προσ[κεφάλαια]
10 καὶ τὸ μέλι. ἔγραψας δέ μοι θαυμάζεις εἰ μὴ κατέχω ὅτι
τούτοις πᾶσι τέλος ἀκ[ολουθεῖ].
ἐπίσταμαι, ἀλλὰ σὺ εἰκανὸς εἶ διοικῶν ἵνα ἀποσταλῆι ὡς
ἀσφαλέστατα.

Verso
1st hand: Ζήνωνι.
2nd hand: Ἱεροκλῆς περὶ Πύρρου.
            Ⳑκθ Ξανδικοῦ γ̄.
            ἐμ Μέμφει.

Hierokles to Zenon greeting. If you are well, it would be excellent. We also are well. You wrote to me regarding Pyrrhos, (telling me) to anoint him (for gymnastic training), if we know with certainty (that he will be a success), but if not certain, to make sure that he not incur useless expense nor be distracted from his studies. Now, so far as my being certain is concerned, (only) the gods know for sure, but it seems to Ptolemy, so far as a man can tell, that Pyrrhos is much better than those presently being trained, who started training a long time before him, and that very soon he will be much beyond them; moreover, he is also pursuing his other studies; and to speak with the gods' leave, I hope to see you crowned. Send a bathing apron to him most quickly and, if at all possible, let it be of goatskin or, if not possible, of thin sheepskin, and a tunic and cloak, and the mattress, bedcovering, [pillows] and honey. You wrote to me that you were surprised that I did not realize that there is a tax on all these things. I know it, but you are well able to manage that it be sent with the greatest possible security.

Outside address: To Zenon.
Docket of receipt: Hierokles about Pyrrhos. (Year) 29, Xandikos 3. In Memphis.

1 Hierokles: the author of PCairZen I 59061, PLond VII 1941, PSI IV 340.
2 PLond VII 1941 has ὅτι νικήσει after ἐπιστάμεθα, i.e., "you told us to train him if we were sure that he will win."
3 μέ: read μή.

16
TOUBIAS TO APOLLŌNIOS
CPJud I 4 (=PCairZen I 59076)

12 May 257 BCE

This and the following letter were sent to Apollonios on the same day by Toubias, and both were written in a fine, large hand, probably that of a Greek scribe. The present letter was written before the following one. Consequently, the elaborate greetings of the health wish in this first letter serve as an introduction to both letters (cf. Edgar's introductory comments in PCairZen 59076). This letter informs Apollonios that four slaves have been sent to him with a eunuch. The phrase, πολλὴ χάρις τοῖς θεοῖς ("many thanks to the gods") seems unexpected in a letter from a Jew, even though he is dictating to a Greek scribe (cf. Tcherikover's comments in CPJud I 4). But Toubias was the father of Joseph, whose descendants championed Hellenism in Coele-Syria.

Τουβίας Ἀπ[ολλωνίωι χαίρειν]. εἰ σύ τε ἔρρωσαι καὶ τὰ σὰ πάντα
καὶ τὰ λοιπά σο[ι κατὰ νοῦν ἐστίν, πο]λλὴ χάρις τοῖς θεοῖς· καὶ αὐτὸς δὲ
ὑγίαινον, σοῦ διὰ π[αντὸς μνείαν ποι]ούμενος, ὥσπερ δίκαιον ἦν. ἀπέσταλκά σοι ἄγοντα Αἰνέ[αν εὐνοῦχον ἕ]να καὶ παιδά[ρια οἰκε]τικά τε
5 καὶ τῶν εὐγενῶν τέσσαρα, ὧν [ἐστὶν] ἀπερίτμητα δύο. ὑπογεγράφαμεν
δέ σοι καὶ τὰς εἰκόνας [[αὐ]]τῶν π[αιδαρ]ίων ἵνα εἰδῆις.
     ἔρρωσο. (ἔτους) κθ, Ξανδικοῦ ι.

Αἶμος ὡς	Ἄτικος ὡς	Αὔδομος ὡς	Ὄκαιμος ὡς
(ἐτῶν) ι	(ἐτῶν) η	(ἐτῶν) ι	(ἐτῶν) ζ
μελαγχρὴς	μελίχρους	μελανόφθαλμος	⟨σ⟩τρογγυλοπρόσωπος
κλαστόθριξ	κλαστόθριξ	κλαστόθριξ	ἔσσιμος γλαυκός
μελανόφθαλμος	ὑπόσιμος	ἔσσιμος πρόστομος,	πυρράκης τετανὸς,
σιαγόνες μείζους	ἡσυχῆι μελανόφθαλμος	οὐλὴ παρ' ὀφρὺν δεξιάν,	οὐλὴ ἐμ μετώπωι
καὶ φακοὶ ἐπὶ σιαγόνι δεξιᾶι, ἀπερίτμητος.	οὐλὴ ὑπ' ὀφθαλμὸν δεξιόν, ἀπερίτμητος.	περιτετμημένος.	ὑπὲρ ὀφρὺν δεξιάν, περιτετμημένος.

Verso
1st hand: Ἀ[πολλωνίωι].
2nd hand: Τουβίας περὶ εὐνούχου
καὶ παιδαρίων δ̄ τῶν
ἀπεσταλμένων αὐτῶι.
(ἔτους) κθ, Ἀρτεμισίου ιϛ, ἐν Ἀλεξ(ανδρείαι).

Toubias to Apollonios greeting. If you are well and if all your affairs and everything else is proceeding according to your will, many thanks to the gods; we also are well, always remembering you, as I should. I have sent to you Aineias leading one eunuch and four boys, houseslaves and of good stock, two of whom are uncircumcised. Moreover, we have appended descriptions of the boys for your information. Good-bye. (Year) 29, Xandikos 10.

Haimos. About ten	Atikos. About eight	Audomos. About ten	Okaimos. About seven
Dark skin	Light skin	Black eyes	Round face. Nose flat
Curly hair	Curly hair	Curly hair. Nose flat	Grey eyes
			Fiery complexion
Black eyes	Nose some-what flat	Protruding lips	Long straight hair
Rather big jaws with moles on the right jaw	Black eyes scar below right eye	Scar near the right eyebrow	Scar on forehead above the right eyebrow
Uncircumcised	Uncircumcised	Circumcised	Circumcised

Outside address: To Apollonios.
Docket of receipt: Toubias, about a eunuch and four boys he has sent.
   (Year) 29, Artemision 16. In Alexandria.

17 TOUBIAS TO APOLLŌNIOS
CPJud I 5 (=PCairZen I 59075)   12 May 257 BCE

This is the second letter of Toubias to Apollonios, with a note appended to the king. Apollonios had asked Toubias to send the king some animals, probably rare ones, and this letter shows that Toubias has complied. Regarding Philadelphos' interest in rare animals, see the introductory comments to CPJud I 5 by Tcherikover.

Τουβίας Ἀπολλωνίωι χαίρειν. καθάπερ μοι ἔγραψας
ἀποστεῖλα[ι
[τῶι βασιλεῖ ξένια ἐν τῶι Ξανδικῶι] μηνί, ἀπέσταλκα τοῦ
Ξανδικ[οῦ]
τῆι δεκάτ[ηι ἄγοντα Αἰνέαν] τὸν παρ᾽ ἡμῶν ἵππους δύο,
κύνας [ἕ]ξ, ἡμιονά[γριον]
ἐξ ὄνου ἕν, ὑποζύγια [Ἀ]ραβικὰ λευκὰ δύο, πώ[λους] ἐξ
ἡμιοναγ[ρίου δύο,]
5   πῶλον ἐξ ὀναγρίου ἕνα· ταῦτα δ᾽ ἐστὶν τιθασά.
ἀπέσταλκα δέ [σοι
καὶ τὴν ἐπι[σ]τολὴν τὴν γραφεῖσαν παρ᾽ ἡμῶν ὑπὲρ τῶν
ξενί[ων]
τῶι βασιλεῖ, ὁμοίως δὲ καὶ τἀντίγραφα αὐτῆς ὅπως εἰδῆις.
ἔρρωσο. (ἔτους) κθ, Ξανδικοῦ ι.
Βασιλεῖ Πτολεμαίωι χαίρειν Τουβίας. ἀπέσταλκά σοι
ἵππο[υς δύο,]
10   κύνας ἕξ, ἡμιονάγριον ἐξ ὄνου ἕν, ὑποζύγια [Ἀρ]αβικὰ
λευκὰ [δύο,]
πώλους ἐξ ἡμιοναγρίου δύο, πῶλον ἐξ ὀναγρίου ἕνα.
εὐτύχει.

Toubias to Apollonios greeting. Just as you wrote to me to send [gifts for the king] in the month [of Xandikos], I have sent our man [Aineas] on the tenth of Xandikos [bringing] two horses, six dogs, one wild mule out of an ass, two white Arab asses, [two colts] out of a wild mule, one colt out of a wild ass; all these are tame. Also, I have sent the letter which I wrote to the king about the gifts, along with a copy of it that you may now. Good-bye. (Year) 29, Xandikos 10.

To King Ptolemy, greetings from Toubias. I have sent [two] horses to you, six dogs, one wild mule out of an ass, two white Arab asses, two colts out of a wild mule and one colt of a wild ass. Farewell.

Outside address: To Apollonios.
Docket of receipt: Toubias, regarding the things he sent to the king and the copy of his letter to the king. (Year) 29, Artemision 16. In Alexandria.

Verso
1st hand: Ἀπολλωνίωι.
2nd hand: Τουβίας τῶν ἀπεσταλμένων
τῶι βασιλεῖ καὶ τῆς πρὸς τὸν
βασιλέα ἐπιστολῆς τὸ ἀντίγραφον.
(ἔτους) κθ, Ἀρτεμισίου ιϛ. ἐν Ἀλεξαν(δρεία).

3 τὸν παρ' ἡμῶν above the line.
9 Both Edgar (cf. PCairZen I 59075) and Tcherikover (cf. CPJud I 5) note that all letters to the
   king, as here, write the king's name before the
   addressor's name in the opening address.

18 PANAKESTŌR TO ZĒNŌN
PSI V 502   received 14 July 257 BCE

Zenon remained in Alexandria for about two months (mid-May to mid-July), after
returning from his tour with Apollonios. Sometime before the twentieth of Daisios (20
July), Zenon had set out with Apollonios again (cf. Edgar, PMich I, pp. 24f.), stopping
for at least ten days at Arsinoe, which was near Alexandria. Subsequent movements
indicate that Apollonios was soon in the midst of another long tour. Zenon continued to
docket correspondence for Apollonios on this second tour until sometime in December
and, then, for the following two months we have no record of his movements. Edgar
suggests that this gap may be due to an illness, since Promethion the banker of Mendes,
writing on Choiach 28 (20 February; cf. PSI IV 333), first expresses concern about
Zenon's recent protracted illness and then relief at hearing of his recovery.

Though Promethion writes as if Zenon were still Apollonios' private secretary,
Zenon may have already been moving into another position. So far as we can tell, he
never returned to Apollonios' retinue following his illness. Rather, he soon became
responsible for Apollonios' personal estates at Memphis and Philadelphia. Before the
end of April 256 BCE, Zenon had replaced Panakestor as the manager of the estate at
Philadelphia.

The present correspondence reveals something of Apollonios' dissatisfaction with
Panakestor, which led to Zenon becoming his replacement. Though Panakestor's covering letter is not illuminating, the appended letter by Apollonios and Panakestor's
appended response show why Apollonios could have been unhappy with him.

Zenon's move to Philadelphia, however, may signal something more than dissatisfaction with Panakestor. Apollonios seems to have decided to devote more attention to his
estates and he chose his best man, Zenon, for this purpose. Zenon was not only a hard-
working lieutenant. His amiable nature made it possible to facilitate working relations
both with native farmers and with state officials. Apollonios himself sends a note of
approval for Zenon's work at Philadelphia (see letter 21 below). In any case, Zenon took
up residence in Philadelphia and, so far as documentation goes, he remained there until
his death.

Παυακέστωρ Ζήνωνι χαίρειν. εἰ ἔρρωσαι καὶ ἐν τοῖς
   λοιποῖς κατὰ λόγον ἀπαλλάσσεις, εἴη ἂν
ὡς ἡμεῖς θέλομεν· ἐρρώμεθα δὲ καὶ αὐτοί. καλῶς ἂν ποιοῖς
   μνημονεύων ἡμῶν. καὶ ὡς ἂν
ποτε εὐκαίρως ὑπολαμβάνηις Ἀπολλώνιον ὑπομνῆσαι
   ὑπὲρ ὧν σοι καὶ ἐμ Μέμφει τὰ ὑπο-

Panakestor to Zenon greeting. If you are well and
you are free from other cares, it would be as we
desire; we ourselves are also well. You would do
well to keep us (me) in mind. And, as you formerly
agreed, to remind Apollonios, at an opportune
moment, about the things which I gave you the

μνήματα ἔδωκα,καὶ ἔφης αὐτῶι σοι ἐπιμελὲς ἔσεσθαι
. [. . .] . ν, σπούδασον μνησθῆναι αὐτῶι
5 ἵνα τὰ προστάγματα λάβηι παρὰ τοῦ βασιλέως καθ[άπ]ερ
ὡμολόγησεν ἡμῖν· οἶδα γὰρ ὅτι σοῦ
βουλομένου ἔσται ἡμῖν πάντα. ὑπογέγραφα δέ [σ]οι καὶ
τῆς ἐλθούσης μοι παρ᾽ Ἀπολλωνίου τὸ ἀν-   ἐπιστολῆς
τίγραφον, ὡσαύτως δὲ καὶ {τ}ῶν ἀπέσταλκα αὐτῶι.
ἔρρωσο. Ⳑκθ, Παχὼνς ῑε.

Ἀπολλώνιος. Κατεπλησσόμην τὴν ὀλιγωρίαν σου ἐπὶ
τῶι μηθὲν γεγραφέναι μήτε περὶ τῆς
συντιμήσεως μήτε περὶ τῆς συναγωγῆς τοῦ σίτου. ἔτι
οὖν καὶ νῦν γράψον ἡμῖν ἐν οἷς ἕκαστά
10 ἐστιν.   Ⳑκθ, Ἀρτέμισι κγ, Φαρμοῦθ λ̄.

Ἀπολλωνίωι. ἐκομισάμην τὴν παροῦ σου ἐπιστολὴν
τοῦ Παχὼνς ῑδ παρὰ Ζωίλου, ἐν ἧι γράφεις
θαυμάζων ὅτι οὐθέν σοι ἀπέσταλκα περὶ τῆς
συντιμήσεως καὶ τῆς συναγωγῆς τοῦ σπόρου. ἡμῖν δὲ
συνέβη παραγενέσθαι εἰς Φιλαδέλφειαν τοῦ Φαμενὼθ
ῑ Ϛ καὶ [ε]ὐθὺ γράψαι Ζωίλωι καὶ Ζωπυρίωνι
καὶ τοῖς βασιλικοῖς γραμματεῦσιν παραγενέσθαι πρὸς
ἡμᾶς, ἵνα τὰ ὑπὸ σοῦ συντεταγμένα οἰκονο-
15 μήσωμεν. Ζωίλος μὲν οὖν ἐτύγχανεν συμπεριοδεύων
Τελέστηι· διὸ ἄσχολος ἦν· οἱ δὲ βασιλικοὶ γραμματεῖς
καὶ ὁ παρὰ Ζωπυρίωνος Παυῆς παρεγένοντο πρὸς ἡμᾶς
μεθ᾽ ἡμέρας ιβ. συναντησάντων δ᾽ αὐτῶν ἐπελθόντες
τὴν γῆν {ε}μετροῦμεν κατὰ γεωργὸν καὶ κατὰ φύλον
ἡμέρας ε̄. τοῦτο δὲ συντελέσαντες μεταπεμψά-
μενοι τοὺς γεωργοὺς τά τε παρὰ σοῦ φιλάνθρωπα αὐτοῖς
ἀπηγγέλλομεν καὶ τὰ λοιπὰ παρακαλέσαντες
ἠξιοῦμεν αὐτοὺς συντιμήσασθαι καθὰ ἡμῖν ἐν τῶι
ὑπομνήματι ἔδωκας, ἢ συνελθόντας μεθ᾽ ἡμῶν
20 ἐντυπὴν ποιησαμένους σύμβολα ποιήσασθαι. οἱ δ᾽ ἐπ[ὶ]
μὲν τοῦ παρόντος ἔφασαν βουλευσάμενοι
ἀποφανεῖσθαι ἡμῖν, μετὰ δ᾽ ἡμέρας δ̄ καθίσαντες εἰς τὸ
ἱερὸν οὐκ ἔφασαν οὔτε δικαίως οὔτ᾽ ἀδίκως
συντιμήσεσθαι, ἀλλ᾽ ἔφασαν ἐκχωρήσειν τοῦ σπόρου·
ὁμολογίαν γὰρ εἶναι πρός σε αὐτοῖς ἐκ τοῦ γενήματος
ἀποδώσειν τὸ τρίτον. ἐμοῦ δὲ καὶ Δάμιδος πολλὰ πρὸς
αὐτοὺς εἰπάντων, ἐπειδὴ οὐθὲν ἠνύομεν, ᾠχόμεθα
πρὸς Ζωίλον καὶ ἠξιοῦμεν αὐτὸν συμπαραγενέσθαι· ὁ δ᾽
ἔφη ἄσχολος εἶναι πρὸς τῆι τῶν ναυτῶν ἀποστολῆι.
25 ἐπανελθοῦσιν οὖν ἡμῖν εἰς Φιλαδέλφειαν μεθ᾽ ἡμέρας γ̄
ἔδοξεν, ἐπειδή, καθάπερ ἐν τῶι ὑπομνήματι
εἴχομεν, συντιμήσασθαι οὐχ ὑπέμενον οὐδὲ προκοπὴν
ποιήσασθαι, αὐτοὺς ἀξιῶσαι δοῦναι ὑποτίμησιν
ἤ ποτ᾽ ἑκάστωι φαίνεται· οἱ δ᾽ ἔδωκαν ἡμῖν ἣν
ἀπεστάλκαμέν σοι πρότερον. ταῦτα δ᾽ οἰκονομήσαντες

memoranda in Memphis, and that you tell him it will be your concern . . . , make an effort to remind him in order that the king receive the instructions just as he agreed with us. For I know that we (I) will have everything that you want. In addition, I have appended for you a copy of the letter which came to me from Apollonios, as well as my response to him. Good-bye. (Year) 29, Pachon 15.

Apollonios. I am astounded by your negligence in not having written either about the valuation or about the gathering of the crops. So, even now, write me immediately how everything is. (Year) 29, Artemisios 23, Pharmouthi 30.

To Apollonios. I received your letter on Pachon 14 from Zoilos, in which you express astonishment that I have sent you no word about the valuation and the gathering of the crops. It happened when we arrived in Philadelphia on Phamenoth 16 that I immediately wrote to Zoilos, Zopyrion and the royal secretaries (asking them) to come to us, in order that we could act according to your orders. Well, Zoilos happened to be making rounds (i.e., on an administrative tour) and so he was busy; but the royal secretaries and the agent of Zopyrion, Paues, arrived after twelve days. We proceeded, in their company, to survey the land for five days according to the individual farmer (tract) and according to the type of crop. When we had completed this we sought out the farmers and related your rescript (φιλάνθρωπα) to them and, after encouraging them in other respects, we asked them to make an agreement on the valuation according to what you specified in your memorandum to us or, having devised some (alternative?) plan to meet with us and contract an agreement. They said that after having deliberated for a while they would give us their answer and, after four days, taking up residence in the temple (i.e., they went on strike), they said they did not want to agree to any valuation, be it fair or unfair, but preferred to renounce their right to the crop. For they alleged there was an agreement between you and them that they would pay one-third of the produce. Moreover, when Damidos and I talked with them at length and accomplished nothing, we went away to Zoilos and asked him to assist us; but he said that he was busy in the dispatch of sailors. Consequent-

ἦμεν πρὸς τῶι τὴν σησαμῖτιν καὶ τὴν ξυλῖτιν μετὰ τῶν
βασιλικῶν γραμματέων γεωμετρεῖν, οἳ τὸν
λόγον ἡμῖν ἔδωκαν τῆι κ̄β̄ τοῦ Φαρμοῦθι. καλῶς ἂν οὖν
ποιήσαις μηδεμίαν ἡμῶν καταγινώσκων ὀλιγωρίαν·
30 οὐ γὰρ ἔστιν σοι ὑπηρετοῦντα ὀλιγωρεῖν. φανερὸν δέ σοι
ἔσται ἐκ τοῦ τὸν σῖτον συναχθήσεσθαι μηδεμιᾶς
οὔσης ἐν τῶι τόπωι χορηγίας.

Verso
1st hand: Ζήνωνι.
2nd hand: Πανακέστωρ. ἀντίγραφον ἐπιστολῆς
τῆς πρὸς Ἀπολλώνιον. Ⳑκθ,
Δαισίου ιδ, ἐν Ἀλεξαν⟨δρείαι⟩.

ly, it seemed necessary for us to return to Philadelphia after three days and, according to (what you recommended) in your memorandum, when they stood firm in refusing to accept the valuation and in not paying anything in advance, we asked them to give a lower valuation (ὑποτίμησις) which was agreeable to each one. The valuations they gave to us we have already sent to you. After we settled these things we (I) began to survey the land to be sown with sesame and the land covered with brushwood with the royal secretaries, who gave the report (on the survey) to us on Pharmouthi 22. Therefore you would do well not to lay any charge of negligence against us (me); for your servant is not negligent. It will be obvious to you from the grain that will be gathered that there is clearly no bounty in the place.

Outside address: To Zenon.
Docket of receipt: Panakestor. A copy of the letter to Apollonios. (Year) 29, Daisios 14. In Alexandria.

---

9   συντίμησις: The "valuation" referred to here is explained by the Revenue Laws in the instructions on gathering the crop of oil plants (cf. PRev 42.3–43.2), in which it is specified that the peasants and other cultivators shall have their produce assessed *before* the harvesting and threshing. In making the valuation prior to harvest, the state was probably trying to eliminate any tricks by the peasants during the harvesting and threshing. But the system was unfair to the cultivators, since any accurate estimate of the crop prior to threshing would have been problematic (cf. Rostovtzeff, *A Large Estate*, pp. 77ff.).

11 παρου: read παρά.
26 ὑποτίμησις: Rostovtzeff (*A Large Estate*, p. 76) noted that he knew of no parallel to this practice and of no analogies for the word ὑποτίμησις used in a similar connection.
28 γῆ ξυλῖτις: This type of land (also called δρυμός) was common during the reign of Ptolemy Philadelphos because it resulted from the land reclamation project in the Fayum, where new villages were being created and where land was being drained and made fit for cultivation. This "brushwood" land was part of the drained lakeshore, overgrown with brush, reeds and weeds (cf. Calderini, "Recerche sul regime," pp. 56ff.).

19 ARTEMIDŌROS TO PANAKESTŌR
PCairZen V 59816   26 December 257 BCE

The writer of this letter is Artemidoros, Apollonios' physician and companion on his inspection tours (also the author of PCairZen 59225 and 59251). The recipient is the Panakestor of the immediately preceding document, who was the manager of Apollonios' estate at Philadelphia. The letter was written shortly before Zenon replaced Panakestor at Philadelphia.

Artemidoros conveys Apollonios' order that no part of the estate be left uncultivated (Apollonios himself says the same in PCairZen 59387). Since many letters of the year preceding Zenon's arrival concern clearing the land of brushwood (cf. PMich I 25),

Apollonios' large land grant from the king was still in the process of being reclaimed (cf. the immediately preceding letter regarding the poor quality of the crops and see the general introduction to letters 5–26 regarding this land grant). The clearing operation, as well as the harvesting of grain and the planting of oil crops (specifically sesame), was the duty of Damis and his two brothers, Etearchos and Sostratos (cf. PSI V 500). Consequently, the manager of the estate was dependent on expert assistants.

This letter was found with Zenon's papers probably because Zenon would have taken over the contents of Panakestor's office when he superseded him as the manager of the estate. Panakestor himself, though relieved of duties at Philadelphia, was not dismissed. He was transferred to the staff of Apollonios' estate in Memphis (cf. PMich I 35.3, PCairZen 59149, 59164). Like Zenon, Panakestor was a native of Caria, though from Kalynda.

᾿Αρτεμίδωρος Πανακέστορι χαίρειν. παραγινομένου μου
ἐγ Βουβάστου εἰς Μέμ[φιν]
ἐνετέλλετο ᾿Απολλώνιος μάλιστα μὲν αὐτὸν διελθεῖν
πρὸς σέ, εἰ δὲ μή, ἀποστεῖλα[ί]
τινα παρ᾿ ἐμοῦ ὃς ἀναγγελεῖ σοι τὰ παρ᾿ αὐτοῦ. ἠκηκόει
γὰρ ὅτι οὐ πᾶσα κατασπείρετα[ι]
ἡ γῆ αἱ μύριαι ἄρουραι. συνέτασσεν οὖν ἀναγγέλλειν σοι
ἵνα ξυλοκοπηθῆι πᾶσα καὶ ποτισθῆι
5 κ[αὶ μάλιστ]α μὲν ὅπως κατασπείρητε πᾶσαν αὐτήν, εἰ δὲ
μή, ὅσην ἂν μὴ[   ]δύν[ηι]
σπείρειν. [. .]σησαμοσπορευθῆι καὶ μὴ ἀργήσηι μέρος
μηθὲν τῆς γῆς. ἐπεὶ [οὖν] αὐτὸ[ς]
οὐ δεδύν[ημαι πα]ραγενέσθαι διὰ τὸ ἐνωχλῆσθαι, γράψας
ἀπέσταλκα [πρὸς] σέ, ἵνα εἰδῆ[ις]
καὶ π[οιῆι]ς οὕτ[ως]. συνέτασσε γὰρ μισθοῦσθαι καὶ
ἐμβάλλειν ἀθρόους[
τοὺς σπεροῦντας σκαλιδευτὰς καὶ τοὺς ὑπουργήσοντας
τούτοις. ἕως οὖν ἔτι ὥρ[α]
10 ἐστὶν σπείρ[ειν], ποιεῖτε οὕτως. ἀνήγγελκα δὲ καὶ Ζήνωνι
καὶ ᾿Αρτεμιδώρωι [τῶ]ι ἐμ Μ[έμφει],
καθότι μοι ᾿Απο[λλώ]νιος ἐνετείλατο, ἵνα χορηγῶσιν ὑμῖν
χαλκόν, ὅσον ἂν χρείαν ἔχη[τε]
εἰς ταῦτα. λαμβάνετε οὖν· δοθήσεται γὰρ ὑμῖν. ἔφασαν δὲ
καὶ νῦ[ν
                    α
Μάρωνι ⱶΜ.
    ἔρρωσο. Ⳑκθ, ᾿Α[πελ]λαίου β.

Verso
1st hand: εἰς Φιλαδέλφειαν.   Πανακέστορι.
2nd hand: Ⳑκθ, ῾Αθὺρ θ. ᾿Αρτεμίδωρος.

Artemidoros to Panakestor greeting. When I was coming from Boubastos to Memphis, Apollonios ordered that, if at all possible, I myself should go over to you or, if not possible, to send one of my people to relay his instructions to you; for he had heard that not all of the 10,000 arouras (about 6,800 acres) was being thoroughly sown. Therefore, he instructed me to tell you that it was all to be cleared of brushwood and irrigated and that, if at all possible, you should sow the whole of it or, if not possible, that whatever you were unable to sow . . . was to be sown with sesame and that no portion of the land should remain uncultivated. Therefore, since I myself have been unable to come because of being sick, I have sent you, by written message, in order that you may know and act accordingly. For he instructed you to hire and put to work (upon the land) numerous . . . and when the sowers are finished (?) people to hoe and people to assist those (who hoe). Therefore, do this while it is still seedtime. Moreover, I have also informed Zenon and Artemidoros, who is in Memphis, about this, just as Apollonios instructed me, in order that they supply you with as much copper as you need for these things. Therefore, get it, for it will be given to you. They said [they had already given] 10,000 drachmas to Maron. Good-bye. (Year) 29, Apellaios 2.

Outside Address: To Philadelphia. To Panakestor. Docket of receipt: (Year) 29, Hathyr 9. Artemidoros.

Letter of Neesis the potter to Zenon. Written in the Egyptian manner with a brush rather than a pen (see illustration, p. 1). Photograph reproduced with the permission of the Rare Book and Manuscript Library, Columbia University.

20 SENCHŌNS TO ZĒNŌN
PMich I 29

July 256 BCE

In this letter, a native Egyptian widow called Senchons ("sister of Chons") complains that Nikias (cf. PMich I 34) has taken her she-ass, which she needs to carry beehives into the pastures. Bees were moved seasonally, probably twice a year, by donkey to honey-bearing fields. The letter suggests that Zenon derived some benefit from the hives and, consequently, that he should render some aid in recovering the ass.

The writing is in broad strokes and indicates that the scribe used a brush rather than a pen. According to Westermann, this type of writing instrument was used by native Egyptian scribes who were accustomed to writing demotic rather than Greek (see his comments in PCol III 52). Compare the photographic reproductions of this document (cf. p. 1 in this volume) and of PCol III 52 (see p. 45 in this volume) with other papyrus documents of the period to see the difference.

Ζήνωνι χαίρειν Σενχῶνς. ἐνήτυχ[όν]
σοι περὶ τῆς ὄνου μου ἣν ἔλαβεν Νικί[ας].
ἴ μοι ἔγραψας περὶ αὐτῆς, ἀπέστ[ιλα]
ἂν 'σοι' αὐτήν. ἴ σοι δοκεῖ, συντάξαι ἀποδο[ῦ]-
5 ναι αὐτήν, ἵνα τὰ ζμήνεα μεταγ[ά]-
γωμεν ἐπὶ τὰ νομάς, μέ σοι παρα-
πόλωνται μέτε σοι μέτε τῶι βα[σι]-
λεῖ. καὶ ἐὰν ἐπιζετῆς τὸ πρᾶγμα,
πεισθήσεις ὅτι χρήσιμοί σοί ἰμεν. κα[ὶ]
10 τὸν δὲ πῶλον αὐτῆς ἀποστηλῶ [σοι]
αὐτόν. δέομαι ὂν σοι καὶ εἰκετεύω,
μέ με παραελκύσης. γυνή ἰμὶ χέ[ρα].
εὐτύχι.

Verso: ∟λ, Παχὼνς κ[.].
Σενχῶνς ὄνου.

To Zenon, greetings from Senchons. I petitioned you about my ass which Nikias took. If you had written to me about her, I would have sent her to you. If it pleases you, command him to return her, in order that we may carry the hives to the pastures, lest they be ruined for you and be of no use to either yourself or the king. And if you examine the matter, you will be persuaded that we are useful to you. And I will send the foal of the ass to you. Therefore, I beg and entreat you, that you not put me off. I am a widowed woman. Farewell.

Docket of receipt: (Year) 30, Pachons 2 . . . Senchons about an ass.

---

3 ἴ for εἴ; similarly in the next line. The scribe does not distinguish ι and ει or ε and η. Thus, Edgar, the editor, says he was a scribe of little education, but one who was more or less acquainted with both Egyptian and Greek and who was able to present native complaints in Greek dress.
4 συντάξαι for σύνταξον.
6–7 τά: read τάς. μέ and μέτε: read μή and μήτε.
8 Read ἐπιζητῆις.
9 Read πεισθήσει and εἰμέν (for ἐσμέν).
10 Corrected from τοῦ δὲ πώλου(?)
11 Read οὖν.
12 Read μή, εἰμί and χήρα.

21 APOLLŌNIOS TO ZĒNŌN
PRyl IV 560

3 October 256 BCE

Zenon's chief sends a brief note of approval regarding a recent activity connected with Zenon's duties as manager of the Philadelphia estate. Since the present note was written on the thirteenth of Mesore and received on the forteenth, Apollonios must have been nearby.

'Ἀπολλώνιος Ζήνωνι χαίρειν. ὀρθῶς
ἐποίησας ἀποστείλας τὸν ἐρέβινθον
εἰς Μέμφιν. .

    ἔρρωσο. Λλ, Λωίου ιϛ, Μεσορὴ ιγ.

Verso
1st hand: Ζήνωνι.
2nd hand: Λλ Λωίου ιδ Μεσορὴ ιδ.
         'Ἀπολλώνιος ἐρεβίνθου.

Apollonios to Zenon greeting. You did right in having sent the chickpeas to Memphis. Good-bye. (Year) 30, Loios 16, Mesore 13.

Outside address: To Zenon.
Docket of receipt: (Year) 30, Loios 14, Mesore 14.
   Apollonios about the chickpeas.

---

5 Λωίοι ιδ ought to be Λωίοι ιζ, by analogy with the double date in Apollonios' note, but Zenon had lived among the native population long enough that he had already lost touch with the corresponding date in the Macedonian calendar.

22 LETTER OF A NON-GREEK TO ZĒNŌN
PCol IV 66   256–255 BCE

Though the writer's name is missing here, the letter makes it evident that he was a non-Greek, and his connection with the camels (lines 3–4) suggests that he was an Arab. He had worked as one of Zenon's company in Syria in 259–258 BCE. His immediate superior was Krotos, an agent of Zenon (see letters 6.2–3, 27–28 and 9.1). After Zenon had returned to Egypt in the spring of 258 BCE to join Apollonios, Krotos had not paid the writer the wages that were due to him. Expecting that Zenon would return to Syria, the writer had held out for some time without receiving pay, but he finally ran away into Syria to seek asylum. Since Krotos had returned to Egypt and was in the Fayum in 255 BCE (see PCairZen II 59176.61, 112, 119; also see letter 23), the affairs in Syria which bear upon his dealings with the non-Greek of this letter would have occurred during 258–256 BCE. And since the writer says he "ran away *into* Syria," he would have been stationed at one of the coastal towns.

When the writer had written previously to Zenon, complaining about his treatment at the hands of Krotos, Zenon had instructed him to come to Philadelphia where he was placed under Jason's supervision. Though negligence also arose in connection with his compensation under Jason, the most offensive part of his treatment was Jason's proposal that he accept the lower grade native wine in lieu of his salary in money. Acceptance of such payment would have amounted, from the petitioner's viewpoint, to an acknowledgment of inferiority and hence he states that he is looked down on as a "barbarian."

According to the editor of this document (see Westermann's comments on PCol IV 66), this is the earliest certain instance in Zenon documents of a native Egyptian/non-Greek's sensitivity to the superior attitude assumed by the Greek ruling caste of Egypt. The non-Greek requests both that inequities of salary be adjusted and that Zenon's assistants treat him with more consideration. When the writer says οὐκ ἐπίσταμαι ἑλληνίζειν ("I do not know how to act the Hellene"), he intends something more general than either Plato's differentiation of barbarian and Greek on the basis of the ability to speak Greek (e.g., *Alcibiades* 1.120B), or Aristotle's differentiation of Greek and barbarian on the basis of the ability to write good Greek (*Rhetoric* 3.5.1407a); he is probably referring to identifiable Greek cultural characteristics, including Greek mannerisms. One may compare this complaint with that of Pyrrhos (PSI IV 443), who also accused Jason of withholding salary but, unlike the writer of the present letter, Pyrrhos did not complain of scornful treatment.

..δ.....Ζήνωνι χαίρειν. καλῶς ποίεις εἰ ἔρρωσαι. ἔρρωμαι δὲ καὶ αὐτός. ἐπίστασαι ὡς κατέλιπές με ἐν Συρίαι
μετὰ
Κρότου καὶ ἐποίουν πάντα τὰ προστασσόμενα τὰ κατὰ ⟨τὰ⟩ς καμήλους καὶ ἤμην σο[ι] ἀνέγκλητ[ο]ς. σου δὲ
προστά-
5 ξαντός μοι ὀψώνιον δίδοναι ἅ συ συνέταξας οὐκ ἐδίδου
μοι οὐθέν. ἐπεὶ δὴ πολλάκ[ι]ς μου δεομένου δίδοναί μοι
ἅ συ συνέταξας οὐκ ἐδίδου μου οὐθὲν Κρότος, ἀλλ᾽
ἐκέλευ-
ἐμ με ἀπαλλάσσεσθαι, χρόνον μὲν οὖν πολὺν ἐκαρτέ-
ρουν σε προσδεχόμενος, ἐπεὶ δὲ τῶν ἀναγκαίων ἐν-
10 δεὴς ἤμην καὶ οὐθὲν ἠδυνάμην οὐθάμοθεν πορί-
ζειν, ἠναγκάσθην ἀποτρέχειν εἰς Συρίαν ἵνα μὴ τῶι
λιμῶι παραπόλωμαι. ἔγραψα οὖν σοι ἵνα εἰδῆις ὅτι Κρότος αἴτιος. σου δὲ πάλιν με ἀποστείλαντος εἰς
Φιλαδέλφειαν
πρὸς Ἰάσονα καὶ ποιουντός μου πάντα τὰ
προστασσόμενα,
15 ἅ συ μοι συνέταξας οὐθέν μοι δίδω⟨σ⟩ι ἤδη μήνων ἐννέα
τὸ ἔλαιον
οὐ δὲ σίτον ἀλλὰ παρὰ διμηνον ὅταν καὶ τὰ ἱμάτια
⟨ἀ⟩πόδωται.
ἐγὼ δὲ καὶ θέρος καὶ χειμῶνα ἐν τῶι πόνωι γίνομαι. ὁ δέ
μοι συντάσ-
σει ὄξος λαμβάνειν εἰς ὀψώνιον. ἀλλὰ κατεγνώκασίμ
μου ὅτι εἰμὶ
                  εἰ σοι δόκει
βάρβαρος. δέομαι οὖν σου σύνταξαι αὐτοῖς ὅπως τὰ
ὀφειλόμενα
20 κομίσωμαι καὶ τοῦ λοιποῦ εὐτάκτωσίν μοι ἵνα μὴ τῶι
λιμῶι παρα-
πόλωμαι ὅτι οὐκ ἐπίσταμαι ἑλληνίζειν. σὺ οὖν καλῶς ἂν
ποιήσαις
ἐπιστροφήν μου ποιησάμενος. ἐγὼ δὲ εὔχομαι πᾶσι τοῖς
θεοῖς καὶ τῶι
δαίμονι τοῦ βασιλέως σε ὑγιαίνειν καὶ ἐλθεῖν τὸ τάχος
πρὸς ἡμᾶς ὅπως
αὐτὸς ἴδηις ὅτι ἀνέγκλητος εἰμί.
25   ἔρρωσο.

Verso: Ζήνωνι

. . . to Zenon greeting. You do well if you are healthy. I myself am also well. You know that you left me in Syria with Krotos and I did all the things that were ordered concerning the camels and I was without reproach toward you. When you sent instructions to give me wages he did not give me anything which you ordered. Indeed when I asked him many times to give me what you ordered Krotos gave me nothing, but he ordered that I be removed (from his presence); I endured manfully, therefore, for a long time waiting for you. But when I became in want of necessities and was unable to procure anything anywhere, I was obliged to run away into Syria lest I perish of hunger. Therefore, I wrote to you in order that you know that Krotos was the cause. When, once again, you sent me to Philadelphia to Jason and I continue to do all the things commanded, already for nine months he has given me nothing of what you instructed concerning me, neither olive oil nor grain except at two month intervals when he also pays for the clothing (allowance). Moreover, I am in drudgery both summer and winter. He instructs me to take sour wine (native/low grade wine) for compensation. Well, they look down on me because I am a "barbarian." Wherefore, I entreat you, if it seems acceptable to you, to instruct them that I am to receive what is still lacking and that henceforth they follow orders lest I perish of hunger because I do not know how to act the Hellene. Therefore, please cause a change of attitude toward me. I pray to all the gods and to the divinity of the king that you be well and that you come to us (me) quickly in order that you yourself may see that I am blameless. Good-bye.

Outside address: To Zenon.

---

3 ἐποίουν πάντα τὰ προστασσόμενα: this phrase reappears in line 14. Regarding the writer's repetitious style, ἅ συ συνέταξας in line 5 is repeated immediately in line 7 and again with slight alteration in line 15; the phrase ἵνα μὴ τῶι λιμῶι παραπόλωμαι in lines 11–12 is repeated in line 20.

11 "I was obliged to *run away* into Syria": Westermann, the editor of PCol IV 66, states that it was rare that an individual sought asylum in the Ptolemaic period, even though it was characteristic of Egypt under Roman rule. We do have examples of groups who sought asylum (*anachoresis*) during the Ptolemaic period in those tem-

ples that were granted asylum status (see letter 18.21 and see the discussion of anachoresis and *ekchoresis* by Westermann ["The Ptolemies," pp. 276ff.], including his citation of extant examples of anachoresis in the Ptolemaic period).

16 "Neither olive oil nor grain": these are two elements of a four-part salary system, which included grain and oil as payment in kind, as well as money (*opsonion*) and clothing allowance (*himatismos*), The same four elements reappear in PSI IV 443 (=PCairZen III 59507). Though the present writer uses *himatia*, instead of *himatismos*, it is clear in his case too that it is a money payment, not the clothing itself.

23 ZĒNŌN TO KROTOS
CPJud I 9a (=PCairZen II 59241)   17 September 253 BCE

In this letter, Zenon instructs Krotos to have Artemidoros make a mattress out of wool acquired from Pasis the Jew. Peisikles, a treasurer or paymaster in Apollonios' household, needs the mattress. It must be long enough to seat two people and must have a double front. Zenon orders Krotos to see that the mattress be completed in fifteen days.

The Krotos of this letter is the commercial agent of Apollonios or Zenon, the Krotos about whom the non-Greek complained in the immediately preceding letter (see also the letters in number 6 of this collection; PCairZen II 59077, 59093; PSI VII 863 [g]). Artemidoros is probably the overseer of Apollonios' Memphis estate (cf. PMich I 35 and PCairZen II 59149), not Artemidoros the physician and companion of Apollonios (letters 19 and 24). Pasis is a Jew with a native Egyptian name (see also CPJud I 9b) who seems to be a shepherd employed by Zenon on the Philadelphia estate.

Tcherikover suggests that though the upper classes of the Jewish population in Alexandria may have aspired to the Hellenized levels of society, most Jewish immigrants to Egypt would have been peasants, like Pasis, or soldiers, mercenaries and prisoners of war. Though Greek names were preferred to Hebrew for newborn Jewish children in Alexandria, Jews who lived outside the Hellenizing centers and in the *chora* (all of Egypt, apart from Alexandria) tended to be assimilated into the native environment (at least in the third and second centuries BCE), to call themselves by native Egyptian names (like Pasis) and to speak the native language (cf. CPJud I, pp. 26ff., 41ff.).

Since this piece of correspondence was found with Zenon's papers, and since it is not a rough draft (i.e., it has an outside address), it must have been returned to Zenon for some reason.

Ζήνων Κρότωι χαίρειν. ὡς ἂν τάχιστα λάβηις τὴν
    ἐπιστολήν,
λαβὲ παρὰ Πάσιτος τοῦ Ἰουδαίου ἐρίων μν(ᾶς) κε καὶ
    ἀπέγδος Ἀρτεμι-
δώρωι ἵνα κατασκευάσηι στρωμάτιον, ὥστε τῶι μήκει ἐπὶ
    δίεδρον
ἢ μικρῶι μεῖζον, διπρόσωπον· χρεία γὰρ αὐτοῦ ἐστιν ὥστε
    Πισικλεῖ.

Zenon to Krotos greeting. As soon as you receive this letter, get twenty-five Minas of wool from Pasis the Jew, (which is) to be contracted by Artemidoros to make a mattress, that is to be long enough to fit a double seat or a little more, (and is) to be covered on both sides. For it is needed by Peisikles. So, as soon as it (the wool) is got, send it to Memphis to Artemidoros, and make an effort that it (the

5 καὶ ὡς ἂν τάχιστα γένηται, ἀπόστειλον εἰς Μέμφιν πρὸς
   Ἀρτεμί-
   δωρον, καὶ πειράθητι ὅπως ἐν ἡμ(έραις) ιε γένηται.
   γεγράφαμεν δὲ
   καὶ Πάσι δοῦναί σοι τὰ ἔρια.
   ἔρρωσο. (ἔτους) λγ, Ἐπεὶφ κη.

Verso: Κρότωι.

mattress) is completed within fifteen days. We (I)
have also written to Pasis to give you the wool.
Good-bye. (Year) 33, Epeiph 28.

Outside address: To Krotos.

---

4 διπρόσωπον: Edgar (cf. comments on PCairZen II
  59241) indicates that this means a mattress (cushion) with a presentable cover on both sides, i.e.,
  like a reversible cushion on a couch.
5 γένηται: Edgar suggests that the meaning here is:
  "as soon as the wool is *got*," but that in line 6 the
  verb means "that the mattress be *made*."

24 ARTEMIDŌROS TO ZĒNŌN
PCairZen II 59251   ca. 13 April 252 BCE

Artemidoros, the private physician of Apollonios (see letter 19 and PCairZen II 59225),
informs Zenon that both he and Apollonios are well and are in the process of returning
to Egypt, after having escorted the queen (the princess Berenike) to the frontier. Edgar
suggests that this text and PCairZen 59242 indicate that the marriage of princess Berenike and Antiochos II was negotiated in 253 BCE and that it took place in the spring of
252 BCE (see his comments in PCairZen II 59242 and 59251). Hence the escort to
which Artemidoros refers in the present letter, and which was probably under the
command of Apollonios, was the same one which accompanied the princess to Syria for
her marriage to Antiochos. The king himself traveled with his daughter as far as Pelusium (see the notes to PCairZen II 59242) and then he entrusted her to Apollonios.
     Since this letter reached Philadelphia in about fifteen days, it probably came by
special courier along with Apollonios' correspondence to the king. Artemidoros
announces that he anticipates being in Philadelphia shortly and he requests Zenon to
buy honey and barley, as well as to take care of various matters on his farm.

Ἀρτεμίδωρος Ζήνωνι χαίρειν. εἰ ἔρρωσαι, εὖ ἂν ἔχοι·   Artemidoros to Zenon greeting. If you are well, it
ἔρρωμαι δὲ καὶ ἐγὼ καὶ Ἀπολλώνιος ὑγίαινεν καὶ   would be excellent; I myself am also well and
τἄλλα ἦν κατὰ γνώμην. ὅτε δέ σοι ἔγραφον, παρεγινόμεθα   Apollonios is healthy and everything else is satis-
εἰς Σιδῶνα, συμπεπορευμένοι τῆι βασιλίσσηι   factory. As I write to you, we are arriving at Sidon,
ἕως τῶν ὁρίων, καὶ ὑπελαμβάνομεν ταχέως παρέσεσθαι   having escorted the princess to the border, and I
πρὸς ὑμᾶς. χαριεῖ οὖμ μοι σαυτοῦ τε ἐπιμελόμενος   assume that we (I) will soon be with you. There-
ἵνα ὑγιαίνηις καὶ ἡμῖν γράφων ἐάν τί σοι βούληι γίνεσθαι   fore, you would do me a favor by concerning
ὧν ἡμεῖς δυνάμεθα. καλῶς δ᾽ ἂμ ποιήσαις ἀγοράσας   yourself with your health and by writing if there is
5 ἡμῖν ἵνα ὡς ἂμ παραγενώμεθα ἔχωμεν μέλιτος τοῦ   anything you want which we are able to get. And
   βελτίστου μετρητὰς γ καὶ κριθῶν ὥστε εἰς τὰ κτήνη   please buy for us (me), in order that I may have
   (ἀρτάβας) χ,   whenever I arrive, three metretas of the best honey
   τὴν δὲ τιμὴν ἀπὸ τοῦ σησάμου καὶ τοῦ κροτῶνος δοὺς εἰς   and six hundred artabs of barley for the animals,
   ταῦτα, καὶ τῆς οἰκίας δὲ τῆς ἐμ Φιλαδελφείαι   giving (paying) the price for these things from (the

ἐπιμελόμενος, ἵνα ὡς ἂμ παραγενώμεθα καταλάβωμεν
αὐτὴν ἐστεγασμένην. καὶ τὰ ζευγάρια δὲ καὶ τὰ ἱερ{ι}εῖα
τοὺς χῆνας
[κ]αὶ τὰ λοιπὰ τὰ ἐνταῦθα ὡς ἂν ἐκποιῆι πειρῶ ἐπισκοπεῖν.
οὕτως γὰρ ἡμῖν μᾶλλον ἔσται τὰ δέοντα.
καὶ τὰ γενημάτια δὲ ἵνα τρόπωι τινὶ συγκομισθῆι ἐπιμελές
σοι ἔστω. καὶ ἐάν τι δέηι εἰς
10 ἀνήλωμα, τὸ ἀναγκαῖον δοῦναι μὴ ὀκνήσηις.
ἔρρωσο. Λλγ, Περιτίου ἐμβολίμου ς̄.

Verso
1st hand: [εἰς Φιλ]αδέλφειαν.   Ζήνωνι.
2nd hand: Λλγ, Φαμενὼθ ς̄.
'Αρτεμίδωρος.

produce of) the sesame and the kroton; moreover,
concern yourself with the house in Philadelphia,
in order that I find it roofed whenever I arrive. And
try, as well as possible, to watch the oxen, the pigs
[the slaughter animals?], the geese and the rest of
the stock there; for by doing so I will have a better
(supply) of the necessities. And make it your concern that the crops be harvested somehow. And if
anything is required for expenses, do not hesitate
to pay what is necessary. Good-bye. (Year) 33,
Peritios intercalary 6.

Outside address: To Philadelphia. To Zenon.
Docket of receipt: (Year) 33, Phamenoth 6.
Artemidoros.

---

2   παρεγινόμεθα (see ἔγραφον also): Edgar suggests that this is a good example of the epistolary imperfect and that it could mean either, "we are on our way to Sidon" (see PCairZen 59247) or "we have just arrived there."

3   τῶν ὁρίων: Edgar thinks the phrase indicates that Coele-Syria still belonged to Egypt (PCairZen II 59251). To explain why the king did not escort the princess beyond Pelusium, however, Bouché-Leclercq (*Histoire des Seleucides,* p. 90) infers that

Coele-Syria had been given away as Berenike's dowry.

6   Zenon was apparently Artemidoros' representative in handling money and selling crops at Philadelphia.

7   Read ἱερεῖα (Edgar, PCairZen 59251), with the meaning "the pigs."

8–10 These lines were added at the bottom of the page (like a postscript), after the farewell and date had been written (see PCairZen II, plate XX).

---

25 APOLLŌNIOS TO ZĒNŌN
PMich I 48   10 September 251 BCE

Apollonios the dioiketes instructs Zenon to buy a number of fowls, apparently for the celebration of an upcoming festival. They are to be sent to Ptolemais at the mouth of the Fayum, perhaps the site of the festival. Edgar suggests that the preparations were prob-ably for the festival known as Πενταετηρίς or Πτολεμαίεια, or, if not for this festival, for the Arsinoeia, which fell near the end of Mesore (see his comments in PMich 48; see PSI 364, PCairZen 59412.26). Apollonios probably wrote this letter in Alexandria, since it took eight days to arrive (e.g., PSI 514 took seven days to reach Philadelphia from Alexandria).

'Απολλώνιος Ζήνωνι χαίρειν. χρείαν ἔχομεν
ὥστ' εἰς σίτευσιν ὀρνίθων υ καὶ τοκάδων ρ.
καλῶς οὖν ποιήσεις ἀγοράσας ἡμῖν καὶ ἀποστείλας εἰς
Πτολεμαίδα τὴν ἐπὶ τοῦ διστόμου πρὸς Διοσκουρίδην
5 τὸν παρ' ἡμῶν.
ἔρρωσο. Λλε, Πανήμου κη, 'Επεὶφ λ.

Apollonios to Zenon greeting. We have need of four hundred fowls and of one hundred hens for fattening. Therefore, please buy them for us and send them to Ptolemais on the fork (of the canal) to our man Dioskourides. Good-bye. (Year) 35, Pan-emos 28, Epeiph 30.

Verso
1st hand: Ζήνωνι.
2nd hand: Ⱶλε, Μεσορὴ ζ.
Ἀπολλώνιος.

Outside address: To Zenon.
Docket of receipt: (Year) 35, Mesore 7. Apollonios.

2   τοκάδων: Though τοκάδες often means "sows" in the Zenon papyri, Edgar suggests that since it is used here in conjunction with "fowls, it probably means "hens" (see his comments in PMich 48; see the use of ὄρνις τοκάς in POxy IX 1207.9 and

τοκάδες with the meaning "geese" in BGU VI 1212d).

4   The town indicated is Ptolemais at the entrance to the Fayum (see the analogous expression in Strabo *The Geography* 17.809, 811).

26 DROMŌN TO ZĒNŌN
PCairZen III 59426

260–250 BCE

In this letter Dromon reports that, according to Zenon's instructions, Zenon's employees will not be bothered. Then he requests Zenon, who is probably in Alexandria, to bring a *kotyle* of Attic honey along when he sails up river; the god has ordered the honey as a medication for Dromon's eyes.

At this time, Dromon was probably living in Memphis and the temple which he would have frequented would have been the great Sarapeum at Saqqarah, where medical prescriptions were communicated to sufferers by means of dreams (see Edgar's comments in PCairZen 59426). The god, either Sarapis or Asklepios, prescribed honey, which is often referred to in Egyptian prescriptions for eye ailments (see the reference to honey as a prescription in letter 8).

Dromon may be the person of that name who, in year 28, was connected to Apollonios' household in Alexandria (see PCairZen III 59355.74).

Δρόμων Ζήνωνι χαίρειν. τοῖς θεοῖς πᾶσιν χάριν ἔχομεν,
εἰ αὐτός τε ὑγιαίνεις καὶ τὰ λοιπά σοι κατὰ λόγον γέγονεν.
ἐρρώμεθα δὲ καὶ αὐτός, καὶ καθότι μοι ἔγραψας τὴν πᾶσαν
ἐπι-
μέλειαν ποιοῦμαι ὅπως ἂν μηθεὶς ἐνοχλῇ τοὺς παρὰ σοῦ.
5   ὡς δ᾽ ἂν ἀναπλέῃς ὑγιαίνων, σύνταξόν τινι τῶν παρὰ
σοῦ
ἀγοράσαι μέλιτος Ἀττικοῦ κοτύλην. χρείαν γὰρ ἔχω πρὸς
τοὺς ὀφθαλμοὺς κατὰ πρόσταγμα τοῦ θεοῦ.
εὐτύχει.

Verso: Ζήνωνι.

Dromon to Zenon greeting. I offer up thanks to all the gods if you yourself are well and if all your other affairs have been as you want. I myself am also well, and just as you wrote I am taking every care that no one bothers your people. Whenever you sail up river in good health, order one of your people to buy me a kotyle of Attic honey; for I require it for my eyes according to the directive of the god. Farewell.

Outside address: To Zenon.

4   ἐνοχλῇ: this may refer to the bother arising from the exaction of taxes (see PCairZen I 59130.19 and letter 15.10–11).

5   "When you are about to sail up *in good health*": see PSI 500.8f. for a similar sentiment regarding travel.

8   εὐτύχει: this is an unexpected closing convention here, since it is used in petitions and in letters where the writer's inferiority is emphasized.

These two letters belong to the archive of the toparch Leon which, in its extant entirety, consists of nine letters: PYale 36–44. All belong to the latter part of the reign of Euergetes (247–221 BCE) and the two principal figures in the correspondence are Leon and Apollonios. Leon's office of toparch is indicated specifically in PYale 37.2 and, though the office of Apollonios is nowhere stated, his activities in PYale 36 suggest that he was an oikonomos (see PYale 36, pp. 98–104). The close relation of the two men is reflected in PYale 42 (=letter 28), allowing the reasonable inference that they were brothers, perhaps sharing an office in Philadelphia (see PYale 37 and 40).

27 APOLLŌNIOS TO LEON
PYale 36   late September 232 BCE

Apollonios forwards an order from the dioiketes, Athenodoros, in Alexandria, who instructed that the sowing schedule for the year 16 be completed immediately and forwarded to the capital. Since Apollonios' letter is dated in Mesore of year 15 (the exact day is lost in lines 7 and 17), and since the dioiketes demanded that the schedule be in his hands before the end of Mesore (lines 11f.), preparation of the sowing schedule would have been a hurried operation. Under such circumstances, the use and threat of police (lines 2 and 13; line 6) is more understandable.

Ἀπολλώνιος Λέοντι χαίρειν. τῆς παρ' Ἀθηνοδώρου τοῦ
    διοικη[τοῦ]
ὑπόκειταί σοι τ' ἀντίγραφον. ἐπιτελέσας οὖν τὴν
    διαγραφ[ὴν τοῦ]
σπόρου μετὰ τῶν εἰθισμένων ἀκολούθως τοῖς
    ἐπε[σταλμένοις]
ἔχ' ἐν ἑτο[ί]μωι, ἵνα πρὸ τοῦ ὡρισμένου καιροῦ καὶ αὐτ[οὶ]
5 ἐπιδῶμεν Λευκίππωι τῶι ἀρχιφυλακίτηι, γινώσκων ὅ[τι
    ἐὰν]
ὑστέρημα γένηται καταποσταλήσει πρὸς τὸν διοικητ[ήν.]
    ἔρρ(ω)σ(ο). (ἔτους) ιε, Μ[εσορὴ .]

Ἀθηνόδωρος Ἀπολλωνίωι χαίρειν. τὴν διαγραφὴν τῆς
    Ε[.
γῆς τοῦ εἰς τὸ ις (ἔτος) σπόρου συντελέσας μετὰ τοῦ [..
10 γραμματέως καὶ τῶν ἄλλων μεθ' ὧν καθήκει πέμψον Υ[..
μάλιστα μὲν συντομώτερον, τὸ δὲ μακρότατον ἕ[ως τῆς .]
τοῦ Μεσορή, κατ' ἄνδρα καὶ κατὰ κώμην καὶ ἐπὶ
    κεφα[λαίου,]

Apollonios to Leon greeting. The copy of the (letter) from Athenodoros the dioiketes is appended below for you. Therefore, after you complete the schedule of the sowing, with the customary people (and) in compliance with the orders given, hold it in readiness, in order that prior to the appointed deadline we ourselves may (be able to) give it to Leukippos, the chief of police; knowing that if a delay occurs, you will be sent down to the dioiketes. Good-bye. (Year) 15, Mesore....

Athenodoros to Apollonios greeting. When you have completed the schedule of the sowing of the ... land for the sixteenth year with the ... secretary and the other customary people, send it if possible sooner, but at the latest by the ... of Mesore, (specified) according to individual farmer and according to village and in summary, to Leukippos the chief of police. For we have written to him, that by this day you will give him these documents

Λευκίππωι τῶι ἀρχιφυλακίτηι. γεγράφαμεν γὰρ αὐτ[ῶι,
ἐπὰν]
ἕως τῆς ἡμέρας ταύτης ἀποδῷις τὰ γράμματα [ταῦτα,]
15 ἀποστεῖλαι εἰς τὴν πόλιν πρὸς ἡμᾶς, συμπέμψαντ[ι τοὺς]
ἀποκαταστήσοντας.
(ἔτους) ιε, Ἐπεὶφ [..]

Verso
1st hand: Λέοντι.
2nd hand: (ἔτους) ιε, Μεσορὴ θ̄. Ἀπολλώνιος ἀντίγρ(αφον)
τῆς παρ᾽ Ἀθηνοδώρου
τοῦ δι(οικητοῦ) ὑπὲρ τῆς
διαγρ(αφῆς) τοῦ σπ(όρου) τῆς εἰς τὸ ιϛ (ἔτος).

to be forwarded to the city to us, in the company of people who will carry them back. (Year) 15, Epeiph ...

Outside address: To Leon.
Docket of receipt: (Year) 15, Mesore 9. Apollonios. Copy of the (letter) from Athenodoros the dioiketes, concerning the schedule of sowing for the sixteenth year.

---

12 κατ᾽ ἄνδρα καὶ κατὰ κώμην: for a similar specification in connection with the sowing and harvesting of crops, see κατὰ γεωργὸν καὶ κατὰ φύλλον in letter 18.17 and κατ᾽ ἄνδρα καὶ φύλλον in PTebt IV 1103.1.

28 NECHTHOSIRIS TO LEON
PYale 42   12 January 229 BCE

Nechthosiris, an Egyptian agent of Leon, has been detained for some time by the dioiketes in Alexandria. He and other servants of Leon in Alexandria have been in need of food and clothing and have been worried about lack of news from Philadelphia. Finally word arrives, but still no supplies. Nechthosiris has good news for Leon and Apollonios, however, Their opponents have been condemned by the *chrematists* (Greek judges in Egypt). Though the king must still review the case, Nechthosiris is confident that Apollonios will be cleared if he comes down to Alexandria. The apparent reference to the oracle of Sarapis in Alexandria (line 9) is significant as an early example of that institution.

Though Nechthosiris has had considerable practice in writing, his style is awkward and repetitious and, along with his grammatical and spelling eccentricities, it suggests that native Egyptians continued to find Greek conventions unnatural. The letter from the widow Senchons, written by a native scribe (letter 20) and the letter from a non-Greek complaining about contemptuous treatment (letter 22) are other examples of this phenomenon.

Νεχθοσῖρις Λέοντι τῶι
ἀδελφῶι χαίρειν. ἔρρωσο καὶ
Ἀπολλώνιος ὁ ἀδ(ελφὸς) καὶ Ἠπιόδωρος
καὶ οἱ παρὰ σοῦ πάντες. ἔρρωμαι δὲ καὶ
5 αὐτός. ἐμοῦ σοι γεγραφότος πλέονας
ἐπιστολὰς καὶ οὐθέμ μοι παρὰ σοῦ τί μοι
προσπεφώνηται, τὸ πλέον ἀγωνιῶν
ἕνεκα τοῦ μηδ᾽ ἕως τοῦ νῦν ἀκηκοέναι
τὰ κατά σε, πρὸς τὸν θεὸν συνεχρώμην πολλάκις.
10 Πρωτολάου δὲ ἀπαγγείλαντος ἡμῖν τὰ
κατά σέ, λίαν ἐχά[ρην.] ἐπὶ οὖν ἀπέσταλκα Διονυσίωι τ[ῶι πα]ρ᾽ ἡμῶν ἀποσ-

Nechthosiris to Leon his brother greeting. May you be well and Apollonios our brother and Epidoros and all your people. I myself am also well. Though I have written many letters to you no word has been declared by you to me; being the more anxious because up to the present I have heard nothing about your affairs, I consulted the god many times. So, when Protolaos reported to us about your affairs, I rejoiced greatly. Therefore, from Thoth onward, I have sent to Dionysios, one of our people, (requesting him) to send me a cloak and tunic, but he has neither sent them nor has he

τῖλαί μοι ἱματίδιον κ[α]ὶ χιτῶνα ἀπὸ θωὺ[θ]
οὔτε ἀπέσταλκεν ἀλλὰ οὐδὲ τοῖς παι-
15 δαρίοις ἀπέσταλκεν σιτ[ά]ρ[ιον] ἕως ἤδη
εἰς τὴν διατροφήν. διὸ ἀξιῶ σαυτὸν
παρενοχλῆσαν, ἐπὶ παραγίνονται εἰς
τὴν πόλιν ἕως ιε τοῦ Χοῖαχ, καὶ σαυτὸν
ἐπιδοὺς ἕως τοῦ μοι ἀποσταλῆναι καὶ
20 τοῖς παιδίοις σιτάριον δῶι. ἐὰν δὲ μὴ
δῶι, γράψομ μοι εἰ ἄν σοι ἀπαντήσει
μηθὲν ὑποστειλάμενος. περὶ δὲ
τῶν κατ᾽ ἐμέ, μὴ ἀγωνία. πάντα λίαν
κατὰ λόγον γέγονεν. κατεγνωσμένοι
25 εἰσὶν ὑπὸ τῶν χρηματιστῶν, καὶ
τ[ού]των χάριν παρακατεσχέ-
[θη]ν ὑπὸ τοῦ διοικητοῦ, μ[ή-]
ποτε ἀξιωθεὶς ἐ[μφ]ανίσηι τῶι
διοικητῆι μὴ δύνασθαι ἀχθῆναι.
30 ὁ γὰρ βασιλεὺς αὐτὸς καθήμενος
διακούει. τὸ δὲ πλέον πάντων ἐπὶ
τῶν θεῶν ἐστιν. περὶ δὲ τοῦ σοῦ ἀδ(ελφοῦ)
[κρ]ίνω αὐτὸν παραγενέσθαι εἰς
[τὴν] πόλ[ι]ν [ἐπ]ὶ τῶν παρόντων,
(vacat)
35 [ἀ]πολυθήσεται γὰρ ἅμα αὐτὸν
καθαρὸν ποιοῦμεν ἐν τῆι πρὸς
[τ]ούτους κρίσιν. εὐχαριστήσεις
οὖν μοι ἐπιμελούμενος τοῦ σώμα-
τ[ο]ς σοῦ [ἵ]να ὑγιαίνης.
40 ἔ[ρρ(ωσο)]. (ἔτους) [ι]η Ἀθυρ κε.

Verso
1st hand: (with the fibers)
τοπάρχηι   Λέοντι
2nd hand: (across the fibers)
Ἀ]πολλωνίου δέησ(ις)
]ΩΝ καὶ τοῦ (ταλάντου) α.
εὐ]θέως παραγενέσθ[αι
]ἔτι τοὺς παρά μου
]άντων τὰ ὁμολογο ύ(μενα).

sent any bread to the servants for their sustenance even up till now. Wherefore, I request that you concern yourself, for they are coming to the city by the fifteenth of Choiach, by seeing to it that these things be sent to me and that he give bread to the servants. If he does not give it, write to me whether he came to you without holding back anything. Concerning my affairs, do not be anxious. Everything has happened according to expectation. They have been convicted by the chrematists, and on this account (or, on their account) I have been detained by the dioiketes, lest having been asked he might make clear to the dioiketes that he (they?) cannot be held (for trial). For the king himself is set to hear the case. The outcome is up to the gods. Concerning your brother, I judge that he should come to the city under the present conditions, for he will be acquitted as soon as we clear him in the suit against them. Therefore, you would favor me by taking care of yourself to stay well. Good-bye. (Year) 18, Hathyr 25.

Outside address: To the toparch Leon.
Docket of receipt: Entreaty about Apollonios . . . the talent . . . to come immediately . . . also my people . . . bringing (?) what was agreed upon.

---

24   "They have been convicted": the editors of PYale 42 notes that this technical use of *katagignosko* is uncommon in the papyri, although common in the authors. (The verb, however, also appears in a legal context in BGU 1004.5 of the third century BCE.)

26–29   If the verb *emphanisei* ("*he* might make clear") were in the first person ("*I* might make clear"), this passage would be sensible, namely, it would be a case of Nechthosiris being kept out of sight by the dioiketes, lest he testify to the dioiketes' lack of jurisdiction. But Nechthosiris did not need to be so exact for Leon, who understood the situation.

30–31   Regarding the use of royal jurisdiction to supersede the authority of the dioiketes, see H. J. Wolff, *Das Justizwesen*, pp. 5–18 and appropriate sections of PRev (e.g., 14.1, 49.20, 93.6, 97.2).

This document belongs to the correspondence of Kleitarchos, who was a government banker in the Koite Toparchy of the Herakleopolite nome at the end of Euergetes' reign. The majority of the correspondence was published in PHib I (66–70b, 160–63 [=PYale 47–49]), though a number of documents were published in the Gradenwitz collection (PGrad 2–5, 9, 11, 197). The editors of PYale (pp. 130–35) reconstruct the following picture of government banking on the basis of Kleitarchos' correspondence.

There were three levels of banking bureaucracy. The area under Kleitarchos' jurisdiction was the toparchy and, since Asklepiades was his superior, we may presume that Asklepiades was the banker in charge of the entire Herakleopolite nome. Both the nome and toparchy levels, represented by Asklepiades and Kleitarchos, were managerial levels. At the third, and lower level were Kleitarchos' subordinates, such as Herakleodoros in the tax office at Phebichis (see PYale 46), who was called the *logeuterion* of the Koite Toparchy in PHib 106.

Moreover, since Herakleodoros worked in the tax office, there is evidence of a close association between the state banking and tax systems. The banking and taxing bureaucracies were carried on by more than one staff, however, since the bankers did not receive taxes directly from the taxpayers, but from the tax office to facilitate the turnover of funds from the collectors to the royal bank.

In the present letter, Asklepiades curtly instructs Kleitarchos to bring up the account of the month Phaophi on Hathyr 8, along with the balance of certain other money.

Ἀσκληπιάδης
Κλειτάρχωι χαίρειν.
παραγίνου τῆι
η τοῦ Ἀθυρ κομίζων
5   τόν τε λόγον τοῦ
Φαῶφι καὶ τὰ περιόν-
τα χρήματα,
[καὶ] μὴ ἄλλως ποιή-
[σηις.]
10   ἔρρωσο. (ἔτους) ιη Ἀθυρ ε.

Asklepiades to Kleitarchos greeting. Come up on the eighth of Hathyr bringing both the account of Phaophi and the remaining (outstanding?) money, and do not act otherwise. Good-bye. (Year) 18, Hathyr 5.

_____

3 The ου of παραγίνου has been corrected from εωθε.

The following documents concern the property of a wealthy woman named Eirene, a resident of the Arsinoite nome, daughter of Orphis and wife of Agamemnon. The six documents concerning Eirene span a five year period (182–178 BCE). They are, in chronological order: PMich III 182, 183; PCol IV 121, 122; PMich III 200, 193. All but two of these, PMich 182 and 200, are included here.

PMich 200 is an annual summary of Eirene's gross income, by far the largest part of which was generated by her orchard, which consisted principally of olive trees. This orchard was the source of 24 talents, 3500 drachmas in 181–180 BCE (PMich 200.19–20 recto; excluding income from inherited property) out of a total yearly income amounting to 28 talents, 4990 drachmas (PMich 200.26). In addition to this olive grove rented from state lands, Eirene's total holdings (see PMich 200.18–32 and the verso) included a vineyard of moderate size rented from state lands (see PMich 182.11, 200.26 recto); property inherited from Eirene's mother (*metrikou*); henna plants rented to a certain Samos; a garden, apparently leased out to a gardener; a building rented to one Theodoros for 5500 drachmas per year; other buildings bringing in rent of 275 drachmas per month and a pigeon house, also rented out (probably for the right to bird droppings as manure).

On the basis of Westermann's extensive comments in PCol IV (pp. 194–202), we gain the following information about the operation of Eirene's holdings. While PCol IV 121 and 122 were written almost a year after PMich 183 and 182, they probably serve as a better introduction to Eirene's method of making money from her properties. We learn that in year 23 of Epiphanes (183–182 BCE), for example, that she had subleased to three contractors (managers of a fruit picking gang who were named Leontiskes, Tesenouphis and Thymos) the right to gather and own the fruits of the orchard. Although the contractual agreement (*homologia*) drawn up between Eirene and these three associates is lost, it seems certain that the crop gatherers had agreed to pay Eirene's rent to the state for the use of the land upon which the orchard grew, as well as to pay an additional sum to Eirene herself. However, something less than thirteen talents of the rent owed to the state still remained unpaid on Tybi 6 of year 24 (10 February 181 BCE; see PCol 121.7). It was this delinquency of a year and a half that called forth the two Columbia letters of Lysimachos, a state official, threatening the three contractors with arrest because of the debt to the crown.

As early as year 21 of Epiphanes (185–184 BCE) Eirene was renting the government land with which the archive is concerned. At that point she herself was responsible to the government for the rent, a considerable part of which remained unpaid until 180–179 BCE (see PMich 200.27 verso, which records her payment in 180–179 BCE of back rent for her tenancy of five years earlier). The available evidence does not show what happened in year 22 (184–183 BCE) but there is no indication that Eirene failed to meet her rental obligations to the state in full. For year 23 (183–182 BCE), we already referred above to the three sublessees' agreement to pay the rent on state property. Then, for year 24 (182–181 BCE), Eirene once again leased the right to gather the fruits of her olive grove to the same three contractors with whom she had made an agreement in the previous year. Once again, the actual contractual agreement is lost though it is mentioned in PMich 182.19. Since the three contractors were still delinquent in paying rent upon the orchard to the state from the previous year (183–182 BCE), it is improbable that the state would accept this group as responsible for the new year's rent. Consequently, it is likely that Eirene herself assumed the obligation of paying rent to the government in year 24.

The strength of Eirene's reputation in the community, which would warrant the state's trust, is indicated by the fact that a few months earlier, in January 182 BCE (see PMich 182.13–14), a certain Nikandros had loaned her 44 talents, 4800 drachmas on the copper standard. In the crop lease with the three contractors which Eirene made in the year 24, the contractors agreed to pay back to Nikandros (Eirene's creditor) both the money she had borrowed from him three months earlier, and the interest on it. On 4 March of that same year, the agreement between the three cultivators and Nikandros, in which they assured Nikandros of paying Eirene's debt, was drawn up (PMich 182). For her part, Eirene assumed the obligation of meeting any remainder not paid by the three to Nikandros. On the very next day, Eirene completed what was required by acknowledging to the three contractors, with her husband acting as her guardian (*kyrios*), that she accepted the financial agreement which they had enacted with Nikandros (PMich 183).

Since the Ptolemaic state had Lysimachos attending to state affairs in the area, it seems almost certain that the complicated maneuvers described above had received government sanction. The state was experienced enough to know the value of continuity in the rental of state land. Thus, the threat of Lysimachos to arrest the three contractors (PCol 121) was not carried out immediately, but was repeated the following month (PCol 122). The unwillingness to implement the threat immediately indicates the practical interdependence of the three elements in the situation: the central government, the entrepreneur Eirene, and the labor contractors who were needed to do the actual harvesting.

Eirene's arrangements for the year 181–180 BCE (year 25 of Ptolemy V Epiphanes and year 1 of Ptolemy VI Philometer) are implied in PMich 200 recto. The orchard of olive trees, as well as figs and pomegranates, seemed to have been under Eirene's direct management; her total income appears in lines 18–19. We learn that she paid the rent on the orchard land for year 1 to the king's account and that she met an outstanding debt on the rent of state land from five years earlier (lines 27–28). Included in her expenditures is an item of ten talents paid "against the mortgage of Nikandros" (line 30), which the three contractors probably left unpaid in 182 BCE.

The sole remaining record of Eirene's affairs is a receipt of the last month of year 4 (year 4 of Philometer, 178–177 BCE), in which Eirene acknowledges that she has received final payment of four talents against the lease of the fruits of her orchard. The lessees were a group of four, which included two contractors which Eirene had formerly employed, Tesenouphis and Leontiskis, and two additional people, Donax and Nikis. This document (PMich 193) is dated to year 4 of an unnamed Ptolemy. The original editor (V. B. Schuman) dated it, on paleographic grounds, to the fourth year of Epiphanes (201 BCE), but this date would separate the document by nineteen years from the earliest of the remaining documents of the group. Consequently, I agree with Westermann (see PCol IV, pp. 194–95, 201–2) that it should be dated to the fourth year of Philometer (178 BCE). Then the entire group would fall within a period of five years instead of twenty-one years.

In addition to Westermann's comments on Eirene as an agricultural entrepreneur (PCol IV, pp. 194–202), see Sarah B. Pomeroy, *Women in Hellenistic Egypt,* pp. 158–60.

30 EIRĒNĒ TO LEONTISKOS, THYMOS AND TESENOUPHIS
PMich III 183   182 BCE

This legal agreement between Eirene and the three contractors, written in the form of a letter, gives Eirene's consent to the terms of a contract drawn up on the preceding day (PMich III 182) between the three contractors and a certain Nikandros, from whom Eirene had borrowed money.

Εἰρήνη Ὄρφεως Μακέτα μετὰ κυρίου τοῦ ἑαυτῆς ἀνδρὸς
   Ἀγαμέμνονος
τοῦ Χρυσέρμου Λαλασσέως Λεοντίσκωι καὶ Θύμωι καὶ
   Τεσενούφει
χαίρειν. συχωρῶ ὑμεῖν διαγράψαι Νικάνδρωι Συρακοσίωι
τὸν φό[ρον το]ῦ ὅλου παραδείσου χαλκοῦ τάλαντα
   τεσσαρά-
5 κοντα ὀκτὼ ἐν τοῖς κατὰ τὴν μίσθωσιν χρόνοις
καὶ οὐθέν ὑμεῖν ἐνκαλέσαι περὶ τούτων ποιησάντων
τὰ κατὰ τὰς συνγραφάς.   ἔρρωσθε. (ἔτους) κγ, Τῦβι
   κθ.

2nd hand: συνχωρῶ κατὰ τὰ προγεγραμένα.

Verso
1st hand: Λεοντίσκωι καὶ
      Θύμωι καὶ Τεσενούφ(ει).

Eirene, daughter of Orphis, a Macedonian woman, with her guardian, her husband, Agamemnon, son of Chrysermos, a native of Lalassis, to Leontiskos, Thymos and Tesenouphis greeting. I agree with you that you are to pay off to Nikandros, Syracusan, the rent of the entire orchard, forty-eight talents of copper, in the times specified according to the lease and, (assuming) you perform the terms of the agreement, that I am not to indict you concerning these matters. Good-bye. (Year) 23, Tybi 29. (second hand) I agree to the above-written statements.

Outside address: To Leontiskos, Thymos and Tesenouphis.

---

3 συχωρῶ for συγχωρῶ (see συνχωρῶ for συγχωρῶ in line 8; συνγραφάς for συγγραφάς in line 7); ὑμεῖν for ὑμῖν (also in line 6).
4 χαλκοῦ: χ corrected from κ.
6 ἐνκαλέσαι for ἐγκαλέσαι; ποιησάντων for ποιησάντων. One would expect a dative to agree with ὑμεῖν, instead of the genitive ποιησάντων. As it is, the construction must be taken as a genitive absolute with ὑμῶν understood.

31 LYSIMACHOS TO LEONTISKOS, THYMOS AND TESENOUPHIS
PCol IV 121   11 January 181 BCE

The editor of this text, Westermann, suggests that the peremptory tone of Lysimachos, both in this and in the following letter, indicates that he was a high official of the central financial bureau. He was sent out to the Arsinoite nome in year 24, specifically with the task of bringing pressure upon tax and rental delinquents in the nome (see his comments in PCol IV 121, pp. 188–90). We noted in the introductory comments to this archive that the three recipients of this letter had agreed with Eirene, in year 23, to pay her rent on the olive orchard that was situated on state land. The crop pickers' difficulty with Lysimachos arose because they did not pay all of the required rent. Lysimachos threatened the three with arrest if they did not send the thirteen overdue talents immediately to Krokodilopolis.

Since the outside docket of receipt shows that the letter was received on the same day on which it was sent, Lysimachos was not far away from the crop pickers. He was probably in Krokodilopolis (line 5) and the three contractors were also somewhere in the Fayum, probably in Philadelphia, near where Eirene's orchard lay (see PMich III 182.12).

Λυσίμαχος Λεοντίσκωι καὶ Θύμωι καὶ Τεσενούφει
χαίρειν. οὐ διαγεγρα-
φηκότες τὰ προσοφειλόμενα πρὸς τὴν μίσθωσιν τοῦ
παραδείσου
σὺν οἷς ἐξεδέξατο ὑμᾶς Ἅρπαλος, (τάλαντα) ιγ,
ἀγνώμονες (ἔσ)εσθε. οὐ μὴν
δ᾽ ἀλλ᾽ ἔτι καὶ νῦν, εἰ μὴ ἅμα τῶι λάβειν τὴν ἐπιστολὴν
ἀνακομίειτε
[[δει]]
5 εἰς Κροκοδίλων πόλιν, ἐξαποστέλουμεν τοὺς ἀνάξοντας
ὑμᾶς [[ε . . . . .]] οὐχ ὡς ὑπολαμβάνετε.
ἔρρωσθε. (ἔτους) κδ, Χοίακ ϛ.

Verso
1st hand: Λεοντίσκωι καὶ
              Θύμωι καὶ Τεσενούφε[ι]
2nd hand: ἀπόδου(ναι) Λυσι(μάχωι)
            διαγ(ραφὴν) μ(ισθωσέως) παρ(αδείσου). Χο(ίαχ) ϛ.

Lysimachos to Leontiskos, Thymos and Tesenouphis greeting. By not having cancelled what is
still owing on the rent of the orchard, along with
what (the amount) Harpholos became surety for
you, (namely) thirteen talents, you will be sense-
less. Certainly, then, if you do not, even now,
deliver (the thirteen talents) to Krokodilopolis, so
soon as you receive this letter, I shall send out
those who will bring you up and not as you expect.
Good-bye. (Year) 24, Choiach 6.

Outside address: To Leontiskos and Thymos and
Tesenouphis.
Docket of receipt: To deliver to Lysimachos can-
cellation of rent upon the orchard. Choiach 6.

---

3   The thirteen talents is the total which the three
    contractors still owed to the state, namely, the
    rent upon Eirene's orchard and another debt for
    which Harpalos was surety.
4   οὐ μὴν δ᾽ ἀλλ᾽ ἔτι καὶ νῦν: see PCairZen III
    59314.2–3, and Mayser, *Grammatik* 2.2.170.
5   Though not indicated in the text, the words τα

ιγ, i.e., "the thirteen (talents)," are written in
small letters, by a second hand, in the left margin
opposite line 5. According to the editor (Westermann), this marginal repetition of the thirteen
talents may have been written by Lysimachos
himself (not his scribe), to indicate that he is still
holding the correspondents liable for the two
debts and that he is not yet proceeding against
Harpalos, the surety for the second amount.
7   Χοίακ: as here, Χοίαχ is sometimes spelled with a
    final κ in papyrus texts.

---

32 SECOND WARNING OF LYSIMACHOS
PCol IV 122   10 February 181 BCE

Only a month after the preceding letter (letter 31), Lysimachos sent out a second one
regarding the delinquent rent owed by Leontiskos and his partners. They were required
to pay the remainder of the debt to Krates, a subordinate of Lysimachos. If they did not
pay the remaining rent on Eirene's orchard for year 23, Krates would bring the contractors to Krokodilopolis under arrest.

In his introductory comments upon this letter, Westermann suggests that the mood
of Lysimachos, though still determined, is milder than in the earlier letter. Since Lysimachos no longer mentions the additional debt for which Harpalos was surety, Westermann conjectures that the partners had paid off the one debt and had possibly paid some
of the back rent on Eirene's orchard from year 23.

An interesting feature of the scribe's writing style (this letter is written by a different
scribe than the preceding letter) is that in ten cases he spaces between words—never
within a word—leaving a blank space of a centimeter in some cases.

Λυσίμαχος Λεοντίσκωι καὶ τοῖς μετόχοις χαίρειν.
ἅμα τῶι λάβειν τὴν ἐπιστολὴν καλῶς ποιήσετε
τὰ προσοφειλόμενα ἐν ὑμῖν πρὸς τὸν φόρον τοῦ κγ
(ἔτους)

Lysimachos to Leontiskos and his partners greeting. Upon receipt of this letter, please pay immediately to Krates what you still owe toward the rent of
the year 23 upon the orchard of Eirene, in order

τοῦ Εἰρήνης παραδείσου ἀπόδοντες Κράτητι παραχρῆμα
5   ὅπως παρακομίση[ι] εἰς Κροκοδίλων πόλιν. εἰ δ᾽ ἄλλως
ἔσται συντετάχαμεν αὐτῶι ἐξαπόστειλαι ὑμᾶς.
ἔρρωσο. (ἔτους) κδ, Τῦβι ς̄.

Verso
1st hand: Λεοντίσκωι
             καὶ τοῖς μετόχοις
2nd hand: . .ρ. [ ] . ς
             τοῦ Εἰρήνης
             παραδείσου

that he may bring it to Krokodilopolis. If anything
other (than this) happens, I have instructed him to
send you out (under arrest). Good-bye. (Year) 24,
Tybi 6.

Outside address: To Leontiskos and his partners.
Docket of receipt: . . . (concerning?) Eirene's
orchard.

---

6   ἐξαποστέλλειν: regarding the technical use of
     this word to designate an order to arrest someone,
     issued by a higher official to a subordinate, or
     with the meaning "to summon before a court"
     (see Semeka, *Ptolemäisches Prozessrecht*, p. 247
     and Berneker, *Zur Geschichte*, pp. 78f.; see also
     the same usage in letter 31.5).

---

33 EIRĒNĒ TO DONAX, TESENOUPHIS, NIKIS AND LEONTISKOS
PMich III 193   178 BCE

In this letter, Eirene acknowledges receipt of a final payment of four talents toward the
twelve talent total paid for fig and pomegranate crops that had been farmed out to the
four contractors. The additional five lines of text in the second column seem to be a
clarifying phrase which should probably be inserted between lines 6 and 7 of column
one. This second column addition, taken together with the absence of the outside
address and the docket of receipt, suggests that our version of the receipt is a first draft
which Eirene herself kept.

Column I

Εἰρήνηι [Ὀρφε]ως Δόνακι
Τεσενού[φει] Νείκει
Λεοντίσ[κω]ι χαίρειν.
ἔχω πα[ρ᾽ ὑ]μῶν εἰς τὸν
5   φόρον τ[ῶν] τε συκίνων
/καὶ ῥο[ίνω]ν καρπῶν
ὧν ἐξ[ειλ]ήφατε
παρ᾽ ἐμ[ο]ῦ εἰς τὸ δ (ἔτος)
(τάλαντα) δ χα(λκοῦ) (γίνονται) ιβ
10   τὰ κατὰ τὴν συγγραφ(ὴν) προδεδηλωμένα.
ἔρ[ρ]ωσ(θε). (ἔτους) δ, Μεσορὴ [[κθ]] λ.

Column II

/ἐν τῶι ὑπ[άρ-]
χοντί μο[ι]
παραδε[ι-]
σωι ελε[
5   νειωι.

Eirene, daughter of Orphis, to Donax, Tesenouphis, Nikis and Leontiskos greeting. I have (received)
from you for the rent of the fig and pomegranate
fruits in my (olive?) orchard, which you have
contracted with me (to pick) in the fourth year, the
four talents of copper, coming to a total of twelve,
as previously specified according to the agreement.
Good-bye. (Year) 4, Mesore 30.

---

10   V. B. Schuman, the editor, notes that line 10 was
     written at the end of line 9 in such a way as to
     keep the right margin intact: τὰ κατὰ τὴν
                                     συγγραφ(ὴν)
                                     προδεδη-
                                     λωμένα

II, 4–5   Schuman notes that a break in the papyrus after
          ελε[makes it impossible to determine whether
          anything else followed these letters in that line. If
          ἐλενείωι is the correct reading, he states that he is
          at a loss regarding its interpretation. I think that
          the word should be restored as ἐλα[ιω]νείωι and,
          accordingly, παραδείσωι ἐλαιωνείωι could be
          translated "olive orchard."

Aroura a unit of land measurement, equal to .68 acre

Artab (literally *artaba*) a dry measure equal to about forty-two quarts (one and one-third bushel), but variable according to the standard employed

Chous a liquid measure, about three quarts

Hin an Egyptian measure, about one pint

Keramion a liquid measure, often used in reference to wine. In PTebt I 118.2, 16 the keramion ("jar") is equal to a six chous jar of wine but the size of the keramion varied like that of the metretes

Kotyle a liquid measure, about one-third quart

Metretes a liquid measure varying in size, but often containing about nine or ten U.S. gallons

Denarius a Roman coin of base alloy, nominally equal to a silver tetradrachm, whose purchasing power was much less than the Ptolemaic drachma

Drachma a Greek coin, silver in the early Ptolemaic period and equal to six obols but later it was more common to reckon by copper drachmas; initially, one silver drachma was equal to sixty of copper and by the end of the second century BCE, the ratio was often as high as 1:500

Mina as a sum of money, equal to one hundred drachmas; as a weight, equal to about twenty U.S. ounces

Obol equal to one-sixth of a silver drachma in Ptolemaic times, one-seventh of a silver drachma in Roman times

Sestertius a small Roman coin, worth one-fourth of a denarius

Stater either a weight or a sum of money; in silver equal to four drachmas, in gold equal to two drachmas

Talent equal to 6000 drachmas; as a weight, originally equivalent to sixty minas but variable according to the standard employed

Tetradrachm a coin of four drachmas

A body of over one hundred papyrus texts, dating from 164–152 BCE, was discovered in the early nineteenth century on the site of the great Serapeum near Memphis. According to F. G. Kenyon ("The Serapeum," p. 1), Arabs found all the documents in a single vessel but, thinking to make more profit by marketing them separately, the collection was scattered among several European museums. The whole collection was reedited by U. Wilcken in volume 1 of *Urkunden der Ptolemäerzeit* (UPZ I). The nine texts included here are intended to represent the correspondence in the larger collection.

Most, if not all, of the Serapeum papyri appear to have become the possession of a certain Ptolemy, the son of Glaukias, a Macedonian allotment-holder (*katoikos*) at the village of Psichis in the Herakleopolite nome. Though his father died sometime during 170–164 BCE (see PLond I 23.5), by 172 BCE Ptolemy had already become a religious recluse, a *katochos*, in the Serapeum. Wilcken has shown that this designation (katochos) means that Ptolemy was being "held fast" by Sarapis, who had somehow signified—whether by dream or inspired utterance—that Ptolemy should remain in the temple precinct so long as the god willed. When the papyri ceased in 152 BCE, Ptolemy was still being held fast and, since his papers were found at the Serapeum, we may conclude that the god never set him free. As some of the following texts illustrate, there were other katochoi, both Greek and Egyptian, in the Serapeum.

We learn from Ptolemy's own family correspondence that he had three brothers (Hippalos, Sarapion and Apollonios) and that he was evidently the eldest son. He often acted as advisor to his brothers, especially to Sarapion and Apollonios. The younger brother, Apollonios, was himself "held fast" by the god during the summer of 158 BCE and, in several cases, he was his older brother's scribe. His grammatical and spelling errors show that he was a poor scholar (see letters 41 and 42).

The largest portion of Ptolemy's papers concern two Egyptian girls, Thaues and Taous, the "twins." Following their father's death, the girls' stepmother had turned them out of the house and into the street. Since Ptolemy had been a friend of their Egyptian father, he procured a post for them in the Serapeum, where twin girls were required in the service of the cult, and he continued to look after them in a paternal manner. In return for service to Isis and Sarapis, they were granted an allowance (*syntaxis*) from the royal treasury of two measures (about eighteen gallons) of sesame and castor oil each year and eight loaves of bread each day. Their service to Asklepios warranted an additional three loaves a day. But through the laxity and/or dishonesty of officials and priests, the twins failed to receive their full allowance of either oil or bread on time. As a consequence, we have the stream of petitions drawn up by Ptolemy, either in the name of the twins or in his own name as their guardian (see letter 37; see in particular, Kenyon, Introduction, PLond I, pp. 1–6).

In addition to the above correspondence which concerned Ptolemy, there are two letters addressed to a certain Hephaistion in the Serapeum: one from his wife, Isias (letter 34), and another from his brother, Dionysios (letter 35). Hephaistion had fled to the Serapeum initially for refuge, apparently to escape some danger, but at the time the letters were received he was in religious detention ($\dot{\epsilon}\nu$ $\kappa\alpha\tau\sigma\chi\hat{\eta}$) to

Sarapis. When his relatives learned that he was voluntarily in detention, they wrote to remind him of family responsibilities at home.

The letter of Herodes to Onias (letter 36) is the only remaining segment of the Serapeum texts to be included below. It is significant because the recipient is probably Onias IV, the founder of the Temple of Onias at Leontopolis and the son of Onias III, the Jewish high priest who had been assassinated only a few years earlier. The letter suggests that Onias had become close friends with the "Philo-Semite" king, Philometer (Ptolemy VI).

Regarding the Serapeum itself and the cult of Sarapis, Ptolemy I (Soter) and his successors used the cult as a syncretistic means of uniting the racially diverse inhabitants of Egypt. There were two primary cult centers, the great Serapeum outside Memphis (see the topographical description by Wilcken in UPZ I, pp. 7–18) and the Serapeum in the native quarter (Rhacotis) of Alexandria. It is conjectured that the name Sarapis ("Serapis" in the Roman period) was a Greek transliteration of the chief deity of Memphis, Oserapis. Oserapis was the living Apis bull who, after death, was identified with Osiris as Osiris-Apis. According to Wilcken, he was not the individual dead bull but the entire series of dead Apis bulls, from the earliest to the most recent. Worship was addressed to the Osiris divinity embodied in the whole line of mummified bulls. The Ptolemies represented him in human shape, in order to make the cult acceptable to the Greek element in Egypt. At Alexandria he was identified above all with Zeus, the world ruler, and was represented as a bearded man in the prime of life. His connection with the great seaport also encouraged belief in his protection of sailors and seafarers. This emphasis is illustrated by subsequent letters, especially those written during the Roman period, by new recruits who traveled to ports like Rome (e.g., see letter 103a).

Some interpreters suggest that Sarapis had become the patron god of Alexandria to such an extent that he absorbed the original patron deity, Agathos Daimon, and that the invocation of Sarapis in a letter may be taken as evidence that the letter was either written in Alexandria or by a citizen from Alexandria (see letters 109, 110, 113). In addition to identification with Zeus at Alexandria, he appears to have been identified also with Asklepios, Dionysios and Helios (i.e., as a god of healing, a god of fertility and an oracular deity). At Memphis, the original native worship of Osiris caused Sarapis to be identified primarily with Pluto, the god of the underworld, rather than with Zeus, the cosmocrator. However, even at Memphis, where there was an Anubieum nearby, worship of Sarapis was not limited to his association with the afterlife. The correspondence of Ptolemy, son of Glaukias, indicates that Sarapis was widely regarded as an oracular deity, who gave revelations through dreams. As a result, the practice of sleeping in the temple precincts to receive such revelation was common.

Though both the Greek and native element worshiped Sarapis at Memphis, elsewhere in Egypt the worship of Sarapis was largely confined to the Greek segment of the population. Even at Memphis the cult was gradually reabsorbed by the original native worship of Osiris-Apis, and the goddess Isis came to replace him in popularity.

During Ptolemy's period of residence at the Serapeum in the mid-second century BCE, there was tension between the Greek and Egyptian elements. After a native rebellion under Dionysios Petosiris in 163 BCE, Ptolemy appealed first to the *strategos* of the nome and later to the king, complaining that he had suffered certain indignities at the time of the rebellion and that he had been attacked by

Egyptians in the temple "because he was a Greek." Once again in 163 BCE he was mistreated and, then, in 158 BCE he was assaulted by Egyptians with "ass drivers' sticks."

The antagonism between the Greek and Egyptian elements, especially in Thebes and the old pharaonic capital of Memphis erupted into broader native revolts during the later Ptolemaic rule of Egypt, as various documents in this collection illustrate (e.g., see letters 43, 56–58). The favor which the Roman government showed to the Greek element only strengthened nationalist feeling, and Osiris, Horus and other native deities reemerged in a general revival of Egyptian sentiment during the Roman period.

In addition to the comments on the Serapeum by Wilcken in UPZ I, see his essay, "Zu den κάτοχοι des Serapeums." See also Bevan, *History of Egypt*, pp. 41–48; Stambaugh, *Sarapis Under the Early Ptolemies;* and Youtie, "The *Kline* of Sarapis." I want to acknowledge Carole Myscofski's collaboration in the translation and commentary of the Serapeum correspondence used in this collection.

34 ISIAS TO HEPHAISTION
SelPap I 97 (=PLond I 42 and UPZ I 59)   168 BCE

This letter was written by Isias to her husband Hephaistion, whom she addressed affectionately and perhaps also literally as "brother." Hephaistion was apparently a κάτοχος, in seclusion at the Memphite Serapeum for religious reasons. Isias begs Hephaistion to return home from the Serapeum. She relates that she and their child have barely survived recent difficulties; that whereas all the others have returned home from religious seclusion, Hephaistion has stayed on; and that the household—in spite of his indifference—is dependent on him.

This is the first of two letters in this collection written to Hephaistion; the second, written by his brother Dionysios and bearing the same date, follows immediately as letter 35. Hephaistion, like the Apollonios of letters 39, 41 and 42 below, was probably living near the temple at Memphis or in the western desert retreat. As indicated above, the duties of the religious recluses to Sarapis are not clearly known. The vow of devotion to Sarapis, however, was a personal act, and was upheld apparently by personal decision. This text, at least, indicates that Hephaistion himself had chosen to remain.

᾿Ισιὰς ῾Ηφαιστίωνι τῶι ἀδελφῶ[ι χαί(ρειν)].
εἰ ἐρρωμένωι τἆλλα κατὰ λόγον
ἀπαντᾶι, εἴηι ἂν ὡς τοῖς θεοῖς εὐχο-
μένη διατελῶ· καὶ αὐτὴ δ᾽ ὑγίαινον
5 καὶ τὸ παιδίον καὶ οἱ ἐν οἴκωι πάντες,
σοῦ διὰ παντὸς μνείαν ποιούμενοι.
κομισαμένη τὴν παρὰ σοῦ ἐπιστολὴν
παρ᾽ ῞Ωρου, ἐν ἧι διεσαφεις εἶναι
ἐν κατοχῆι ἐν τῶι Σαραπιείωι τῶι
10 ἐν Μέμφει, ἐπὶ μὲν τῶι ἐρρῶσθα[ί] σε
εὐθέως τοῖς θεοῖς εὐχάριστουν,
ἐπὶ δὲ τῶι μὴ παραγίνεσθαί σε [π]ά[ντ]ων
τῶν ἐκεῖ ἀπειλημμένων παραγεγο[νό]των

Isias to Hephaistion greeting. If you are well and your other affairs turn out in a like fashion, it would be as I have been continually praying to the gods; I myself am also well and the child and all in the household are continually thinking of you. When I received your letter from Horos, in which you make clear that you are held fast (i.e., in the possession of the god) in the Serapeum in Memphis, I gave thanks immediately to the gods that you are well; but when you did not come back when all of the others who had been in seclusion returned, I was unhappy, for I have steered myself and your child through such a critical time—

ἀηδίζομαι ἕ[νε]κα τοῦ ἐκ τοῦ το⟨ιο⟩ύτου
15 καιροῦ ἐμαυτήν τε καὶ τὸ παιδί[ον σ]ου
διακεκυβερνηκυῖα καὶ εἰς πᾶν τι
ἐληλυθυῖα διὰ τὴν τοῦ σίτου τιμὴν
καὶ δοκοῦσα νῦν γε σοῦ παραγενομένου
τεύξεσθαί τινος ἀναψυχῆς, σὲ δὲ
20 μηδ᾽ ἐντεθυμῆσθαι τοῦ παραγενέσθαι
μηδ᾽ ἐνβεβλοφέναι εἰς τὴν ἡμετέραν περί-
στασιν, ὡς ἔτ[ι] σοῦ παρόντος πάντων ἐπεδεομην,
μὴ ὅτι γε τοσούτου χρόνου ἐπιγεγονότος
καὶ τοιούτων καιρῶν καὶ μηθὲν σοῦ ἀπεσταλκότος.
25 ἔτι δὲ καὶ ῞Ωρου τοῦ τὴν ἐπιστολὴν παρακεκο-
μικότος ἀπηγγελκότος ὑπὲρ τοῦ ἀπολελύσθαι σε
ἐκ τῆς κατοχῆς παντελῶς ἀηδίζομαι.
οὐ μὴν ἀλλ[ὰ] ἐπεὶ καὶ ἡ μήτηρ σου τυγχάνει
βαρέως ἔχουσα, καλῶς ποιήσεις καὶ διὰ ταύτην
30 καὶ δι᾽ ἡμᾶς παραγε[ε]νόμενος εἰς τὴν πόλιν, εἴπερ μὴ
ἀναγκαιότερόν σ[ε] περισπᾷ. χαριεῖ δὲ καὶ τοῦ
σώματος ἐπιμελ[ό]μενος ἵν᾽ ὑγιαίνηις.
ἔρρωσο. (ἔτους) β, Ἐπεὶφ λ̄.

Verso: ῾Ηφαιστίωνι.

having come into all of this because of the price of grain—and it seems that some relief would have accompanied your arrival, but you did not even consider returning nor did you give any consideration to our circumstances. Even while you were here, I was in need, not to mention the great time that has elapsed and such critical periods of time, with your having sent nothing. Moreover, now that Horos, who brought the letter, has reported about your release from possession (by the god), I am altogether unhappy. Not only this, since your mother is also grieved, please—both for my sake and for hers—come back to the city, unless something more urgent restrains you. You will favor me by taking care of yourself, in order to stay well. Good-bye. (Year) 2, Epeiph 30.

Outside address: To Hephaistion.

---

18   Read νῦν.
31   Read χαῖρε.

35 DIONYSIOS TO HEPHAISTION
UPZ I 60 (=Vat., Graec. 2289)   168 BCE

In this second letter to Hephaistion, his brother Dionysios acknowledges that the family has received Hephaistion's letter (the same letter to which Isias refers in letter 34). He then calls on Hephaistion to end his period of seclusion at the Serepeum and to return home as his comrades had. Dionysios reiterates the struggles that Isias, the wife of Hephaistion, and his child have been through, and he points out that it is customary to come home after having survived personal dangers.

Διονύσιος ῾Ηφαιστίωνι τῶι ἀδελφῶι χαίρειν.
εἰ ἐρρωμένωι σοι τἆλλα κατὰ λόγον ἀπαντᾶι,
εἴη ἂν ὡς βούλομαι, καὶ αὐτὸς δ᾽ ὑγίαινον καὶ
Εὐδαιμονὶς καὶ τὰ παιδία καὶ ᾿Ισιὰς καὶ τὸ παιδίον σου
5 καὶ οἱ ἐν οἴκωι πάντες. κομισάμενος τὴν
παρὰ σού ἐπιστολήν, ἐν ἧι διεσάφεις διασεσῶισθαι
ἐγ μεγάλων κινδύνων καὶ εἶναι ἐν κατοχῆι,
ἐπὶ μὲν τῶι ἐρρῶσθαί σε τοῖς θεοῖς ἐπευχαρίστουν,
ἠβουλόμην δὲ καὶ σὲ παραγεγονέναι εἰς τὴν
10 πόλιν, καθάπερ καὶ Κόνων καὶ οἱ ἄλλοι οἱ ἀπει-
λη[μμέν]οι π[ά]ντες, ὅπ[ω]ς καὶ ἡ ᾿Ισιὰς τοῦ
παιδίου σου εἰς τὰ ἔσχατα ἐληλυθότος διασεσωι-
κυῖα αὐτὸν ἐκ παντὸς τρόπου, ἔτι δὲ καὶ τοιούτους

Dionysios to Hephaistion greeting. If you are well and if your other affairs turn out in a like manner, it would be as I wish; I myself am also well as are Eudaimones and the children and Isias and your child, and the entire household. When I received your letter, in which you made clear that you had come safely through great danger and that you were being held fast (or, "in the possession" of the god), for this, that you are well, I gave thanks to the gods; yet I wish that you would come back to the city, just as Konon and all the others who had been detained (by the god), in order also that Isias who, when your child had passed through the most

ἰδοῦσά σε
καιροὺς ἀνηντληκυῖα νῦγ γε τύχηι τινὸς
15 ἀναψυχῆς. οὐ γὰρ πάντως δεῖ στενῶς ἐπανά-
σε
γοντά προσμένειν ἕως τοῦ πορίσαι τι καὶ κατε-
νεγχεῖν, ἀλλὰ πᾶς τις πειρᾶται, ὁπηνίχ᾽ ἂν
ἐκ κινδύνων διασωθῆι, ταχέως παραγίνεσθαι
καὶ ἀσπάζεσθαι τήν τε γυναῖκα καὶ τὰ παιδία
20 καὶ τοὺς φίλους. καλῶς οὖν ποιήσεις, εἴπερ μὴ καί σε
τι
ἀναγκαιότερόν περισπᾶι, συντόμως πειραθεὶς
παραγενέσθαι, [[. .]] καὶ τοῦ σώματος ἐπιμελόμενος,
ἵν᾽ ὑγιαίνηις.   ἔρρωσο. (ἔτους) β, Ἐπεὶφ λ̄.

Verso: Ἡφαιστίωνι.

extreme (circumstances), preserved him from every manner of difficulty, and even yet patiently endured such crises, would now, at least, on seeing you, meet some relief. For, it is not at all necessary that you postpone your return until you have earned something to bring home, but anyone would try, at the very moment he has been rescued from danger, to return speedily and greet wife and children and friends. Therefore, please try, unless something more urgent detains you, to return immediately, . . . and take care of yourself to stay well. Good-bye. (Year) 2, Epeiph 30.

Outside address: To Hephaistion.

14 Read νῦν.
17 Read ὁπηνίκα.

36 HERODES TO ONIAS
CPJud I 132 (=UPZ I 110)   164 BCE

The present letter was the first of three from the dioiketes Herodes, written on a papyrus text that was seven columns long. Following the precedent of Tcherikover (CPJud I 132), we have reprinted only the first of the three letters, the correspondence with Onias (lines 1–19), because of the possibility that Onias was the famous Jew of the same name (Onias is a Greek transliteration of חוניך).

Who was this Onias? The dioiketes' polite tone in addressing Onias, which contrasts sharply with the manner in which he addressed the recipients of the remaining two letters (Dorion in lines 20–192 and Theon in lines 193–213), led Wilcken to conclude that Onias was a high-ranking state official, probably a strategos (UPZ I 110). To be more specific, Onias might have been the strategos of the Heliopolite nome (the district next to Memphis). But Tcherikover suggests that Onias was even more important. He notes that the mention of the king's health, together with the health of the king's brother, the queen, and the royal children, is unique in the whole of official correspondence. As a consequence, Tcherikover concluded that Onias was a member of the court, known personally both to the king and to the dioiketes. Moreover, since the name Onias occurs at a time when the king in question was a "Philo-Semite" Ptolemy VI Philometer (see CPJud I, pp. 20ff.), it seems quite likely that Onias was the high priest, the founder of the well-known "Temple of Onias" in Leontopolis. Since, according to 2 Macc 4:34, Onias III was killed by Andronikos in Daphne near Antiocheia (ca. 170 BCE) the Onias of our letter, and the founder of the temple, would be Onias IV, son of Onias III.

One piece of evidence that is antithetical to this theory is the statement by Josephus (*Jewish Antiquities* 12.387) that Onias IV left Palestine for Egypt after the execution of Menelaus and the nomination of Alkimos to the office of high priest, namely, after 162 BCE. Our document, on the other hand, would have already been written prior to this date. Tcherikover proposes, however, that Josephus may have placed the flight of Onias

IV wrongly at the later date. In fact, it could have happened before 164 BCE; the flight could have occurred immediately after the assassination of Onias and, indeed, the assassination may have been the cause of the flight. It would be a very unusual coincidence if there were two people of high social standing with the same name, so near the same date, who were both friends of the king and living at or near Memphis.

Ἡρώιδης Ὀνί[αι] χαίρειν. ἔρρωται μὲν βασ[ιλεὺς]
Πτολεμαῖος καὶ βασιλεὺς Πτολεμαῖος ὁ ἀδελφὸς κ[αὶ]
βασίλισσα Κλεοπάτρα ἡ ἀδελφὴ καὶ τὰ τέκνα καὶ
τὰ πράγματ᾽ {ατ} αὐτοῖς ἔχει κατὰ τρόπον· ἰ δὲ
5 καὶ σὺ ὑγιγαίνις καὶ τἆλλά σοι κατὰ λόγον ἐστίν, εἴ-
η ἂν ὡς βουλόμεθα, καὶτοὶ δ᾽ ἱ(ι)κανῶς ἐπανή-
γομεν. τῆς πρὸς Δωρίωνα τὸν ὑποδιοικητὴν
ἐπιστολῆς ὑπόκιταί σοι τὸ ἀντίγραφον. διαλα-
βὼν οὖν ὡς ἡ περὶ [τ]ῶν κατὰ τὸν σπόρον φρον-
10 τὶς κοινῆι πᾶσιν ἐπιβάλλει τοῖς τῶν πραγμά-
των κηδομένοις, καλῶς ποιήσεις τὴν πᾶσαν προσενεγκάμενος ἐκτένειαν καὶ πρ[ο]νο-
ηθείς, ὅπως μήτε{ν} τῶν ἀδυνατούντων γε-
ωργεῖν περισπᾶται μηθεὶς μήτε τῶν δυνα-
15 μένων σκεπάζηται κατὰ μηδεμίαν παρ-
εύρεσιν, ἕκαστα δ᾽ ἐπιτελεσθῆι κατὰ τὸν ὑπο-
δεδειγμένον ἐν τῶι πεμφθέντι σοι παρ᾽ ἡμῶν
ὑπομνήματι τρόπον. ἐπιμελόμενος δὲ καὶ σαυτοῦ, ἵν᾽ ὑγιγαίνηις.   ἔρρωσο. (ἔτους) ϛ Μεσ[ορ]ὴ κδ.

Herodes to Onias greeting. King Ptolemy is well and king Ptolemy his brother and Queen Cleopatra the sister and the children, and their affairs are satisfactory; if you too are well and everything is satisfactory to you, it would be as we wish; we too are recovering well. The copy of the letter to Dorion the *hypodioiketes* is for you. Therefore, since you realize that consideration regarding those engaged in sowing is a common responsibility for all those who are concerned about the state (administration), please apply all zeal and take all precaution, in order neither that those who are unable to work in the fields be impressed nor that those who are able be protected (e.g., by patronage) on any pretext whatever; but that each thing be completed according to the manner in which it was indicated in our memorandum which was sent to you. Also, take care of yourself, to stay well. Good-bye. (Year) 6, Mesore 24.

4 Read εἰ.
5 Read ὑγιαίνεις (also in line 19).
6 Read καὐτοί.

37   A PETITION FROM THE SERAPEUM TWINS
PMilligan 5 (=PParis 26)   163–162 BCE

The majority of extant documents from the Serapeum concern the grievances of two sisters, the twins Thaues and Thaus (or Taous). Kenyon provides a rather full reconstruction of their affairs (PLond I, pp. 2–6). The twins acted as attendants in the Serapeum, perhaps originally in connection with the Apis bull funerary rituals (see Crawford, "Ptolemy, Ptah and Apis," p. 9). As attendants, they were entitled to payments in oil and bread. Both in the present letter and in others, the girls protest that they have not been properly paid. A certain Ptolemy, who was among those in religious detention in the Serapeum, wrote this petition and the others on behalf of the twins.

The twins address their plea to King Ptolemy VI Philometer and Queen Cleopatra, recounting their efforts, up until the day before the letter was written, to regain the food allowance owed to them. They turn appropriately to the monarchs, on whose behalf they serve the worship of the celestial king and queen, Osiris and Isis. The temple officials mentioned in this text were responsible to the crown: the (financial) administrators (τοῖς χειρισμοῖς, lines 19 and 34) were appointed administrators; the supervisors (ἐπιστάτης, lines 23f., the "supervisor" of the sacrifices) supervised the rituals and ritual objects; the curator(s) (ἐπιμελητής, lines 24 and 43) oversaw the public buildings; and the strategos was the military governor.

Column I

Βασιλεῖ Πτολεμαίῳ καὶ Βασιλίσσῃ Κλεοπάτρᾳ τῇ
  ἀδελφῇ,
θεοῖς Φιλομήτορσι, χαίρειν. Θαυὴς καὶ Ταοῦς δίδυμαι, αἱ
  λειτουργοῦσαι
ἐν τῷ πρὸς Μέμφει μεγάλῳ Σαραπιείῳ· καὶ πρότερον μὲν
  ὑμῖν
ἐπιδημήσα[σι]ν ἐν Μέμφει καὶ ἀναβᾶσιν εἰς τὸ ἱερὸν
  θυσιάσαι
5 ἐνετύχομεν, καὶ ἐπεδώκαμεν ἔντευξιν, προφερόμεναι μὴ
  κομίζεσθαι
τὴν καθήκουσαν ἡμῖν δίδοσθαι σύνταξιν τῶν δεόντων ἔκ
  τε τοῦ
Σαραπιείου καὶ Ἀσκληπιείου. Μέχρι δὲ τοῦ νῦν οὐ
  κεκομισμέναι
ἐκ πλήρους ἠναγκάσμεθ' ὑπὸ τῆς ἀνάγκης ἐπειγόμεναι,
  ὡς ἂν
ὑπὸ τῆς λιμοῦ διαλυόμεναι, πάλιν ἐντυχεῖν ὑμῖν, καὶ δι'
  ὀλίων
10 τὴν τῶν ἀδικούντων ἡμᾶς φιλαυτίαν ἐχθεῖναι. ὑμῶν γὰρ
  ἐκτιθέντων
ἔτι ἀπὸ τῶν ἔνπροσθεν χρόνων σύνταξιν τῷ τε Σαραπιείῳ
καὶ τῷ Ἀσκληπιείῳ, καὶ ἐκ τούτων καὶ τῶν πρὸτοῦ
  γενηθεισῶν
δ[ι]δύμων κομισαμένων τὰ ἑαυτῶν καθ' ἡμέραν δέοντα,
  καὶ ἡμῖν,
ὅταν ἔβημεν κατ' ἀρχὰς εἰς τὸ ἱερόν, παραχρῆμα μὲν
  ὀλίας ἡμέρας,
15 ὑπέδειξαν ὡς ἂν εὐτακτηθησομένων ἡμῖν τῶν
  καθηκόντων,
τὸν δὲ λοιπὸν χρόνον οὐκ ἐξετίθεσαν. διὸ καὶ πρὸς τοὺς
ἐπιμελητὰς ἐπέμπομεν τοὺς ἐντευξομένους,
καὶ ὑμῖν, καθ' ἃς ἐποεῖσθ' ἐν Μέμφει παρουσίας,
  ἐνεφανίζομεν
ὑπὲρ τούτων. τῶν δὲ πρὸς τοῖς χειρισμοῖς ἐν τῷ Σαραπιείῳ
20 καὶ Ἀσκληπιείῳ τεταγμένων κατατετολμηκότων καὶ τὰ
ὑφ' ὑμῶν ἡμῖν χρηματιζόμενα ἐκφερομένων καὶ οὐδεμίαν
εὐλάβειαν προορωμένων· ἡμῶν δὲ τοῖς δέουσι θλιβομένων
καὶ Ἀχομάρρῃ μὲν τῷ ἐπιστάτῃ τοῦ ἱεροῦ πλεονάκι
  διεστάλμεθα
ἀποδιδόναι ἡμῖν· καὶ τῷ υἱῷ δὲ Ψινταέους τοῦ ἐπιστάτου
  τῶν

To King Ptolemy and Queen Cleopatra the sister, gods Philometores, greeting. Thaues and Taous, who are twins, perform religious duties in the great Serapeum at Memphis. And, formerly, when you stayed in Memphis and went up to the temple to sacrifice, we petitioned you and presented a petition to you, carrying before you our plea that we had not received the required stipend which was to be given to us by the Serapeum and the Asklepeum. But since, up to the present, we have not received this in full, we have been compelled, pressed by necessity, being undone as we are by hunger, to petition you once again and to put before you in a few words the selfishness of those who are treating us unjustly. For you had already set aside an allocation in earlier times for the Serapeum and the Asklepeum and from this (allocation) the twins who preceded us also received the daily necessities; and they indicated also to us, when we first went into the temple, straightways for a few days, that whatever was fitting for us would be done in good order, but it has not been carried through during the intervening time. Wherefore, we both sent people (on our behalf) who petitioned the directors (curators), and we reported on these things to you, when you happened to be present in Memphis. And when those who were appointed to the (financial) administration of the Serapeum and Asklepeum showed us great cruelty and were removing privileges granted by you to us, and were paying no regard to religious duty, being oppressed by necessities, we several times asked Achomarres, the supervisor of the temple, to deliver (our allowance) to us. And we approached the son of Psintaes, the supervisor of the sacrifices, when he was going up into the temple the day before yesterday, and gave him information about each of these things. And when he had summoned Archomarres, he ordered him to give all that was owed to us. But the latter, who is the most unfeeling of all men, promised us that he would comply with what was prescribed but, when the son of Psintaes had departed from

25 ἱερῶν, ἀναβάντι πρώην εἰς τὸ ἱερόν, προσήλθομεν, καὶ
  περὶ ἑκάστων
  μετεδώκαμεν. καὶ προσκαλεσάμενος τὸν Ἀχομάρρην
  συνέταξεν ἀποδοῦναι ἡμῖν τὰ ὀφειλόμενα. ὁ δέ, πάντων
  ἀνθρώπων ἀγνωμονέστατος ὑπάρχων, ἡμῖν μὲν ὑπέσχετο
  τὸ προκείμενον ἐπιτελέσειν· τοῦ δὲ τοῦ Ψινταέους υἱοῦ ἐκ
  τῆς

Column II

30 Μέμφεως χωρισθέντος, οὐκέτι
  οὐδένα λόγον ἐποήσατο. οὐ μόνον δ᾽ οὗτος
  ἀλλὰ καὶ ἄλλοι τῶν ἐκ τοῦ Σαραπιείου
  καὶ ἕτεροι τῶν ἐκ τοῦ Ἀσκληπιείου
  ὄντες πρὸς χειρισμοῖς, παρ᾽ ὧν ἔθος ἐστὶν
35 ἡμᾶς τὰ δέοντα κομίζεσθαι, ἀποστε-
  ροῦσιν, ὧν τά τε ὀνόματα καὶ τὰ ὀφειλόμενα,
  διὰ τὸ εἶναι πλείονα, οὐκ ἐκρίναμεν κατα-
  χωρίσαι. δεόμεθα οὖν ὑμῶν, μίαν
  ἔχουσαι ἐλπίδα τὴν ὑφ᾽ ὑμῶν ἐσομέ-
40 νην ἀντίληψιν, ἀποστεῖλαι ἡμῶν
  τὴν ἔντευξιν ἐπὶ Διονύσιον τῶν φίλων
  καὶ στρατηγόν, ὅπως γράψῃ Ἀπολλωνίῳ
  τῷ ἐπιμελητῇ, ἐπιλαβόντα παρ᾽ ἡμῶν
  τὴν γραφὴν τῶν ὀφειλομένων ἡμῖν
45 δεόντων καὶ τίνα πρὸς τίνας χρόνους
  προσωφείληται καὶ ὑπὸ τίνων,
  ἐπαναγκάσῃ αὐτοὺς ἀποδοῦναι ἡμῖν,
  ἵνα, πᾶν τὸ ἑξῆς ἔχουσαι, πολλῷ μᾶλλον
  τὰ νομιζόμενα τῷ Σαράπει καὶ τῇ Ἴσει
50 ἐπιτελῶμεν ὑπέρ τε ὑμῶν καὶ τῶν
  ὑμετέρων τέκνων. ὑμῖν δὲ γίνοιτο
  κρατεῖν πάσης ἧς ἂν αἱρῆσθε χώρας.
       εὐτυχεῖτε.

Memphis, he no longer took any account of the matter. And not only this man but also others associated with the Serapeum and others with the Asklepeum who are in the administration, from whom it is customary for us to receive our necessities, are cheating us, whose names and obligations, on account of being so numerous, we decided not to record. Therefore, we entreat you, having this one hope, the aid which comes from you, to send our petition to Dionysios a member of the court and strategos, in order that he may write to Apollonios the curator (of the Serapeum) so that he, in turn, having received from us the written list of what allowances are owed to us, and for what length of time and by whom, may compel them to pay it to us in order that, when we have everything in order, we may much better fulfil the customary duties to Sarapis and to Isis on behalf of you and your children. May it be granted to you to rule all the land (territory) that you desire. May you prosper (fare well).

---

6 σύνταξιν: a customary term for a contribution from the treasury for religious purposes; see Otto, *Priester und Tempel* 1:366ff.

9 Read δι᾽ ὀλίγων (see 1 Pet 5:12). See ὀλίος for ὀλίγος also in line 14.

38 DIONYSIOS TO PTOLEMAIOS
SelPap I 98 (=PParis 49; UPZ I 62)   ca. 160 BCE

The writer of this letter, a certain Dionysios, is not the strategos of the same name (see letter 37.41–42) but a minor official in Memphis, who supervised scribes in some capacity. The recipient, Ptolemy, is the religious recluse (katochos), and scribe, who wrote the preceding petition (letter 37) and other pieces of correspondence on behalf of the twins. He is also the recipient of letters 40–42.

Dionysios writes to Ptolemy, reporting on his recent encounter with the latter's brother (Sarapion of letter 40?). The brother had asked to have some reports transcribed and had offered to pay for them. Dionysios turned down payment for the work and asked, in exchange for the favor, that the youth pick up a quarter artab of sesame from him the next morning and have it ground into paste. Since the youth did not return, Dionysios inquires, in the present letter, whether the youth were ill, ashamed, or had some other reason for disappearing.

The *tritomon* that the brother proposed to bring to Dionysios is an unknown Greek word and, consequently, it is translated in various ways. Wilcken suggests that it is some type of payment or bribe, which the brother offered for transcribing his reports, but Hunt and Edgar, the editors, translate it as a third section of a roll and suggest that the term probably refers to a certain quantity of papyrus.

Διονύσι[ος Πτολε] μαίωι χαίρειν καὶ
ἐρρῶσθα[ι]. τοι[αύ] την ἐμαυτοῦ
ἐλευθερ[ιότ]η[τ]α, [ο]ὐ βαναυσίαν
ἐκτέθεικα πᾶσιν ἀνθρώποις,
5   μάλιστα δὲ σοὶ κ[α]ὶ τῷ σῷ ἀδελφῶι
διά τε τ[ὸν] Σάραπιν καὶ τὴν σὴν
ἐλευθε [ρία]ν καὶ πεπείραμαι,
ἀφ᾽ οὗτε συνεστάθης μοι, εἰς πᾶν
τό σοι χρήσιμον ἐμαυτὸν ἐπιδιδόναι.
10   τοῦ δὲ ἀδελφοῦ σου συμπεσόντος μοι
τῆι ιζ τοῦ Μεχεὶρ
καὶ ἀξιώσαντός με ὅπως, ἐὰν ἐνέγκηι
τρίτομον, μεταλάβωσιν αὐτῶι οἱ πα-
ρ᾽ ἐμοῦ γραμματεῖς πάντας τοὺς
15   χρηματισμούς, εἶπα αὐτῶι μὴ ἐμὲ
ἀξιοῦν, ἀλλὰ δόξαντα ἀδελφὸν αὐτοῦ
ἐν τῆι αὐλῆι εἶναι παραγίνεσθαι,
μονογράφοις δὲ μηθὲν διδόναι γράφειν
μηδὲ ἀναλίσκειν χαλκοῦς, καὶ ἀπέλυσα
20   εἴπας αὐτῶι ὀρθρίτερον ἐλθεῖν, ὅπως
λαβὼν παρ᾽ ἐμοῦ ἐν Μέμφει σησάμου
τέταρτον τρίψῃ μοι {ἐν Μέμφει} τρίμμα
διὰ τὸ εἰς τὴν πόλιν με θέλειν δοῦναι
ἀπενεγκεῖν. ὁ δέ, φαίνεται, τὴν
25   ἡμέραν ἐκείνην ἀσχοληθεὶς ᾔσχυνται
συμμεῖξαί μοι. εἴπερ οὖν ἐστιν αὕτη
ἡ αἰτία καὶ διὰ τοῦτο οὐκέτι ἥκει πρὸς ἐμὲ
αἰσχυνθείς, παρακαλέσας αὐτὸν
ἀπόστειλον πρὸς ἐμέ· γίνεται γὰρ
30   ἐντραπῆναι. ἐγὼ γὰρ νὴ τοὺς θεοὺς
ἀγωνιῶ μή ποτε ἀ[ρ]ρωστεῖ τὸ παιδάριον
καὶ οὐκ ἔχω σχολὴν ἀναβῆναι πρὸς ὑμᾶς.
εἰ δὲ δι᾽ ἄλλο τι οὐκ ὀπτάνεταί μοι, γίνωσκε
σαφῶς ὅτι, ἐὰν ἀναβῶ κἀγὼ προσκυνῆσαι,
35   πρὸς σὲ οὐ μὴ εἰσέλθω, εἰς δὲ
[[εἰς]] τὰ Πρωτάρχου καταλύσω. ὑγίαινε
[δὲ...

Verso: Πτολεμαίωι.

Dionysios to Ptolemy greeting and health. My very strong liberality, not vulgarity, I have displayed to all men, and most of all to you and to your brother, for the sake of Sarapis and because of your own liberal nature and I have tried, from the time that you were introduced to me, to devote myself to everything that is useful to you. And when your brother met me on the seventeenth of Mecheir and asked me whether, if he brought a third section of a roll (tritomon), my scribes would undertake the transcription of all his business transactions, I told him not to ask me, but rather to come as if he were assuming that he had a brother at court, and to give nothing to professional scribes to write nor to waste coppers on them; and I sent him off, telling him to come early the next morning in order to take from me a quarter of an artab of sesame to be ground into paste for me in Memphis, because I wanted it to be given to someone to carry it back to the city. But, evidently, since he had no time on that day he has been ashamed to meet with me. Therefore, if that is the cause and because of this, having become ashamed, he no longer will come to me, encourage him and send him to me; for it happens that one may feel shame. For, by the gods, I am anxious lest the lad be ill and I do not have the leisure to come up to you. But if I do not see him for some other cause, understand clearly that, if I come up to worship, I will certainly not enter (your door), but will lodge with Protarchos. Keep well . . .

Outside address: To Ptolemy.

39 BARKAIOS TO APOLLŌNIOS
UPZ I 64 (=PParis 42)   156 BCE

The recipient of this letter, Apollonios, is the younger brother of Ptolemy the katochos. He is also the co-recipient with Ptolemy of letter 40 and the addressor of letters 41 and 42 (both addressed to Ptolemy). In the present correspondence, Barkaios, who is also called Ammonias, thanks Apollonios for notifying the authorities about the escape of prisoners on the temple grounds. The prisoners escaped from a prison attached to the police station, which was located in the precinct of the temple of Anubis. The temple lay on the edge of the desert, near the Serapeum. The strategos himself, when he visited the Serapeum, resided at the Anubieum, and we hear in letter 42.19–23 that the strategos will spend two days in the temple "drinking."

Along with his notice of the prisoners' escape, Apollonios had also reported that his brother Sarapion had been mistreated by a prison guard. This Sarapion is the young brother mentioned in letter 38 (160 BCE) and the addressor of letter 40 (154 BCE), who notifies Ptolemy and Apollonios of his intention to marry. Here, Barkaios informs Apollonios that Sarapion had admitted he was not harmed by the guard. Barkaios adds that Apollonios will receive a reward for his service and that similar notification in the future will not go unnoticed.

Barkaios was clearly an official or warden of the prison, and though he addresses Apollonios as brother, the appellation clearly indicates familiarity, social equality or, perhaps, even the common religious ties of the correspondents. It is not to be taken literally.

Βαρκαῖος ⟨ὁ⟩ καὶ Ἀμμώνιος Ἀπολλωνίωι τὰ ἀδελφῶι
   χαίρειν.
εἰ ἐρρωμένως σοι καὶ τᾶλλα κατὰ λόγον ἐστίν, τὸ δέον ἂν
   εἴηι καὐτοὶ δὲ
ὑιαίνομεν. λίαν σοι χάριν μεγάλην ἐσχήκαμεν σημήνας
   ἡμῖν
τὰ κατὰ τοὺς ἀλάστορας τοὺς διηλμένους ἐκ τῆς φυλακῆς,
   προσδι-
5 εσάφεις δὲ καὶ τὸν ἀδελφόν σου Σαραπίωνα ἀδικεῖσθαι
   ὑπὸ Ἁ[ρ]παήσιος
φυλακίτου. μεταπεμψάμενος οὖν αὐτὸν καὶ τὸν
   φυλακίτην
ἐπετίμων αὐτῶι καὶ ὁ ἀδελφός σου ἀνθωμολογεῖτο μὴ
   ἠδικῆσθαι ὑπ᾽ αὐ-
τοῦ, καὶ παρεκάλεσα αὐτὸν ἔρχεσθαι, περὶ ὧν ἂν
   βούληται. χαριεῖ δὲ
συμπαραστὰς ἡμῖν ἐν τοῖς λοιποῖς καὶ παρατηρήσας τοὺς
   ἀλάστορας,
10 καὶ ἐὰν τολμήσωσι καὶ καταβῶσι ἐκτὸς τοῦ ἀσύλου,
   διασάφησόν μοι,
ὅπως παραγενηθεὶς σύν σοι γενόμενος πράξωμέν τι, καί
   υοι
στεφανίον ἐστιν χα(λκοῦ) ⟨ταλάντων⟩ γ, ὡς περὶ ἰδίου
   πράγματος διαβαίνων, καὶ ἡμῖν

Barkaios, also called Ammonios, to his brother, Apollonios, greeting. If you are well and everything else (or, your other affairs) is agreeable, it is as it should be. We also are well. We had great thanks for you when you reported to us about the wretches who had escaped from the prison. You made quite clear in addition that your brother Sarapion was mistreated by Harpaesis the guard. Therefore, after I summoned him and the guard, I censured him (the guard) and your brother confessed that he had not been harmed (?) by him, and I encouraged him to come to me, about whatever he wanted. You would do us a favor by assisting us in the future and by watching the prisoners closely, and if they dare to go down outside the sanctuary, inform me, in order that, having been assisted by you, we would be enabled to do something. And there is a reward for you of three copper talents, so that your own status is improved and you will have favored us greatly. Also you would favor us by taking care of yourself to stay well. Good-bye. (Year) 26, Phaophi 4.

Outside address: . . . to Apollonios.

ἔσει μεγάλως κεχαρισμένος. χαρίζοι⟨ο⟩ δ᾽ ἂν καὶ τοῦ σώματος
ἐπιμελόμενος, ἵν᾽ ὑιαίνῃς.   ἔρρωσο. (ἔτους) κϛ, Φαῶφι δ.

1 Read τῷ.
2 Read ἐρρωμένωι.
3 Read ὑγιαίνομεν, σημήναντι.
14 Read ὑγιαίνῃς.

Verso: . . . .   Ἀπολλωνίωι

40 SARAPION TO PTOLEMAIOS AND APOLLŌNIOS
SelPap I 99 (=UPZ I 66; PParis 43)   154 BCE

With this note Sarapion announces to his older brothers that he will be married shortly. In preparation for that ceremony he evidently requires half a chous of olive oil. He invites Apollonios to attend the celebration, but Ptolemy is not invited, apparently because he was being "held fast" to the Serapeum by the god and, consequently, would have been unable to attend.

Σαραπίων Πτολεμαίωι καὶ Ἀπολλωνίῳ τοῖς ἀδελφοῖς χαίρειν. εἰ ἔρρωσθαι, ἔρρωμαι δὲ καὐτοί. συγγέγραμμαι τῆι Ἑσπέρου θυγατρί, μέλλω δὲ ἰσάγειν
ἐν τῷ Μεσορὴ μηνί. καλῶς ποιήσεις ἀποστεῖλαί μοι ἱμίχουν
ἐλαίου. γέγραφ᾽ ἱμεῖν ἵνα εἰδῆται.
5   ἔρρωσο. (ἔτους) κη Ἐπεὶφ κα.
(Added on left) παραγε⟨νομε⟩νου δὲ εἰς τὴν ἡμέραν Ἀπολλώνιος.

Verso: Πτολεμαίωι, Ἀπολλωνίωι.

Sarapion to his brothers, Ptolemy and Apollonios, greeting. If you are well, (it would be excellent); I myself am well. I have contracted with the daughter of Hesperos and intend to marry her in the month Mesore. Please send half a chous of olive oil to me. I wrote to you in order that you may know. Good-bye. (Year) 28, Epeiph 21.

Postscript added on left: Come for the (wedding) day, Apollonios.

Outside address: To Ptolemy and Apollonios.

1 Read ἔρρωσθε. According to Hunt and Edgar (SelPap I 99), εὖ ἂν ἔχοι should be understood with this health wish.
2 Read καὐτος.
3 Read ἡμίχουν.
4 Read ὑμῖν, εἰδῆτε.

41 APOLLŌNIOS TO PTOLEMAIOS
UPZ I 68 (=PParis 44)   3 August 152 BCE

At the time of writing, Apollonios is in the Herakleopolite nome, perhaps in the city of Herakleopolis, attending to business affairs. We know that the father of Apollonios and Ptolemy had been a Macedonian allotment-holder (katoikos) at the city of Psichis in the Herakleopolite nome. Apollonios, then, seems to be attending to family property and to other family business matters.

Though the letter is primarily concerned with these transactions, Apollonios informs Ptolemy near the close of the letter that he has had a bad dream in which he is being chased by a certain Menedemos. He adds that he has also grown anxious about his brother Ptolemy and a certain Apollonios. According to Wilcken, the editor, this is the same Apollonios to whom our Apollonios wrote, on the same day as the present letter, in UPZ I 69. Namely, he was the *epistates* of the Anubieum near Memphis. The anxiety which Apollonios expresses here about that Apollonios and about his brother Ptolemy is probably unrelated to the bad dream about Menedemos.

Apollonios wrote another letter, also close in time to this one, to his brother Ptolemy, in which he refers to a "runaway" who is causing difficulty for him. That letter follows immediately in this collection (letter 42) and the runaway there is to be identified with the Menedemos. He is an irritant in both cases, but he seems not to be the most significant cause of difficulty for Apollonios. At present, we do not know the circumstances of the grave troubles in the following letter, nor the cause of concern for Ptolemy and Apollonios (the epistates) in the present letter.

Regarding the troublemaker Menedemos, it was common in the early interpretation of these texts to identify him with the Menedemos who was a subordinate of the strategos, in correspondence written ten years earlier (see UPZ I 7.18). But Wilcken was probably correct in rejecting this connection, since that Menedemos was associated with the Anubieum near Memphis. The Menedemos of this letter, on the other hand, was a fugitive operating in the Herakleopolite nome.

Ἀπολλώνιος Πτολεμαίωι τῶι πατρὶ χαίρειν. εἰ ἔρρωσαι,
  ἔρρωμαι δὲ καὐτός,
εἴε ἂν ὡς βούλομαι καὶ τὰ ἄλλα σοι καιτὰ λό[γ]ον ἀπαντᾶ.
  γίνωσκέ με πεπορεῦσθαι εἰς Ἡρα-
κλέους πόλιν ὑπὲρ τῆς οἰκίας. τοὺς χαλκοὺς οὓς κέχρηκας
  Πετοσίριος καὶ Σεμφθῆαι κεκόμισ⟨μαι⟩
καὶ Σαραπίωνι
τὰς μὲν (δραχμὰς) Ἀ, ἃς δέδωκας Πετενήθι χῆνα
  ἀγωράζει⟨ν⟩, τί κελεύ[ι]ς περὶ τούτων, ἀπόστιλόν μοι
  ἐπισ-
5 τόλιον ἔχωντα Πολυδεύκην ταχὺ καὶ ἢ ἕτερον θέλις
  λέγειν, λέγε. ἐγὼ γὰρ ἐνύπνια
ὁρῶ πονηρά, βλέπω Μενέδημον κατατρέχοντά με.
  Δ[ιασά]φ[η]σόν μ[ο]ι τὰ περὶ Ἀπολλώνιον
καὶ τὰ περὶ σαυτὸν ἀκριβῶς, ὅπως εἰδῶ, ἀγωνιῶ γὰρ
  περὶ σοῦ.   ἔρρωσο. (ἔτους) κθ, Ἐπεὶφ η̄.

Verso: τῶι πατρὶ Πτολεμαίωι.

Apollonios to his father, Ptolemy, greeting. If you are well, I too am well, (and) it would be as I desire and (I hope that) everything else is agreeable to you. Know that I have gone to Herakleopolis about the house. I have received back the coppers which you loaned to Petosiris and Semphth and Sarapion. Send me a letter quickly by means of Polydeukes, explaining what you want done with the one thousand drachmas which you gave to Petenethis to buy a goose and if you have anything else you want to say, say it. For I have a bad dream, (in which) I see Menedemos chasing me. Make clear to me exactly how the affairs of Apollonios and of yourself are going, in order that I may know, for I am concerned about you. Good-bye. (Year) 29, Epeiph 8.

Outside address: To my father Ptolemy.

2   Read εἴη, κατά.
3   Read Πετοσίρει.
4   Read ἀγοράζειν.
5   Read ἔχοντα, εἰ, θέλεις.

APOLLŌNIOS TO PTOLEMAIOS
SelPap I 100 (=PParis 47; UPZ I 70)

152 BCE

Apollonios addresses his elder brother respectfully as father, just as he did in the immediately preceding letter. In this instance, however, the tone of the letter is very harsh. Whereas Ptolemy believed devoutly that the god communicated his will through dreams, in a moment of angry disillusionment, Apollonios writes a bitter denunciation of his brother's prophetic dreams. He alleges that affairs have gone just the opposite of what his brother has predicted. His mood appears even to degenerate to sarcasm on the outside address where, in addition to naming his recipient, he adds: "to those who tell the truth" (soothsayers?). Apollonios' aggravation is reflected also in the omission of both opening and concluding health wishes in the letter.

The runaway to which Apollonios refers in line 15 is, as noted in the introduction to the preceding letter, a certain Menedemos. This reference to the troublesome runaway suggests that the present letter was written relatively close in time to letter 41 (=UPZ 68) and UPZ 69. Wilcken, the editor, suggests that in this instance Apollonios is writing from Memphis rather than from the Herakleopolite nome, since he refers to the strategos coming up to the Serapeum in lines 19–23 (UPZ I 70). If this is the case, one wonders why Apollonios sent a letter, since he would have been close by his brother, who was in the Serapeum. The nature of his difficulty is also puzzling. Though he talks about the gravity of the situation, he does not identify the problem. Ptolemy, of course, would have understood the circumstances.

Ἀπολλώνιος Πτολεμαίωι
τῶι πατρὶ χαίρειν. ὀμνύ-
ο τὸν Σάραπιν, ἰ μὴ μικρόν
τι ἐντρέπομαι, οὐκ ἄν με
5 ἴδες τὸ πόρσωπόν μου
πόποτε, ὅτι ψεύδηι
πάντα καὶ οἱ παρὰ σὲ
θεοὶ ὁμοίως, ὅτι ἐν-
βέβληκαν ὑμᾶς εἰς ὕλην
10 μεγάλην καὶ οὗ δυνάμε-
θα ἀποθανεῖν, κἂν ἴδης
ὅτι μέλλομεν σωθῆναι,
τότε βαπτιζώμεθα.
γίνωσκε ὅτι πιράσεται
15 ὁ δραπέ[τ]ης μὴ ἀφῖναι
ἡμᾶς ἐπὶ τῶν τόπων
ἵναι· χάριν γὰρ ἡμῶν
ἠζημίοται εἰς χαλκοῦ
(τάλαντα) ιε. ὁ στρατηγὸς ἀνα-
20 βαίνει αὔριον εἰς τὸ Σαραπι-
ῆν καὶ δύο ἡμέρας ποι-
εῖ ἐν τῶι Ἀνουβιείωι
πίνων. οὐκ ἔστι ἀνακύ-
ψαι με πόποτε ἐν τῇ Τρικομίαι
25 ὑπὸ τῆς αἰσχύνης, ἰ καὶ
αὐτοὺς δεδώκαμεν
καὶ ἀποπεπτώκαμεν
πλανόμενοι ὑπὸ τῶν

Apollonios to his father, Ptolemy, greeting. I swear by Sarapis, if it were not that I still have a little reverence (for you), you would never see my face again; because you deceive completely and likewise your gods, for they have thrown us into a great slough in which we may die, and when you see (i.e., have a vision) that we are about to be saved, then we are immersed. Know that the runaway will try to hinder us from staying in these parts, for on account of us he has suffered a financial loss of fifteen copper talents. The strategos is coming up to the Serapeum tomorrow and will spend two days in the Anubieum drinking. I will never be able to hold up my head in Trikomia because of the shame, that we have given ourselves away and have been deluded, being lead astray by the gods and trusting dreams. May you fare well.

Outside address: To those who speak the truth (on the left side of the verso). To Ptolemy, greeting.

---

2 Read ὀμνύω.
3 Read εἰ (also in line 25).
5 Read πρόσωπον.
9 Read ἡμᾶς.
13 Read βαπτιζόμεθα.
17 Read εἶναι.
18 Read ἐζημίωται.

θεῶν καὶ πιστεύοντες
30 τὰ ἐνύπνια.   εὐτύχει.

Verso: πρὸς τοὺς   Πτολεμαί-
τὴν ἀλή-   ωι χαίρε[ι]ν.
θειαν λέγοντες.

20   Read Σαραπιεῖον.
23f.   "hold up my head": the imagery suggests rising up out of the water or, figuratively, out of difficulties. The previous image of sinking in lines 9–10 and 13 appears still to be operative here.
24   Read Τρικωμίαι.
28   Read πλανώμενοι.
33   Read λέγοντας.

In this letter of a Greek soldier, written in Upper Egypt (Thebes), the writer informs his parents that his detachment of troops, loyal to Ptolemy VIII (Euergetes II [145–116 BCE]), is about to attack the town of Hermonthis, which was being held for Queen Cleopatra II. News has come that Paos, the governor (strategos) of Thebes, is about to bring a sufficient force to crush Hermonthis. The document vividly illustrates the internal strife of the royal family during this period.

The strife appeared forty years earlier when, in 170 BCE, Antiochos IV Epiphanes invaded Egypt and took the young king Ptolemy VI Philometor as prisoner. In Philometor's absence, soldiers and citizens of Alexandria overthrew his advisors and placed his younger brother (later known as Ptolemy VIII or Euergetes II) on the throne. Since it was advantageous for Antiochos Epiphanes to have Egypt divided against itself, he allowed Philometor to rule in Memphis. But during the winter of 169–168 BCE the two brothers agreed to reign together as joint kings in Alexandria; their sister Cleopatra II completed the family trio as Philometor's wife. This uneasy truce continued for five years until 163 BCE when, through Roman intervention, it was determined that Philometor would rule Egypt and Cyprus, and "Ptolemy the brother" would rule Cyrene.

When Philometor died in battle in Syria (145 BCE), at first Cleopatra II ruled Egypt alone. But there was little hope that she would continue to rule single-handedly, since "Ptolemy the brother" waited at Cyrene to seize the throne. Alexandria itself was divided into two parties—one loyal to the queen and the other eager to have the brother back. Eventually, Cleopatra II, the widow of her elder brother, became her younger brother's wife.

Josephus tells an interesting story about Ptolemy's return to Egypt. Because the Jewish element in Alexandria had backed the queen, Ptolemy VIII tried to have the Jews trampled upon by his elephants. But he gave up his vendetta, according to Josephus, because his mistress, variously called Ithake and Eirene, interceded (Josephus *Against Apion* 2.50–56. Compare this account with 3 Maccabees 5–7 which attributes this action to Ptolemy IV Philopator).

After taking office, Ptolemy added to the existing tension by violating his sister's daughter (i.e., his niece), whom he later took publicly as his wife. When they married, Ptolemy, his niece, and Cleopatra were all regarded as sovereigns of Egypt.

The growing tension between Cleopatra II and her brother seems to have come to a head in 131–130 BCE, the period in which the present letter was written. The resultant state of violence and confusion, designated the *amixia* in the papyri (see, e.g., PTebt I 61b.31 [118–117 BCE], 72.45 [114–113 BCE]), continued officially until 124 BCE when Cleopatra II agreed to a reconciliation with her brother. The violence continued unofficially in parts of the kingdom until 118 BCE (as evidence of the ongoing factions, see MChr 11 [123 BCE], PSI III 171 [122–121 BCE]).

At last in 118 BCE a series of royal decrees to regulate conditions throughout the kingdom was issued in the name of all three sovereigns (see PTebt I 5 [118 BCE]). Many of the decrees (*prostagmata*) were indulgences (*philanthropa*) or remissions of penalties. The first decree announced a general amnesty for all except the perpetrators of the most serious crimes up to the year 52 of Ptolemy VIII. The necessity of such concessions was occasioned by land grants having been made by each of the rival governments to its own constituencies, which were not acknowledged as valid by the other. In general, the series of decrees acknowledged present ownership of land as valid, regardless of whether the land came as a grant to Euergetes' supporters or to Cleopatra's partisans.

Regarding the further discussion of this period, see Bevan, *History of Egypt*, pp. 306–25; PTebt I 5 (118 BCE), pp. 17–20 and appendix I, pp. 553f.

Ἐσθλάδας τῶι πατρὶ καὶ τῆι μητρὶ χαί(ρειν)
καὶ ἐρρῶσθαι. ἐπεὶ πλειονάκις σοι γράφω περὶ τοῦ διανδραγαθήσαντα
σαυτοῦ ἐπιμέλεσθαι μέχρι τοῦ
5   τὰ πράγματ' ἀποκαταστῆναι,
ἔτι καὶ νῦν καλῶς ποιήσεις παρα-
καλῶν σαυτὸν καὶ τοὺς παρ' ἡμῶν.
προσπέπτωκεν γὰρ Παῶν ἀνα-
πλεῖν ἐν τῶι Τῦβι μ(ηνὶ) μετὰ δυνάμεων
10   ἱκανῶν πρὸς τὸ καταστεῖσαι τοὺς
ἐν Ἑρμώνθει ὄχλους, χρήσασθαι δ' αὐτοῖς
{αὐτοῖς} ὡς ἀποστάταις. ἐπισκοποῦ δ[ὲ]
καὶ τὰς ἀδελφὰς [[αδ]] καὶ Πέλοπα
καὶ Στάχυν καὶ Σεναθῦριν.
15   ἔρρωσο. (ἔτους) μ, Χοίαχ κγ̄.

Verso: ἀπόδος [ε]ἰς
Παθῦρ(ιν)
τῶι πατρί.

Esthladas to his father and mother greeting and
good health. Since I wrote to you often about
acting consistently in a brave manner so as to take
care of yourself until matters return to normal, so
also once again please encourage yourself and our
people. For it has become known that Paos is
sailing up in the month of Tybi with sufficient
forces to put down the mobs at Hermonthis and to
deal with them as rebels. In addition, look after my
sisters and Pelops and Stachys and Senathyris.
Good-bye. (Year) 40, Choiach 23.

Outside address: Deliver to Pathyris to my father.

While not so numerous as the papers of Zenon, a considerable number of documents belong to the archive of Menches, village scribe of Kerkeosiris for at least the second time (119–111/110 BCE). Menches' papers are part of an extensive collection of papyri which were excavated by Grenfell and Hunt in the winter of 1899–1900 at the ancient village of Tebtunis, on the southern fringe of the Fayum. Papyri discovered on the site date from the third century BCE up to the Roman period. Texts of the late second to early first centuries BCE, including the Menches archive, were published as volume one of *The Tebtunis Papyri* (1902); papyri from the Roman town were published as PTebt II (1907); documents from the third and second centuries BCE were published in two parts (1933, 1938) as PTebt III; and, more recently, the papyri which appeared only as "Descriptions" at the back of PTebt I—primarily documents of the Menches archive—were published as PTebt IV (1976).

Menches' tenure as village scribe (119–111/110 BCE) coincides with the end of the internal strife between Cleopatra II and Euergetes II, and with the proclamation of their decrees in 118 BCE regulating the ownership and use of land. The total area of the village where Menches lived was 4700 arouras (about 3150 acres), the largest part of which was designated crown land (*basilike ge*).

For our purpose, a practical way of classifying this land of Kerkeosiris is to divide it into that from which the crown could expect to collect rent, primarily rent in grain, and that which was exempt from rent. Exempt from rent, for example, was the land used for roads, waterways, threshing floors; land that was too sandy for productivity and useful only for grazing; land held by the temples, and the allotments (kleroi) granted to military and civil officials as part of the privileges of their station. The land from which the state could expect to collect rent was let out by state officials to tenant farmers who paid a substantial share of the crop as the grain rent, in addition to a series of taxes on the land. Land which could be cultivated at a profit was designated *sporimos* ("fit for sowing") and useless crown land was called *hypologos* ("unproductive" or "deduction"), because it represented a "deduction" which officials responsible for the rent could substract from the sum which they would otherwise have to deliver. Occasionally, the designation "unproductive" refers to land which was once productive but had fallen out of cultivation either as a result of the revolt from 131–118 BCE or for various other reasons. Unproductive land was further classified according to whether it went out of cultivation before or after the revolt, as a way of designating which land would best repay the state's attempts at reclamation. The editors of PTebt IV list the following ways in which the government reclaimed derelict land: long-term leases were granted at nominal rent to people willing to bring the land back into cultivation; military *klerouchs* would rent such land both for profit and to pay certain dues to the state; officials, such as Menches, could be required to reclaim derelict land as part of the conditions of their appointment to office.

Regarding the normal conditions under which crown land was leased, the tax rolls and land surveys of Kerkeosiris suggest that although a plot of land's worth was reassessed from year to year, the renewal of a lease for such land was automatic to the former holder and to his heirs so long as they desired renewal and continued to pay dues. It is less clear how much personal choice was allowed to the tenant in the kind of crop which he was permitted to grow on the land. We do know that grain began to be harvested in the month of Pharmouthi (18 April–17 May in this period) and was largely completed by the end of Payni (mid-July). Rent on the crop was due by the end of the calendar year and could be paid in installments. This government land was farmed by persons of various vocations, including priests, soldiers, and village officials, in addition to peasants. It is somewhat striking that no woman is listed either as renting crown land or as holding land in any other capacity, such as we found in the example of Eirene (letters 30–33).

Crawford concludes in her study of Kerkeosiris that the quality of life there was not only poor by modern standards but that the villagers were in a state of despair (*Kerkeosiris,* p. 139). The editors of PTebt IV, J. G. Keenan and J. C. Shelton, (Introduction, pp. 16–18), while somewhat more reserved about the evidence for determining the psychological state of the inhabitants, tend to be less severe in their evaluation. In particular, they take issue with the suggestion that peasant life was uncertain and regimented, and suggest that there is only one instance (at least during the years covered by their volume) of compulsory cultivation at Kerkeosiris. They consider the long note on βία given by Grenfell and Hunt (PTebt I 61b.33, pp. 211f.) to be a more accurate appraisal of peasant life in the village.

A more detailed survey of the land at Kerkeosiris and its holders, along with the documentary evidence, may be found in PTebt I (appendix I, "The Land of Kerkeosiris and its Holders," pp. 538–80) and in PTebt IV (Introduction, pp. 1–18). Regarding the sale of derelict land by the state, see Keenan's comments on PTebt IV 1101, along with his bibliography on the subject.

44 ASKLĒPIADĒS TO MARRES
PTebt I 10   119 BCE

Asklepiades, a royal secretary (*basiliko-grammateus*), notifies Marres, the district scribe (*topogrammateus*), of the appointment of Menches by the dioiketes to the post of village scribe (*komogrammateus*). This document is actually a renewal of Menches' appointment since we learn from PTebt I 9, written four months earlier, that he already held the office of village secretary. In that letter Menches promised, in the event of being reappointed, to pay fifty artabs of wheat and fifty artabs of various leguminous seeds (lentils, peas, etc.). Grenfell and Hunt suggest that, because of these promises, Menches' letter of application may have been offered as a bribe to superiors in the village to secure their favorable intervention with the dioiketes. At least some officials at the time were in the habit of requiring subordinates to pay for the rights to their office, in return for which they offered their intercession with higher levels of bureaucracy. The evidence for this practice is indicated by a specific prohibition against it in the decrees of Cleopatra II and Euergetes II (see, in particular, PTebt I 5.184–86).

In the present letter Menches is required to reclaim ten arouras of land which had gone out of cultivation, at a rent of five artabs per aroura. A lower rate, or even complete exemption for a time, was usually allowed when land was being reclaimed (e.g., see PTebt I 61b.59). In the case of Menches, the higher rent should probably be regarded as a fee for holding office. He retained this office for a little more than nine years and, as already noted, he had held the same post earlier but, since PTebt 9 is the earliest mention of Menches in the archive, we do not know how long that earlier term of office lasted.

Ἀσκληπιάδης Μαρρεῖ χαίρειν. Μεγχῆι τῶι ὑπὸ τοῦ
διοικητοῦ
καθεσταμένωι πρὸς τῆι κωμογραμματείαι Κερκεοσίρεως
ἐφ᾽ ὧι κατεργᾶται
τοῖς ἰδίοις ἀνηλώμασιν ἀπὸ τῆς ἀναφερομένης περὶ τὴν
κώμην
ἐν ὑπολόγωι γῆς (ἀρούρας) δέκα (ἀρταβῶν) πεντήκοντα,
ἂς καὶ παραδώσει
5 ἀπὸ τοῦ νβ (ἔτους) εἰς τὸ βασιλικὸν κατ᾽ ἐνιαυτὸν ἐκ
πλήρους ἢ τὰ ἀπολείψοντα
ἐκ τοῦ ἰδίου μετρήσει, μετά[δ]ος τὰ τῆς χρείας γράμματα
καὶ φρόντισον
ὡς τὰ τῆς ὑποσχέσεως ἐκπληρωθήσεται.
ἔρρωσο. (ἔτους) να, Μεσορὴ γ.

Verso: τοπογρ (αμματεῖ) Μαρρεῖ.

Asklepiades to Marres greeting. Menches has been appointed as village secretary of Kerkeosiris by the dioiketes, for which he will cultivate at his own expense ten arouras of land from the area about the village reported to be unproductive at a rent of fifty artabs, which he shall deliver annually in full from the fify-second year to the crown or else he shall pay what is lacking out of his own means. Transmit the papers of his appointment and make sure that the terms of his engagement are fulfilled. Goodbye. (Year) 51, Mesore 3.

Outside address: To the district secretary, Marres.

45 MENCHĒS TO HĒRŌDES AND AMMŌNIOS
PTebt I 12   118 BCE

In the present document we have the first draft of two letters to Herodes and Ammonios respectively, Menches' brothers. Since these letters are dated, Menches must have intended to keep them for his file. The omission of the outside address, numerous abbreviations and various errors or corrections in the letter testify to their rough draft status. Both refer to the same information and were probably dispatched near or at the same time.

Menches informs Herodes in the first letter that he himself must join the royal secretary to survey the village, though he has requested a delay of three days for this task. He asks Herodes to do something for him regarding this survey but the request is unclear because of lacunae in the text. In the second letter he asks Ammonios to send Dionysios with a *periphora*, apparently a surveying instrument, and to instruct Dionysios to delay the survey until some pressing business is settled. In addition to these two brothers, who probably held minor offices, we hear of two other brothers, Polemon, an epistates, (see PTebt 15.7 and letter 48 here) and Mousaios, about whom little is known (see PTebt 55). We learn from PTebt I 11.1 that Menches was the son of Petesouchos.

[Μεγ]χῆς Ἡρώδει τῶι ἀδελφῶι [χαίρε]ιν
[κ]αὶ ἐρρῶσθαι. γείνωσκε Ἀμμώνιον τὸν
[. . . .] παρ᾽ ἡμῶν ὢν ἐν τοῖς Ἀμεννέως
[τοῦ βα(σιλικοῦ)] γρ(αμματέως) γεγραφὼς ἡμῖν περὶ τοῦ
συνέχεσθαι
5 [Ἀρω]τεῖον τὸν τοῦ Πετεαρφρείους [[συνέχεσθαι]]
[ὑπὸ το]ῦ βα(σιλικοῦ) γρ(αμματέως) χάριν τῆς
εὐθυμετρίας τῆς κώ(μης) καὶ
[τοῦ] σχοι (νισμοῦ), καὶ ἐμοὶ δὲ γεγράφηκεν συμμείσγειν
[αὐτοῖ]ς. ἠξίωκα ἐπισχῖν μοι ἕως τῆς κα.

Menches to Herodes his brother greeting and good health. Know that Ammonios, (until recently?) one of our agents, who is in the office of Amenneos the royal secretary, has written to us about Aroteios the son of Petearphreios being detained by the royal secretary for the survey of the village and the measurements. Moreover, he has also written me to join them. I requested that he wait for me until the twenty-first. Therefore, whenever you receive this letter . . . , and for the rest take care of yourself

[ὁπό]τ᾽ οὖν ἐὰν λάβ[η]ς τὴν ἐπιστολὴν ἕως
10 [.........]σ.[...]...] ας τὸν Ἀρωτεῖον ἐπιτε-
..ν....[....]εσ[...]τα καὶ πταρτιδισ
......αι ἀν[τιλ]ογείαι, τὰ ἄλλα σαυτοῦ ἐπιμε (λόμενος)
ἵν᾽ ὑγ(ι)αίνης.   ἔρρω[σ]ο. (ἔτους) νβ, Μεσο(ρὴ) ιη.

Μεγχῆς Ἀμμωνίωι τῶι ἀδελφῶι
15 πολλὰ χαίρε[ι]ν. ἐκομισάμην τὸ παρὰ σοῦ γρ(αφὲν)
ἐπισ(τόλιον)
δι᾽ οὗ διεσάφις τά τε ἄλλα καὶ περὶ τοῦ..ολισ-
σου. περιφορὰν δὲ δὸς Διονυσίωι χά{ι}ριν
τῆς εὐθυμετρίας καὶ ὅτι συμμίσγειν
ἅμα ἡμέρα, ἐπὶ οὐ καὶ σὺ οὐκ ἀγνοεῖς ἐν ἧι
20 ἐσμεν ἀσχολί(αι) καὶ διότι ἐν τῆι τ[ο]ῦ στρα(τηγοῦ)
ἐσμεν φ(υλακῆι?), παρακεκληκὼς δὲ τὸν
Διονύσιον ἐπισχεῖν μέχρι τοῦ με ἀπὸ τῆς
ἀσχολίας γενέσθαι τῆι[ι κ]α. ἀποδέχομαι δὲ τὰ
παρὰ σοῦ λίαν [[λια]], καὶ ὑπερευχαριστῶι παρηγγέ(λθαι)
25 Ἀθεμμεῖ τῶι [..].(   ) ἀναβῆναι. καὶ σὺ περὶ ὧν ἐὰν
[βούλ]ηι διασάφησον, τὰ δ᾽ ἄλλα χα{ι}ριεῖ σαυτοῦ
ἐπιμ(ελόμενος).

in order that you stay well. Good-bye. (Year) 52, Mesore 18.

Menches to Ammonios his brother many greetings. I received the note you wrote through which you inform me, among other things, about the . . . . Give the turn-table (?) to Dionysios for the survey and (tell him) that he is to join them as soon as it is daybreak, for you also are not ignorant about how busy I am and (know) that I am in the company of the strategos. Entreat Dionysios to wait until I have completed this business on the twenty-first. I approve your (views/recommendations?) completely, and am extremely thankful that Athemmeos the . . . has been instructed to go up. You also, in turn, must let me know what you would like, and for the rest favor me by taking care of yourself.

46 MENCHĒS TO HŌROS
PTebt IV 1099 (=PTebt I 142)   114 BCE

In this letter, Menches notifies Horos, the crown secretary, that the workers on crown land, the *basilikoi georgoi*, have retired (*anakechorekenai*, line 4) to the temple at Narmouthis. This anachoresis (asylum/sanctuary) had occurred while Menches was in Ptolemais Euergetis, the nome capital eighteen miles from Kerkeosiris, where his accounts were being audited.

Keenan suggests in his comments on this letter (PTebt 1099, p. 28) that the flight of the crown tenants to the temple at Narmouthis indicates that none of the Kerkeosiris temples possessed the status of granting asylum (see Otto, *Priester und Tempel* 2:298, n. 6; Rostovtzeff, *Social and Economic History* 3:1549, n. 180), but were all of second or third rank status. Though we do not know the cause of the workers' flight, its effect must have been only temporary, since late in the same year these crown tenants were paying rents on time at the usual rates (see PTebt IV 1105, 1193). Keenan notes further that the only other known instance of anachoresis at Kerkeosiris concerned long-term leases under special conditions. For a brief survey of the Egyptian natives' right of anachoresis (the "going up" to the temple for asylum) in the Ptolemaic period, see Westermann ("The Ptolemies," pp. 276–78), who suggests that anachoresis in this period was a group protest against some threatened or actual injustice of administrative officials or private employers (see the examples which he cites, p. 277, n. 24; see letters 18 and 22 of this collection).

Since the present letter is the clean copy of PTebt I 26.11–24, a copy of the first draft is included in this collection (47.11–24) for comparison.

M[εγχῆ]ς κωμ{μ}ογραμματεὺς Κερκεοσίρεως τῆς
 Πολέμωνος μ[ε]ρίδος Ὥρωι
χ[α] ἰρ[ειν.] ὄντι μ[οι] ἐν Πτολεμαΐδει [Εὐ] εργέτ[ι]δι
 πρὸς τῆι ἐ[πιδόσει] τῶν ἐ[παιτου-]
μένων λόγων προσέπεσεν ἡμῖν τοὺς ἐκ τῆς κώμη[ς
 βασι]λικοὺς γεωργοὺς
ἀνακεχωρηκέναι ἐπὶ τὸ ἐν Ναρμοῦθι ἱερόν. καλῶς [ἔ]χειν
 [ὑπέ]λαβον προσαν[ε-]
5 νέγκαι ὅπως εἰδῆς.
  ἔρρωσο. (ἔτους) δ, Φαῶφι κ̄.

Verso: Ὥρωι.

Menches, village secretary of the division of Polemon, to Horos greeting. While I was in Ptolemais
Euergetis for the delivery of the accounts which
were demanded, I learned that the crown tenants
of the village had retired to the temple which is in
Narmouthis. I thought it right to report in order
that you would know. Good-bye. (Year) 4, Phaophi
20.

Outside address: To Horos.

47 A COPY OF TWO LETTERS
PTebt I 26

114 BCE

We know from the immediately preceding letter that lines 11–24 of the present text are
a rough draft of that piece of correspondence. The abbreviated address in line 11 is one
indication that the letter is a first draft. The body of the present letter is more extensive
than the fair copy (see in particular the addition in lines 16–18 and the specification of
the date when the crown tenants took up asylum in the temple in line 20).

   Since Horos' letter in lines 1–10 is written in the same hand as lines 11–24 it also was
copied in Menches' office. It is not known why this letter would have been copied by
Menches unless, perhaps, he was unable to retain the original for one or another reason.
Horos, the crown secretary, directs both the village secretary, Menches, and the district
secretary (Marres?—see letter 44 above) to join the people who are to participate in the
downward voyage.

Ὧρος τοῖς τοπογρ(αμματεῦσι) καὶ κω(μο)γρ(αμματεῦσι)
 χ[αί]ρειν.
ὡς ἂν ἀναγνῶτε τὴν ἐντ[ολὴν]
συμμείσγετε τεταγμένοι[ς
πρὸς τὸν κατάπλουν ἀκολού-
5 θως οἷς γέγραφεν Εἰρηναῖος [ὁ] συγγε(νὴς)
καὶ διοικη (τής). ἀπεστάλκαμεν
δὲ τούτων χάριν τοὺς τὰ γρ(άμματα)
ἐπιδικνύοντας. τοῦ γρ ( ) με ( )
καὶ ποιήσειν ἀκολούθως.
10   (ἔτους) δ, Φαῶφ(ι) ιθ.

Ὥρωι χαίρειν. ὄντι μοι ἐν
{ἐν} Πτολεμαΐδει Εὐ{γ} εργέτιδι πρὸς
πῆι ἐπιδόσει τῶν ἐπαιτου-
μένων λόγων προσέπεσεν ἡμῖν
15 πε[ρ]ὶ τοῦ τοὺς ἐκ τῆς κώμης
 [β]ασιλικοὺς γεωργοὺς ἐγκαταλει-

Horos to the district secretary and to the village
secretary greeting. As soon as you read this order
join those who have been instructed to sail down
river in accordance with what Eirenaios the king's
kinsman and dioiketes wrote. We have sent for this
purpose those who are showing the letters (letter
bearers). . . . and act accordingly. (Year) 4, Phaophi
19.

To Horos greeting. While I was in Ptolemais
Euergetis for the delivery of the accounts which
were demanded, I learned that the crown tenants
from the village, having left their prescribed occupations, had retired to the temple in Narmouthis
on the nineteenth of the month written below.
Therefore I thought it right to report this in order
that you would know. Good-bye. (Year) 4, Phaophi
20.

[πο]ντας τὴν ἐπικειμένην
ἀσχολίαν ἀνακ[ε]χωρηκέναι
ἐπὶ τὸ [ἐν Ν]αρμούθι ἱερὸν
20 τῆι ιθ τοῦ ὑποκειμένου
μηνός. καλῶς ἔχει[ν οὖν]
ὑπέλαβον [[δι]] προσανεν[εγκεῖν]
ὅπως εἰδῆς.
    ἔρρωσο. (ἔτους) δ, Φαῶφι κ.

13 πῆι: the mistake of π for τ is apparently due to careless writing.

48 POLEMŌN TO MENCHĒS
PTebt I 17

114 BCE

This and the following letter were written to Menches by his brother Polemon, the epistates of the village (the village "chief of police"). Polemon announces the approaching visit of the *epimeletes* (a representative of the financial administration in the nome; see Bevan, *History of Egypt*, p. 143) and warns Menches to put his account in order.

Πολέμων Μεγχεῖ χαίρειν. ἐπεὶ
διέγνωσται τὸν ἐπιμελητὴν
παραγίνεσθαι ἅμ' ἡμέραι τῆι ιε εἰς
Βερενικίδα τῆι δὲ ις παράγειν
5 τὴν κώμην εἰς Θεογο{γο}νίδα, στόχασαι
ὡς πάντα τὰ ἐνοφειλόμενα περὶ τὴν
κώμην ἐν μέτρωι ἔσται ὅπως
μὴ ἐπικατασχὼν αὐτὸν εἰς δα-
πάνας ἐμπέσῃς οὐκ ὀλίας.
10   ἔρρω(σο). (ἔτους) γ, Παῦ(νι) ια.

Verso: κω(μο)γρ(αμματεῖ)   Μεγχεῖ.

Polemon to Menches greeting. Since it is decided that the epimeletes will proceed as soon as it is daybreak on the fifteenth to Berenikis and to pass by the village enroute to Theogonis on the sixteenth, see to it that all the arrears from around the village will be in order lest in detaining him you incur no little expense. Good-bye. (Year) 3, Payni 11.

Outside address: To the village secretary, Menches.

49 POLEMŌN TO MENCHĒS
PTebt I 19

114 BCE

Polemon urges Menches to hasten the collection of taxes. Three of Polemon's letters to Menches (letters 48, 49; see PTebt 18) are similar in mood and subject matter, urging haste in the performance of one or another of his responsibilities. Though Menches did not always record a letter's receipt, whenever he did record its arrival, it was marked like the present letter, on the inside and immediately above the beginning of the letter. This practice is unlike that of the earlier letters of this collection, which docket the letter's receipt on the outside with the address.

ἐλ(ήφθη) (ἔτους) γ, Παχ(ὼν) [..].

2nd hand:
Πολέμων Μεγχεῖ τῶι ἀδελφῶι χαίρειν. ἐκομισάμεθα τὰ παρὰ σοῦ ἡμῖν γραφέντα καὶ
ὑπὲρ ὧν ἐσήμαινες πέμψαι γεωργῶν

5 ἀπροσδέητοί ἐσμεν. τοῦ δὲ Ἀσκληπιάδου
ἐπιτετακότος τὰ πράγματα καὶ προσαγειοχότος
ἐκτὸς τῶν ὑποκε[ιμ]ένων ἄλλας (πυροῦ) (ἀρτάβας) Ἀ
χωρὶς ἀργυρίου βεβουλήμεθα σπεῦσαι.
ὑπὲρ δὲ ὧν σημαίνεις κωμογραμματέων

10 μόλις ἕως τῆς κε χωρισθήσονται. σὺ δὲ
ὀρθῶς ποιήσεις τὸ προσάγγελμα μὴ ἐλατ-
τώσας παρὰ τὸ πρῶτον ὅπως εὐπροσω-
πῶμεν, καὶ ἐν τοῖς δὲ ἄλλοις χαριῆι κατατα-
χήσας τὰ τῆς εἰσαγωγῆς. ἐπιμελόμενος δὲ

15 καὶ σαυτοῦ [ἵν' ὑ]γιαίνῃς,
ἔρρωσο. (ἔτους) γ, Παχὼν ιθ.

Verso: Μεγχεῖ.

Polemon to Menches his brother greeting. I received what you wrote to me, and about the cultivators whom you stated you were sending, I do not need them. Since Asklepiades has pressed on matters and has demanded in addition to what is prescribed another one thousand artabs of wheat, besides money, I have become anxious to make haste. Regarding the village secretaries to whom you refer they will hardly leave until the twenty-fifth. You will act correctly in not decreasing the report from the first one, in order that we may make a good showing, and for the rest it would be gratifying if you accelerated the collection of taxes. In addition, take care of yourself in order that you stay well. Good-bye. (Year) 3, Pachon 19.

Outside address: To Menches.

---

1   ἐλ(ήφθη): The docket has ελ followed by the date. This ελ is an abbreviation of ἐλήφθη (see PSI III 169, note to line 1), not ἐλ(άβομεν) or ἔλ(αβον), the possible resolutions suggested by the original editor of PTebt I 19 (see Keenan's comments on PTebt IV 1100, note to line 1 and see *Bulletin of the American Society of Papyrologists* 7, p. 97).

9–10   The departure of the village secretaries is probably for Alexandria (see PTebt I 26.4, 28.7, 58.44).

50   TO MENCHĒS FROM HŌROS
PTebt I 48

ca. 113 BCE

This is a petition to Menches regarding an assault, from the komarch and the elders of the crown cultivators. The addressors had attempted to collect fifteen hundred artabs of grain from the farmers, as well as an extra levy of eighty artabs for the approaching visit of the king (Soter II). While collecting the grain, the petitioners were attacked by fellow villagers, led by a certain Lykos. Apparently, the offenders were brought before an official on the day following the attack but at this point the papyrus becomes fragmented. Owing to its fragmentary condition we cannot date this petition to the year or even to the month. However, an attack by an armed band is also the subject of a series of five petitions addressed to Menches (PTebt I 45, 46, 47; IV 1095, 1096). This attack occurred on the eighth of Mesore of the year 4 (23 August 113 BCE). If the attack mentioned in the present letter occurred within the same year, as seems likely, it would have preceded that raid by a few months (since the month Pachon is still future in this letter and Pachon preceded Mesore by three months).

In the five aforementioned petitions, crown cultivators complained that their houses had been broken into and looted by a certain Pyrrhichos (a cavalryman) and one Herakleios, who headed a large armed band. The households had been plundered while the farmers were at work in the fields (see PTebt 47.3ff.) or assisting in the collection of land rents (PTebt 45.9ff., 1095.8–10 and note). The purpose of the present attack is not so clear, though it may be in resistance to the collection of rent and, in particular, the special tax for the king's visit.

Commenting on the payment for the king's visit (*parousia*) in line 14, Grenfell and Hunt suggested that ἐπιγεγραμμένην . . . ἀγοράν ("the specified . . . provisions") in lines 12–14 indicates a special impost, in contrast to regular taxes (see their note on ἐπιγραφή in PTebt I 5.59). The preparation for such visits, whether from the king or other officials, is a subject often mentioned in Ptolemaic papyri (see PTebt I 5.184). The burdensome obligations and abuses which often accompanied these visits is the subject of one of the decrees of Euergetes II and Cleopatra II (PTebt 5.178–87). The preparations for a visit from a Roman senator is the subject of letter 51.

Μεγχεῖ κωμογραμματεῖ
Κερκεοσίρεως
παρὰ ῞Ωρου κωμάρχου καὶ τ[ῶν
πρεσβυτέρων τῶν γεω(ργῶν) τῆς αὐτῆς.
5   κεχειρογραφηκότων ἡμῶν
Πολέμωνι τῶι τοπάρχηι
περὶ τοῦ παραδώσειν εἰς [τὸ
βασιλικὸν ἕως ι τοῦ Παχὼν
πυροῦ (ἀρτάβας) ᾽Αφ περὶ ὧν καὶ προσ-
10 εδρευόντων διά τε νυκτὸς
καὶ ἡμέρας μέχρι τοῦ τὸ προκείμενον ἐκπληρῶσαι καὶ τὴν ἐπιγεγραμμένην πρὸς τὴν τοῦ βασι-
λέως παρουσίαν ἀγορὰν (πυροῦ) (ἀρταβῶν) π,
15 τῆι δὲ γ τοῦ ὑποκειμένου μηνὸς
ὄντων πρὸς τῆι παραδόσει
τῶν ἐκφορίων καὶ τοῦ ἀλοητοῦ
ἐπελθὼν ἐπὶ τὴν ἅλω Λύκος
σὺν ἄλλοις ἐν ὅπλοις καὶ σπασαμένων
20 τὰς μαχαίρας ἐπιλαβομένων τοῦ
ἑνὸς ἡμῶν ῞Ωρου κωμάρχου καὶ
τούτου ἀγωγὴν μετὰ σκυλμοῦ
ποιουμένων ῥίψαντα τὸ ἱμάτιον
εἰς φυγὴν ὁρμῆσαι, καὶ ἡμᾶς τε
25 σὺν τοῖς λοιποῖς γεωργοῖς ὑπόπτως
σχόντας συνδεδραμηκέναι,
διὰ δὲ ταύτην τὴν αἰτίαν ἐμπο-
δισθῆναι ἐν τοῖς κατὰ τὴν παρά-
δοσιν τῶν ἐκφορίων καὶ τῶν ἄλλων
30 ἐπιγεγραμμένων. τῆι δὲ δ
συμψήσαντες τὸν Λύκον κ[αὶ
[τοὺς σὺν αὐ] τῶι ἐπὶ τ[ὸν] . [. . .

To Menches, village secretary of Kerkeosiris, from Horos, Komarch, and the elders of the cultivators (crown tenants) of the same village. We have committed ourselves in writing to Polemon the toparch about the transmission of fifteen hundred artabs of wheat by the tenth of Pachon to the treasury, concerning which we have also been working constantly night and day until we complete the aforesaid obligation along with the eighty artabs of wheat for the provisions specified for the visit of the king. On the third of the month indicated below, while engaged in the collection of the rents and the threshing expenses, Lykos came to the threshing floor with others who were armed and when they drew their swords they seized one of us, Horos the Komarch and, attempting to carry this one off forcibly, he took to flight so as to throw off his garment and we, along with the other cultivators, having become mistrustful, ran off along with him, on account of this reason we were hindered with regard to the collection of the taxes and the other prescribed things. On the fourth we forced Lykos and his associates (to appear) before the . . .

This is a copy of a letter to Asklepiades, the "overseer of the revenues" (see PTebt 27.98; 64b.14; 72.259, 275) and not the crown secretary of the same name in letter 44 above. The letter was enclosed in a letter by Hermias (probably the Hermias of PTebt 27.27) to Horos, a crown secretary (the Horos of letters 46 and 47 above), announcing the visit of a Roman senator, Lucius Memmius. The letter suggests how the senator is to be received and entertained. It was expected that, as a tourist (see *epi theorian* in line 6), he would be guided to the usual sights of the Fayum, which are discussed by Herodotus (Godley, *Herodotus* 2.148–49) and Strabo (*The Geography* 17.811–12), such as the Labyrinth and the sacred crocodiles. Near the end of the letter, the required supplies are detailed, but these particulars are much fragmented.

We may assume that this notice of the Roman senator's arrival also reached Menches' office and was copied there, since this document is copied on the verso of the same papyrus which contains PTebt 75 on the recto, a report by Menches of crown land which was derelict in 112 BCE.

῾Ερμ(ίας) ῟Ωρωι χαί(ρειν). τῆς πρὸς ᾿Ασκλη(πιάδην)
ἐπισ(τολῆς) ἀντίγρ(αφον) ὑπόκι(ται).
[φρόν]τισον οὖν ἵνα γένη(ται) ἀκολούθως.   ἔρρω(σο).
[(ἔτους)] ε Ξαντικοῦ ιζ, Μεχεὶρ ιζ.

᾿Ασκλη(πιάδει). Λεύκιος Μέμμιος ῾Ρωμαῖος τῶν ἀπὸ
συνκλήτου ἐν μίζονι ἀξιώματι κα[ὶ] τιμῆι
5 κείμενος τὸν ἐκ τῆς πό(λεως) ἀνάπλουν ἕως τοῦ
᾿Αρσι(νοΐτου) νο(μοῦ)
ἐπὶ θεωρίαν ποιούμενος μεγαλο{υ}πρεπέστερον
ἐγδεχθήτωι, καὶ φρόντισον ὡς ἐπὶ τῶν
καθηκόντων τόπων αἵ τε αὐλαὶ κατασκευασ-
[θ]ήσ[ο]νται καὶ αἱ ἀπὸ τούτων ἐγβα(τηρίαι) ε[.]ιε[...]
10 π....συντελεσθήσονται καὶ αὐτῶι προσ-
ενεχθήσεται ἐπὶ τῆς ἐγβα(τηρίας) τὰ ὑπογεγρ(αμμένα)
ξένια,
καὶ τ[ὰ] εἰς τὸν τῆς αὐλῆς καταρτισμὸν
καὶ τὸ γεινόμενον τῶι Πετεσούχωι καὶ τοῖς κροκο(δείλοις)
ψωμίον καὶ τὰ πρὸς τὴν τοῦ λαβυρίνθου θέαν
15 καὶ τὰ.[..].[..σ]ταθησόμενα θύματα καὶ τῆς
θυσί[α]ς.....χ.ηκ.ν[...]ται, τὸ δ' ὅλον ἐπὶ πάν[των]
τὴν μεγίστην φροντίδα ποιουμένου τοῦ εὐδοκοῦν[τ]α
τὸν ἄνδρα κατασταθῆ[ναι] τὴν πᾶσαν προσένεγκαι
σπουδὴ[ν]...

Hermias to Horos greeting. The copy of the letter to Asklepiades is appended. Take care, therefore, that it (the instructions of the letter) happen accordingly. Good-bye. (Year) 5, Xandikos 17, Mecheir 17.

To Asklepiades. Leukios Memmios, a Roman who is a member of the senate occupying a position of great dignity and honor, is making a voyage upstream from the city (Alexandria) to the Arsinoite nome to see the sights. Let him be received with the greatest possible magnificence and take care that his chambers be readied at the appropriate places along with the landing-places to them and that the gifts written below be presented to him at the landings, and the furnishings for the chamber, and the customary morsels for Petesouchos and the crocodiles, and that the things required for viewing the Labyrinth and the offerings and sacrifices be provided; and in general take the greatest possible care that the man be made satisfied in everything, applying the utmost zeal that . . .

---

8   αὐλαί here probably means "guest-chambers" (especially for spending the night) and the singular of this noun has the same nuance in line 12.

19   The original text extends an additional six lines to line 25 but, because they are so fragmented, they are not included here. Among other things, the presents (ξένια) that are referred to in line 11, which were to be specified subsequently, would have been listed in these lines.

52 PETESOUCHOS TO MARRĒS
PTebt I 56

late II BCE

Petesouchos, a cultivator at Kerkesephis, requests aid from a certain Marres, who is probably a farmer at Kerkeosiris, because the land at nearby Kerkesephis has been flooded. The names Petesouchos and Marres are so common in the Menches correspondence and in other documents discovered at Kerkeosiris that even though Petesouchos identifies himself as the son of Marres (see the designation in PTebt 86.19, 109.14) and Marres is identified as the son of Petosiris (see PTebt 13, introduction; 84.40, etc.) we cannot be certain that these are the same people who are so described elsewhere. The popularity of the name Petesouchos is surely due to the fact that Souchos was one of the primary gods worshipped in the area; Petesouchos is a local form of Souchos at Kerkeosiris (see the reference to the god Petesouchos in letter 51.13).

This document is contemporaneous with Menches' correspondence. Grenfell and Hunt fix its approximate date by means of a fragmentary letter, PTebt I 260, which was cartonnage from the same mummified crocodile. The fragment is dated μ[.], i.e., some year between the fortieth and forty-ninth regnal year of Euergetes II.

Πετεσοῦχος Μαρρήους γ[εωρ]γὸς
τῶν ἐκ Κερκεσήφεως {[εω]ς}
Μαρρῆτι Πετοσείριος τῷ[.]
[   ]
5   καὶ ἀδελφῷ χαίρειν. γείν[ωσ]κε δὲ
περὶ τοῦ κατακεκλῦσθαι τὸ πεδίον
ὑμῶν καὶ οὐκ ἔχομεν ἕως τῆς
τροφῆς τῶν κτηνῶν ἡμῶν.
καλῶς οὖν ποήσῃς εὐχαριστῆσαι
10 πρῶτον μὲν τοῖς θεοῖς δεύτερον
δὲ σῶσαι ψυχὰς πολλὰς ζητή[σ]α[ς
μοι περὶ τὴν κώμην σου εἰς τὴν
τροφὴν ἡμῶν γῆς ἀρούρας πέ[ν-
τε ὡς ἕξομεν ἐξ αὐτῶν τὴ[ν
15 τροφὴν ἡμῶν. τοῦτο δὲ ποήσας
ἔσῃ μοι κεχαρισμένος εἰς τὸν
ἅπαντα χρόν[ον].
        ἔρρωσο.

Petesouchos, son of Marres, one of the cultivators from Kerkesephis, to Marres, son of Petosiris who . . . and his brother greeting. Know that our plain has been flooded and that we do not have even enough food for our cattle. First of all, therefore, please give thanks to the gods and, secondly, save many lives by seeking out for me in the area of your village five arouras for our sustenance so that we may obtain our food from them. If you should do this, I would be favored (by you) for all time. Goodbye.

7   Read ἡμῶν.

Verso: Some effaced lines.

53 PHILOXENOS TO APOLLOS
PTebt I 34

ca. 100 BCE

Philoxenos, apparently an official of some status, instructs his brother Apollos to secure the release of someone who had been arrested for debt. Philoxenos' interest in the man's release has been occasioned by a letter from Demetrios, either an official or someone of importance, who has written that the person in detention is under his "protection." This practice of obtaining the patronage of influential persons is also illustrated by PTebt 40, where a collector of the taxes on beer and the mineral natron entreats a crown secretary to be put under his protection as a means of being fairly treated by village officials. Officials themselves sometimes resorted to such measures, as illustrated by Menches' application for office, referred to above (see PTebt I 9 and the introduction to letter 44). The abuses to which the practice led are made evident by the decrees pronounced against such bribery by Euergetes II and Cleopatra II in 118 BCE (see PTebt I 5, especially the notes to lines 19–22 and 186).

Since the conventional closing matters are omitted (e.g., farewell and date), since there is no outside address, and because various later insertions appear on the document, this letter is probably a first draft.

Φιλόξενος Ἀπολλῶτι τῶι
ἀδελφῶι χαίρειν καὶ ἐρρῶσθαι.
ἅμα τῶ σε λαβῖν τὸ ἐποστόλιν
συνελθεῖν Ὥρω Κότνι
5 πρὸς Ἑρμίαν τὸν κωμογρ(αμματέα)
χάριν τοῦ παρ' αὐτοῦ ἀπηγμένου
καὶ πρὸς Χαιρήμωνα τὸν
πράκτορα. ἀπολυθήτωι δὲ
καὶ μη παρανοχλεί⟨σ⟩θω ὑπ' οὐδενὸς
10 διὰ τὸ γεγραφηκέναι ἡμῖν
Δη⟨μή⟩τριος περὶ αὐτοῦ, ὄντα δὲ αὐτοῦ
ὑπὸ σκέπην καὶ γεωργό⟨ν⟩.
γράφω σοι δὲ διαστολὰς αὐτοῖς
δοῦναι.

Philoxenos to Apollos his brother greeting and good health. As soon as you receive this letter, go together with Horos, the son of Kotys, to Hermias, the village secretary, on account of the person arrested by him, and to Chairemon the collector of taxes. Moreover, let him be released and not be bothered by anyone because Demetrios has written to me about him, that he is under his (Demetrios') protection and is his cultivator. I am writing to you to give these instructions to them.

---

3 This line is a later insertion (παρ' αὐτοῦ and περι αὐτοῦ are above the line in lines 6 and 11 respectively).

9 Read παρενοχλεί⟨σ⟩θω (read Δημήτρειον in line 11).

54 POSEIDŌNIOS TO THE PRIESTS AT TEBTUNIS
PTebt I 59   99 BCE

Poseidonios, probably an important official in Alexandria, writes to priests at Tebtunis, assuring them of his good will. Since the principal temple at Tebtunis was the temple of Soknebtunis, these priests probably served that deity. Grenfell and Hunt note that this papyrus was found tied up with eight good-sized demotic rolls in the remains of a building in the Tebtunis cemetary. Since several of those demotic rolls belonged to the reign of Ptolemy Alexander, they suggest that the year 16 in the present letter should also be dated to the reign of Alexander.

Ποσειδώνιος τοῖς ἐν Τεπτύνει
ἱερεῦσι χαίρειν καὶ ἐρρῶσθαι, ὑγίαινον
δὲ καὶ αὐτός. καταντήσαντος γὰρ
εἰς τὴν πόλιν Σοκονώφεως
5 καὶ Ὥπεως τῶν ἐξ ὑμῶν
καὶ ὑποδεικνυ⟨όντ⟩ων ἣν ἔχετε

Poseidonios to the priests in Teptunis greeting and good health. I myself am also well. Having come down to the city (Alexandria), Sokonophis and Opis, who are members of your body, also suggest the hereditary friendship which you have toward me from of old. So, whatever you should need,

πρὸς ἡμᾶς ἄνωθεν πατρικὴν
φιλίαν, ἐν οἷς ἐὰν προσδεῆσθέ
μου ἐπιτάσσοντές μοι προθυ-
10 μότερον διὰ τὸ ἄνωθεν φοβεῖσθαι
καὶ σέβεσθαι τὸ ἱερόν.
ἔρρωσθ(ε). (ἔτους) ις, Φαῶφι
θ.

Verso: παρὰ   τοῖς ἐν Τε⟨π⟩τύνει ἱερεῦσι.
Ποσειδω(νίου).

instruct me and I will gladly oblige, because of old
I revere and worship the temple. Good-bye. (Year)
16, Phaophi 9.

Outside address: To the priests of Teptunis. From
Poseidonios.

1 Τεπτύνει: Grenfell and Hunt (PTebt I 59) note
that though this spelling is rare in the Ptolemaic
period, it tends to supersede Τεβτῦνις in the
Roman era.

55 PETESOUCHOS TO HIS BROTHERS AND FRIENDS
SelPap I 103 (=PGrenf II 36)   95 BCE

Petesouchos, the son of Panebchounios, who writes this letter to his brothers Peteharsemtheos and Paganis, is mentioned with his brothers elsewhere in the documents of
PGrenf II (25–27, 29, etc.). He is involved in various loans of money from 103 BCE
onward. The documents in PGrenf II, like the present text, contain numerous spelling
errors and confused grammatical constructions, as Grenfell pointed out (see PGrenf 25,
introductory comments). These errors indicate that Petesouchos and his brothers may
belong to the native Egyptian element in Thebes.

The present letter consists largely of greetings and farewells, along with assurances of
the writer's welfare. Lines 9–18 contain ambiguous information about certain people
being killed by someone who has shown favor to the writer and his associates. Petesouchos elsewhere mentions that a certain strategos is his protector. Perhaps he is referring to the same person here. We know from the immediately following set of documents (letters 56–58) that the Thebaid area was in revolt once again in 88 BCE (see letter
43 and the comments on the revolt in Thebes, 130–118 BCE). The evidence is too scant,
however, to determine whether the violence reported in the present letter had anything
to do with the disturbed condition of Thebes which later issued into the revolt of 88
BCE.

The Greek text has been altered here on the basis of the corrections made by Hunt
and Edgar in SelPap I 103.

Πετοσοῦχος Πανεβχούνιος Πετεαρσεμθεῖ
καὶ Παγάνει Πανεβχούνιος καὶ
Παθήμει Παρᾶ καὶ Πετεαρσεμθεῖ
Ἀρσενούφ[ι]ος καὶ Πετεαρσεμθεῖ
5   Ψεννήσι[ο]ς καὶ Ὥρωι Πατῆτος χαίρειν
καὶ ἐρρῶσθαι. ἔρρωμαι δὲ καὶ αὐτὸς
καὶ Ἐσθαῦτις καὶ Πατοῦς καὶ Ἀλμέντις
καὶ Φίβις καὶ Ψενοσῖρις καὶ Φάφις
καὶ οἱ παρ' ἡμῶν πάντες. μὴ λυ-
10 πεῖσθε ἐπὶ τοῖς χωρισθεῖσι. ὑπε-
λαμβάνοσαν φονευθήσεσθαι. οὐθὲν
ἡμῖν κακὸν ἐπύησεν, ἀλλ' ἐκ τῶν

Petosouchos, son of Panebchounios, to Peteharsemtheos and Paganis, sons of Panebchounios, and
Pathemis, son of Paras, and Peteharsemtheos, son
of Harsenouphis, and Peteharsemtheos, son of
Psennesis, and Horos, son of Pates, greeting and
good health. I myself am also well, along with
Esthautis and Patous and Almentis and Phibis and
Psenosiris and Phaphis and all our people. Do not
be grieved at the departed ones. They were
expected to be killed. He did nothing bad to us but,
quite to the contrary, he has taken care of us.
Concerning this matter, if you want, write to me.

ἐναντίων ἐπιμεμέληται.
περὶ ὧν, ἐὰν αἱρῆτε, γράψατέ
15 μοι. ἠκούσαμεν τὸν μῦν κατα-
βεβρωκέναι τὸν σπόρον. καλῶς
ἡμῖν ὧδε, ἢ ἐν Διὸς πόλει ἐὰν
αἱρῆσθε, πυρὸν ἀγοράσαι ἥκατε.
τὰ δ᾽ ἄλλα χαρίζοισθ᾽ ἑαυτῶν ἐπι-
20 μελόμενοι ἵν᾽ ὑγιαίνητε.
ἔρρωται Ὧρος καὶ Πετοσῖρις.
ἔρρωσθε. (ἔτους) ιθ, Παχὼν η.

Verso: παρὰ   Πετεαρσεμθεῖ Νεβχούνιος
         Πετεσούχου
         τοῦ Νεβχούνιος.

We heard that the mice have eaten up the crop. Please come here to us or, if you prefer, to Diospolis to buy grain. For the rest, you would favor us by taking care of youselves that you stay healthy. Horos and Petosiris are well. Good-bye. (Year) 19, Pachon 8.

Outside address: To Peteharsemtheos the son of Nebchounios. From Petesouchos, the son of Nebchounios.

1   Read Πετεσούχος: see this spelling on the verso and elsewhere when the name occurs in PGrenf II.
2   The name Paganis elsewhere appears as Phagonis in PGrenf II.
7   Esthautis and Almentis are revised readings offered in SelPap I 103.
9   Read ἡμῖν.
11 Read ὑπελάμβανον.
12 Read ἐποίησεν.
18 Read ἥκετε.
23 Nebchounios is apparently a variant for Panebchounios (see line 25 also).

We noted in letter 43 that civil war erupted in Egypt in 131–130 BCE because of the tension between Cleopatra II and Euergetes II, with inhabitants dividing up into factions behind one or the other ruler. The Thebaid seems to have been especially agitated during that period. But in 88 BCE, a state of antidynastic agitation of the native Egyptians, comparable to the great revolt of 131–130 BCE, occurred. On this occasion, the Thebaid area was the very center of the revolt. The following comments describe something of the background to that rebellion.

As mentioned earlier, Euergetes II took a niece, known as Cleopatra III, to be his wife. He, Cleopatra III, and his sister-wife, Cleopatra II, were all three regarded as co-sovereigns of Egypt. At Euergetes' death in 116 BCE, the niece-wife, Cleopatra III, wanted to make her younger son, Alexander, co-regent with herself. Cleopatra's decision led to such vehement popular opposition, however, that she was forced to call her elder son, designated Soter II, from Cyprus to rule in place of Alexander. Soter II's nickname, the occasion of which is no longer known, was Lathyros, "Chick-pea." Initially, this young man of twenty-five or so was unable to withstand his mother's wishes, with the result that he could not even alter her decision to take away his sister-wife, Cleopatra IV (to whom, according to Justin, he was much attached). A younger sister, Cleopatra Selene, replaced Cleopatra IV as co-regent.

Ten years later, by 108–107 BCE, "Chick-pea" had managed to assert himself enough against his mother that she found it necessary to accuse him of trying to murder her. She worked so successfully on the feelings of the Alexandrian population that Soter found it necessary to flee overseas. Thereupon, Cleopatra summoned her younger son, Alexander, from Cyprus to become co-regent. Eventually, Soter reestablished himself well enough in Cyprus, a Ptolemaic dependency, that Cleopatra could not dislodge him.

When Cleopatra III died in 101 BCE, the younger son, Ptolemy Alexander, continued to rule Egypt until 89 BCE when his army turned against him. Though he fled to Syria to raise a new force of mercenaries to reenter Alexandria, he was driven out of Alexandria once again, and, subsequently, was killed in a sea battle with the Alexandrian admiral Chaereas.

Thus, for the second time, Soter came from Cyprus to rule Egypt. The eight years following Soter's return were years of internal agitation and nationalism, which had arisen already in the waning years of Alexander's rule. During that period new native leaders had emerged who hoped to establish a new line of pharaohs. The ancient city of Thebes was the seat of this nationalistic movement, but by the time Soter returned to the throne in 88 BCE, the whole Thebaid was in a state of rebellion.

A series of letters, all written by a certain Platon, throw some light on the situation. Three of these five letters are included in this collection. In the first two letters below (letters 56–57), we learn that the town of Pathyris is still supporting the Ptolemaic dynasty. In the first letter (PLond II 465), Platon, presumably the *epistategos* of the Thebaid, encourages the village to hold on for a while and to rally behind their military leader, Nechthyris. In the second letter (PBour 10), written on the same day and addressed to Nechthyris himself, Platon instructs Nechthyris on the various aspects of the village's defense. At this time, Soter's return to Egypt seems not to have been known in the Thebaid, since Platon continued to date his correspondence by the regnal year of Alexander. A third letter (PBour 11), not included here, was written by Platon two days later and, though rather fragmentary, contains clear instructions to Nechthyris regarding the rations which the village's inhabitants were to provide for themselves in the present circumstances. A fourth letter (edited by F. Bilabel in PBad II, pp. 22ff.), also fragmentary, undated, and not included below, is addressed "to the priests and the other inhabitants at Pathyris." This letter appears to be similar to the first in encouraging the villagers to rally behind Nechthyris. In the fifth letter (PBour 12 and letter 58 below), which is written seven months later than the earliest correspondence (1 November 88 BCE), we learn that the town is still holding out for the Ptolemaic dynasty and that Soter's return to Egypt is now known. Platon suggests that his return will make a considerable difference in the overthrow of the revolt. Pausanias, the second century CE traveler and geographer, states that it took three years for Soter to subdue the rebellion and that, when finally accomplished, he inflicted a terrible punishment on Thebes (*Description of Greece* 1.9.3).

The following bibliographical details pertain to the discovery of the Platon correspondence. The text of PLond II 465 (letter 56) was not actually published but a brief description was given by Sir F. G. Kenyon (PLond II, pp. xli). Grenfell, however, saw the relationship between it and a Platon letter, edited by P. Jouguet, announcing the arrival of Soter II (*Bulletin Correspondance Hellénique* 21:141–47=Wilcken, WChr 12; reedited by Collart as PBour 12), and he edited the letter extensively in "A New Papyrus." A third letter by Platon, written only two days after PLond 465, and dealing with the rations of the inhabitants of Pathyris, while more fragmentary, was edited by Wilcken (*Archiv* 7:298f.). A fourth letter, again somewhat fragmentary, was edited by F. Bilabel (PBad II, pp. 22ff.). Then, in 1922, Paul Collart published all five letters with commentary in the *Recueil d'Etudes Egyptologiques* dedicated to J.F. Champollion (pp. 273–82). Three of the same letters were republished in PBour, p. 54–59. Bevan commented on the five letters while discussing Egyptian nationalism in the Thebaid (*History of Egypt*, pp. 335–37) and Pierre Jouguet's study of the Ptolemies' relationship with the native Egyptian element is also germane to the Platon correspondence (see *Les Lagides et les indigènes égyptiens*, pp. 419–45).

56 PLATŌN TO THE INHABITANTS OF PATHYRIS
SelPap II 417 (=PLond II 465)   28 March 88 BCE

The nearly identical nature of this and the immediately following letter strongly suggests that they were written on the same day. Consequently, we accept Collart's corrections of the text and his date (see *Recueil d'Etudes Egyptologiques*, p. 276), as he altered Grenfell's edition. SelPap II 417 follows Collart's edition. The restoration of the month as Φα]με(νώθ) was advocated already by Grenfell, though he dated the document a year later.

Platon addresses the inhabitants of Pathyris in the present letter, encouraging them to remain loyal to the crown and to rally behind their appointed commander, Nechthyres, until such time as he himself can come to Pathyris.

[Π]λάτω[ν τοῖς ἐν] Παθύρει
[κ]ατοικ[οῦσι χαίρει]ν καὶ
ἐρρῶσθαι. [ἐξωρμη]κότες
[ἐγ] Λάτων πόλ[εως] ἀντιληψό-
5 [μ]ενοι τῶν ἐν[εστη]κότων
[κα]τὰ τὸ συμφ[έρον] τοῖς
[π]ράγμασι, ἐκρ[ίνα]μεν σημῆναι
καὶ παρακαλέσαι εὐψυχο-
[τ]έρους ὑπάρχοντας
10 ἐφ ἑαυτῶν εἶνα[ι] καὶ συν-
γίνεσθαι Νεχθύρει τῶι
ἐφ᾽ ὑμῶν τεταγμένωι
μέχρι τοῦ [καὶ ἡμᾶ]ς ὅ τι
τάχο[ς παρεῖν]αι τοῖς τόπο[ις].
15   ἔρρ(ωσθε). [(ἔτους) κϛ, Φα]με(νὼθ) ιϛ.

Verso: τοῖς ἐν Παθύρει
[κατοι]κοῦσι.

Platon to the inhabitants in Pathyris greeting and good health. Having set out from Latonpolis in order to take charge of the things that have arisen in a way that is advantageous to state affairs, I decided to notify you and to exhort you to be supportive of one another, remaining courageous, and to assist Nechthyres who has been appointed commander over you until I myself can come to you as quickly as possible. Good-bye. (Year) 26, Phamenoth 16.

Outside address: To the inhabitants in Pathyris.

---

15 (Year) 26: i.e., year 26 of Ptolemy Alexander, who was still king when the revolt broke out or thought, at least, in the Thebaid to still be ruling in Alexandria. Grenfell noted in his edition of this text that the restoration Φα]με(νὼθ) can hardly be doubted, since this abbreviation is common, while the customary abbreviation of Μεσορή is Μεσο(ρή) and that of Μεχείρ is Μεχ(είρ).

The return of Soter II, referred to in letter 58, did not affect the revolt which, unlike the earlier revolt in 131–130 BCE (a partisan rebellion; the parties sided with one or another Ptolemy), was a native uprising against foreign rule. Consequently, when Soter came to Egypt, Platon promptly transferred his allegiance from Alexander to Soter.

57 PLATŌN TO NECHTHYRES
PBour 10   28 March 88 BCE

Paul Collart states, in his Introduction to Platon correspondence in PBour (pp. 54–55), that the indolent Alexander assumed no responsibility for quelling the mutiny in Thebes and that, in fact, he attached little importance to the Thebaid. Consequently, the jurisdiction of the Thebaid, and certainly any measures for dealing with revolt there, became the singular responsibility of Platon, the epistrategos over Thebes, and his subordinates.

In the present letter, Platon instructs Nechthyres to take such urgent measures as will insure the security of the area, including the surveillance of the environs, the protection of loyal subjects and the detention of any rebels. In short, Nechthyres was to make all the preparations for a state of siege. Collart suggests, in his editorial comments on this text, that the earlier revolt of 131–130 BCE had taught the Ptolemies a valuable lesson. In a revolt of the native Egyptian population it was advantageous to enlist members of the native element against the insurgents. The advantage became evident through the appointment of the Egyptian, Paos, to the the post of *strategos* over the Thebaid in that earlier revolt (see the introduction to letter 43). A second Egyptian, Phommus, was serving in the same capacity from at least 116–111 BCE and in the present correspondence another native, Nechthyres, is the military commander at Pathyris.

Πλ[άτω]ν Νεχθύρει
χαί[ρειν]. ἐξωρμή-
κα[μεν] ἐγ Λατων-
πόλ[εως ἀντιληψό-]
5   με[ν]οι τῶν ἐνεστη-
κ[ότων] κατὰ τὸ
σ[υμφέρο]ν τοῖς πράγμασι
κ[αὶ γεγ]ραφότες
[τοῖς κα]τοικοῦσι
10   συ[γγ]ίνεσθαί σοι.
καλῶς ποιήσεις
συντηρῶν τὸν
τόπον καὶ προ-
ιστάμενος·
15   [το]ὺς δ' ἐπιχει-
[ροῦ]ντας μὴ
[ὑπα]κούειν σου
[. .].τέραι στάσει
[. .].ομένους
20   [ἀσ]φαλισάμενος
[μέ]χρι τοῦ καὶ
[ἡμᾶ]ς ὅτι τάχος
[ἐπι]βαλεῖν πρὸς σέ.

[ἔρρω]σο. Ⳑ κϛ, φαμε(νὼθ) ιϛ.

Verso: ἀπόδ(ος) Νεχθύρει.

Platon to Nechthyres greeting. We have set out from Latonpolis to take charge of the circumstances that have arisen in a way that is advantageous to state affairs and have written to the inhabitants to assist you. You will do well if you attend closely to the place and guard it. And if there are some who try to disobey you . . . in sedition, hold them until we come to you as quickly as possible. Good-bye. (Year) 26, Phamenoth 16.

Outside address: Deliver to Nechthyres.

---

8   γεγραφότες: the message of this note is at first almost identical to the preceding one (letter 56), except that in that case the letter was addressed to the inhabitants of Pathyris, rather than to their military leader. The two texts may be used to correct and complement each other.

12   συντηρῶν: apparently the military jurisdiction of Pathyris had been placed entirely in Nechthyres' hands. According to Collart, the editor, since Platon does not refer to any armed troops in his company the revolt may have taken him by surprise while he was making the customary tour of the area under his jurisdiction.

58   PLATŌN TO THE PRIESTS OF PATHYRIS
PBour 12

1 November 88 BCE

Collart, the editor of PBour 12, suggests that since Platon does not refer to the letter's point of origin, it must have been sent from Ptolemais, the residence of the epistrategos of the Thebaid. The letter is significant because it indicates that Soter, who had now returned to power, had decided to take a more personal role in suppressing the Thebaid revolt. While his intervention may only reflect his disregard for an epistrategos appointed by his brother, it seems more likely that the severity of the uprising, which now included the entire Thebaid area, called for more drastic measures. Consequently, the king had organized a military expedition, under the leadership of General Hierax, specifically to overthrow the revolutionaries. In spite of his advancing age, Soter accompanied his troops as far south as Memphis.

Πλάτων τοῖς ἐν Παθύρει
ἱερεῦσι καὶ τοῖς ἄλλοις
τοῖς κατοικοῦσι

Platon to the priests and other inhabitants at Pathyris greeting. Philoxenos my brother wrote me in a letter, which Orses has delivered to me,

χαίρειν. γέγραφεν
5 ἡμῖν Φιλόξενος
ὁ ἀδελφὸς δι᾽ ὧν κεκό-
μικεν ἡμῖν Ὄρσης
γραμμάτων περὶ τοῦ
τὸν μέγιστον Θεὸν
10 Σωτῆρα Βασιλέα
ἐπιβεβληκέναι
εἰς Μέμφιν, Ἱέρακα δὲ
προκεχειρίσθαι
μετὰ δυνάμεων
15 μυρίων ἐπὶ κατα-
στολὴν τῆς Θηβαΐδος.
ὅπως οὖν εἰδότες
εὐθαρσεῖς ὑπάρ-
χητε ἐκρίναμεν
20 σημῆναι.

ἔρρ(ωσθε). Ⳑλ, φαῶφι ιθ.

Verso: τοῖς ἐν Παθύρει
ἱερεῦσι καὶ τοῖς ἄλλοις.

that King Soter, the very great God, has arrived at Memphis and that Hierax has been appointed, with considerable forces, for quelling the Thebaid. Therefore, knowing that you would be encouraged (by such news) I decided to notify you. Good-bye. (Year) 30, Phaophi 19.

Outside address: To the priests and the others in Pathyris.

---

21 (Year) 30: this letter is only seven months later than the two immediately preceding letters (56–57), which are dated "year 26." This last letter, however, refers to the regnal year of a different king, Soter II, whose rule had been interrupted by his queen mother (see the general introduction above to the Platon correspondence).

Greek silver *tetradrachm* struck at the Alexandria mint 305–283 BCE. *Obverse:* diademed head of Ptolemy I (Soter), who reigned from 323–283 BCE. *Reverse:* eagle standing on thunderbolt, the legend translating as "of King Ptolemy," and the monogram in the left field identifying the person in charge of the mint.

Roman silver *denarius* minted in 28 BCE, one year before Octavian received the title of Augustus, an event that marked the beginning of imperial Rome. *Obverse:* The inscription records Octavian's current rank as CAESAR and his sixth year as consul (COS VI). *Reverse:* Crocodile with open jaws that bears the inscription AEGYPTO CAPTA. The coin commemorates Octavian's defeat of Cleopatra VII of Egypt in 31 BCE and the subsequent annexation by Rome of Ptolemaic Egypt.

Photographs courtesy of Numismatic Fine Arts, Beverly Hills.

59 APOLLŌN TO PETESOUCHOS
PTebt I 37

The exact sense of this letter is unclear, primarily because lines 6–9 are obscure. If the words "works" in line 7 and "extension" in line 8 are correct, apparently Kephalas and his partners, from whom some payment was due, had asked Demetrios (an official) for an extension because of some burden which had been imposed upon them. Demetrios agreed to the cultivators' proposal initially but afterwards he became embarrassed about the extention and instructed Apollon to take soldiers and "ravage" the cultivators, from whom the fine was to be exacted. Apollon instructed Petesouchos, in turn, to implement the order, claiming that he himself was too busy at present to attend to the matter.

Grenfell and Hunt suggest that the "ninth year" must refer to the reign of Neos Dionysos rather than to the earlier reign of Soter II, because of the date of other documents found in the same crocodile (see introductory comments to PTebt I 103).

Ἀπόλλων Πετεσούχωι
χαίρειν. γίνωσκε Κεφα-
λᾶν καὶ Πετεσοῦχον καὶ
τοὺς μετόχους προσελη-
5 λυθέναι Δημητρίῳ
περὶ ὧν ἐὰν ὀμόσω-
σι ἔργων ἐμβεβλῆ-
σθαι εἰς τὴν γῆν καὶ παρα-
τάσις δοῦναι αὐτοῖς.
10 καὶ γὰρ μεγάλως ἠρυ-
θρίακε καὶ ἐντέ-
ταλται μοι παραλα-
βὼν στρατιώτας
ἐκπορθῆσαι αὐ-
15 τούς. ἐγὼ οὖν περι-
σπώμενος περὶ
ἀναγκαίων γέγρα-
φά σοι ἵνα ἱκανὸς
γένῃ, καὶ πράξας
20 ἔχε ἀπὸ τοῦ χαλ-
κοῦ (τάλαντον) α ἕως
καταβῶ καὶ λάβωι.
ἐὰν δὲ ἀμελήσῃς
ἀναγκασθήσομαι
25 ἐγὼ ἐ[λθεῖ]ν αὔριο[ν.
[ἔρρωσο]. (ἔτους) θ, Χο⟨ί⟩αχ [. .

Verso: Πετεσούχωι.

Apollon to Petesouchos greeting. Be aware that Kephalas and Petesouchos and their partners have applied to Demetrios about the works, swearing indeed that they (the works) had been imposed unfairly against their land and that he should give them an extension of time (for payment). For now he has become greatly embarrassed (about granting the extension) and has commanded me to take soldiers and ravage them. Therefore, since I am occupied with things that must be done, I wrote to you in order that you handle the matter, and when you accomplish it, keep out one talent of copper until I come down and get it. If you should be negligent about this, I myself will be compelled to come tomorrow. (Good-bye). (Year) 9, Choiach . . .

12   Read παραλαβόντι.
26   Owing to the threatening tone of the letter in the closing instructions (lines 23–25), it may well be the closing farewell was omitted, even though we have followed the original editor in restoring it above.

Lysimachos informs Taarmiusis, who is probably his wife, that he cannot travel before a certain date because of oracular advice from the god Soknebtunis. Soknebtunis, like Petesouchos in earlier texts of this collection, was a local form of the crocodile god Sebek, probably the most popular god of the Fayum (see PFay, Introduction, p. 22). The word "sister" in the present letter is, like "brother," a term of endearment and equality. But since marriage between brother and sister was not uncommon in Egypt, Taarmiusis may be the sister of Lysimachos as well as his wife. The fragmented condition of the papyrus makes many of its details unintelligible; only the first seven lines and the conclusion are very certain.

We have seen various references to the advice of the gods in this collection (see especially the Serapeum correspondence, letters 34–42), which indicates that the practice of consulting local oracles must have occurred frequently. Though no actual questions to oracles contemporaneous with our text have been published, to my knowledge, a number from the following two centuries are available. Four examples of these petitions to the oracle are presented below, two each from POxy and PFay (see also BGU I 229–30). A fifth document, a Christian prayer, is also illustrated below. Its style and form are clearly analogous to questions to pagan deities.

Questions to oracles must have been brief and stylized, as the examples below illustrate, consisting of three elements: (1) the opening address to the god: "To B"; (2) the petitioner's question; and (3) the inquiry about an answer to the question (see the convention τοῦτό μοι σύμφωνον ἔνεκε in POxy 1148.8–10 which is equivalent to τοῦτό μοι ἐξόνιγκον in BGU 229.4, 230.4 and to τοῦτο ἐκξένειγκον καὶ συμφονησάτο in PFay 138.3f.). Κρίνειν is the technical term for the oracle's answer in PTebt 284.2f. (see PFay 138.1) and χρηματίζειν serves the same purpose in PFay 137.2.

The POxy questions were addressed to the oracle of Sarapis. The PFay questions, which were discovered in the central chamber of the temple at Bakchias (northeast corner of the Fayum), were addressed to Sokanobkoneos, another local form of the crocodile god, and to the Dioscouroi.

Λυσίμαχος Τααρμιύσι
τῆι ἀδελ(φῆ) χαίρειν. ἐπικέ-
κριταί μοι μὴ καταβῆ-
ναι ἔως τῆς κε, καὶ
5   ὡς θέλει ὁ Σεκνεβτύ(νις)
ὁ κύριος θεὸς καταβή-
σομαι ἐλευθέρως. σὺ δὲ
ἱκανήν μου σὺν τοῖς
παιδίο(ι)ς περὶ τῆς λιτα-
10 νήας....ἐὰν ἐξ εὐ-
τυχίας...τὰ παιδία
καὶ α.....ωσιν μη-
δὲ π............
λην κ.....ἐὰν κατα-
15 βῶ. καὶ σεαυτῆς ἐπιμ(ελομένη) ἵν' ὑ(γιαίνης)
ἔ[ρ]ω(σο). (ἔτους) ιβ, Χοί(αχ) κ.

Lysimachos to Taarmiusis his sister greeting. It has been determined for me that I should not come down until the twenty-fifth, and as Soknebtunis the Lord God wills it I will come down freely. And you are able, together with my children, concerning the supplication . . . if by good fortune . . . the children and . . . if I should come down. And take care of yourself that you stay in good health. Goodbye. (Year) 12, Choiach 20.

---

1   Taarmiusis is also a name that appears in PTebt II 283.3 but the editors of the two texts thought they were different people.

2   ἐπικέκριται: the editors, Grenfell and Hunt, suggested that this could be restored as ἐπ(ε)ὶ κέκριται, in which case the καί at the end of line 4 would introduce the apodosis and the condition would read: "Since it has been determined for me not to come down until the twenty-fifth, then I will come down freely as the Lord God Soknebtunis desires it."

TO SARAPIS HELIOS
POxy VIII 1148

I CE

Κύριέ μου Σαράπι Ἥλιε
εὐεργέτα. εἰ βέλτειόν
ἐστιν Φανίαν τὸν υἱό(ν)
μου καὶ τὴν γυναῖκα
5 αὐτοῦ μὴ συμφωνῆσαι
νῦν τῷ πατρὶ α(ὐτοῦ), ἀλλὰ
ἀντιλέγειν καὶ μὴ δι-
δόναι γράμματα; τοῦ-
τό μοι σύμφωνον ἔνεν-
10 κε. ἔρρω(σο).

My Lord Sarapis Helios, benefactor. (Say) whether it is better for Phanias my son and his wife not to agree now with his father, but to oppose him and not make a contract. Tell me this truly. Good-bye.

TO ZEUS HELIOS SERAPIS
POxy VIII 1149

II CE

Διὶ Ἡλίῳ μεγάλωι
Σεράπ[ι]δι καὶ τοῖς
συννάοις. ἐρωτᾷ
Νίκη εἰ σ[υ]μφέρει
5 μοι ἀ[γο]ράσαι παρὰ
Τασαρ[α]μίωνος ὃν
ἔχει δοῦλον Σαραπί-
ωνα τ[ὸ]ν κα[ὶ Γ]αΐωνα.
[τοῦτό μ]οι δός.

To Zeus Helios great Serapis and his fellow gods. Nike asks whether it is advantageous for her to buy from Tasarapion her slave, Sarapion, who is also called Gaion. Grant me this (answer).

TO SOKANOBKONEOS
PFay 137

I CE

Σοκωννωκοννῖ θεῶι με⟨γά⟩λο μεγάλωι. χρημάτισόν μοι, ἢ μείνωι
ἐν Βακχιάδι; ἢ μέλ⟨λ⟩ω ἐντυνχ-
άνιν; τούτωι ἐμοὶ χρημάτισον.

To Sokanobkoneos the great, great God. Answer me, should I stay in Bakchias? Or should I meet (him?)? Answer me this.

1 Read Σοκανοβκονεῖ θεῷ μεγάλῳ.

TO THE LORDS DIOSCOUROI
PFay 138

I or II CE

Κύριοι Διόσκουροι, ἢ κρείνεται
αὐτὸν ἀπελθεῖν ἰς πόλειν;
τοῦτο ἐκξένεigκον καὶ

O lords Dioskouroi, is it determined that he should depart to the city? Bring this to pass and let him make an agreement with your (?) brother.

συμφονησάτο πρὸς
5 τὸν ἀδελφόν σου.

3 Read ἐξένεγκον.
4 Read συμφωνησάτω or συμφωνήσατε. The subject of συμφωνησάτω seems to be the person
   mentioned in line 2. However, ἀδελφόν σου in
   line 5 (one of the Dioscouroi or αὐτόν) is obscure.

CHRISTIAN PRAYER
POxy VIII 1150

VI CE

+
+ Ὁ θεὸς τοῦ προστάτου ἡμῶν
   τοῦ ἁγίου Φιλοξένου, ἐὰν
   κελεύεις εἰσενεγκεῖν
   εἰς τὸ νοσοκομῖόν σου Ἀνούπ;
5 δεῖξον τὴν δύναμ[ὶ]ν σου
   καὶ ἐξέλθη τὸ πιττ[ά]κ[ιον.

O God of our patron saint Philoxenos, do you
command us to take Anoup to your hospital? Show
your power and let this request be granted.

1 A Christian symbol is written in the left margin
   and immediately above line one.

61 ATHĒNAGORAS TO THE PRIESTS IN THE LABYRINTH
SelPap I 104 (=BSAA xiv, p. 194)

I BCE

Athenagoras, the chief of the public physicians maintained by the state, writes to temple
attendants, apparently mummy-dressers, about an employee or servant who has died in
their district. The editors of SelPap 104 suggest that, strictly speaking, the *stolistai* were
temple attendants responsible for clothing the images of the gods. In the present case,
however, they seem to be involved in one or another aspect of embalming and burial,
and it is likely that not all of these attendants were actually priests.

The Labyrinth where the priests served is the funeral temple of Amenemhet III: one
of those well-known Egyptian sights, along with the sacred crocodiles, popularized by
Herodotus and his successors (see letter 51 above in which a Roman senator is sche-
duled to view these sights).

Ἀθηναγόρας ὁ ἀρχίατρος τοῖς ἱερεῦσι τῶν
ἐν τῶ[ι] Λαβυρίνθωι στολιστῶν καὶ τοῖς
στολ[ισ]ταῖς χαίρειν. ἐπεὶ Ἡρακλείδης
ὁ πα[ρ’ ἐ]μοῦ ἐπὶ τῶν τόπων τετελεύτηκ(εν)
5 καὶ ἔ[σ]τιν ἐν ταῖς παρ’ ὑμεῖν νεκρίαις,
τού[τ]ου δὲ χάριν πέπομφα Νικίαν καὶ Κρόκ(ον),
καλῶς ποιήσετε προέμενοι τὸ σω-
μάτι[ο]ν μηθὲν πράξαντες καὶ συν-
καταστήσατε αὐτοῖς ἕως Πτολεμαΐδος.
10 γέγραφαν δὲ ὑμεῖν καὶ οἱ ἀπ’ Ἀλεξανδρείας
στολ[ισ]ταὶ περὶ αὐτοῦ. ἐπιμέλεσθε δὲ
ἑαυ[τῶ]ν ἵν’ ὑγιαίνητε.
     ἔρρωσ(θε). (ἔτους) ιδ, Ἁθὺρ κε̄.

Athenagoras, the chief physician, to the priests of
the stolistai at the Labyrinth and to the stolistai
greeting. Since my man Herakleides has died in
your area and is in your cemetaries there, I have
sent for this reason Nikias and Krokos. Please
deliver the body without fee and help them in
carrying it as far as Ptolemais. The stolistai from
Alexandria have also written to you about him.
Take care of yourselves to stay well. Good-bye.
(Year) 14, Hathyr 25.

Outside address: To the priests of the stolistai and
   to the stolistai.

Verso: τοῖς ἱερεῦσι τῶν στολιστῶν
καὶ τοῖς στολιστα[ῖς].

5 Read ὑμῖν.
10 γέγραφαν is the corrected reading by the editors
of SelPap 104. The original edition had [[γ]] ἔγρ-
αψαν.

62 APOLLŌNIOS TO THOŌNIS
PRyl IV 593

6 August 35 BCE

Although this document is largely intact and there are few textual difficulties, we know so little about the circumstances of the letter that its meaning is not entirely clear. It is a private letter dealing with some business matter(s). Apollonios instructs Thoonis to deliver a fleece to someone from whom, in turn, he receives the original of a document that Thoonis had sent to Apollonios. One cannot tell whether this document was connected specifically with the delivery of the fleece. The editors of PRyl 593, Roberts and Turner, noted that since the name Thoonis was common in Oxyrhynchos, the letter may well have originated there.

Ἀπολλώνιος Θοώνει
χαίρειν. περὶ οὗ σοι
ἐντέταλκα πόκου
μεγάλου π[. .]λου τῶι
5 ἐπιστάτηι τοῦ παιδίου
δὸς τῶι ἀποδιδόντι σοι
τὸ πιττάκιον αὐτὸν
ὧν μοι πεποίηκας
ἐπαγγελιῶν ἵνα μὴ
10 μέμψεις ἔχωμεν
πρὸς ἑαυτούς.
ἔρ(ρωσο). (ἔτους) ιζ β, Με(σορὴ) ι.

Apollonios to Thoonis greeting. Concerning the large fleece, about which I instructed you, give it to the slave overseer who will return the actual promissory note (?) to you in which you made your offers to me, lest we have complaints against each other. Good-bye. (Year) 17-2, Mesore 10.

---

3 Read ἐντέταλκα.
7 πιττάκιον: the context of the text is not detailed enough to show what type of document is designated by *pittakion*, a word whose meaning varies from century to century and from one context to another. The original editor rendered the word as "memorandum."
12 (Year) 17-2: see T.C. Skeat, "Reigns of the Ptolemies," p. 40, for the explanation of this type of dating formula.

BGU IV 1203–9, is a series of seven letters stuck together on a roll, all but one addressed to a certain Asklepiades. Though various business matters are discussed in the correspondence, it is clear that they are private letters and consist, for the most part, of correspondence between family members. The central figure in the archive is Asklepiades who received or wrote (BGU 1203 seems to be a first draft by Asklepiades himself) all of the letters and who kept them in his file. His sister Isidora is next in importance after Asklepiades; she is the addressor of four of the seven letters. Another brother, Paniskos, is mentioned in four separate letters; Petechon, a recently deceased brother, and perhaps the husband of Isidora, is cited in 1209; and, while the usage may be figurative, Tryphon is identified as yet another brother in 1208 and 1209. Other names are mentioned in the correspondence, some two or more times, but, apart from the identification of Philon as an oikonomos, we do not know their official status or their relation to the family. From the nature of the subjects discussed in the correspondence, it seems the family was relatively wealthy.

The editor of BGU IV 1203–9, Schubart, indicated that the correspondence was part of the papyrus cartonnage from Abusir-el-malaq (Hellenistic Busiris), a town located to the east and slightly to the south of the Fayum (see the map on p. 155). The only place name actually cited in the correspondence, however, is Hermopolis, located more than one hundred miles south of Busiris (see BGU 1204.30).

Three of the seven letters from Asklepiades' files are included in this collection: BGU 1204, and 1206–7.

63 ISIDŌRA TO ASKLĒPIADES
BGU IV 1204   2 October 28 BCE

Isidora writes to her brother Asklepiades, notifying him that a letter to Paniskos has been sent under the same seal, and that she needs a response from Paniskos regarding a broken boat. This same Paniskos is mentioned in BGU 1205.10, 15 and 1207.8. BGU 1206.4f. indicates specifically that he is a brother.

Ἰσιδώ[ρα] Ἀσκληπιάδηι τῶι ἀδελφῶι
χαίρε[ιν] κα[ὶ ὑ]γιαίνειν διὰ παντός.
τὰ πρὸς Πανίσκον γράμματα συνεσφράγισμαι
ὑμεῖν. τὴν οὖν ἀπάντων ἀντιφώνησιν
5 ἐν τάχ[ει πέμ]ψον διὰ τὸ τὸ πλοῖον
χωρίζεσθαι. καὶ σὺ δὲ διανδραγάθει.
ἕως οὗ ἂν παραγένηται, καὶ σεατοῦ
[ἐπιμελοῦ ἵν᾽] ὑγιαίνῃς, ὃ δὴ μέγιστόν ἐστι.
ἔρρω(σο). Lγ, Φαῶ(φι) ε.
10 τὸ ἐνκοίμητρον τοῦ
παιδίου πέμψον.

Isidora to her brother Asklepiades greeting and may you always be well. I enclosed under the same seal to you the letter to Paniskos. Therefore, whenever you meet him, send his reply in haste on account of the fact that the boat is broken. Moreover, continue to act steadfastly, until whatever time he arrives, and take care of yourself to stay well, which is most important. Good-bye. Year 3, Phaophi 5.

Postscript: Send the child's mattress (?).

4 Read ὑμῖν.
6 χωρίζεσθαι: Schubart, the editor, notes that this is a very uncertain reading. Διανδραγαθεῖν, though generally a little used word, is used with some frequency by Isidora in her correspondence with Asklepiades. Nonetheless, the exact attitude which she is enjoining by the word is not clear.
10–11 Τὸ ἐνκοίμητρον: though this word probably refers to something that people slept on, the same word means "counterpane" in PCairZen 48.4 (III BCE).

64 ISIDŌRA TO ASKLĒPIADES
BGU IV 1206   2 November 28 BCE

This is another letter of Isidora to Asklepiades written in a different hand than letter 63. BGU 1203–4 and 1207 are all written by a writer described by Schubart as "hand a." Though Isidora addresses two of the three (1204, 1207), the fact that Asklepiades addresses the third indicates that an employee or servant of the well-to-do family probably wrote all three letters.

In the present letter, as well as BGU 1205, however, another writer penned the correspondence. Schubart called this writer "hand b." Since both of these letters name Isidora as the addressor, she may well have written them in her own hand. Note that a shortened form of Asklepiades' name occurs, Asklas, and that Isidora's own name is spelled differently than in letters written by hand a. The two hand b letters by Isidora are longer and, perhaps, more familial in tone (note the wish for health expressed as a prayer in 1205 and 1206).

    Ἰσιδώιρα Ἀσκλᾶτι τῶι ἀδελφῶι
    χαίρειν καὶ διὰ παντὸς ὑγειαί⟨νειν⟩
    καθάπερ εὔχομαι. κεκόμισμαι
    ἃ ἐγεγράφις. ὁ ἀδελφοὺς Πανίσ-
5   κος γέγραφε Νουμήνιν πεπομ-
    φέναι Φίλωινα τὸν οἰκονόμον
    ἐπ᾽ αὐτὸν κατασπουδέως ἐ-
    πεὶ τὴν διοίκησιν, οὔπωι σε-
    σήμαγκε τί ἐκβέβη[κ]ε. περὶ
10 δὲ Ἀρήου αὐτὸς Πατρ .. γράφι
    ἐπ᾽ αὐτὸν χάριν το[ῦ π]αραγρά-
    φεσθαι πυρούς. σὺ δὲ καὶ Ἁρα-
    μώιτης διανδραγα[θ]εῖτε ἐν
    τῆι εἰσαγῆι τῆς τιμῆς [τ]οῦ
15 φακοῦ καὶ ὀλύρας. ἐάν τι
    ἄλλο προσπέσῃ σημανῶι σοι,
    καὶ σεατοῦ ἐπειμελοῦ, ἵν᾽ ὑγιαί-
    νῃς.
        ἔρρωσο. Ⳑγ, Ἀθὺρ ϛ̅.
20   πρωι ..

Verso: Ἀσκλᾶτι τῶι ἀδελφῶ [ι].

Isidora to her brother Asklas greeting and may you always be well, just as I pray. I received what you had written. Our brother Paniskos wrote that Noumenios has sent Philon the oikonomos zealously to the treasurer (?) himself, but in no way has he indicated what has been shipped. Regarding Areos, Patr . . . himself writes on his behalf because the wheat is being registered. You and Haramoitis must continue diligently to record the worth of the lentil and the olyra. If anything else should happen, I will tell you, and take care of yourself to stay well. Good-bye. Year 3, Hathyr 6 early.

Outside address: To my brother Asklas.

---

4 Read ἀδελφός.
5 Read Νουμήνιον.
7 Read κατασπουδαίως. Read ἐπί.
14 Read εἰσαγωγῆι.

ISIDŌRA TO ASKLĒPIADES
BGU IV 1207

received 5 November 28 BCE

As the addressor's date shows (line 14) this letter was sent three days before letter 64, but its present position on the roll to which it was attached by Asklepiades indicates that it actually arrived later. Though fragmented near the beginning, it appears that Isidora is acknowledging the receipt of certain things which Asklepiades had sent to her. Owing to the private and haphazard nature of postal service, it was probably necessary to take inventory when parcel post arrived. The middle of the letter is very similar to letter 64 in reporting that Paniskos, the brother of Isidora and Asklepiades, has apparently been accused of some type of financial (tax?) irregularity; Philon, the oikonomos (see letter 64), has been sent to intercede on behalf of Paniskos. The fact that Asklepiades is exhorted both here and in 64 to attend diligently to the way in which he records the value of certain crops suggests that Paniskos' difficulty arose for an analogous reason. After closing the letter, Isidora added a somewhat puzzling postscript about the receipt and transfer(?) of silver drachmas.

ἐλ(ήφθη) ∟γ, Ἀθὺρ θ̄ διὰ Πτολ(λίωνος).
......
 Ἰσιδώραι Ἀσκληπιάδηι τῶι ἀδελφῶι χαίρειν
 καὶ ὑγιαίνειν [δι]ὰ παντ[ός ..] κ[. . . . .] μη .. ἐγεγράφεις
5 κεκ [όμισμαι . . . . περι] στρώματα
 σανδύκινα [. . . . .] .. ωνια ι ἀεροε[ι]δῆ γ
 περιστρώμα[τα] συκανιωνια β. περὶ δὲ
 Πανίσκου τοῦ ἀδελφοῦ πέπομφε Νουμήνι[ος]
 Φ[ί]λωνα τὸν ἀδελφὸν αὐτοῦ ἐπ' αὐτὸν
10 κα[τὰ σπουδὴν] ἐπὶ τὴν διοίκησιν. συ οὖν καὶ
 [Ἁραμώτης] ἀνδραγαθεῖτε καὶ εἰσάγεσθε
 τ[ιμὴν φ] ακοῦ ὀλυρίω, καὶ τἆλλα σατοῦ δὲ
 ἐπιμ[ελοῦ] ἵν' ὑ (γιαίνῃς).
  ἔρρωσο. ∟γ, Ἀθὺρ γ̄.
15 ἐὰν δέ τι προσπ[έ]σηι σημανῶ ὑμεῖν,
 [εἰ δ]οκεῖ ἄγεσθε ἕως γράψω
 κεκόμισμαι διὰ τοῦ χειριστοῦ ἀργυ(ρίου) ⊢. ʽβω
 καὶ κομίζει σοὶ Πτολλίων ἀπολογη . . . .
 ἐὰν οὖν πέμπῃς [ἀρ]γύριον μελη .. τέλος
20 εἰκοστόν.

Verso: Ἀσκληπιάδηι.

Docket of receipt: Received year 3, Hathyr 9 through Ptollionos.

Isidora to her brother Asklepiades greeting and may you always be well. . . . I received what you had written: . . . red bed coverings, . . . three light-colored (?) . . . two mulberry-colored(?) bed coverings. Regarding our brother Paniskos, Noumenios has sent Philon his brother zealously on his behalf to the treasurer. Therefore you and Haramotes must continue to be diligent and record the value of the lentil to the olyra. And, for the rest, take care of yourself to stay well. Good-bye. Year 3, Hathyr 3.

Postscript: If anything should happen, I will tell you. If you should decide to transport (silver) in order that I should write you, I have received by means of the worst silver 802 drachmas and Ptollion receives. . . . Therefore, if you should send silver, make sure that it . . . the twentieth.

---

1 ἐλ(ήφθη): ελ is an abbreviation of ἐλήφθη, not ἐλάβομεν or ἔλαβον, as the editor Schubart originally conjectured. See the justification of the present reading on letter 49, note to line 1.
3 Read Ἰσιδώρα.
11 *Haramotes* is restored from letter 64.12f.
15 Read ὑμῖν.

66 A LETTER TO AGCHASIOS AND THAMINES
PPrinc III 160

late I BCE

The wife of Kolanos (see the verso) informs Agchasios and Thamines that she has asked Pnepheros for a contract. She would like for them to pick it up and hold it for her until she can come to get it. For other examples of this unusual salutation (i.e., "*From* A to B . . ."), see Exler, *Ancient Greek Letter*, pp. 49f.

Παρὰ Σ[. . . .] Ἀγχασίωι καὶ Θαμίνει χαίρειν
καὶ ἐρρ[ῶσ]θαι. ἔρρωμαι δὲ καὶ αὐτός. γεγράφαμεν
Πνεφ[ε]ρῶτι ὅπως δὴ αἰτῆι συγγραφήν.
καλῶς [οὖ]ν ποιήσεις κομίσα⟨ς⟩ καὶ ἔχε μέχρι
5 τοῦ ἐ[μὲ π]αραγενέσθαι.

Verso
1st hand: Ἀγχασίωι.
2nd hand: γυναῖκα Κολάνου.

From S(. . .) to Agachasios and Thamines greeting and good health. I myself am also well. We (I) have written to Pnepheros in order to ask for a contract. Therefore, please get it and hold it for me until I arrive.

Outside address: To Agchasios.
Docket of receipt: The wife of Kolanos.

67 DIOGENĒS TO DIONYSIOS
POxy VII 1061

22 BCE

Diogenes writes to Dionysios, urging his assistance in the measurement of unirrigated land and in the payment of taxes upon it. Diogenes had written previously about the same matter, but since it had not been attended to yet, he has now sent someone, out of necessity, to attend to the matter on his behalf. Diogenes had apparently hoped that with this extra incentive Dionysios would finally help him.

Though Diogenes addresses Dionysios as brother, it is evident that the term is to be taken figuratively as a designation of familiarity and equality, not as an indication of actual relationship. This is clear by Diogenes' reference to Apollonios, the brother of Dionysios, as "your" brother. On the other hand, it is evident that the men and their families were well acquainted, as the closing salutations show.

Διογέν[η]ς Διονυσίωι τῶι ἀδελφῶι πλεῖστα
χα(ίρειν) καὶ ὑγιαίνειν. ἐπειδὴι καὶ ἄλλοτέ σοι
ἐγράψαμεν καὶ οὐ διῃτησαι ἡμᾶς καὶ Ἀπολλωνίωι τῶι ἀδελφῶ σου τὰ νῦν ἀνάγκην ἔσχον
5 παρακαλέσαι Πτολεμαῖον Πτολεμαίου νεώτε(ρον)
ὅπως συντύχηι Δίωι καὶ Διογένει Δημητ(ρίου)
ἕως ἂν μετρηθῆι ἡ ἄβροχος ἦι ἐν ταῖς
ζ (ἀρούραις) καὶ μετρη(θῆ) τὸ ὑπερ α(ὐτοῦ) δη(μόσιον) διὰ
τοῦ Διονυσίο(υ)
καὶ τὸ κατάλοιπον ἀποδοθῆι τῶι Πτολε-
10 μαίωι. ἐρωτηθεὶς οὖν συνπροσέσηι τῶι
Πτολεμ[α]ίωι καὶ Ἀπολ[λ]ώνιος ὁ ἀδελφός σου
ἕως μοι τοῦτο τελέσητε, διαφέρετε γὰρ
τοῦ Πτολεμαίου ἐμπειρίᾳ, κἂν δέον ἦν
Πτολεμαίω τῶι ἄλλωι ἀδελφῶι τοῦ Πτο-
15 λεμαίου πρεσβυτέρ[ω]ι συντυχεῖν περὶ

Diogenes to his brother Dionysios many greetings and good health. Since I wrote to you formerly and you did not make arrangements for us and (I wrote) to your brother Apollonios, I now found it necessary to entreat Ptolemy, the younger son of Ptolemy, to meet Dios and Diogenes, the son of Demetrios, until the unwatered land which is in the seven arouras be measured and that the taxes on it be measured through Dionysios, and that the remainder be paid to Ptolemy. Therefore, I request that you will accompany Ptolemy, in the company of your brother Apollonios, until you accomplish this for me. For you excel Ptolemy in experience, and if he has to meet Ptolemy, the older brother of Ptolemy, about this, (see to it) that he meet him and that he pursue the matter zealously until it is

τούτου, συντύχηι καὶ σπουδάσει ἕως
ὅτου τελεσθῆ[ι. ἐὰ]ν οὖν σοι φαίνηται
καὶ ὑπὲρ τούτων καὶ ὑπὲρ ὧν ἄλλων
σε διὰ γραπτοῦ ἠρώτησα ἀντιφωνῆ-
20   σαί μοι, ἔσῃ μοι κεχαρισμένος, καὶ σὺ
δὲ γράφε ὑπὲρ ὧν ἐὰν θέλῃς καὶ ἥδιστα
ποιήσωι. ἔγραψα δὲ καὶ Δίωι τῷ τοῦ χι-
ριστοῦ περὶ τούτου, ᾧ καὶ συντεύξηι.
ἀσπάζου τοὺς σοὺς πάντας. ἀσπάζε-
25   ταί σε Ἀθηναροῦς καὶ τὰ παιδία τὰ λοιπά.
ἐπιμελοῦ σεα(υτοῦ) ἵν᾽ ὑγι[α(ίνῃς)].   ἔρρωσ{σ}ο.
(ἔτους) η, Ἐπε[ὶφ.

Verso: Διονυσίωι τῷ καὶ Ἀμόιτι Πτολεμαίου ἀδελφῶι
Ἀπολλωνίου
κωμογραμμάτεως Θώλθεως παρόντος
ἐχομέ(νως) Θέωνο(ς) Ἰσχυρίω(νος).

accomplished. Therefore, if it seems good to you to reply to me, both about these things and the other matters about which I asked you through letter, I will be favored by you, and you also must write about whatever you want and I will do it most willingly. Moreover, I wrote to Dios, the son of the administrator, about this, whom also you will meet. Salute all your people. Athenarous and the rest of the children salute you. Take care of yourself to stay well. Good-bye. (Year) 8, Epeiph . . .

Outside address: To Dionysios, who is also called Amois, son of Ptolemy and brother of Apollonios the village secretary of Tholthis, who is staying near Theon, the son of Ischyrion.

---

3   Read δεδιῄτησαι (see POxy VII 1061, note to line 3).
16   συντύχηι: A. S. Hunt, the original editor, suggested that perhaps the third person was employed because the writer was thinking primarily of Apollonios. It seems more likely that the third person must be understood in the context of Diogenes' appeal for Dionysios to accompany Ptolemy. In this case, Dionysios is encouraged to make sure that Ptolemy should meet (*syntyke*) Ptolemy.
22   Read χειριστοῦ.

68 BASSOS TO HERAKLEIDĒS AND TRYPHŌN
PRyl IV 603   7 BCE

Here, Bassos, an official, responds to a letter from two minor officials at Oxyrhynchos. They have informed Bassos that local villagers have not completed work on the embankments used for irrigation. In a curt reply, he instructs the men to attend to the project themselves and to make sure that it is finished.

This document was attached to a ledger where documents dealing with state business were kept. On either side of the text are fragments of other letters; on the right side, part of thirteen lines remain and on the verso of this fragment is the address; Ἡρᾶι γραμματεῖ Διοσκουριδ(οῦ) βασιλ(ικοῦ) γρ(αμματέως) Ὀξυρυγχ(ίτου). It may well be, as the editors, C. H. Roberts and E G. Turner, suggest, that the Heras in the address is the Herakleides of the present letter. The Dioskourides of the same address may be the royal secretary of that name who appears in POxy IX 1188 (13 CE). If these conjectures are correct, then Herakleides (Heras) would be associated with the secretary's office at Oxyrhynchos.

The editors of PRyl 603 refer to our letter as forming part of an εἰρόμενον. The designation was used in Hellenistic and early Roman times to refer to a collection of documents compiled as rolls and kept at local record offices. Generally speaking, εἰρόμενα were rolls of abbreviated or abstracted copies of contracts (abbreviated for the sake of space and to preserve only the salient details), not a compilation of the full text of the actual documents (see the comments on PMich II 121 recto, and on PTebt III, pt. I 815; Boak, "The Anagraphai," pp. 164–67; Segré, "Note sul documento," pp. 97–107. As examples of such compilations, see also PLond III 1179, PFlor I 51, BGU VI 1258). Though the series of texts to which our letter belongs was kept on a roll at the local office, like the abstracted contracts and documents to which we have referred, it is the actual correspondence, not a copy, and it does not appear to be abbreviated.

Βάσσος ['Η]ρακλείδηι καὶ
Τρύφωνι   χαίρειν.
περὶ τῶν ἐποικίων ὡς τὰ
χώματα οὐκ ἀγείοχαν
5 ἐγράψατέ μοι· τοῦτο δὲ
οὐκ ἦν καθ' ὑμᾶς σήμερον
ἡμέρᾳ τοιαῦτά μοι γράφειν·
διὸ ἔτι καὶ νῦν ἔχετε τὰ
γενήματα αὐτῶν καὶ
10 στρατιώτην καὶ αὐτοὺς
τοὺς ἀνθρώπους οὓς
ὀχλῆσαι δύνασθε· ὥστε
ἐκτελέσατε συμβουλεύωι.
2nd hand: ἔρρωσθε. (ἔτους) κγ, Καίσαρος, Μεσορὴ κγ.

Verso: 'Ηρακλείδηι καὶ Τρύφωνι εἰς 'Οξυρυγχ(ίτην)

Bassos to Herakleides and Tryphon greeting. You wrote to me about the villages, that they have not brought (the soil for) the embankments. It was not (appropriate) for you to write such things to me today. Wherefore, even as late as it is, hold their crops and (take along) a soldier and the men themselves as many as you are able to trouble. I advise that you complete the work. Good-bye. (Year) 23 of Caesar, Mesore 23.

Outside address: To Herakleides and Tryphon at the Oxyrhynchite nome.

4   Read ἀγείοχασι.
5   Read συμβουλεύω. The editors of PRyl 603 theorize regarding lines 12–13 that the writer initially intended to close the letter with the imperative ἐκτελέσατε alone and that συμβολεύω was added only as an afterthought. If this was not the author's intention, he suggests that perhaps the imperative should be emended to the subjunctive, ἐκτελέσητε, on the supposition that the writer was translating, all too literally, *suadeo ut peragatis*.

69 APHYNCHIS TO APIS
POxy XLI 2979   September/October 3 BCE

Aphynchis writes to Apis, urging him to follow through on his offer to lease land to Aphynchis for the current year. To carry through on the matter, Aphynchis instructs Apis either to come down himself to make the lease or to send his servant on his behalf. The writer of this letter often divides words awkwardly between lines.

'Αφύγχις "Απει[[σ]]τι χαίρειν καὶ
ὑγιαίνιν. ἐπεὶ 'Ωρος υἱός μου
καταβὰς ἀπὸ τῆς πόλεως ἔλ-
εγέν μοι ὅτι ἔλεγες αὐτῷ μν-
5 ησθῆναί μοι περὶ ἧς ἔχεις ξυ-

Aphynchis to Apis greeting and good health. Since Horos my son who came down from the city said that you told him to remind me about sowing your land, that you would give (lease) all of it to me for the year, if you have the time, consequently, come

λαμῆς πᾶσαν δοῦναί μο[ι] ἐ-
ν τῷ ἔτει, [ἐ]ὰν οὖν εὐκαιρῇς
καταβῆναι καὶ μισθῶσαί μοι
ἦτε συ ἦ τὸ παιδίον σου διὰ τὸ ἐ-
10 μὲ περὶ τὰ κτή[νη] στρέφεσθαι
καὶ μὴ σχολάζειν. μὴ οὖν ἄλλως ποήσῃς ἐπεὶ καὶ ἄλλοι π-
αράκι'ν'ταί μοι, κατ᾽ ἐγλογὴν δὲ
σε αἱρετίζομαι. βουλευσάμε-
15 νος οὖν περὶ τούτου τὴν τα-
χίστην ἀντιφώνησόμ μοι
ἵνα μὴ ἐκπέσω. καὶ σεαυ(τοῦ) ἐπιμέλου ἵν᾽ ὑγι(αίνῃς).   ἔρρ[[ο]]ʽωʼσο.
(ἔτους) κη Καίσαρος, Φαῶφι. .

Verso: Ἄπειτι.

down and lease it to me, either you or your servant because I am occupied with the cattle and do not have the leisure for it. Therefore, do not act otherwise since others are also urging me, though you are my first choice. Therefore, after thinking about this, answer me immediately lest I miss (the opportunity). And take care of yourself to stay well. Good-bye. (Year) 28 of Caesar, Phaophi . . .

Outside address: To Apis.

---

2   Read ὑγιαίνειν.
3   καταβάς: the editor of POxy 2979, G. M. Browne, notes that *kata* in compounds often denotes movement from city to village (see H. C. Youtie, "The *Kline* of Sarapis," p. 15, n. 36).
9   τὸ παιδίον σου: the original editor translates this as "your boy." It seems more likely that the writer intends the more common meaning of the word in the papyri, "servant" (see line 2 where υἱός is used with reference to the writer's own son).
17 ἐκπέσω: by analogy with PTebt I 50.27–28, perhaps something like τοῦ καιροῦ should be supplied.

70   ANTAS TO PHAUSTOS
POxy IV 742   2 BCE

In this letter, Antas instructs Phaustos to get reeds from Pothos. Phaustos is to put aside part of the reeds until Antas can pick them up for his trip up river. The remainder are to be given to a friend to deliver to Antas. Though fragmented near the close, the primary purpose of the letter seems clear enough. On the other hand, we do not know the nature of the relationship between the corresponding parties nor, for that matter, the purpose of the reeds.

Ἄντας Φ[αύσ]τωι πλεῖστα χαίρειν.
παράλαβε παρὰ Πόθου τὸν κάλα-
μ[ο]ν πανα[ρ]ιθμῶι καὶ ἀπόστειλόν
μ[ο]ι πόσας δέσμας παρείληφες
5 καὶ θὲ[ς]ς αὐτὰς εἰς τόπον ἀσφαλῶς ἵνα τῇ ἀναβάσει αὐτὰς
ἄξωμεν. παράδος δέ τινι
τῶν φίλων ἀριθμῷ αὐτὰς ἵνα

Antas to Phaustos many greetings. Get from Pothos the whole amount of reeds and send me (word) how many bundles you received and put them in a safe place in order that we may take them along on the journey up. Give some of them to one of our friends in order that the friend, in turn, may deliver them safely to us, and if you can manage it . . . take pains to . . . I have bought from (Pothos?)

πάλιν φ[ί]λος ἡμεῖν παραδοῖ
10 ἀσφ[αλῶς,] καὶ ἐάν τι δύνῃ
σὺ ἐ[....]ναί μοι δὸς ἐργασί-
α[ν......]σα ἐμὲ ἠγορακέναι
παρ[ὰ...ο]υ τὴν χιλίαν δέσμην
(δραχμῶν) δ[εκάπ]εντε. μὴ ἀμελήσῃς.
15   ἔρρωσο.
(ἔτους) κη [κα]ίσαρος, Παῦνι α.

Verso: Φαυστῶι [......]ετ ενν .( ) εἰς Νέκλη.

the one thousand bundles for fifteen drachmas. Do not neglect this. Good-bye. (Year) 28 of Caesar, Payni 1.

Outside address: To Phaustos ... at Nekle.

---

9   Read ἡμῖν.

71 PART OF A LETTER TO A FRIEND
POxy IV 743   2 BCE

This letter, written in two columns, is very fragmented throughout most of the first column. The letter indicates that a certain Damas has been sent to attend to a number of neglected business matters. The writer asks the letter's recipient to aid Damas in whatever way he may need assistance. Since we have neither the letter opening nor the outside address, we do not know the name of either the writer or the recipient. It is clear from the letter itself, however, that the correspondents are friends and social equals. Though Damas is sent in the service of the writer, the manner in which he is recommended to the friend, along with various other stylistic features, cause the letter to resemble a letter of introduction.

Column I

Parts of 16 lines
17] θέλω δέ σε καὶ τὸν Καίσαρος
]ἀναγνοῦναι, δεῖ γάρ σε

Column II

εἰ καὶ π[ρ]ὸς ἄλλους εἶχον πρᾶγμα
20 βοηθὸν αὐτοῦ γ[ε]νέσθαι διὰ ἣν
ἔχομε(ν) πρὸς ἑαυτοὺς φιλίαν. καὶ
γὰρ ἐγὼ ὅλος διαπον[ο]ῦμαι εἰ Ἑλε-
νος χαλκοὺς ἀπόλε[σ]εν, παραγενομ(ένου)
γὰρ Δαμᾶτος εἰς Ἀλεξάνδρειαν ἦλ-
25 θαμεν ἐπὶ Ἐπαφρόδειτον καὶ εὑρέ-
θη μήτε εἰληφὼς μήτε δεδωκώ(ς).
ὥστ' ἂν τοῦτό σε θέλω γεινώσκειν
ὅτι ἐγὼ αὐτῷ διαστολὰς δεδώκειν
τὸ βαδίσαι εἰς Τακόνα χάριν τῶν ἐκ-
30 φορίων καὶ τὰ νῦν ἐπειπέπομφα
αὐτὸν πάντα συνλέξαι καὶ περὶ πάντων αὐτῷ τὴν ἐπιτροπὴν δέδωκα.

I wish you and the ... of Caesar to read this(?), for you must assist him because of our friendship even though I have had trouble(?) with others. For I am worn down completely by the fact that Helenos lost the money, because when Damas arrived at Alexandria we came to Epaphrodeitos and it was learned that he had neither received nor paid anything. Consequently, I want you to know this that I have given instructions to him that he proceed to Takona on account of the rents and now have given him authority over the whole matter. Whatever he may stand in need of from you, assist him in that, as he will be as agreeable for you as he is for me. Because I was distracted by my (aforesaid) situation, I was unable to meet Apollonios the Libyan in order to tell him these same things. And you must write to me about whatever you want and I will willingly do it, for Damas has agreed (to do) all things for me. It is well that he arrive as quickly as possible, for he will instruct you. Take care of yourself to stay well. Look after all your folks. Good-bye. (Year) 29 of Caesar, Phaophi 6.

ἐν οἷς ἐὰν σοῦ προσδεῆται συνπροσ-
γενέσθαι αὐτῶι ὡς ἀνθομολογη(σομένῳ)
35 ὑπέρ σου οὕτως ὡς ὑπ(έρ) μου. ἐν τῷ δέ
με περισπᾶσθαι οὐκ ἠδυνάσθην
συντυχεῖν Ἀπολλω(νίῳ) τῷ Λιβικῷ ἵνα
αὐτῷ αὐτὰ ταῦτα ὑποδίξω. καὶ σὺ
δὲ ὑπὲρ ὧν ἐὰν θέλῃς γράφε μοι καὶ ἀνό-
40 κνως ποήσω, Δαμᾶς γάρ μοι ἀνθωμολ(ογήσατο)
πάντα. καλῶς δὲ γέγονεν τὸ ταχὺ
αὐτὸν ἐλθεῖν, ὑφηγήσεται γάρ σοι.
[σ]εατο(ῦ) ἐπιμε(λοῦ) ἵν᾽ ὑγι(αίνῃς). ἐπισκοπ(οῦ) τοὺς
σοὺς πάντε(ς).
ἔρρω[σο.]   (ἔτους) κθ Καίσαρος, Φαῶ(φι) ϛ.

18 Hunt and Grenfell, the editors of POxy 743, suggest that probably some word like οἰκονόμον should be supplied, i.e., "the *household* of Caesar."
22 Read ὅλως.
23 Read ἀπώλεσεν.
34 ἀνθομολογη(σομένῳ): see PTebt I 26.6; PParis 42.7.
43 Read πάντα(ς).

72 HILARION TO ALIS
POxy IV 744

1 BCE

This frequently reprinted text concerns a native of Oxyrhynchos who, at the time of writing, is away in Alexandria trying to earn a livelihood for the family at home. Though the writer, Hilarion, addresses Alis as sister, it is clear that she is his wife. "Sister" might be only an endearing form of address, as suggested previously, but it is probably to be taken literally here, i.e., this is a brother and sister marriage. Berous, who is also greeted at the beginning and who is called "my lady," is probably the mother of the two correspondents. Apollonarion, in turn, is the child of the couple.

Alis, who had apparently become concerned about Hilarion's extended stay in Alexandria and by the fact that he had neither written nor sent money home, conveyed her worry to Aphrodisias, who was going to Alexandria. When he arrived at the city Aphrodisias carried these concerns to Hilarion. Consequently, the present letter is written by Hilarion in response to Alis' concern. We do not know why Hilarion's fellow laborers were returning home and he was not, nor do we know why his wages have not yet been paid.

As confirmation of the practice of exposing infants, mentioned in lines 8–10 of the present letter, Deissmann cites a striking parallel in Apuleius' *Metamorphoses*: "a man setting out on a journey orders his wife, who is in expectation of becoming a mother, to kill the child immediately if it should prove to be a girl" (*Ancient East*, p. 170).

Ἱλαρίων{α} Ἄλιτι τῇ ἀδελφῇ πλεῖστα χαίρειν καὶ Βεροῦτι τῇ κυρίᾳ μου καὶ Ἀπολλω-
νάριν. γίνωσκε ὡς ἔτι καὶ νῦν ἐν Ἀλεξαν-
δρε(ί)ᾳ (ἐ)σμεν· μὴ ἀγωνιᾷς ἐὰν ὅλως εἰσ-
5 πορεύονται, ἐγὼ ἐν Ἀλεξανδρε(ί)ᾳ μένω.
ἐρωτῶ σε καὶ παρακαλῶ σε, ἐπιμελή-
θ(ητ)ι τῷ παιδίῳ καὶ ἐὰν εὐθὺς ὀψώνιον λάβωμεν ἀποστελῶ σε ἄνω. ἐὰν
πολλὰ πολλῶν τέκῃς, ἐὰν ᾖ{ν} ἄρσε-

Hilarion to his sister Alis many greetings, likewise to my lady Berous and to Apollonarion. Know that we are even yet in Alexandria. Do not worry if they all come back (except me) and I remain in Alexandria. I urge and entreat you, be concerned about the child and if I should receive my wages soon, I will send them up to you. If by chance you bear a child, if it is a boy, let it be, if it is a girl, cast it out. You have said to Aphrodisias, "Do not forget me."

10   νον, ἄφες, ἐὰν ᾖ⟨ν⟩ θήλεα, ἔκβαλε.
      εἴρηκας δὲ Ἀφροδισιᾶτι ὅτι μή με
      ἐπιλάθῃς. πῶς δύναμαί σε ἐπι-
      λαθεῖν; ἐρωτῶ σε οὖν ἵνα μὴ ἀγω-
      νιάσῃς.
15   (ἔτους) κθ Καίσαρος, Παῦνι κγ.

Verso: Ἱλαρίων Ἄλιτι ἀπόδος.

How can I forget you?. Therefore I urge you not to worry. (Year) 29 of Caesar, Payni 23.

Outside address: Deliver from Hilarion to Alis.

---

2   Read Ἀπολλωναρίῳ.
8   Read σοι.
8-10 ἐὰν πολλὰ πολλῶν τέκῃς: this is the corrected reading in SelPap I 105, where Grenfell and Hunt translate πολλα πολλῶν as "if by chance." The original editor of POxy 744 construed πολλαπολλων, by contrast, as a misspelling of Apollonarion (see line 2). Witkowski (*Epistulae privatae*, pp. 97f., 131ff.) thought the phrase implied a wish and so he translated it as something like "great, good luck."
9-10 ἦν ..., ... ἦν: the imperfect form is apparently a mistake, an illiterate spelling of ᾖ (according to Deissmann, *Ancient East*, p. 169, n. 6).

Five letters in volume 2 of the Tebtunis Papyri were written to Akousilaos, often addressed simply as Akous. Though the letters span a rather long period from 3–27 CE, the evidence strongly suggests that Akousilaos and Akous were the same person. For example, PTebt 408, 409 and 289, though they span twenty years, were found together. Further, both variations of the name which we find elsewhere in the correspondence occur together in 409, where the dioiketes is called both Akousilaos and Akous. Even though there is a break of eleven years between PTebt 409 (5 CE) and 410 (16 CE), and Akous is designated dioiketes in 409 but toparch in 410, two men referred to in 410, Soterichos the stonemason and Lysimachos the village secretary, are also mentioned in earlier correspondence with Akous. Lysimachos appears both in 408 and 409; Soterichos appears in 408. The coincidences seem so striking as to assure us that Akousilaos the dioiketes and Akousilaos the toparch are one and the same.

The editors of this correspondence, Grenfell and Hunt, suggest that since Akous first occupied the office of dioiketes and later the position of toparch, the office of toparch was superior to the office of dioiketes at this time. In the days of the early Ptolemies, by contrast, the office of dioiketes was occupied by such figures as Apollonios, who was the chief financial minister under Ptolemy Philadelphos (see letters 5–26).

Four of the five letters to Akous are included here. The fifth, PTebt II 462, is listed only in the "Descriptions" of PTebt II, p. 308. There we are told that the letter consists of fourteen fragmented lines and that it is dated to the thirteenth year of Tiberius (27 CE). The first three letters in this collection are cordial in tone and appear to be written by friends and social peers of Akous. The last, on the other hand, which is quite threatening, is written by the strategos who accuses Akous of negligence in the performance of his duties.

73   HIPPOLITOS TO AKOUSILAOS
PTebt II 408   3 CE

Hippolitos entreats Akousilaos to curb the generosity of the writer's sons who, out of affection for Soterichos' people, would like to give away wheat to them. We do not have detailed information about the nature of the friendship between Hippolitos and Akous, because this is the only place where the writer's name occurs together with Akous'. The familiarity of the two is evident in Hippolitos' use of endearing terms in his opening salutation, and by his offer to repay the favor which he asks of Akous.

Two people who are mentioned here, Soterichos and Lysimachos, do appear elsewhere in the correspondence. Lysimachos is identified as the village secretary (komogrammateus) in PTebt 410 (letter 76) and the manner in which he is referred to there, as well as in PTebt 409 (letter 75), suggest that he and Akous worked closely with each other. Soterichos is identified as a stonemason in PTebt 410 (letter 76).

Ἱππόλιτος Ἀκουσιλά-
ω τῷ φ[ι]λτάτῳ πλεῖ-
στα χαίρειν. ἐπιστά-
μενος πῶς σε τίθε-
5 μαι κὲ φιλῶ, παρα-
καλῶ σε περὶ υἱῶν
μου τῆι φιλοστορ-
γίᾳ τῶν περὶ Σωτή-
ριχον μὴ ἐᾶσαι
10 πυρὸν αὐτοῖς δοθῆ-
ναι. ἔγραψα δὲ καὶ
Λυσ[ι]μάχῳ τῶι φιλ-
τάτῳ μου περὶ τῶν
αὐτῶν ὡς καὶ σοί. μὴ
15 οὖν ἄλλως ποιήσῃς,
καὶ σὺ δὲ περὶ ὧν βούλε[ι]
γράφε, τὰ δ᾽ ἄλλα ἵν᾽ ὑ(γιαίνῃς).
ἔρρ(ωσο). (ἔτους) λβ Καίσαρος, Ἐπεὶφ ιε.

Verso: διο[ι]κ[ητ]ῆι Ἀκ[ο]υ[σιλάω.

Hippolitos to his dearest Akousilaos many greetings. Since you know how I respect and love you, I urge you regarding my sons not to allow them to give wheat to Soterichos' people out of their (the sons') affection for them. I also wrote to my beloved Lysimachos about the same people as well as to you. Therefore, (see that) you do not act otherwise, and you too must write about whatever you want; for the rest, (take care) to stay well. Goodbye. (Year) 32 of Caesar, Epeiph 15.

Outside address: To the dioiketes, Akousilaos.

3   Read ἐπιστάμενον.
5   Read καί.
7-10 As the editors of PTebt 408, Grenfell and Hunt, suggested, αὐτοῖς probably refers to Soterichos' dependents. The writer's wish is that his sons be prevented from giving wheat to these dependents, τῶν περὶ Σωτήριχον (τῶν is an objective genitive after φιλοστοργία). Hippolitos would probably not have objected to wheat being given to the sons, as would be the meaning if αὐτοῖς referred to the sons and τῶν were a subjective genitive.

74   DŌRIŌN TO AKOUSILAOS
PTebt II 409   5 CE

Dorion reminds Akousilaos that he had been given twelve drachmas, which were to be forwarded to Lysimachos who, in turn, was supposed to send three sound he-asses (?) to Dorion. Lysimachos is apparently the person of the same name in the immediately preceding letter, written two years earlier. It appears that Akous and Lysimachos had some type of working association in the sale of asses. This is the only occasion in which Dorion's name occurs.

Δωρίων Ἀκουσιλάωι [τ]ῶι
διοικητῆι πλεῖστα χαίρειν
καὶ διὰ παντὸς ὑγιαίνειν. ἐπὶ
τῆς πόλεώς σε ἠρώτησα δούς σοι
5 (δραχμὰς) ιβ ὅπως Λυσιμάχῳ δοῖς καὶ ἐ-
ρωτήσῃς αὐτὸν οἱ περ ἐμοῦ ὅπως
γ τελήους μοίκλεας συντόμως
πέμψῃι, εἰδὼ[ς ὅ]τι ἐξ[ι]ουσίαν
αὐτῶν ἔχει καὶ Λυσίμαχος καὶ σύ.
10 [σὲ] δὲ ἠρώτησα, φί[λτ]ατέ μου,

Dorion to Akousilaos the dioiketes many greetings and continued good health. At the city I gave twelve drachmas to you and asked that you give them to Lysimachos and that you ask him on my behalf to send three he-asses without blemish immediately, because I knew that both Lysimachos and you had an ample supply of them. I asked you, my dear friend, because I knew that it was convenient for you and that I will have sound animals, without blemish and good-tempered, on

εἰδὼς ὅτι ἐπιτ[ηδιό]ν [σο]ι [κ]αὶ
καλοὺς ἕξωι καὶ τελήους καὶ εὐ-
νοικοὺς διὰ σέ.   ἔρρω(σο). (ἔτους) λδ Καίσαρος,
    Π[α]ῦ(νι) κα.

Verso: εἰς] π[ό]λιν Ἀκοῦτι διοικητῆι.

account of you. Good-bye. (Year) 34 of Caesar, Payni 21.

Outside address: To Akous, dioiketes, at the city.

6   Read ὑπέρ.
7   The editors of this text suggested that μύκλους should be read instead of μοίκλεας; noting that according to Hesychius the Phocaeans called a he-ass μύχλος.

75   HERMIAS TO AKOUSILAOS
PTebt II 410   16 CE

By the time this letter was written, some eleven years later than the preceding one (letter 74), Akous no longer occupied the office of dioiketes but now held the position of toparch. Apparently, it is in his capacity as toparch that he is requested by Hermias to do something about the encroachment of a neghbor upon the property of Soterichos. This is the only time that we hear from Hermias in letters sent to Akous. It is not clear why he has intervened on behalf of Soterichos.

Ἑρμίας Ἀκουσιλάωι τῶι
φιλτάτωι πλεῖστα χαίρειν.
Σωτηρίχω[ι] τῶι λάξωι
.. [.] πρόσεχε χάριν οὗ
5   παρορίζεται ὑπὸ γίτονος
ἐωνημένου τῶν γιτνιωσῶν
αὐτῷ ε ... [.] Λυσιμάχω
τ[ῷ]ι [κωμο]γραμματεῖ. μν[ή-]
σθητι ὡ[ς] ἐν τῷ Τρ[ι]στόμω με
10   ἐφιλοτ[ι]μοῦ σὺν ἐμοὶ μεῖναι.
ἐρωτῶ σε ταχύτερον συσ-
χεῖν τ[ὸ] πρᾶγμα ἵνα κδ ἐρχό-
μενος πρὸς ἐμὲ ὁ Σωτήριχος
[ἀνθο]μολογήσηται περὶ τῆς
15   σπ[ο]υδῆς τὰ διπ ( ).   ἔρρω(σο).
    (ἔτους) γ Τιβερ[ίο]υ Καίσαρος Σεβαστοῦ,
    μη(νὸς) Νέου Σεβα(στοῦ) ιζ.

Verso: Ἀκουσιλάω]ι τοπάρχηι Τεβτύνε(ως).

Hermias to his dearest Akousilaos many greetings. Be concerned about Soterichos the stonemason on account of (his) being encroached upon by a neighbor who has bought some of the adjoining property, . . . (and inform?) Lysimachos the village secretary. Remember how eager you were in Tristomos to remain with me. I ask you to conclude the matter very quickly in order that when Soterichos comes to me on the twenty-fourth he may give an account concerning your zeal. . . . Good-bye. (Year) 3 of Tiberius Caesar Augustus, the seventeenth of the month Neos Sebastos.

Outside address: To Akousilaos, toparch of Tebtunis.

The editors of PTebt 410, Grenfell and Hunt, note that the following corrections have been made on the text: οy of υπο γιτονος has been corrected in line 5; in line 11 the first τ or ταχυτερον has been corrected from χ and the second σ of συσχειν has been corrected; the ν of ερχομενος is corrected in line 12.

76 APOLLŌNIOS TO AKOUS
PTebt II 289
23 CE

This letter from the strategos to Akous is very different in mood from the three preceding letters. The strategos demands a supplementary and up to date report on tax payments. It is obvious from his threat to dismiss Akous, should the report not be satisfactory, that Akous is being accused of negligence in the performance of his office.

['Α]πολλώνιος στρατηγὸς 'Ακοῦτι
τοπάρχῃ Τεβτύνεως χαίρειν.
ἐξαυτῆς πέμπε μοι πρόσγραφον
τῶν μέχρι τῆς σήμερον διαγεγρ(αμμένων)
5   κατ᾽ εἶδος, οὕτως γὰρ γνώσομαι
πότερον ἐπὶ τόπων σε ἐάσω
πράττοντά τι ἢ μεταπεμψάμε(νος)
πέμψωι τῶι ἡγεμ[όνι] ὡς ἀ[με-]
λοῦντα τῆς εἰσπρά[ξεως].
10   ἔρρωσο.
(ἔτους) ἐνάτου Τιβερίου Καίσαρος Σεβαστοῦ,
Μεχ(εὶρ) κα.

Verso: ['Ακοῦτι] τ[ο]π[ά]ρ[χ(η)] Τεβτύν(εως).

Apollonios, strategos, to Akous, toparch of Tebtunis, greeting. Send at once to me a supplementary statement of what has been entered (paid), up to date and according to class; for I will know by this means whether I will allow you to manage things where you are or to summon you in order to send you to the prefect for negligence in the collection of taxes. Good-bye. Ninth (year) of Tiberius Caesar Augustus, Mecheir 21.

Outside address: (To Akous), toparch of Tebtunis.

---

3   See BGU II 457 (II CE) for an example of a πρόσγραφον submitted by a village secretary (see also POxy III 513.34 [II CE]).

In this letter of recommendation, Apollonios introduces a member of his household to the good graces of the strategos Sarapion, who is also addressed as *gymnasiarch*. This particular combination of offices is striking. Whereas the office of strategos (governor) was civil and military and rendered in the service of Rome, the office of gymnasiarch was an honorary position associated with the metropolis (the capital of each nome) and was not a position in government. There were some six metropolitan committees or offices, five of which continued from Ptolemaic times, all of which were concerned with metropolite social caste and its attendant activities within each nome capital. A gymnasiarch, who usually held his office for one year, had the responsibility of assuring the day-to-day operation of the gymnasium and, in particular, providing the basic supplies of such operation, e.g., fuel for hot water and oil for anointing and illumination.

The oddity in the description of Sarapion as strategos and gymnasiarch is that he combines the two functions simultaneously. J. G. Tait ("Strategi and Royal Scribes," pp. 166ff.) gave evidence to show that from the time of Augustus' reform onward, governors (strategoi) were never placed in charge of a nome where they had either previously lived or held property. A gymnasiarch, by contrast, would have held office in his own metropolis. One might make the case that Sarapion was governor in one nome and, though absent, discharging the financial obligations of the gymnasiarch in another capital. Or, one could argue, as Tait does, that the office of gymnasiarch was in this case only an honorary title given to Sarapion by the gymnasium of the place where he had been appointed strategos. But it seems more likely, as the editors of this text, Rees, Bell and Barns, suggest, the Augustan rule to which we referred had not yet been enforced. Namely, Sarapion may well have been both strategos and gymnasiarch in the same nome where he lived.

Ἀπολλώνιος Σαραπίωνι τῶι
[σ]τρατη[γῶι] καὶ γυμνασιάρχωι
πλεῖστα χ[αίρ]ειν καὶ διὰ παντὸς
ὑ[γ]ιαίνειν. Ἰ[σί]δωρος [ὁ] φέρων σοι
        τ
5 τὴν ἐπισ[[θ]]ολὴν ἔστιν μου ἐκ τῆς
οἰκίας. ἐρωτηθεὶς ἔχε αὐτὸν
συνεσταμένον, καὶ ὑπὲρ ὧν ἐὰν
σοι προσέλθῃ, εἰς τὴν ἐμὴν καταλο-
γήν ποήσον αὐτῶι. τοῦτο δὲ ποήσας
10 ἔσῃ μοι κεχαρ[ισ]μένος. καὶ σὺ δὲ
περὶ ὧν ἐὰν αἴρῃ σήμανον, καὶ
ἀνόκνως ποήσωι πρὸς αὐτῶν ὅμοια.
ἐπιμέλου σεαυτοῦ ἵν᾽ ὑγι(αίνῃς).   ἔρρωσο.
(ἔτους) λϛ Καίσαρος, Φαῶπ(ι) κϛ

Verso: ἀπόδ(ος)   [Σ]αραπίων[ι στ]ρ[ατη]γ[ῷ].

Apollonios to Sarapion, the strategos and gymnasiarch, many greetings and continual good health. Isidoros, who carries this letter to you, is a member of my household. Please regard him as recommended and, about what he should approach you, do it for him on my account. By doing this, I shall be favored by you. Moreover, in turn, you indicate whatever you should choose, and I shall act accordingly without hesitation. Take care of yourself to stay well. Good-bye. (Year) 36 of Caesar, Phaophi 26.

Outside address: Deliver to Sarapion the strategos.

     τ
5 ἐπισ[[θ]]ολήν: the writer himself corrected the original error with the raised letter.
6 ἐρωτηθείς: the editor of this text translated this passive participle as "please" (i.e., "Please consider him introduced to you, and . . ."). For support of this meaning he offered the following examples of the same usage: PGen 74.8; POxy II 269, col. II, line 4 (57 CE); BGU II 596.9; and see Deissmann, *Bible Studies*, p. 195; Meecham, *Light from Ancient Letters*, pp 57f., 122.
14 Read Φαῶφι.

78 THEŌN TO HIS BROTHER HĒRAKLEIDĒS
POxy IV 746

16 CE

Theon writes to his brother Herakleides, a basiliko-grammateus (royal secretary), to recommend the letter carrier, Hermophilos. The same Theon may also be the author of the following letter of introduction; the brother who is recommended to the dioiketes is, as here, also named Herakleides. Grenfell and Hunt, the editors of this letter, found it surprising, and rightly so, that a basiliko-grammateus would have more than one nome under his jurisdiction, as the outside address appears to indicate.

Θέων Ἡρακλείδηι τῶι ἀδελφῶι
πλεῖστα χαίρειν καὶ ὑγιαίνειν.
Ἑρμόφιλος ⟨ὁ⟩ ἀποδ[ι]δούς σοι τὴν
ἐπιστολήν [ἐ]στ[ι] . [. .] . κ[. .]μ . φ[.]ηρι

5 [.]ερίου, καὶ ἠρώτησέν με γράψαι σοι.
[π]ροφέρεται ἔχειν πραγμάτιον
[ἐν τῆι] Κερκεμούνι. τοῦτο οὖν ἐὰν
σοι φα[ί]νηται σπουδάσεις κατὰ τὸ
δίκαιον. τὰ δ' ἄλλα σεαυτοῦ ἐπιμελοῦ

10 ἵν ὑγιαίνῃς.
     ἔρρωσο.
   (ἔτους) γ Τιβερίου Καίσαρος Σεβαστοῦ, Φαῶφι γ.

Verso: Ἡρακλείδηι βα(σιλικῶι) γρ(αμματεῖ)
       Ὀξυ(ρυγχίτου) (Κυνοπ)(ολίτου).

Theon to his brother Herakleides many greetings and good health. Hermophilos, who carries this letter to you, is (the friend or relative) of . . . erios, and he asked me to write to you. He (Hermophilos) declares that he has business at Kerkemounis. Therefore, if it meets with your approval, you will make an effort to assist him, as is right. For the rest, take care to stay well. Good-bye. (Year) 3 of Tiberius Caesar Augustus, Phaophi 3.

Outside address: To Herakleides, the basiliko-grammateus of the Oxyrhynchite and Kynopolite nomes.

4f. The description of Hermopilos as a friend or relative of someone whose name ends in "erios" is conjectural, owing to the fragmented condition of line 4 and the beginning of line 5.

79 THEŌN TO TYRANNOS
POxy II 292

ca. 25 CE

In this second letter of introduction (see letter 78), Theon introduces his brother Herakleides to the dioiketes, Tyrannos. This letter is in the same hand as POxy 291, which immediately follows and which is also addressed to Tyrannos. Because of the fine, bold, semi-uncial hand of the writer, the editor of the two texts suggests that both were written by a professional scribe who was probably attached to the strategos.

Θέων Τυράννωι τῶι τιμιωτάτωι
     πλεῖστα χαίρειν.
Ἡρακλείδης ὁ ἀποδιδούς σοι τὴν
ἐπιστολήν ἐστίν μου ἀδελφός·

5 διὸ παρακαλῶ σε μετὰ πάσης δυνά-
μεως ἔχειν αὐτὸν συνεσταμένον. ἠρώτησα δὲ καὶ Ἑρμί[α]ν
τὸν ἀδελφὸν διὰ γραπτοῦ ἀνηγεῖ[σθαί
σοι περὶ τούτου. χαρίεσαι δέ μοι τὰ μέγιστα

10 ἐὰν σου τῆς ἐπισημασίας τύχηι.

Theon to his esteemed Tyrannos many greetings. Herakleides, who carries this letter to you, is my brother. Wherefore, I entreat you with all my power to regard him recommended. I have also asked your brother Hermias through correspondence to talk with you about him. You will grant the greatest favor to me if he receives your attention. Above all I pray that you may have health and fare most excellently, unharmed by enchantment (the evil eye). Good-bye.

πρὸ δὲ πάντων ὑγια⟨ί⟩νειν σε εὔχ[ο-
μαι ἀβασκάντως τὰ ἄριστα
πράττων.   ἔρρω(σο).

Verso: Τυράννωι διοικ(ητῇ).

Outside address: To Tyrannos, dioiketes.

___

9   σοι περί is inserted above the line. Read χαρίσει.
12 ἀβασκάντως: this expression or wish occurs with
    some frequency in letters, generally near the
    closing, and seems to imply enchantment with
    the evil eye.

80 CHAIREAS TO TYRANNOS
POxy II 291

25–26 CE

Chaireas, the strategos of the Oxyrhynchite nome (see POxy 246.1) instructs Tyrannos, a dioiketes, to make sure that the list of arrears on the payment of grain and money be collected, so that everything is ready for Chaireas when he arrives. Tyrannos, the dioiketes, was also the recipient of letter 79.

We noted above (see the introduction to letters 73–76) that already in the early Roman rule of Egypt the status of dioiketes had been diminished considerably. The tone of letter 76, and of the present letter, shows that the office of dioiketes at this time was inferior to the office of strategos. One may note that even in the Ptolemaic period there seem to have been officials besides the chief minister of the treasury at Alexandria, with the same title of dioiketes. Other financial officials of the nome, such as the *oikonomos* and the *antigrapheus*, served under the control of these officials. Even when allowance is made for a subordinate form of the office, however, it still had been diminished in its status by the time of the Roman rule.

Χαιρέας Τυράννωι τῶι φιλτάτωι
          πλεῖστα χαίρειν.
τ[ὴν] ἔκθεσιν τοῦ ιβ̄ (ἔτους) Τιβερίου
Καί[σαρ]ος Σεβαστοῦ σειτικὴν καὶ
5   ἀρ[γ]υρικὴν εὐθέως γράψον,
ἐ[πεὶ] Σεουῆρος μοι ἐνετείλατο
πρὸς ἀπαίτησιν· καὶ προέγρα-
ψ[ά σοι] ἀνδραγαθῖ[ν] καὶ ἀπαιτεῖν
μ[έχ]ρι ὑγια[ί]νων παρ[α]γένωμαι.
10 [μὴ ο]ὖν ἀμελήσῃς καὶ τὰ ἀπὸ
[. (ἔτους) μ]έχρι ῑᾱ (ἔτους) ἑτο[ῖ]μα ποίησον
[εἰς τὴ]ν ἀπαίτησιν σιτικὰ καὶ
[ἀργυρικά].
          ἔρρωσο.

Verso: Τυράννωι   διοικητῆι.

Chaireas to his dearest Tyrannos many greetings. Write out immediately the list (of arrears) both on grain and money for the twelfth year of Tiberius Caesar Augustus, since Severus has instructed me on their return of payment. I already wrote to you previously to be firm and to demand payment until I myself should arrive in sound health. Therefore, do not neglect this matter, but make ready the account on grain and money from the . . . up to the eleventh year for the return of payment. Good-bye.

Outside address: To Tyrannos, dioiketes.

___

3   ἔκθεσιν: κ is written above χ which has not been
    deleted. Regarding the above meaning of *ekthesis*
    as "list of arrears," see POxy II 272, note to line
    18.
4   Read σιτικήν.
8   Read ἀνδραγαθεῖν.

HERMOGENES TO THE PROPHET, HARUŌTĒS
POxy XII 1480

32 CE

Priests of a certain rank in Egypt were called prophet; nominally they were interpreters of oracles and revelations. In this poorly spelled letter from a certain Hermogenes to a prophet named Haruotes, Hermogenes informs Haruotes what he has been doing on his behalf. Apparently, Haruotes was seeking to delay the payment on something, which was of concern to such state officials as the *eklogistes* (the auditor of the nome tax accounts; see POxy XII 1436, note to line 23) and the komogrammateus (village secretary).

Ἑρμογένης Ἀρυώτῃ
τῷ προφήτῃ καὶ φιλ-
τάτῳ πλῖστα χαί(ρειν)
καὶ διὰ παντὸς ὑγιέ(νειν).
5 οὐκ ἠμέλησα περὶ
οὗ μοι ἐπιτέταχας·
ἐπορεύθην πρὸς
Ἑρμογένην τὸν κω-
μογρ[α]μματέαν, καὶ
10 ὁμολόγησέ μοι ποῆσε
τὴν ἀναβολήν· πεπόη-
τε εἰς τὸν ἐκλογιστήν.
λυπὸν ἠὰν δύνῃ ἐ[π]ισ-
τολὴν λαβῖν παρ' αὐ-
15 τοῦ τοῦ ἐκλογισ[τοῦ
ὡς Ἑρμογένει, ἵν[α
μὴ σχῆ τ[...]..[..,
παρακαλῶ [σε με-
γάλως π[έμψαι
20 τῷ υἱῷ μ[ου φά-
σιν μοι λ[......
περὶ αὐ[τοῦ ...,
καὶ γράψ[ον μοι περὶ
ὧν ἠ[ὰ]ν δύν[ω-
25 με κα[ὶ] ἡδή[ως
ποήσω.   ἔρρω[σο.
(ἔτους) ιη Τιβερίου Καίσαρος
Σεβαστοῦ, Μεχ(εὶρ) ιθ.

Verso: [ἀπόδ(ος) Ἁ]ρυώτῃ προφήτῃ παρὰ
Ἑρμογ(ένους) Ἡρακ(λ   ).

Hermogenes to Haruotes the prophet and my dear (friend), many greetings and continual good health. I was not negligent about what you instructed me to do; I proceeded to Hermogenes the komogrammateus and he agreed to allow the delay (of payment?). He progressed (with the matter) as far as the eklogistes (?). For the rest, if you can get a letter from the eklogistes himself as well as from Hermogenes, lest he have the . . . , I strongly encourage you to communicate with my son for me . . . and write to me about whatever I could do and I shall do it willingly. Good-bye. (Year) 18 of Tiberius Caesar Augustus, Mecheir 19.

Outside address: Deliver to Haruotes the prophet from Hermogenes, son of Herakl . . .

---

4   Read ὑγιαί(νειν).
10   Read ὡμολόγησε . . . ποῆσαι.
11   Read πεπόηται. ἀναβολήν: the editor of this text suggests that since this word is generally used in a literal sense in the papyri (e.g. with ναυβίων in BGU II 593.3), the meaning here is uncertain.
13   Read λοιπὸν ἐάν.
13–14 τ of ἐ[π]ιστολήν is corrected from κ.
24–25 Read ἐ[ὰ]ν δύν[ω]μαι . . . ἡδέ[ως.
27   The second ι of τιβεριον is corrected from ο.
29   The second α of παρά is above the line.

These four letters, three from the Rylands collection (PRyl II 229–31) and one from the British Museum collection (PLond III 893), were all written by Ammonios to Aphrodisios. The occupation of both men and the specific nature of their business relationship is unclear, though the tone of the correspondence indicates that they were social peers and friends.

Aphrodisios is referred to as epistates on the outside address of letter 82. The original editors of the letter (PRyl II 229) translated epistates as "agent," namely, agent on behalf of Ammonios. However, epistates refers much more often to a type of public office in the papyri than to a private occupation. In any case, Ammonios' instructions to Aphrodisios are personal and concerned with farm stock and produce. Consequently, it appears that Aphrodisios was a steward over the farm that belonged to Ammonios, and, perhaps, to other individuals as well.

Ammonios, for his part, was probably an absentee owner of farm property and livestock. It is more difficult to determine his ordinary occupation apart from the farm, though he is on board a boat in letter 82 and pressing grapes in letter 85. Letters from Alypios to Heroneinos in the third century CE (see PFlor II 127, 137, 142, 162; PRyl II 238; PFay 133), in which Heroneinos is the steward (φοοντιστής) of Alypios' farm, are analogous to this letter.

82   AMMŌNIOS TO APHRODISIOS
PRyl II 229   38 CE

In this letter, Ammonios notifies Aphrodisios about three business matters which concerned him, but which were being transacted through Herakleos and Ophelion. Then, he instructs Aphrodisios to follow up on one of these matters and to attend to other things which, for the most part, involved provisions required for feeding farm animals.

'Αμμώνιος 'Αφροδισίωι τῶι
  φιλτάτωι χαίρειν.
ἔγραψα ἐπιστολὴν πρὸς 'Ηράκλη(ον)
τὸν π[ρ]οβατοκτη(νοτρόφον) ἵνα δοῖ σοι ὄνον,
5 καὶ 'Ωφελίωνι ἐνετειλάμην
ἵνα καὶ αὐτὸς δοῖ ἑτέραν καὶ τοὺς
ἄρτους μοι πέμψηι. ἐπεὶ οὖν
ἔπεμψάς μοι (ἀρτάβας) γ ἐρωτῶ σε
ἐκ παντὸς τρόπου εὐθέως μοι
10 πέ[μ]ψαι τὰς ἄλλας (ἀρτάβας) γ καὶ τὸ
ὀψάριον, ἐπεὶ ἐν πλοίῳ εἰμί.
περὶ δὲ τῆς τροφῆς τῶν χοιριδίω(ν)
καὶ τοῦ λοιπ(οῦ) τῆς τιμῆ(ς) τοῦ χόρτου πρό-
χρησον ἕως οὗ παραγένωμαι,

Ammonios to his dearest Aphrodisios greeting. I wrote a letter to Herakleos the herdsman to give an ass to you and I instructed Ophelion also to give another to you and to send the loaves to me. Therefore, since you (already?) sent three artabs, I ask you by all means to send the remaining three artabs immediately and the pickled fish, since I am on board a boat. Concerning the pigs' fodder and the rest of the price of the hay, make the advance (payment) until I arrive, for I expect to make an account with you. I entrusted everything to you. Therefore urge your wife with my words in order that she be concerned about the pigs; also take care of the calf. By all means, Aphrodisios, send the

15   δοκῶ γὰρ συναιρόμενος πρὸς σὲ
     λογάριον. παρεδεξάμην σοι πάντα.
     παρακάλεσον οὖν τὴν γυναῖκά
     σου τοῖς ἐμοῖς λόγοις ἵνα ἐπιμελῆ-
     ται τῶν χοιριδίων· ἐπιμελοῦ δὲ
20   καὶ τοῦ μόσχου. πάντω(s) δέ, Ἀφροδίσιε,
     τοὺς ἄρτους μοι πέμψον καὶ τὸ ὀψάριον,
     ἐὰν δὲ θέλῃς γράψον μοι τίνι
     δῶ εἰς τὸν χόρτο(ν) καὶ εἰς τροφὴ(ν) ἄλλας (δραχμὰς) κ.
         ἔρρω(σο). (ἔτους) β Γαίου Καίσαρος Σεβαστοῦ
         Γερμανικο(ῦ), Μεχ(εὶρ) κς.

Verso: Ἀφροδισίωι ἐπιστάτῃ.

loaves and the pickled fish to me, and if you would, write me to whom I should pay the further twenty drachmas for the hay and the fodder. Good-bye. (Year) 2 of Gaius Caesar Augustus Germanicus, Mecheir 26.

Outside address: To Aphrodisios, epistates.

---

8   The first ε of επεμψας is corrected from τ.
22-24 Owing to the lack of space at the bottom, these
     lines were written in the top margin.

83   AMMŌNIOS TO APHRODISIOS
PRyl II 230   40 CE

Ammonios informs Aphrodisios that he has received a letter, apparently from Aphrodisios, and that he is complying with what Aphrodisios had written. Then he instructs Aphrodisios to get an unguent, an item of great concern, since Ammonios interprets failure to get it as an act of alienation. Finally, Ammonios greets the family of Aphrodisios and it is likely that Aphrodisios' "sister" is also his wife.

     Ἀμμώνιος Ἀφροδισίωι τῶι
         φιλτάτωι χαίρειν.
     ἐκομισάμην ἐπιστολὴ(ν) περὶ τοῦ
     πέμψαι με ἐπὶ τοὺς ἄρτους τῇ ε.
5   πέμψω οὖν τοὺς ὄνους τῆι η
     πρὸς σὲ π[ά]ντως. παρακληθ[εὶ]s
     οὖν ἐκ παντὸς τρόπου ποίησον
     γενέσθαι μοι τὸ ζμῆμα ἀπὸ τοῦ
     ὀρόβ[ο]υ, μὴ [ο]ὖν ἄλλως ποιή[σ]ῃ(s) μὴ ἵνα
10   δόξωμέν σε εὐθέως ἠλλάχθαι
     τὰ πρὸς ἡμᾶς. ἀσπάζου Θέρμιο(ν) τὴ(ν)
     ἀδελφὴν καὶ τὰ παιδία σο(υ).   ἔρρω(σο). (ἔτους) ε,
     μη(νὸς) Νέ(ου) Σεβαστοῦ ς Σεβαστῆι.

Verso: Ἀφροδισίωι τῷ φι[λ]τ(άτῳ).

Ammonios to his dearest Aphrodisios greeting. I received a letter instructing me to send for the loaves on the fifth. Accordingly, I will send the donkeys to you promptly on the eighth. Please make every effort to get the unguent for me from the vetch (lentil?) plant; do not act otherwise, lest we think that suddenly you have become alienated toward us. Salute Thermion, your sister, and children. Good-bye. (Year) 5, Neos Sebastos 6.

Outside address: To my dearest Aphrodisios.

---

6   The παρα of παρακληθείς is written over ex-
     punged letters.
9   Read ἵνα μή.
13   Σεβαστῆι: see the explanation on PRyl II 144,
     note to line 5.

84 AMMŌNIOS TO APHRODISIOS
PRyl II 231

40 CE

Like the two preceding letters, this one is concerned with affairs on Ammonios' farm, to which Aphrodisios is urged to attend. The writer's sense of urgency is communicated both by the relative brevity of the letter and by the sequence of subject matters, e.g., the closing greetings are given following the farewell, and a postscript is appended to the date.

Johnson, Martin, and Hunt, the editors of this text, observed how Ammonios' haste in writing has made the letters much larger than they would normally be (see line 13).

Ἀμμώνιος Ἀφροδισίωι τῷ φ[ι]λτ(άτῳ)
    χαίρειν.
τ[οὺ]ς ἄρτους καλῶς ποιήσεις εἰπὼ(ν)
γενέσθαι καὶ τὴν ἐλᾶν μοι
5 ταρειχεύσας καὶ πέμψας
μοι φάσιν ἵνα πέμψω ἐπὶ
αὐτούς. τὸν πυρὸν τὸν ἐν
τῷ θησαυρῶι μεταβαλοῦ
δι[ὰ] τὴν βροχὴν τὸν πάντα.
10   ἔρρωσο. ἀσπάζου Θέρμιον
καὶ τὰ παιδία σου.
    (ἔτους) ε, μη(νὸς) Σωτῆ(ρος) κα.
κατὰ σπουδὴν δέ σοι ἔγραψα.

Ammonios to his dearest Aphrodisios greeting. Please order that the loaves be made and that my olives be pickled and send me word in order that I may send for them. Get all the grain in the granary moved because of the inundation. Good-bye. Salute Thermion and your children. (Year) 5, Soter 21.

Postscript: I wrote to you in haste.

---

4 Read ἐλαίαν.
12 The month Soter appears to correspond to Phaophi in the Egyptian calendar (see PRyl II 149, note to line 10).

85 AMMŌNIOS TO APHRODISIOS
PLond III 893

40 CE

Originally, this letter was published independently of PRyl II 229–31, but it clearly belongs to the Ammonios-Aphrodisios correspondence. The editors of PRyl 229–31, Johnson, Martin, and Hunt, note that this text is the earliest instance of dating by both the Roman and Egyptian calendars (lines 7–8, 10). The sixteen-day divergence between the two systems, indicated here, is consistent with evidence from other sources (see PLond I 130; PFay 139, introduction). Because the letter refers to grape-pressing, the month Drousieus (line 18) would have been equivalent to either Payni or Epeiph, but it is more likely that it corresponded to Epeiph and that it preceded Mesore.

The details of this letter are ambiguous. We do not know, at the beginning, what could have been communicated about a certain Seras or what connection, if any, this matter had with Ammonios' instruction that the young one (a child?) be sent to him. It is clear that at the time of writing, Ammonios was moving about from one place to another in his grape-pressing. Some type of difficulty, which had been brought to the attention of the chief of police, Pholos (see PRyl II, p. 118), seems to be one of the more pressing occasions of the letter.

This letter, like the immediately preceding one, appears to be written in some haste. Further business is taken up after the closing greeting, and a postscript added in the top margin follows the farewell and date.

καὶ ἄρτων ἀρτάβ(ας) τέσσαρε(ς) [[σὺν σεαυτ(ῷ)]]
  [ ] ἔνεγκον.
Ἀ[μμ]ώνιος Ἀφροδισίωι τῷ φιλ(τάτῳ) χα(ίρειν).
Διομ[ή]δης ὁ Φόλου λέγει μὴ μετα-
5 δεδωκέν[α]ι [σ]ε αὐτῶι ὑπὲρ Σεράτος, διὸ
καλῶς π[οιή]σεις ἐξαυτῆ(ς) πέμψας μοι τὸν
μεικρόν, καὶ ἐλθὲ εἰς Βουβάστον τῇ δ,
ἐπεὶ τρυγῶ ἐκεῖ, ἥ ἐστι(ν) Αἰγυπ(τίων) κ, καὶ
ἀγόρασόν μοι ὀψάρια τῇ η καὶ ἔνεγκο(ν)
10 ... ε[ἰς Β]ερενικίδ(α) Αἰγι(αλοῦ) τῇ ι ἥ ἐστι κϛ·
τρυγῶι ἐκεῖ, ἔρχου. Ζηνόδ[ο]το(ς)
[π]ολλὰ κατηγόρησεν ἐπὶ Φόλω
ὡς μὴι τὰ ὑπὸ σ[οῦ] εἰρημένα γ[.].
ν....ι......ω( ) ποιη(σ) πέμψαι μ[ο]ι
15 διά τινος τῶ(ν) φυλά̣κ(ων) τὸν μεικρόν.
ἀσπάζο(υ) Θέρμιον. ἀπαίτησον χεῖραν (δραχμῶν) μ
καὶ (δραχμὰς?) ϛ ἐπομ(ένας) καὶ τὸ λοιπ(ὸν) τὰ ὀφειλόμε(να).
ἔρρωσθε.
(ἔτους) δ, μη(νὸς) Δρουσιέ(ως) κη.

Ammonios to his dearest Aphrodisios greeting. Diomedes, the son of Pholos, says you have not communicated with him about Seras. Wherefore, please send the young one (child?) to me immediately, and come to Boubastos on the fourth, or the twentieth by the Egyptian calendar, since I am pressing grapes there, and buy some pickled fish for me on the eighth and bring (them along?) ... to Berenikis of the Shore on the tenth, which is the twenty-sixth. I am pressing grapes, so come. Zenodotos made many denunciations before Pholos ... please send the young one to me by means of one of the guards. Salute Thermion. Collect (the loan) of forty drachmas and the six drachmas resulting (the interest) and any remainder that is owed. Good-bye. (Year) 4, Drousieos 28.

Postscript: And bring the four artabs of loaves.

---

1 The editors of PRyl 229–31 note that an oblique stroke precedes καί, probably in order to call attention to the postscript.

4 The Pholos both here and in line 12 is probably the Gaius Iulius Pholus who was an *epistates phylakiton* at the time (see PRyl II, p. 118).

4–5 The editors of PRyl 229–31 translate these lines as follows: "Diomedes son of Pholus says that you have given him nothing on account of Seras."

7 Read μικρόν (also in line 15).

9 ὀψάρια: the editors translate this as "relishes" (see letter 82.11, 21 where the editors also translate ὀψάριον as "relish").

14 The editors of PRyl 229–31 noted that neither πάντω(ς) ποίη(σον) nor καλῶ(ς) ποιή(σεις) are consonant with the fragmented remains of the line.

Various primary documents, as well as certain accounts by ancient historians, indicate that a pogrom against the Jews began in Alexandria in 38 CE. Three documents which illustrate the situation are included here. But before giving a brief account of these texts, as well as of a few other primary documents which bear on the situation, it will prove helpful to describe something of the social and political background which contributed to the pogrom.

Augustus confirmed for Alexandrian Jews all the privileges which they had enjoyed under the Ptolemies, including the right to have their own council of elders. In such circumstances, the Jews, or at least those of high economic and social standing in the community, considered themselves full-fledged Alexandrians and equivalent in class with the Greeks who were members of the polis (Alexandrian citizens).

Various factors converged which both jeopardized Jewish status and created tensions with the Greek element in the city. On the one hand, Augustus aggravated the Greeks by removing their right to have a council (boule), a traditional organ of self-government. This action was apparently a punishment on Alexandrian Greeks (presumably the other two Egyptian cities with the status of Greek polis, Naukratis and Ptolemais, retained their council) for their rather negative response, first to Caesar and, then, to Augustus himself. The Jews' continuous right to their council of elders aggravated Augustus' denial of the Greeks' request to a council. On the other hand, when Augustus imposed the poll tax (*laographia*) on Egypt in 24–23 BCE, only two groups were exempt from taxation: Roman citizens and urban Greeks (i.e., Greeks who were members of the polis and, consequently, with citizenship status). Since only a few members of the Jewish community were members of the polis, the Jews were effectively degraded to the level of the Egyptian natives. This meant, among other things, that Jews were excluded from military and civil service. It was only through Alexandrian citizenship that Egyptian Jews could aspire to Roman citizenship. To be sure, Jews could enroll in Roman military auxiliary units but, in this case, Roman citizenship was attained only at the end of one's service, not at the moment of enlistment as when one enrolled in the Roman legions.

It is little wonder, then, that the Jews tried to extricate themselves from the poll tax and the unfavorable social status which it represented. The primary documents of the period, which we will discuss shortly, show some of the means whereby the Jews tried to establish their Alexandrian citizenship. Of course, such efforts created further tensions with the Greeks.

The tensions between Jews and Greeks in Alexandria had reached such a point that open violence broke out in 38 CE. When Caligula succeeded Tiberius as emperor in 37 CE, the Jews wanted to send a delegation to Rome to congratulate him on his accession to the throne and more importantly, from their viewpoint, to request that they be exempted from the poll tax. The prefect of Egypt at the time, a certain Flaccus, thwarted the action because he favored certain anti-Jewish activists among the Greeks. When King Agrippa, the grandson of Herod, arrived in Alexandria enroute to Judea on 1 August 38 CE, Greek agitators disrupted a Jewish parade in his honor. Flaccus did not intervene with troops and a pogrom against Jews erupted.

In the wake of that action, the Jews sent an embassy to Caligula in 39–40 CE, attempting once again to have the poll tax lifted and to make a case, through diplomatic means, for the status of Alexandrian Jews. This embassy was led by the distinguished Jew, Philo, a Hellenistic-Jewish philosopher. Caligula was antagonistic to the petition and, following his death, rioting broke out in Alexandria once again. But this time the Jews were responsible for initiating the attack.

Hence, it happened that both the Greeks and the Jews sent an embassy to the new emperor Claudius, congratulating him on his accession and petitioning him for favors. It appears from Claudius' response to the Greeks in letter 88 that the primary purpose of the hearing which he granted to the two groups was to talk about the most recent hostilities in Alexandria. He resolved, without desiring to make any detailed examination of the matter, that further hostilities could not be allowed and that Jews and Greeks had to respect each others' privileges, as these were determined by Rome. Claudius confirmed the former religious and legal status of the Jews but he refused, with finality, to grant Alexandrian citizenship to them. So far as the Greeks were concerned, while acknowledging, at least implicitly, that the Jews were the agitators in the most recent riots and while granting certain favors, he refused, for the present, to allow the Greeks to have a council (boule). A boule was finally granted to Alexandria in 200 CE, when Severus established such councils in all of the nome capitals. Alexandrians could hardly rejoice at this time, however, since their city was placed on a par with country towns.

The following documents, arranged in chronological sequence, illustrate the Jewish troubles in Alexandria during the early Roman rule.

(1) The so-called *Boule*-papyrus (PSI X 1160=Musurillo I=CPJud II 150), probably 20–19 BCE. In this text, a spokesman on behalf of the Alexandrians (citizens of the polis) addresses the emperor, requesting that Alexandria be permitted its traditional council. A council was necessary, according to this spokesman, because undesirable and ineligible aliens were entering the privileged ranks of Alexandrian citizenship by getting themselves inscribed with *epheboi* on the public records. By this means, these "uneducated and uncultured" people were escaping the laographia.

Since the native Egyptians in Alexandria seem never to have constituted a serious political threat, it is likely that the principal targets of the letter were the Jews who were penetrating Greek society.

(2) BGU IV 1140 (=CPJud II 151 and letter 86), 5–4 BCE. This is a petition to the Roman prefect in Egypt from an Alexandrian Jew. The petitioner's attempt to remove the poll tax represents precisely the kind of activity about which the spokesman of the *Boule*-papyrus complained.

(3) BGU IV 1079 (=CPJud II 152 and letter 87), 41 CE. In this letter, written when tensions between Greeks and Jews in Alexandria were at their height, a Greek merchant warns his servant or agent, who is in Alexandria at the time of writing, about going to the Jews to ask for a loan.

(4) PLond VI 1912 (=CPJud II 153 and letter 88), 41 CE. This is the famous letter of the emperor Claudius to the Alexandrians. As suggested above, this letter resolved with finality the Jewish struggle for civic rights by determining that Jews were not citizens.

(5) The so-called "Acts of the Alexandrian ('Pagan') Martyrs" (Musurillo, texts I–XI; see CPJud II 154–59). These semi-literary stories, though not directly dependent on material from official protocols, are based in part on historical documents. The heroes of these accounts were sentenced to death by Roman emperors because they defended the rights of Alexandrian Greeks before the Caesars. At the same time, the authors of these works were anti-Semitic and, consequently, cast light on the Jewish troubles in Alexandria during the early Roman period. It seems that Claudius' execution of Isidoros and Lampon in 41 CE provided the initial occasion for this martyr literature. Our extant texts are from the second to third centuries CE.

Various editions of the primary texts, as well as a spate of interpretations, could be cited in connection with the Jewish troubles in Alexandria. Only a few bibliographical sources are cited here. The above spectrum of primary documents is edited by V. Tcherikover ("'The Jewish Question' In Alexandria," CPJud II, sect. 8; see texts 150–59, pp. 25–107). An extensive edition of Claudius' letter to the Alexandrians has been made by H. I. Bell in PLond VI, with the covering title, *Jews and Christians in Egypt* (see Alexandrian martyr literature, PLond VI 1912, pp. 1–37). An edition of the *Boule*-papyrus and of the Alexandrian martyr literature has been made by H. A. Musurillo (*Acts of the Pagan Martyrs*). Of the large number of interpretive works on the Jewish troubles in Alexandria, the following two, while helpful, are relatively non-technical and brief: A. Segré, "Status of the Jews," pp. 375–400; N. Lewis, *Life in Egypt*, pp. 25–31 (the section entitled "Urban Greeks and Jews").

86 TO GAIUS TYRRANIUS FROM HELENOS
CPJud II 151 (=BGU IV 1140)   5–4 BCE

This petition from Helenos is addressed to the prefect of Egypt, who was prefect from 7 to 4 BCE. Though only the opening eight to nine lines are relatively complete, it seems clear that the request is occasioned by an alleged injustice done to Helenos by Horos, a financial official of the government. More particularly, the document shows, according to Tcherikover (introductory comments to CPJud II 151), that Helenos was being forced to pay the poll tax (laographia). This is evident in the triple citation of the tax (lines 17, 21, 22) and in Helenos' reference to the fact that men of sixty years were exempt from it.

Helenos contends that since he is the son of an Alexandrian citizen, he has lived in Alexandria all of his life and he had enjoyed a Greek education, he is assured of citizenship. On the other hand, the financial officer (the oikonomos?) was probably right in requiring Helenos to pay the poll tax. This is evident in the fact that the scribe replaced the title suggested by Helenos, "an Alexandrian," with another designation which corresponded to the actual legal status of the plaintiff, "a Jewish inhabitant of Alexandria." The reluctance of Helenos to agree with the new formulation of his civic status, as defined by the scribe, probably accounts for the confused wording of the petition. The argument of Helenos, according to H. I. Bell (*Jews and Christians*, p. 12), seems to have run: "I am an Alexandrian, the son of an Alexandrian, and *in any case* I am over age." The illogicality of such an argument is obvious, according to Tcherikover, but it does illustrate the lengths to which Jews in the period would go in the struggle to claim civic rights and to avoid the degradation of status which payment of the poll tax implied (see CPJud II, pp. 61ff.).

The order to pay the poll tax was directed to Helenos and not to his father. In the cancelled lines, 24–25, Helenos emphasizes that he was not disturbed with the poll tax by previous prefects. But, if Tryphon, the father, was an Alexandrian citizen, why was Helenos, the son, obliged to pay the tax? The most probable explanation is given by Tcherikover (CPJud II, p. 32), who suggests that Helenos' mother was probably not the daughter of a citizen. Since the Alexandrians appear to have adopted the law of Athens for their city (see PHal=*Dikaiomata*, 64ff.; POxy XVIII 2177), citizenship would have been granted only to persons whose mother and father were both citizens.

The administrator of the Roman emperor's Privy Purse also adopted this policy in Egypt, as indicated in the *Gnomon of the Idios Logos* (=BGU V 1210), a papyrus roll which sets out numerous rules and restrictions pertaining to status and interclass relationships. All the clauses of the *Gnomon of the Idios Logos* that deal with mixed marriages presuppose that the children follow the status of the inferior partner. N. Lewis rightly concludes, on the basis of these stringent regulations, that a prime objective of Augustus (an objective maintained for two hundred years by successors) was to impede social mobility and to keep the various strata of the population as discrete and immutable as possible (*Life in Egypt*, p. 32).

So far as Alexandrian Jews were concerned, the marriage of Jews who were Alexandrian citizens with Jews who were merely members of the Jewish community was probably common, since Jewish marriage law was not bound by the status of Jews in the Greek polis. But once the poll tax was enacted, status became much more pronounced and Jews like Helenos would have been tempted to violate the law if one of the parents had Alexandrian citizenship.

Γαίωι Τυρρανίωι

᾿Ιουδαίου τῶν ἀπὸ ᾿Αλεξανδρε(ίας)
παρὰ ῾Ελένου το(ῦ) Τρύφωνο(ς) [[᾿Αλεξανδρέω(ς)]].

μέγιστε
ἡγεμὼ(ν) [[βελτιστε]], ὧν ἐκ πατρὸς ᾿Αλεξανδρέ(ως)
[[καὶ]] διατρείψας ἐνταῦθα τὸν πάντα χρόνον
5 μεταλαβὼν καθ᾿ ὃ δυνατὸν {καὶ} τῷ πατρὶ
[τῆ]ς ἀρεσκούσης παιδείας, κινδυνεύω
οὐ μόνον τῆς ἰδίας πατρίδος στερηθῆ-
ναι ἀλλὰ καὶ εἰς τὸν [...]..(...)..ενοιαι.τον
...ειν βίαν. συμβέβηκε γὰρ ῟Ωρον

β
10 δ[η]μόσι(ον) οἰκονόμ[ον.....]....τυ
τρ..πο τῆ(ς) αἰτίας ἔν[εκα.....].αι τὸν
πατέρα μου ἔχειν πρὸς τὸν πάτριον αὐτοῦ
[[.υμνασιον ἔτι δὲ καὶ]] σχῆμα [....]μιον]]
..τικον ἀνηρπακω [[......χειρισας]]

χειρισας ιδα
[[.........]]..τὴν ἀπὸ τῆς ἐφηβεί(ας)

με
15 [[.............]]...............

To Gaius Tyrranius from Helenos, the son of Tryphon, an Alexandrian (cancelled), a Jewish inhabitant of Alexandria. Most mighty governor, although my father was an Alexandrian and I have resided here all my life, having partaken of an acceptable education so far as my father's means allowed, I am in danger not only of being deprived of my own homeland but also. . . . For it has turned out that Horos, the public administrator, . . . on the ground that . . . my father has, with a view to his ancestral bearing (?), . . . even yet . . . forcibly . . . from the ephebate . . . Caesar . . . written . . . poll tax . . . from Mecheir to . . . the remaining time of the poll tax on account of the (age limit) of sixty, I request you, savior of all, not to disregard (my plea), just as I have been undisturbed both by the first governors and the same by you . . . (cancelled)

2 Τρύφων: a common Greek name among Jews. ᾿Ιουδαίου τῶν ἀπὸ ᾿Αλεξανδρε(ίας): see the extensive note by Tcherikover (CPJud II 151, note to line 2).

[[.......]]
κον. Καίσαρος [...]τικου [.......γ]εγραμμέ-
[[.....]]
[....]...στι λαογραφίας [.......]........
.............τη[.......]ἀπὸ Μεχεὶρ
πρὸς τέλει ἕως....[...
          ἕως
20 ἀπὸ [[τοῦ]]. ιβ(ἔτους) [..]...ρ....ουν[...
          περαιουν...ν
[[τῆ(ς) λαο(γραφίας)]] [[δὲ τοῦ]] ἐλλείποντος χρόνου
    τῆς
λαογραφίας διὰ τὸ τῶν ἑξ(ή)κοντα, ἀξιῶ σε
τὸ(ν) πάντων σωτῆ(ρα) μὴ παρι(δεῖν) [[καθὼς καὶ ὑπὸ
    τῶν]]
[[πρώτων ἡγεμόνων ἀπαρενόχλητος γέγο-]]
25 [[να καὶ ὑπό σου τὸ ὅμοιον οὐδὲ σοί........]]
[[....των........]]τον υπ.............

4 καί: the scribe cancelled the wrong καί. Though καί is useless in line 5, here it is required.

6 τῆς ἀρεσκούσης παιδείας: Tcherikover conjectures that Helenos received the regular education of a Greek youth in a gymnasium and as ephebos (the mutilated word in line 13, which he translates as "gymnasium," is used in support of this view). Thus, he contends that the case of Helenos confirms the statement of the spokesman of the Alexandrians in the *Boule*-papyrus (CPJud II 150=PSI X 1160) about persons who avoided the payment of the poll tax by being listed with the epheboi even though they were subject to it.

11ff. There appears to be a hint of something done to the father of Helenos, but one cannot determine from the fragmentary condition of the text what relationship, if any, this had for the status of Helenos himself. Tcherikover translates these lines: "... on the ground of ... my father to his ancestral gymnasium ... forcibly ... from the ephebate. ..."

87 SARAPIŌN TO HĒRAKLEIDĒS
CPJud II 152 (=BGU IV 1079)   4 August 41 CE

Sarapion, the author of this letter, is described in another letter as an *emporos*, a wholesale merchant (BGU IV 1078). In that other piece of correspondence, written two years earlier, Sarapion was writing from Alexandria to his wife in the country (chora). It appears both from that letter and the present one that whereas Sarapion's residence was in the chora, he maintained business connections in Alexandria. Herakleides, to whom the present letter is addressed, was apparently a servant or business agent of Sarapion in Alexandria. He seems to have run short of money, perhaps because of an unsuccessful business transaction (see lines 16ff.), and was now attempting to secure the required financial aid from Ptollarion that would allow him to continue his operations in Alexandria.

The warning about the Jews in lines 23–26 has been interpreted in a variety of ways. Wilcken, for example, suggested in his edition of this text that it is the oldest example of anti-Semitism in business affairs (WChr 60; see *Archiv* 4:567ff.). Others have suggested that the warning has nothing to do with business affairs but served merely as a reminder of the present political hostilities between Jews and Greeks in Alexandria (see Tcherikover, introductory comments to CPJud II 152). Given the context of this warning, Sarapion apparently assumes that if Herakleides cannot secure help from Ptollarion, he will borrow money from Jewish moneylenders in Alexandria. But this need not mean that Sarapion's comment was intended as a warning against Jewish dishonesty in business. The Jews had violently attacked their enemies in February or March, at the beginning of Claudius' reign, which was only a few months prior to this letter. It was probably still considered quite dangerous for a Greek to enter the Jewish quarter.

Σαραπίων ʿΗρακλείδῃ τῷ
ἡμετέρῳ χα(ίρειν). ἔπεμψά σοι

Sarapion to our own Herakleides greeting. I sent two other letters to you, one through Nedymos,

ἄλλας δύο ἐπιστολάς,
διὰ Νηδύμου μίαν, διὰ
5 Κρονίου μαχαιροφόρου
μίαν. λοιπὸν οὖν ἔλα-
βον παρὰ το(ῦ) Ἄραβος τὴν
ἐπιστολὴν καὶ ἀνέ-
γνων καὶ ἐλυπήθην.
10 ἀκολούθει δὲ Πτολλ-
αρίωνι πᾶσαν ὥραν· τά-
χα δύναταί σε εὔλυτ-
ον ποῖσαι. λέγε αὐτῷ· "ἄ-
λλο ἐγώ, ἄλλο πάντες·
15 ἐγὼ παιδάριν εἰμί· παρὰ
τάλαντόν σοι πέπρακα
τὰ φο[ρτ]ία μου· οὐκ οἶδα
τί μ[ε ὁ] πάτρων ποίσει·
πολλοὺς δανιστὰς ἔχο-
20 μεν· μὴ ἵνα ἀναστατώ-
σῃς ἡμᾶς." ἐρώτα αὐτὸν
καθ' ἡμέραν· τάχα δύνα-
ταί σε ἐλεῆσαι. ἐὰν μή, ὡς
ἂν πάντες καὶ σὺ βλέ-
25 πε σατὸν ἀπὸ τῶν Ἰου-
δαίων. μᾶλλον ἀκολουθῶν
αὐτῷ δύνῃ φιλιάσαι αὐτῷ.
ἴδε ἢ δύναται διὰ Διοδώρου
ὑπογραφῆναι ἡ τάβλα διὰ
30 τῆς γυναικὸς τοῦ ἡγεμ-
όνος. ἐὰν τὰ παρ(ὰ) σατοῦ ποί-
σῃς, οὐκ εἶ μεμπτός.
ἀσπάζου Διόδωρον μεγάλω(ς).
ἔρρω(σο). ἀσπάζου Ἁρποχράτιον.
35 (ἔτους) α Τιβερίου Κλαυδίου Καίσαρο(ς)
Σεβα(στοῦ) Γερμανικοῦ Αὐτοκρά(τορος), μηνὸ(ς)
Καισαρείου ῑα.

Verso: [ἀπόδος εἰς] Ἀλεξά(νδρειαν)
εἰς Σεβα(στὴν) Ἀγορὰ(ν) εἰς τ[ὴν] . . . .
. . . θήκην ὥστε Ἡρακλ(είδῃ) πα(ρὰ) Σαραπίω(νος)
. . . . ωνος το(ῦ) Σωσιπάτρου.

one through Kronios the swordsman (military policeman?). Finally, then, I received your letter from the Arab and was upset upon reading it. Follow Ptollarion all the time; perhaps he can resolve your difficulty. Tell him "It is one thing for everyone else, another for me; I am (only) a slave; I have sold my merchandise to you for a talent too little; I know not what my patron will do to me; we have many creditors; do not drive us out (of business)." Ask him daily. Perhaps he may take pity on you. If not, like everyone else, see to it that you too (keep) yourself away from the Jews. It would be better, if you are able, through following him to make friends with him. Or, see whether it is possible by Diodoros to get the tablet signed through the wife of the commander (?). If you should do your part, you are not to be blamed. Salute Diodoros heartily. Good-bye. Salute Harpochration. (Year) 1 of Tiberius Claudius Caesar Augustus Germanicus, the Emperor, the eleventh of the month Kaisareios.

Outside address: Deliver to Alexandria, at the marketplace of Augustus, to the . . . store for Herakleides, from Sarapion, the son of . . . on, the son of Sosipatros.

---

9   ἐλυπήθην: the υ is corrected from η.
11 πᾶσαν: σ is corrected from ρ.
13 Read ποιῆσαι.
15 Read παιδάριον.
15–16 παρὰ τάλαντον is an obscure phrase, which interpreters have puzzled over. Tcherikover states that, since the aim of the sentence is to prove the miserable condition of Herakleides, the phrase must refer to some losses through business transactions with Ptollarion: "I have sold my merchandise to you for a talent too little." He suggests that this may be a proverb, since a talent would be an enormous sum.
18 Read ποιήσει.
25 Read σαυτόν (read σαυτοῦ in line 31).
28 Read εἰ.
29–30 διὰ τῆς γυναικὸς τοῦ ἡγεμόνος: Tcherikover notes that the usual translation of this phrase is "through the wife of the *prefect*" (see SelPap I 107). By contrast, he suggests that it is quite improbable that the wife of a prefect would have been assigned the role of signing documents for the benefit of small merchants in Alexandria. Consequently, he proposes that in this instance ἡγεμών has the alternative meaning of "legionary commander" or "commander" in a broader, unspecified sense.

CLAUDIUS TO THE ALEXANDRIANS
CPJud II 153 (=PLond VI 1912)   10 November 41 CE

This well-known letter of the emperor Claudius, especially the passage dealing with the Jews, has been reprinted and interpreted many times. Two of the more thorough, critical editions are by H. I. Bell (PLond VI 1912, *Jews and Christians*) and V. Tcherikover (CPJud II 153). Tcherikover also provides an extensive bibliography of the interpretation of the letter (see CPJud II, pp. 36f.).

The letter was written in response to honors voted Claudius and to requests presented to him by the Greek embassy. The embassy was sent from Alexandria in 41 CE to congratulate him on his accession to the throne. The letter was first made public in Alexandria but was copied and sent to the chora, namely, Egypt outside Alexandria.

So far as its details are concerned, the actual letter is preceded by a brief edict of the prefect of Egypt, ordering its publication (lines 1–13). Following the prefect's edict, the letter itself opens with the more or less conventional words of diplomatic courtesy, including an enumeration of the twelve members of the Greek embassy (lines 14–29). Thereupon, the emperor confirms the honors voted for him by the Alexandrians (lines 29–51), before responding to their requests (lines 52–72). In the remaining part of the body (lines 72–104), Claudius addresses the question of the Jews' privileges and limitations in Alexandria, and he insists that both the Greek and Jewish elements of the city be respectful of one another. Finally, the letter closes on a personal note with the farewell and with the emperor's thanks to two friends who were members of the Greek delegation (lines 105–9).

Our version of the letter, which was preserved and found in Philadelphia in the Fayum, was made by a rather careless scribe. The original was probably either written in Latin and then translated into Greek at the Imperial Chancery in Rome, before being sent on to Alexandria, or originally composed in Greek, but a Greek influenced by Latin (see Tcherikover, CPJud II, pp. 37–38).

The decisions announced in the letter are prudent and politically expedient, whether they directly reflect Claudius' attitude or a cooperative effort made in concert with his secretariat. The document reverses the more Hellenistic tendencies of Gaius Caligula and reestablishes the principles laid down by Augustus. Claudius grants to the Alexandrians only those rights dictated by political necessity. His insistence that both Alexandrians (i.e., inhabitants with citizenship status) and Jews keep the peace is intended to settle hostilities once and for all. His acceptance of the honors voted to himself as emperor is restrained.

Some of the early details of the letter are discussed in notes which follow the translation. Here, we will limit ourselves to an examination of the latter part of the letter which deals with the Jews.

The subject of lines 72ff. is neither civic rights nor religious freedom, but the question of responsibility for the renewed outbreak of hostilities between Greeks and Jews in Alexandria since Claudius became emperor. Claudius' comments indicate that both Greeks and Jews had stated their case before him and that he was presiding over the discussion in the role of supreme judge. It also seems clear to the editor of this text, Tcherikover, that though Claudius knew the Jews were actually responsible for the renewal of aggression, he refused to make a detailed inquiry in the interests of the common peace. The Greeks were obviously guilty of initiating hostilities against the Jews from 38 CE onward in the time of Gaius Caligula. Thus, the fact that the Greek embassy was arguing forcefully for an exact inquiry at this point indicates that they were only interested in establishing the guilt of the Jews in the most recent aggression under Claudius.

This line of interpretation is supported by Claudius' prohibition, in lines 96ff., against Jews of Egypt and Syria entering Alexandria. These Jews had entered Alexandria to help their brethren prepare for renewed aggression. In fact, the Jewish historian, Josephus, identifies the Jews as the aggressors (*Jewish Antiquities* 19.278) and it is most likely that the emperor would have known what Josephus' sources knew. Why, then, did Claudius not identify the Jews more explicitly as those responsible for the recent conflict? Because, then, he would have done exactly what the Greek embassy wanted and he was anxious to restore peace, not to perpetuate hostilities.

On the other hand, Claudius' unwillingness to name the Jews explicitly as aggressors does not justify the interpretation of certain scholars that Claudius was a "philo-Semitic" emperor. When he states in lines 74ff., "*Although* your ambassador . . . argued forcefully, *notwithstanding* I have not wished to make an exact inquiry," he is acknowledging that the Jews are the aggressors. Moreover, he seems to add for the Alexandrians' benefit: "but I have stored up within me an immutable wrath against those who renewed the conflict." Nonetheless, the threat is directed to both sides, since Claudius could not know who would disturb the peace next. Though he had addressed only the Alexandrians (i.e., the Greek element) up to line 80, from that point onward he addresses both Greeks and Jews.

Why address the Jews in a letter sent in response to representatives of the polis? The war against the Jews was an issue that extended beyond the boundaries of the Greek city-state and affected the inhabitants of Alexandria in general. The double address, Ἀλεξανδρεῖς μέν (line 82) . . . Ἰουδέοις δέ (line 88), indicates that Ἀλεξανδρεῖς is used with the nuance, "citizens of Alexandria," which one finds in official documents (see letter 87.2: Ἀλεξανδρέως altered to Ἰουδαίον τῶν ἀπὸ Ἀλεξανδρείας). It follows, consequently, that from Claudius' viewpoint the Jews were not, apart from a few exceptions, Alexandrian citizens. But, by ordering the Alexandrians not to dishonor Jewish rites in the worship of their God and to allow them to observe the customs that they had practiced under Augustus, Claudius was confirming the religious and national ἔθη which had been granted to Jews by Augustus, but which had been abolished under Gaius.

There is one final interpretive issue that ought to be discussed. To what is Claudius referring to in lines 90–91 when he speaks of two embassies "as if they lived in two (separate) cities"? In his edition of PLond VI 1912, Bell explained the "two embassies" as representing, respectively, the Alexandrians and the Jews. This explanation leads to the conclusion that the Jewish element in the city had no right to send an independent embassy to the emperor. Tcherikover rightly rejected this interpretation, however, because the Acts of the Alexandrian ("Pagan") Martyrs illustrate that such embassies were always sent (see CPJud II 154–59; H. A. Musurillo, *Acts of the Pagan Martyrs*) and Claudius himself speaks of both Greeks and Jews pleading their cause before him as if the Jewish embassy were legal. Consequently, Tcherikover argued that Claudius' reproof was addressed only to the Jews who themselves had sent two separate embassies. Claudius' accusation, that they behaved as if they were representing "two (separate) cities" suggests that there was a considerable difference of opinion between the two Jewish embassies.

And what was the basis of the disagreement? It was suggested above that the occasion of the present letter was not the question of Jewish civic rights but the matter of ascertaining the guilty party in the recent hostilities in Alexandria. One Jewish contingent, which represented the interests of wealthy Jews who were strongly influenced by Hellenistic culture, was represented most notably by Philo. This contingent would have contended that Greek society as such was not hostile to the Jews but only the criminal policy of one Roman prefect (Flaccus)—who misused his power and who had aligned himself with a little group of political gangsters—was responsible for the anti-Semitic feeling of the Alexandrians.

But, even while Philo and his contingent were in Rome pursuing this line of argument, it came to light that there were Jews in Alexandria who, supported by brethren from elsewhere in Egypt and Palestine, were employing arms successfully against their enemies. This element probably did not belong to "high society" but, like the initial stage of the Maccabbean revolt, to the broad masses of Jewish population, which sought to defend the Jewish religious tradition against its idolatrous enemies. According to Tcherikover's notes on lines 90–91 of CPJud II 153 (pp. 50–53), it is not too much to suggest that this element captured the leadership of the Jewish community after its successful fight against the Greeks in 41 CE. This group, then, sent the second embassy to Rome. Unlike Philo, who attributed the problem to a small group of Greeks that incited a well-intentioned populace, these Jews painted an appalling picture of a general hatred of Alexandrian Jews. It was apparently the impression created by this second Jewish embassy which led Claudius to characterize the Jews as a "wide-spread plague infecting the whole inhabited world." We may also infer that friction between the two Jewish embassies had reached the dimensions of a public disturbance. Claudius' solution to the internal conflict was to prohibit the sending of two separate Jewish embassies in the future. So far as the warlike contingent was concerned, it was obvious that Claudius would tolerate no future violence against the Greeks.

Following the example of Bell, I have divided the translation according to the various subjects taken up in the letter.

Column I

Λούκιος Αἰμίλλιος ʿΡῆκτος λέγει·
ἐπειδὴ τῇ ἀναγνώσει τῆς ἱεροτάτης
καὶ εὐεργετικωτάτης ἰς τὴν πόλειν
ἐπιστολῆς πᾶσα ἡ πόλεις παρατυχεῖν
5 οὐκ ἠδυνήθη{ν} διὰ τὸ πλῆθος αὐτῆς,
ἀναγκαῖον ἡγησάμην ἐκθεῖναι
τὴν ἐπιστολὴν ἵνα κατ᾽ ἄνδρα ἕκαστον
ἀναγεινόσκων αὐτὴν τήν τε μεγαλιότητα
τοῦ θεοῦ ἡμῶν Καίσαρος θαυμάσητε
10 καὶ τῇ πρὸς τὴν πόλειν [[ὁμοίᾳ]] εὐνοίᾳ
χάριν ἔχητε. (ἔτους) β Τιβερίου Κλαυδίου
Καίσαρος Σεβαστοῦ Γερμανικοῦ Αὐτοκράτορος, μηνὸς
Νέου
Σεβαστο(ῦ) ιδ.

Column II

Τιβέριος Κλαύδιος Καῖσαρ Σεβαστὸς Γερμανικὸς
Αὐτοκράτωρ ἀρχ{ι}ιερεὺς
15 μέγειστος δημαρχικῆς ἐξουσίας ὕπατος ἀποδεδιγμένος
Ἀλεξανδρέων

A. THE PREFECT'S PROCLAMATION

Lucius Aemilius Rectus says: since the entire population was unable to be present, because of its size, at the reading of the most sacred and beneficent letter to the city, I considered it necessary to display the letter (publicly) in order that each person upon reading it individually may marvel at the greatness of our deified Caesar and be grateful for his good will towards the city. (Year) 2 of Tiberius Claudius Caesar Augustus Germanicus, the Emperor, the fourteenth day of the month Neos Sebastos.

B. THE EMPEROR'S LETTER

I. The address

Tiberius Claudius Caesar Augustus Germanicus the Emperor, Pontifex Maximus, holder of the tribunician power, consul designate, to the city of the Alexandrians greeting.

τῇ πόλει χαίρειν. Τιβέριος Κλαύδιος Βάρβιλλος,
    Ἀπολλώνις Ἀρτεμιδώρου,
Χαιρήμων Λεονίδου, Μάρκος Ἰούλιος Ἀσκληπιάδης,
    Γάιος Ἰούλιος Διονύυσιο(ς),
Τιβέριος Κλαύδιος Φανίας, Πασίων Ποτάμωνος,
    Διονύσιος Σαββίωνος,
Τιβέριος Κλαύδις ⟨Ἀρχίβιος⟩, Ἀπολλώνις Ἀρίστονος,
    Γάιος Ἰούλιος Ἀπολλώνιος, Ἑρμαίσκος

20 Ἀπολλωνίου, ὑ πρέσβεις ὑμῶν, ἀναδόντες μοι τὸ
    ψήφισμα πολλὰ περὶ
τῆς πόλεως διεξῆλθον, ὑπαγόμενοί μοι δῆλον πρὸς τὴν εἰς
    ἡμᾶς
εὔνοιαν ἣν ἐκ πολλῶν χρόνων, εὖ εἴστε, παρ᾽ ἐμοὶ
    τεταμιευμένην⟨ε.⟩
εἴχεται, φύσει μὲν εὐσεβεῖς περὶ τοὺς Σεβαστοὺς
    ὑπάρχοντες, ὡς
ἐκ πολλῶν μοι γέγονε γνόριμον, ἐξερέτως δὲ περὶ τὸν ἐμὸν

25 οἴκον καὶ σπουδάσαντες καὶ σπουδασθέντος, ὧν εἶνα τὸ
    τελευ-
ταῖον εἴπωι παρεὶς τὰ ἄλλα μέγειστός ἐστιν μάρτυς οὕμος
    ἀδελφὸς
Γερμανικὸς Καῖσαρ γνησιωτέραις ὑμᾶς φωναῖς
    προσαγορεύσας.
διόπερ ἡδέως προσεδεξάμην τὰς δοθείσας ὑφ᾽ ἡμῶν μοι
    τιμὰς
καίπερ οὐκ ὢν πρὸς τὰ τοιαῦτα ⟨ρ⟩ ῥᾴδιος. καὶ πρῶτα μὲν
    Σεβαστὴν

30 ὑμεῖν ἄγειν ἐπιτρέπωι τὴν ἐμὴν γενεθλείαν ὃν τρόπον
    αὐτοὶ προ-
είρησθαι, τὰς τὲ ἑκα⟨τασ⟩σταχοῦ τῶν ἀνδριάντων
    ἀναστάσεις
ἐμοῦ τε καὶ τοῦ γένους μου ποιήσασθε συνχωρῶι· ἐγὼ
    ὁρῶι γὰρ
⟨ὅτι⟩ πάντη μνημεῖα τῆς ἡμετέρας εὐσεβείας εἰς τὸν ἐμὸν
    οἴκιον
ὑδρόσασθαι ⟨ἐ⟩σπουδάσαται. τῶν δὲ δυοῖν χρυ[σῶ]ν
    ἀνδριάντων

35 ὁ μὲν Κλαυδιανῆς Εἰρήνης Σεβαστῆς γενό[με]νος,
    ὥσπερ ὑπέθετο
καὶ προσελειπάρη[σ]εν ὁ ἐμοὶ τιμ[ι]ώτατος Βάρβιλλος
    ἀρνουμένου
μου διὰ τὸ φορτικότε[ρο]ς δ[οκ]εῖ[ν,] ἐπὶ Ῥώμης
    ἀνατεθήσεται,

Column III

ὁ δὲ ἕτερος ὃν τρόπον ὑμεῖς ἀξιοῦτε πομπεύσει ταῖς
    ἐπονύμαις
ἡμέραις παρ᾽ ὑμῖν· συνπομπευέτωι δὲ [[καὶ αυ]] αὐτῶι καὶ
    δίφρος

II. The Preamble

Tiberius Claudius Barbillus, Apollonios son of Artemidoros, Chairemon son of Leonideas, Marcus Julius Asklepiades, Gaius Julius Dionysios, Tiberius Claudius Phanias, Pasion the son of Ptoamon, Dionysios the son of Sabbian, Tiberius Claudius Archibios, Apollonios the son of Aristion, Gaius Julius Apollonios, Hermaiskos the son of Apollonios, your ambassadors, having delivered to me your decree, spoke at length about the city, directing my attention to your good will towards us, which, you may be sure, has been stored up by me (in my memory) for a long time. For it arises because you are reverent by nature regarding the Augusti, as has become well known to me through many examples, and specifically through being zealously disposed toward, and zealously reciprocated by, my own family, concerning which, to speak only about the most recent example, and to pass by the others, the best witness is my brother, Germanicus Caesar, who addressed you with the most genuine words of mouth. Wherefore, I willingly accepted the honors given by you to me, even though I have no taste for such things.

III. The Honors Confirmed

In the first place, then, I permit you to observe my birthday as a deified Augustus in the manner that you yourselves have proposed. I agree to the erection in their various places of the statues of me and my family; for I see that you are zealous to set up on every side memorials of your reverence for my family. Concerning the two golden statues, the one representative of the Pax Augusta Claudiana shall be set up at Rome, as my most honored Barbillus proposed and entreated, though I preferred to deny (the request) because it seemed too offensive and the other, in the manner you requested, shall be carried in your processions on name days, and let a throne accompany it, adorned with whatever ornamentation you desire. It would probably be foolish, while allowing such honors, to refuse to establish a Claudian tribe and to sanction groves according to the custom of Egypt. Wherefore, I also grant these things to you. If you wish, you may also set up the equestrian statues of Vitasius Pollio my procurator. As for the erection of the four-horse chariots which you wish to set up to me at the entrances of the

40 ᾧ βούλεσθαι κόσμωι ἠσκημένος. εὐῆθες δ' ἴσ{σ}ως
τοσαύτας
προσ[ι]έμενον τειμὰς ἀρνήσασθαι φυλὴν Κλαυδιανὰν
καταδῖξαι
ἄλση τε κατὰ νόμον παρεῖναι τῆς Αἰγύπ⟨τ⟩ου· διόπερ καὶ
ταῦτά [[ημιν]]
θ' ὑμεῖν ἐπιτρέπωι. εἰ δὲ βούλεσθαι καὶ Οὐειτρασίου
Πωλείωνος
τοῦ ἐμοῦ ἐπιτρόπου τοὺς ἐφίππους ἀνδριάντας
ἀναστήσατε. τῶν δὲ
45 τετραπώλων ἀναστάσε[ι]ς ⟨ἃς περὶ τὰς εἰσ⟩βολὰς τῆς
χώρας ἀφιδρῦσέ μοι βούλεσθαι
συνχωρῶι, τὸ μὲν περὶ τὴν Ταπόσιριν καλουμένην τῆς
Λιβύης,
τὸ δὲ περὶ Φάρον τῆς Ἀλεξανδρείας, τρίτον δὲ περὶ
Πηλούσιον
τῆς Αἰγύπ⟨τ⟩ου στῆσαι. ἀρχ⟨ι⟩ιερέα δ' ἐμὸν καὶ ναῶν
κατασκευὰς
παρετοῦμε, οὔτε φορτικὸς τοῖς κατ' ἐμαυτὸν ἀνθρόποις
50 βουλόμενος εἶναι τὰ ἱερὰ δὲ καὶ τὰ τοιαῦτα μόνοις τοῖς
θεοῖς
ἐξέρετα ὑπὸ τοῦ παντὸς αἰῶνος ἀποδεδόσθαι κρίν[ω]ν.
περὶ δὲ τῶν αἰτημάτων ἃ παρ' ἐμοῦ λαβεῖν ἐσπουδάκα-
τε οὕτως γεινώσκωι· ἅπασι τοῖς ἐφηβευκώσει ἄχρει τῆς
ἐμῆς ἡγεμονείας βαί[[βον]]βαιον διαφυλάσσωι τὴν
Ἀλεξανδρέων
55 πολειτείαν ἐπὶ τοῖς τῆς πόλεως τειμείοις καὶ
φιλανθρόποις
πᾶσει πλὴν εἰ μή τινες ὑπῆλθον ὑμᾶς ὡς ἐγ δούλων
γ[ε]γονότες ἐφηβεῦσαι, καὶ τὰ ἄλλα δὲ οὐχ ἧσσον εἶναι
βούλομε
βέβαια πάνθ' ὅσα ὑμεῖν ἐχαρίσθη ὑπό τε τῶν πρὸ ἐμοῦ
ἡγεμόνων
καὶ τῶν βασιλέων καὶ τῶν ἐπάρχων, ὡς καὶ [ὁ] θεὸς
Σεβαστὸς ἐβεβαίωσε.

Column IV

60 τοὺς δὲ νεοκόρους τοῦ ἐν Ἀλεξανδρείᾳ ναοῦ ὅς ἐστιν τοῦ
θεοῦ
Σεβαστοῦ κληροτοὺς εἶναι βούλομε καθὰ καὶ ὑ ἐν
Κανόπωι
τοῦ αὐτοῦ θεοῦ Σεβαστοῦ κληροῦνται. ὑπὲρ δὲ τοῦ τὰς
πολει-
τεικὰς ἀρχὰς τριετῖς εἶναι καὶ πάν⟨υ⟩ ἐμοὶ [[υ]] καλῶς
βεβουλεῦσθαι
δοκεῖται, ὑ γὰρ ⟨ἄρ⟩χοντες φώβωι τοῦ δώσειν εὐθύνας ὧν
κακῶς
65 ἦρξαν μετριώτεροι ἡμεῖν προσενεκθήσονται τὸν ἐν ταῖς
ἀρχαῖς χρόνον. περὶ δὲ τῆς βουλῆς ὅ τι μέν ποτε σύνηθες

country, I accede, for one to be set up at Taposiris, the Libyan town of that name, one at Pharos in Alexandria, a third at Pelousion in Egypt. But the (appointment of a) high priest to me, and the construction of temples, I deprecate, not wishing to be offensive to my contemporaries and because I consider temples and the like to be set apart in all ages for the gods alone.

IV. The Favors Asked

Concerning the requests which you have been anxious to receive from me, I decide as follows. To all those who have been registered as epheboi up to the time of my principate I preserve their Alexandrian citizenship as certain, with all the privileges and indulgences of the city, except some who secretly entered among you, though born of slave parents, having contrived to become epheboi, and I decide no less that the other things be confirmed which were granted to you by emperors, kings and prefects, in the same way as the deified Augustus confirmed them.

It is my will that the *neokoroi* of the Alexandrian temple of the deified Augustus be chosen by lot, just as they are chosen by lot in Kanopos for the same deified Augustus.

Concerning (your suggestion that) the municipal magistrates be triennial, it seems to me you have decided well, for magistrates will behave more moderately through fear of the account they will have to render for what was done badly during their term of office.

Regarding the senate, what indeed your custom was under ancient kings, I have no means of saying, but that you did not have one under the Augusti before me you are well aware. Because this is now a new matter, being formulated for the first time, and it is uncertain whether it will be advantageous to the city and to my own interests, I wrote to Aemilius Rectus to examine the matter and to inform me whether it is necessary that the senate be constituted and the manner, if then it should be appropriate to so assemble, according to which it will be constituted.

V. The Jewish Question

As to who should be held responsible for the disorder and sedition against the Jews or, rather, if

ὑμεῖν ἐπὶ τῶν ἀρχαίων βασιλέων οὐκ ἔχωι λέγειν, ὅτι δὲ ἐπὶ τῶν

πρὸ ἐμοῦ Σεβαστῶν οὐκ εἴχεται σαφῶς οἴδατε. καινοῦ δὴ πράγματος νῦν πρότων καταβαλλομένου ὅπερ ἄδηλον εἰ συνοί-

70 σει τῇ πόλει καὶ τοῖς ἐμοῖς πράγμασει ἔγραψα Αἰμιλλίωι Ῥήκτωι

διασκέψασθαι καὶ δηλῶσέ μοι εἴται καὶ συνείστασθαι τὴν ἀρχὴν δεῖ,

τόν τε τρόπον, εἴπερ ἄρα συνάγειν δέν, καθ᾽ ὃν γενήσεται τοῦτο.

τῆς δὲ πρὸς Ἰουδαίους ταραχῆς καὶ στάσεως, μᾶλλον δ᾽ εἰ χρὴ τὸ ἀληθὲς

εἰπεῖν τοῦ πολέμου, πότεροι μὲν αἴτιοι κατέστησαν, καίπερ

75 ἐξ ἀντικαταστάσεως πολλὰ τῶν ἡμετέρων πρέσβεων φιλοτειμηθέντων καὶ μάλιστα Διονυσίου τοῦ Θέων[ο]ς, ὅμως

οὐκ ἐβουλήθην ἀκριβῶς ἐξελένξαι, ταμιευόμενος ἐμαυτῶι κατὰ τῶν πάλειν ἀρξαμένων ὀργὴν ἀμεταμέλητον· ἁπλῶς δὲ προσαγορεύωι ὅτι ἂν μὴ καταπαύσηται τὴν ὀλέ-

80 θριον ὀργὴν ταύτην κατ᾽ ἀλλήλων αὐθάδιον ἐγβιασθήσομαι

δῖξαι ὑόν ἐστιν ἡγεμὼν φιλάνθροπος εἰς ὀργὴν δικαίαν μεταβεβλη-

μένος. διόπερ ἔτι καὶ νῦν διαμαρτύρομε εἶνα Ἀλεξανδρεῖς μὲν

πραέως καὶ φιλανθρόπως προσφέροντε Ἰουδαίο(ι)ς τοῖς τὴν αὐτὴν πόλειν ἐκ πολλῶν χρόνων οἰκοῦσει

Column V

85 καὶ μηδὲν τῶν πρὸς θρησκείαν αὐτοῖς νενομισμένων τοῦ θεοῦ λοιμένωνται, ἀλλὰ ἐῶσιν αὐτοὺς τοῖς ἔθεσιν χρῆσθαι ὗς καὶ ἐπὶ τοῦ θεοῦ Σεβαστοῦ, ἅπερ καὶ ἐγὼι διακούσας ἀμφοτέρων ἐβεβαίωσα. καὶ Ἰουδέοις δὲ ἄντικρυς κελεύωι μηδὲν πλήωι ὧν πρότερον

90 ἔσχον περιεργάζεσθαι μηδὲ ὥσπερ ἐν δυσεὶ πόλεσειν κατοικοῦντας δύο πρεσβείας ἐκπέμπειν τοῦ λοιποῦ, ὦ μὴ πρότερόν ποτε ἐπράκθη, μηδὲ ἐπισπαίειν γυμνασιαρχικοῖς ἢ κοσμητικοῖς ἀγῶσει, καρπουμένους μὲν τὰ οἰκῖα ἀπολά⟨υ⟩οντας δὲ

95 ἐν ἀλλοτρίᾳ πόλει περιουσίας ἀπθόνων ἀγαθῶν, μηδὲ ἐπάγεσθαι ἢ προσείεσθαι ἀπὸ Συρίας ἢ Αἰγύπ⟨τ⟩ου καταπλέοντας Ἰουδαίους, ἐξ οὖ μείζονας ὑπονοίας ἀνανκασθήσομε λαμβάνειν. εἰ δὲ μή, πάντα τρόπον αὐτοὺς ἐπεξελεύσομαι καθάπερ κοινήν

100 τεινα τῆς οἰκουμένης νόσον ἐξεγείροντας. ἐὰν τούτων ἀποστάντες ἀμφότεροι μετὰ πραότητος

the truth be told, the war, although your ambassadors, and especially Dionysios the son of Theon, argued forcefully, notwithstanding, I have not desired to make a detailed examination (of the hostility), but I have stored up within me an immutable hostility against those who renewed the conflict. Simply stated, if you do not lay to rest this destructive and obstinate hostility against one another, I shall be forced to show what a benevolent ruler can become when turned to (inflict) a justified wrath. Wherefore, still even now, I entreat you that, on the one hand, the Alexandrians behave gently and kindly towards the Jews, who have inhabited the same city for many years and that they not be destructive of any customs observed by them in the worship of their god, but that they be allowed to observe their customs as during the time of the deified Augustus, which I too have confirmed, having heard both sides. On the other hand, I order the Jews, unreservedly, not to waste effort seeking more than what they formerly had, nor for the future to send two embassies as if they lived in two (separate) cities, a thing which was never done before, nor to force their way in to contests (presided over by) the *gymnasiarchoi* and the *kosmetai*. Rather, they must enjoy the advantages which derive from their own status and, indeed, they have a plentiful abundance of good things in an alien city. Nor are they to bring in or to admit Jews who are sailing down from Syria or Egypt, by means of which I will be forced to conceive an even more serious suspicion. Otherwise, I will take vengeance against them in every respect, just as though they were a widespread plague infecting the whole inhabited world. (But) if you both (Alexandrians and Jews) forsake such things and are willing to live with gentleness and kindness toward one another, I, for my part, will have the greatest consideration for the city, just as one which has a long-standing familial status with us.

Conclusion

I bear witness to my friend, Barbillus, who has always had consideration for you before me and who, on this occasion, has fully advocated your case, as well as to my friend, Tiberius Claudius Archibios. Good-bye.

καὶ φιλανθροπείας τῆς πρὸς ἀλλήλους ζῆν ἐθελήσητε,
καὶ ἐγὼι πρόνοιαν τῆς πόλεως ποιήσομαι τὴν ἀνατάτωι
καθάπερ ἐκ προγόνων οἰκίας ὑμῖν ὑπαρχούσης.

105 Βαρβίλλωι τῶι ἐμῶι ἑτέρωι μαρτυρῶι ἀεὶ πρόνοια[ν]
ἡμῶν παρ᾽ ἐμοὶ ποιουμένωι, ὃς καὶ νῦν πάσηι φιλο-
τειμείᾳ περὶ τῶν ἀγόνα τὸν ὑπὲρ ὑμῶν κέχρ[ητε],
καὶ Τιβερίωι Κλαυδίωι Ἀρχιβίωι τῶι ἐμῶι ἑτέ[ρωι].
ἔρρωσθαι.

---

2 Read ἱερωτάτης.
4 Read ἀναγινωσκοντες.
9 Wilcken (*Archiv* 7:308ff.) proposed θε⟨ί⟩ου as an emendation for θεοῦ, indicating that there were no further examples of emperors being offically designated θεός in Egypt and that Claudius himself refused to accept divine honors in the letter. By contrast, Tcherikover produces examples of Augustus being called θεός in Egypt (POxy 143; BGU 1200–1201), although he too alleged that he did not care for divine honors. Tcherikover states further that it was common in the Orient to deify the living king (see CPJud 153, note to line 9).
16–19 Regarding the members of the embassy, see Tcherikover (CPJud 153, note to lines 16–19) and Bell (PLond VI 1912, note to lines 16–19).
17 Read Λεωνίδου.
19 Read Ἀρίστωνος.
20 Read οἱ.
21 Read με for μοι?
23 Read εἴχετε. φύσει μὲν κτλ.: diplomatically, the Imperial Chancery used a polite, but inappropriate, formula, since the anti-Roman feelings of the Alexandrians were well known at Rome. Regarding this matter, see the introduction to CPJud II 154–59, pp. 57–59.
24 Read γνώριμον, ἐξαιρέτως.
27 γνησιωτέραις . . . φωναῖς: Alexandrians had cheered Germanicus when he visited the city in 19 CE, seeing him perhaps as a possible rival of Tiberius. Claudius refers to Germanicus' speech by means of the phrase, γνησιωτέραις φωναῖς, which Bell translates as "by word of mouth" (i.e., in person). Grenfell and Hunt (SelPap II 212) translate the phrase as "more clearly-stamped as his own," indicating that Germanicus addressed the Alexandrians in their native tongue whereas Claudius' letter was composed in Latin. Tcherikover argues that both translations assume that Claudius was drawing an unfavorable comparison between himself and Germanicus, and that such a line of argument is unlikely. He suggests that the Greek comparative is used here merely for the purpose of strengthening the meaning of the word and so he translates the phrase as "in the most sincere language."
28 Read ὑμῶν.
29 Read πρῶτα.

30 Read προῄρησθε.
32 Read ποιήσασθαι.
33 Read ὑμετέρας.
34 Read ἱδρύσασθαι ἐσπουδάσατε.
35ff. The statue designated *Pax Augusta Claudiana* personified the peace established by the reign of the emperor. Claudius' fear of erecting a personification of peace in Rome stemmed from the full title, Pax Augusta Claudiana, which sounded too arrogant and implied a parallel between Claudius and the deified Augustus.
37 Read φορτικώτε[ρο]ς, ἐπί.
38 Read ἐπωνύμαις.
40 Read βούλεσθε (also in lines 43 and 45).
45 Read ἀφιδρῦσαι.
49 Read παραιτοῦμαι, ἀνθρώποις.
51 Read ἐξαίρετα.
53 Read ἐφηβευκόσι. The epheboi were youths (sometimes registered as very small children) qualified by descent (i.e., their parents were Alexandrian citizens) to receive citizenship and to qualify for education in the Greek gymnasium.
60 νεοκόροι: these were temple overseers, who were usually appointed for a limited period.
61 Read κληρωτούς, βούλομαι, οἱ, κανώπωι.
64 Read δοκεῖτε, οἱ, φόβωι.
65 Read προσενεχθήσονται.
66–73 Claudius deliberately avoids the question of whether Alexandria had possessed a city council (boule) under the Ptolemies, but the publication of the *Boule*-papyrus (PSI X 1160=Musurillo 1= CPJud II 150), from about 20–19 BCE, shows that there had been an Alexandrian city council under the late Ptolemies, and Claudius would have known this fact.
68 Read εἴχετε.
69 Read πρῶτον.
71 Read δηλῶσαι, τε.
72 Read δέοι.
79 Read καταπαύσητε.
81 Read οἶον, φιλάνθρωπος.
82 Read διαμαρτύρομαι.
83 Read φιλανθρώπως προσφέρωνται.
86 Read λυμαίνωνται.
87 Read οἷς.
88 Read Ἰουδαίοις.
89 Read πλείω.
92 Read ὅ, ἐπράχθη, ἐπεισπαίειν.
93 Read ἀγῶσι.
95 Read ἀφθόνων.
98 Read ἀναγκασθήσομαι.
103 Read ἀνωτάτω.
104 Read οἰκείας ἡμῖν.
105 Read ἑταίρωι (also in line 108).
106 Read ὑμῶν.
107 Read τὸν ἀγῶνα, κέχρ[ηται].

Mystarion, a native Egyptian, sends his servant (who is also the letter carrier) to Stotoetis, a chief priest, to get sticks for his olive gardens. A. Deissmann, commenting on this letter, suggested that it was in the wider sense a letter of recommendation (*Ancient East*, p. 171). Though Blastos is described as Mystarion's servant, this hardly amounts to a specification of his credentials. Blastos is merely identified as the one who is authorized to carry the sticks back to Mystarion. Consequently, in my opinion, the letter does not qualify as a letter of introduction (e.g., see the preceding letters of recommendation: letters 11 and 77–79).

Μυσταρίων Στοτόητι τῶι
ἰδίωι πλεῖστα χαίρειν.
ἔπεμψα ὑμεῖν Βλάστον τὸν ἐμὸν
χάριν διχίλων ξύλων εἰς τοὺς
5 ἐλαιῶνάς μου. ὅρα οὖν μὴ αὐτὸν
κατάσχῃς. οἶδας γὰρ πῶς αὐτοῦ
ἑκάστης ὥρας χρήζωι.

In another hand: ἔρρωσο.
L ια Τιβερίου Κλαυδίου Καίσαρος Σεβαστοῦ
10 Γερμ[α]νικο[ῦ] Αὐτοκράτορο[ς], μη(νὶ) Σεβα(στῶι) ιε.

Verso: Στοτόητι λεσώνῃ εἰς τὴν νῆσον τ[?].

Mystarion to his own Stotoetis many greetings. I sent my man Blastos to you on account of (my need of) forked (?) sticks for my olive gardens. Therefore, see that you do not detain him. For you know that I need him every hour. In another hand: Good-bye. Year 11 of Tiberius Claudius Caesar Augustus Germanicus Imperator, in the month Sebastos 15

Outside address, endorsed in the first hand: To Stotoetis, chief priest, at the island t(. . . ?).

5 Read διχήλων. This word, which has the meaning of "two" pincers or prongs, seems to have the more general meaning of "forked" here.

11 λεσώνη: regarding the use of this word as a title of the Egyptian priesthood, see U. Wilcken, *Archiv* 2:122–23.

1.	Hoe	5.	Head of wooden rake	10, 11, 12	Wooden mallets
2.	Sickle	6	Balance	13, 14	Spindles
3.	Knife	7, 8	Combs	15, 16, 17	Combs for carding wool
4.	Drill	9	Wooden funnel		

Photograph reproduced with the permission of the Committee of the Egypt Exploration Society.

Pompeius and other members of his family are known to us from PMert II 63 and three letters of the Oslo collection published by S. Eitrem and L. Amundsen ("Three Private Letters," pp. 177–83). All four letters are addressed to Pompeius. Though only one is dated (PMert 63 [18 January 57 CE]), the repetition of people's names and what appears to be the same chronological setting indicate that all were written in the mid-first century.

Pompeius belonged to one of the privileged classes which lived in the metropolis (capital) of the Arsinoite nome (see the introduction to letters 90 and 91). In their notes on POsloInv 1460 (letter 92), Eitrem and Amundsen suggest that the addressor, a certain Heraklous, may have been the wife of Pompeius ("Three Private Letters," p. 180). We know from another letter, POsloInv 1475 (letter 91) that a sister named Charitous also lived in the same city and perhaps in the same house. We learn from the letter which is not included here that some children were still living at home (POsloInv 1444.13). On the other hand, letter 90 indicates that other children were grown and living in another town in the Arsinoite nome. The names of three sons, at least two of whom were living in that town, are: Pompeius (see letters 90.11, 26; 91.14), Syrion (letters 90.22, 91.15) and Onamastos (referred to as the letter carrier in letter 90.17f. The verso of the same letter seems to read: "Deliver to Pompeius . . . father of Onomastos"). Herennia, who wrote two letters to Pompeius (letter 90 and POsloInv 1444), is a daughter, who also lived in the town and in the house with the three brothers (was one a husband?). Thaisous may be yet another daughter (see letter 91.15 and POsloInv 1444.8). Though it is not certain that any are cited by name, there were also grandchildren of Pompeius living in the same village with Herennia and the brothers. One cannot tell with certainty whether the person described in the two letters by Herennia as "Pompeius the young ("little"?) one" is the son of Pompeius (i.e., Pompeius "junior") or the grandson. It is interesting, in any case, that two people who appear to be somewhat young (Pompeius the young and Syrion) are living with the daughter Herennia. This correspondence further confirms the need to be careful in interpreting familial designations.

Since Pompeius appears to be moving back and forth between his home in the metropolis and the village where his daughter Herennia lives, he apparently had some type of business operation (perhaps a farm?) in the village.

In the first letter below, Herennia informs her father that a religious contribution is being exacted for the shrine of Souchos and that she is awaiting his advice on the matter. In the second piece of correspondence, Charitous, a sister of Pompeius, writes to him while he is away in the village of Herennia, informing him that she has attended to some matter about which he expressed concern. Heraklous notifies Pompeius, in the third letter, that she has been bothered by a certain Serapous ever since someone named Apeis died. Apparently, Apeis' death occasioned some dispute over an inheritance. Heraklous desired the assistance of Pompeius in the matter and wanted him to return home as quickly as possible.

HERENNIA TO POMPEIUS
PMert II 63

18 January 57 CE

Herennia informs her father Pompeius, in this badly spelled letter, that though an offering is being exacted for the shrine of Souchos, she has not yet paid but is awaiting her father's decision on the matter.

The nature of "the pious offering" ($\epsilon\dot{v}\sigma\epsilon\beta\epsilon\iota a$), referred to in lines 5–6, is ambiguous. However, the editor of PMert 63 appears to be close to a correct explanation when he suggests that this "pious contribution" was neither a tax nor a regular exaction but an irregular contribution levied on special occasions by the priesthood (e.g., before great festivals). It is noteworthy that the privileged classes that would normally be exempt from such contributions—designated as the "Romans, the Alexandrians (the Greek citizens of Alexandria) and the inhabitants in the Arsinoite nome"—are also subject to the levy here. We know that Roman citizens and Alexandrians were exempt from the poll tax and that they had certain other privileges (see the introduction to letter 88). Moreover, we might expect Romans and Greeks to be exempt from the maintenance of sanctuaries devoted to Egyptian deities. It may be the native priests were turning to the privileged classes on this occasion, as the result of an economic depression in Egypt during the reign of Nero (see PMert 63, introductory comments). Herennia and her family belonged, apparently, to one of the aforementioned privileged classes.

In lines 19–23 Herennia alerts her father to the inclusion of a letter from Syrion but, following a blank space of about three lines, she herself closes the letter by extending greetings to people where the father is staying. It may be Syrion was only a child and that he was supposed to scrawl something in the blank space. The photograph of the text in PMert II seems to reveal faint markings about one-third of the way over beneath the written lines of text (Plate XI, following p. 42) but, until such markings are actually confirmed, the reference remains puzzling.

[Ἑ]λενία Πονπηγίωι τῶι πατρὶ
[π]λεῖστα χαίριν καὶ διὰ παντὸς
[ὑ]γιαίνιν. ἠγόρακά συ
[τ]ας ἐλέας. αἰτοῦσι παν-
5 [τ]αχόθην εἰς τὴν εὐσέ-
βιαν τ[ο]ῦ ναοῦ Σούχου,
πάντος ἀνθρώπους,
καὶ Ῥωμαίους καὶ Ἀλεξαν-
δρεῖς καὶ κατυκοῦτος ἐν
10 τῶι Ἀρ[σ]ενοείτηι. αἰτοῦσι
Πονπ[ή]γιν. οὐ δέδωκα
δὴ ὡς σήμερον προσ-
[δ]εχωμένυ ὅτι ἐλεύσῃ·
ἢ σὺ φροντίσας πείησον, ἂν
15 δὲ μή, [αὐτὴ]ν δ[ί]δομεν· καὶ
ὑγεὴς κεκόμισμαι τὴν
ἐπιστολὴν παρὰ τοῦ Ὀνο-
μά[σ]του. εὐχώμετά σε
ἵνα καλῶς ἔχην. ἵνα ⟨μὴ⟩
20 ἐπιλάθῃς τῶν τέκνω⟨ν⟩
σου, κόμισαι ἑτέραν ἐπισ-

Herennia to her father Pompeius many greetings and continual good health. I have bought the olives for you. They are asking on all sides for the pious offering for the shrine of Souchos; asking everyone, even Romans and Alexandrians and inhabitants (settlers) in the Arsinoite nome. They are asking Pompeius. I have not paid, since I was expecting that you would come today (?). Either give heed and attend to it, or if you do not, we will pay it. Also, I received the letter safely from Onomastos. We pray that you may be well. Lest you forget your children, receive another letter from your son Syrion. (Blank space of about three lines) We send our regards to you and to Charitous and her children. Moreover, little Pompeius sends his regards to you. (Year) 4 of Nero Claudius Caesar Augustus Germanicus Imperator, Tybi 23.

Outside address: Deliver to her father Pompeius from Herennia . . . to the father of Onamastos (?) . . . deliver to the house of Nemesous.

{σ}τολὴν Συρίωνος τοῦ υἱοῦ
σου.

ἐπισ{σ}κοπούμεθά σε καὶ
25 Χαριτοῦν καὶ τὰ τέκνα
αὐτήν. καὶ Πονπήγις ὡ μι-
κρὸς ἐπισ{σ}κοπῖται ἡμᾶς.
(ἔτους) δ Νέρωνος Κλαυδίου Καίσαρος
Σεβαστοῦ Γερμανκοῦ Αὐτοκράτορος,
30 Τῦβι κγ.

Verso: δῦς Πονπηγίωι πατρὶ
παρὰ Ἑλενίας ιτ[.......].ελνν
τῶι πατρὶ Ὠνομάστου
α[...].[....]..οσε.[..].[ἀπό]δ̣ο̣ς
ε[ἰς τὴν ο]ἰκίαν Νεμεσοῦ[τος].

1 [Ἑ]λενία (see also line 31): POsloInv 1475.13f.
(letter 91) and POsloInv 1444.1 show this spelling to be a corruption of Ἑρεννία. The scribe
employed for the present letter misspelled both
the name of Herennia and that of Pompeius.
Herennia is the addressor, both here and in
POsloInv 1444, and she was assisted in both cases
by an "unprofessional" scribe. She herself added
the valediction in POsloInv 1444.14 (see PMert
II 63, note to line 1 and see Mayser, *Grammatik*
1.1.161f.).
   Read Πομπηίωι: for the spelling, Πονπηγίωι,
see also line 31 (see Πονπήγιν, line 11). Regarding the intrusive γ, see Mayser, *Grammatik*
1.1.142f.
2 Read χαίρειν.
3 Read ὑγιαίνειν, σοι.
4 Read ἐλαίας.

4f.   Read πανταχόθεν.
5f.   Read εὐσέβειαν.
7   Read πάντας.
9   Read κατοικοῦντας.
10   Read Ἀρσινοίτηι.
11   Read Πομπήιον.
12f. Read προσδεχομένη.
13   Read ὅτι ἐλεύσει (?).
14   Read ποίησον.
16   Read ὑγιῆ (?).
17f. Read Ὀνομαστοῦ.
18   Read εὐχόμεθα.
18f. εὐχώμετά σε ἵνα καλῶς ἔχην: the editors of
      PMert 63, Rees, Bell and Barns, suggest that this
      clause is almost certainly a confusion of two con-
      structions. Namely, ἔχην should either be ἔχειν
      (see Mayser, *Grammatik* 2.3.202, 204) or it
      should be ἔχῃς (see POxy IX 1217.5).
21f. Read ἐπιστολήν.
26   Read αὐτῆς, Πομπήιος ὁ.
26f. Πονπήγις ὡ μικρός: see POsloInv 1475.14 (letter
      91) and POsloInv 1444.11.
27   Read ἐπισκοπεῖται ὑμᾶς: the editor of PMert 63
      suggests that ἐπισκοπεῖσθαι usually means "send
      regards to" in letters (see POslo III 153, note to
      line 16). The translation, "look after," by Grenfell
      and Hunt, the editors of POxy II 293.16 and of
      POxy 294.31, is doubtful (see also POxy IV
      743.43).
29   Read Γερμανικοῦ.
31   Read δοῖς (*sic*), Πομπηίωι.
32   Read Ὀνομαστοῦ (?). Onomastos is an uncom-
      mon name, occuring only twice in Preisigke's
      Namenbuch.

91 CHARITOUS TO POMPEIUS
POsloInv 1475

mid-I CE

Charitous writes to her brother, Pompeius, informing him that she had attended to a
matter about which he had written. It seems Pompeius feared that he had incurred
some obligation which would be on record in the office of the basiliko-grammateus (the
crown secretary).

Pompeius was temporarily away from home, probably staying at the town, and in the house of his daughter Herennia. Sometimes a man who is addressed as "brother" by a woman will also be her husband. In the present instance, however, even though Charitous clearly misses her brother and wishes that he would return home, Pompeius is probably not her husband. The manner in which Herennia extends separate greetings to Charitous and her children in the preceding letter (letter 90.24–26), when she writes to her father, makes it unlikely that Charitous was the wife of Pompeius.

Since the office of the basiliko-grammateus was located in Pompeius' place of residence, his city would have been the metropolis (capital) of the Arsinoite nome (see letter 90.9f. as evidence that it was the Arsinoite nome).

Χαρ[ιτοῦ]ς Πομπηίωι τῶι
    ἀδελφῶι χαίρειν.
θέλω σε γε[ι]νώσκειν ὅτι περὶ
οὗ μοι ἔγραψας, ἐμέλησέ
5 μοι· ἀπῆλθον πρὸς Ζωιλᾶν
τὸν τοῦ Ἀργαίου καὶ ἀπῆλθεν
εἰς τὰ τοῦ βασιλικοῦ γραμματέως καὶ ἐπέσκεπται
καὶ οὐχ εὗρεν τὸ ὄνομά
10 σου ἐν τῶι τόμωι γε-
γραμμένον. λοιπὸν οὖν
ταχύτερον ἀνάβα παρά σε.
ἀσπάζου τὰ παιδεία Ἑρεν-
νίας [κ]αὶ Πομπ[ῆιν] καὶ
15 Συρίωνα καὶ Θαισ[οῦν κ]αὶ
τὰ τέκνα αὐτῆς καὶ
τὸν ἄ[ν]δρα αὐτῆς καὶ
πάσας [τ]ὰς φί[λ]ας μο[υ.
    ἔρρω(σο).

Verso: ἀ]πόδ(ος) παρὰ Χαριτοῦτ(ος) Πομπηίωι τῶι ἀδελφῶι.

Charitous to her brother Pompeius greeting. I want you to know that I attended to the matter about which you wrote to me. I went to Zoilas, the son of Argaios, and he went to the office of the basiliko-grammateus and he inquired and did not find your name written on the roll. At last, then, come up very quickly to your home. Salute the children of Herennia and Pompeis and Syrion and Thaisous and her children and husband and all my friends. Good-bye.

Outside address: Deliver from Charitous to her brother Pompeius.

5ff. ἀπῆλθον . . . καὶ ἀπῆλθεν . . . καὶ ἐπέσκεπται καὶ οὐχ εὗρεν: the editors of POsloInv 1475 (Eitrem and Amundsen, "Three Private Letters," p. 178) note that the parataxis here indicates immediately subsequent (and sequential) actions.

13 Read παιδία.

14 Pompeis: the son of the addressee (see letter 90.11).

15 Thaisous: see POsloInv 1444.8.

92 HĒRAKLOUS TO POMPEIUS
POsloInv 1460

mid-I CE

Heraklous informs Pompeius that he must come to her immediately to settle some business matter occasioned by the death of a certain Apeis. In their edition of this letter in "Three Private Letters," (pp. 179–81), Eitrem and Amundsen suggest that the matter at issue may concern an inheritance. The documents called "memoranda" may concern the transference of property (e.g., household possessions, house mortgage) on which the sales tax (ἐγκύκλιον) should have been paid when the transaction was registered. Acting on behalf of Heraklous, Argyrios had gained access to the public office where such transactions were recorded and had learned that no sales tax had been paid. Consequently, the transactions in question were invalid and this seems to agree with what Heraklous had been maintaining against Serapous, who was making some claim against the property. Serapous emphasized that there were "two" memoranda, evidently thinking that the second one would prove her claim. Pompeius probably knew exactly what Heraklous was writing about, but we can only speculate.

Eitrem and Amundsen suggest that Heraklous may be the wife of Pompeius ("Three Private Letters") She is elsewhere referred to in the correspondence but not named (see POsloInv 1444.11f.). In this case, Serapous pestered Heraklous more easily in Pompeius' absence.

ʽΗρακλοῦς Πομπηίωι χα(ίρειν)
καὶ διὰ παντὸς ὑγιαίνειν. εὐθέως ἄν σοι
ἔλθῃ ἡ [ἐ]πιστολή, εὐθέως παραγείνου. ἐξ ὅτου
Ἄπεις ἐτελεύτησεν, οὐκ ἀφεῖ Σεραποῦς
5   ἐν τῇ οἰκίᾳ χειμάζει με. ἐξ ὅτου ʼνκλεῖ
ὅτι· φέρετε τὰ ὑπομνήματα, ἔσταται λέγ[ο]υσα
ὅτι· δύο ὑπομνήματα. οὐ δίδω. Ἀργύριο[ς
ἐκκεκοίρουκεν ἡμᾶς λέγων ὅτι· οὐ δεδ[ώ-
κατε ἐνκύκλ[ιο]ν. ἐὰν σοι ἔλθῃ ἡ ἐπ[ισ]τολή,
10   εὐθέω[ς πα]ραγείνου· εἰ δὲ μὴ, ἐγὼ ὑπά-
γω ἐκ τῆς οἰκίας. ἐὰν μὴ ἔλθῃς, ἐγὼ
καθίσασα οἶκον ἐλεύσομαι εἴς σε, εἰν'
ἢ τηγ[.........................

Verso:].˙˙
                        ]εἰς τὸ . . .

Heraklous to Pompeius greeting and continual good health. Just as soon as this letter arrives, come immediately. Ever since Apeis died, Serapous does not leave off troubling me at home. Ever since then she taunts me: "produce the memorandum," she stands there saying, "Two memoranda." I do not give them. Argyrios has utterly confirmed (?) us, saying: "You have not paid the sales tax." Whenever this letter arrives, come immediately. If you do not come, I will leave the house. If you do not come, after arranging about the house, I will come up to you in order to . . . (The papyrus breaks off here).

Outside address: (Only traces regarding the letter's destination).

2   Read ἐάν: sometimes ἐάν in Hellenistic Greek seems to be synonymous with ὅταν (see also the translation of ἐάν in line 9), e.g., see POxy IV 744.7; John 14:3: ἐὰν πορευθῶ . . . πάλιν ἔρχομαι; 1 John 2:28: ἵνα ἐὰν φανερωθῇ, σχῶμεν παρρησίαν (text rec. ὅταν)..
3   ἐξ ὅτου=ἀφ' ὡς or ἀφ' ὅτε (see POxy III 528.7, 9).
4   Read ἀφίει.
5   Read χειμάζειν, ἐγκαλεῖ.
8   Read ἐκκεκύρωκεν: Eitrem and Amundsen note that though ἐκκυροῦν is not in the Greek dictionary, it must denote "confirm utterly" (or "ratify completely").
12   Read ἵν'.

LETTER TO DIONYSIOS THE PHYSICIAN
PMert I 12

This letter is striking because of its literate, almost philosophical, expression of cordiality and friendship. The recipient of the letter was a physician, and the literary flavor of the letter suggests that the writer was also well educated and may have been a physician himself. Apart from the opening expression of friendship occasioned by the receipt of a letter from the addressee, the writer gave his opinion on certain prescriptions of plaster which the addressee had sent to him. In need of yet another remedy, the writer requested a plaster that could be used to cauterize soles of the feet. While the writer may have required this prescription for his own use, it seems more likely that it was required for one or more of his patients. Many native Egyptians went barefoot and we often hear about sore feet.

The original editors of this text, Bell and Roberts, were aided in interpreting the medical references by a physician, Dr. E. T. Withington (see introductory comments to PMert I 12).

Χαιρᾶς Διονυσίωι τῶι φιλτάτωι
πλεῖστα χαίρειν καὶ διὰ πάντο(ς)
ὑγιαίνειν. κομισάμενός σου ἐπι[στολ(ὴν)]
οὕτως περιχαρὴς ἐγενόμη[ν ὡς εἰ]
5 ὄντως ἐν τῇ ἰδίᾳ ἐγεγόνειν, ἄ[νευ]
γὰρ ταύτης οὐθέν ἐστιν. γράφειν δέ
σοι μεγάλας εὐχαριστίας παρετέο(ν)·
δεῖ γὰρ τοῖς μὴ φίλοις οὖσι διὰ λόγων
εὐχαριστεῖν. πείθομαι δὲ ὅτι ἐν
10 γαληνείᾳ τινὶ ἐνεισχύω, καὶ εἰ μὴ
τὰ ἴσα σοι παρασχεῖν, βραχεία τινὰ
παρέξομαι τῇ εἰς ἐμὲ φιλοστοργίᾳ.
ἀντιγράφια δέ μοι δύο ἔπεμψας,
τὸ μὲν τῆς Ἀρχαγαθήου τὸ δὲ τῆς
15 ἑλκωτικῆς. ἡ μὲν Ἀρχαγάθις ὑγιῶς
περιέχει, ἡ δὲ ἑλκωτικὴ ῥητείνης
συνσταθμίαν οὐ περιέχει. ἐρωτῶ
δέ σε περὶ ἑλκωτικῆς γενναίας
δυναμένης ἀκινδύνως πέλματ(α)
20 ἑλκῶσαι ... χ[ὰ]ρ [κ]ατ' ἀνάγκην
ἐπείγομαι. περὶ δὲ τῆς σκληρᾶς
ἔγραψας δύο γένη εἶναι. τὸ τῆς δια-
λυτικῆς μοι γραφίον πέμψον· ἔστιν
γὰρ καὶ ἡ τετραφάρμακος σκληρά.
25 ἡ δὲ ἐπιστολὴ αὕτη ταύτῃ σοι ἐσφράγι(σται).
ἔρρωσο καὶ μέμνησο τῶν εἰρημ(ένων)
ε (ἔτους) Νέρωνος τοῦ κυρίου, μηνὸς Γερμανικοῦ ᾱ.

Verso: Διονυσίωι ἰατρῶι.

Chairas to his dearest Dionysios many greetings and continual good health. When I received your letter, I was as exceedingly joyous as if I had actually been in my own native place; for without (the joy of) that there is nothing. And I can disregard writing to you with great gratitude, for it is (only) required that one express thankfulness with words to those who are not friends. I am confident that I can persevere with sufficient tranquillity, and if not able to render something equivalent, I will be able to render some humble return for your warm affection toward me. You sent two prescription copies, one of the Archagathian, the other of the caustic plaster. The Archagathian is of the right consistency (rightly compounded), but the caustic does not include the correct amount (relative weight) of resin. I request your advice regarding a suitable caustic that can be used safely to cauterize the soles of the feet; for I am pressed by necessity (for a prescription). Regarding the stiff plaster, you wrote that there are two kinds. Send the prescription of the resolvent type; for the four-drug plaster is also stiff. This letter for you is sealed with this (?). Good-bye and remember what I have said. (Year) 5 of Nero the lord, the month of Germanicus 1.

Outside address: To Dionysios, physician.

5f. ἄνευ κτλ.: strictly speaking, this is not an explanation of delight at receiving the letter, but the letter makes present the writer's home town (native place) and all that it means to him emotionally. In short, "there is no place like home."

6-9 The editors of PMert 12 suggest that the essential idea here is that whereas verbal thanks may be paid to perfectly indifferent people, they are an inadequate expression of intimate friendship. Deeds are the appropriate medium of friendship (see the following sentence).

10 Read ἐνισχύω: this word usually refers to a condition or opinion of a group, but here it must refer to the state of Chairas himself, i.e., he "continues" in serenity. The editors of PMert 12 suggest that he is "getting up his strength" (after an illness?).

11 Read βραχέα.

13 ἀντιγράφια: this is evidently the diminutive form of ἀντίγραφος (the use of γραφῖον in line 23 favors this interpretation of ἀντίγραφια. The editors note that the writer probably wrote αντιρραφια, but it is difficult to see what that word could mean in this context.)

14 Read Ἀρχαγαθείου (and Ἀρχαγάθειος in line 15): a well-known plaster, the name of which was derived from its inventor, Archagathos.

15 Read ἑλκωτικῆς: see PMert 12, note to line 15 regarding the meaning of this word.

16 Read ῥητίνης.

23 Read γραφεῖον.

94 INDIKĒ TO THAÏSOUS
POxy II 300

late I CE

Indike informs Thaisous that she has sent a breadbasket with a camel driver (probably from a passing caravan) and instructs Thaisous to send word whether she has received it. Private post was carried either by one's own messenger or by people who happened to be traveling in the direction of the letter. As the present letter implies, such delivery could be risky business and, consequently, it was important to notify the intended recipient that something had been sent.

Since Indike greets Thaisous as "her lady" and Theon as "lord," Indike is probably either the daughter or a servant of the couple. The other people to whom salutations are extended in the closing are probably family members in the household of Thaisous and Theon.

Ἰνδικη Θαεισοῦτι τῇ κυρίᾳ
    χαίρειν.
ἔπεμψά σοι διὰ τοῦ καμηλείτου
Ταυρείνου τὸ πανάρι(ο)ν, περὶ οὗ
5 καλῶς ποιήσεις ἀντιφωνήσασά
μοι ὅτι ἐκομίσου. ἀσπάζου Θέωνα
τὸν κύριον καὶ Νικόβουλον καὶ Διόσκο-
ρον καὶ Θέωνα καὶ Ἑρμοκλῆν τοὺς
ἀβασκάντους. ἀσπάζεται ὑμᾶς
10 Λογγεῖνος.   ἔρρω(σο).
    μη(νὸς) Γερμανικ(   ) β̄.

Verso: εἰς τὸ γυμνάσι(ον)   Θέωνι Νικοβούλ(ου)
    ἐλεοχρείστηι.

Indike to her lady Thaisous greeting. I sent the breadbasket to you by means of Taurinos, the camel driver; regarding which, please send word to me that you received it. Salute my lord Theon and Nikoboulos and Dioskopos and Theon and Hermokles, may all be free from harm. Longinus salutes you. Good-bye. The month Germanic (. . .) 2.

Outside address: At the gymnasium. To Theon the son of Nikoboulos, the olive oil supplier.

---

1 Read Θαισοῦτι.

3 Read καμηλίτου.

4 Read Ταυρίνου. πανάριον=Latin *panarium* (Greek ἀρτοφόριον).

11 Γερμανικ( ) may be either Γερμανικ(οῦ) (Egyptian Thoth; see PFay 110.33 and letter 95) or Γερμανικ(είου) (Egyptian Pachon).

12 Read ἐλαιοχρίστηι.

The following six letters (letter 97 has two entries) belong to a group of letters which were unearthed in the winter of 1898–99 in the ruins of a small village in the northwest corner of the Fayum (see the map of the Fayum, p. 155). The archive consists of thirty-five letters, two contracts, and one column of an account of wages which were paid to seasonal farm laborers. Of these documents, the editors of PFay have published fourteen letters (PFay 110–23), the account of wages (PFay 102), and one of the contracts (PFay 91). The remainder are catalogued and explained briefly in the "descriptions" at the end of the volume.

The principal figure in the correspondence is Lucius Bellenus Gemellus, the head of the family, and the one by whom the bulk of the letters were written. His own letters span a period from 94–110 CE, a period during which he was a prosperous old farmer in the Fayum. Most of them were addressed either to Epagathos, a steward on four of his farms, or to his son Sabinus. Other family members mentioned in the correspondence are Gemella, probably a married daughter of Gemellus (letter 97a.15=PFay 113); a little boy whom Gemellus speaks of affectionately as "the little one" (letter 97a.18), who is probably the son of Gemella; Marcus Antonius (?) Maximus, a brother (PFay 116.18); two sons in addition to Sabinus, Harpokration and Lykos (letter 99=PFay 123); a fourth son, whose name is lost because of a break in the papyrus (letter 99.27); Geminus who, like Epagathos, was probably a trusted servant (PFay 121); and, finally, another servant, a certain Pasis (PFay 119.33–34).

Gemellus himself was probably born about 32 CE, because he gives his age as "about sixty-seven years" in a contract made in 99 CE (PFay 91.12). He appears to have been of Graeco-Egyptian descent and to have served in one of the two Roman legions stationed in Egypt (see the editors' interpretation of PFay 91.11). After having served the customary twenty years, he would have been discharged as a veteran and it was this service which gave to him his Roman citizenship and which accounts for his Roman name, which was the badge of such citizenship. It is unlikely that he received citizenship upon enlistment, since that privilege was reserved for Greeks who were members of the polis, most notably at Alexandria (see the comments on Alexandrian citizenship in the introduction to letters 86–88).

Gemellus owned and worked, or supervised work, on seven small farms. The correspondence itself does not reveal how many or which ones of these farm plots were inherited, which ones may have been bought while enrolled in the legion, and which ones were granted as reward for military service. It seems reasonable to assume, however, that the military service accounts for a considerable portion of the land. Gemellus lived at the village of Aphroditopolis and managed the farms near Aphroditopolis and Psennophris, in the division of Herakleides of the Arsinoite nome. Four other farms, near the villages of Euhemeria, Dionysias, Apias, and Senthis, were under the management of a steward, Epagathos. These were located in the division of Themistes, some fourteen to fifteen miles west and perhaps a little south of Aphroditopolis. Epagathos lived at Euhemeria, which was the center of the operations for the four farms that he managed. It seems the storehouses and draft animals for the whole of Gemellus' holdings were centered at Euhemeria.

The remaining holding was a vegetable garden at Psinachis, under the supervision of one Pasis.

One of the two plots managed directly by Gemellus, the farm at Psennophris, was, like the garden at Psinachis, either planted with vegetables or olive trees, since he was manuring the property (grain fields were not manured in Egypt, except by pasturing animals on the land prior to planting). The grain fields were located primarily at the Euhemeria center.

The general impression that one gains of Gemellus from his correspondence is that he was a shrewd business man with a keen attention to detail, who was insistent upon punctuality (e.g., see letter 96). He could express strong disapproval when the actions of his lieutenants dissatisfied him. On the other hand, the more genial side of Gemellus is exhibited in his frequent instructions regarding supplies for the celebration of some festival (see letter 98.11=PFay 117, 118.16, 119.28) or the birthday of a family member (97a.14=PFay 113; 97b.20=PFay 114; 115.8). Even these occasions could be used to enhance business, however, as the example of the fall celebration of the Isis cult illustrates (it began on Hathyr 17, or 12 November). Gemellus customarily sent presents to certain nome officials (see PFay 118.13–15) on this festival. Clearly, Gemellus was of a naturally keen business nature and his experience in the Roman army only enhanced his understanding of how to deal with petty bureaucrats and subordinates. He also stayed in contact with higher officials of the Arsinoite nome, as letter 98 indicates. In his latest extant letter to Sabinus (108 CE), he informs his son that Elouras, the royal scribe of the nome, had been appointed to perform the duties of the strategos, Erasus, by mean of a letter from the prefect. Regarding that appointment, he offers the following advice: "If it seems good to you, send an artab of olives and some fish, since we have need of him."

The latest letter from Gemellus is in 110 CE (PFay 118), when he was about seventy-seven years old. His age is reflected in his shaky and nearly illegible handwriting but, as the editors suggest, it was probably never very good, any more than his atrocious spelling and grammar. Gemellus probably died in this same year or shortly thereafter. According to Westermann, his death would explain why the son Sabinus wrote instructions to Epagathos (PFay 122) instead of Gemellus, and it would account for a letter from a brother, Harpokration, who asks for a decision on a proposed action (letter 99; "An Egyptian Farmer," p. 190). These two letters, which are dated about 100 CE by the original editors, Grenfell, Hunt and Hogarth, are placed by Westermann in 110 CE or shortly thereafter ("An Egyptian Farmer," p. 190).

Three summary explanations of the Gemellus archive are: the introductory comments by the editors of PFay 110; Westermann, "An Egyptian Farmer"; and the chapter, "Lucius Bellenus Gemellus," in Lindsay's *Daily Life*, pp. 258–65.

95 LUCIUS BELLENUS GEMELLUS TO EPAGATHOS
PFay 110   94 CE

Gemellus sends a number of instructions to Epagathos regarding agricultural affairs on the farm near Euhemeria and also on the farm at nearby Dionysias. Epagathos is instructed to allow water in upon all the grain fields so that the sheep might be folded there. This was at the high period of the annual flood (Thoth: 29 August–27 September), about a month before planting. Evidently, the sheep grazed there to fertilize the land, which was the only manuring that the grain fields received. The original editors, Grenfell, Hunt and Hogarth, suggested that the sheep would not have been let into these fields until the water had subsided. But they wrongly assumed, it appears, that during inundation the fields would have been continually covered with a sheet of water. Westermann suggested, by contrast, that the more natural implication of Gemellus' instruction that the sheep were to be turned in upon the fields is that the water was only allowed to soak in and then it was drained off in a few days, i.e., the flood was controlled completely ("An Egyptian Farmer," pp. 183–86).

There were olive groves at Euhemeria and Dionysias (possibly also at Psennophris). They formed a significant source of income for Gemellus. Generally speaking, olive culture was not (and still is not) an important agricultural product in Egypt, but Gemellus lived in the one place, the Fayum, where olive trees produced well enough in quantity and quality to be used for the manufacture of olive oil. We learn here that olive groves were to be irrigated for the second time of the season in Thoth (September; cf. lines 14–20). According to PFay 118 they were also irrigated in Hathyr (November). Consequently, olive groves were irrigated in the four to five months during which the fruit developed. In Choiach (December) and early Tybi (January), olives in the Fayum were ripe and ready for harvest (see letter 98: it is on Tybi 19 that Gemellus sends to Euhemeria for fresh olives for the house). The different types of work required in the care of olive groves at this time are rehearsed by Westermann ("An Egyptian Farmer," pp. 183ff.).

This handwriting does not belong to Gemellus, but the letter was written by a scribe who, according to the editors, wrote in a well-formed, uncial hand of a literary type.

λούκιος Βελλῆνος Γέμελλος
Ἐπαγαθῶι τῶι ἰδίωι χαίρειν.
εὖ ποιήσεις κομισάμενός μου
τὴν [ἐ]πιστ[ο]λὴν ἀναγκάσας
5 ἐκχωσθῆναι τὸ ἐν αὐτῶι κόπριον
ἵνα καταβ[ο]λαῖον γένηται ὃ λέγεις
ταμε[ῖ]ον, κ[α]ὶ τὰ κύκλωι τοῦ ἐλαιουργίου ἔξωθεν σκάψον ἐπὶ βάθος
ἵνα μὴ εὖ ὑπερβατὸν ἦι τὸ ἐλαι-
10 ουργῖον, καὶ χώρισον τὸ κόπριον
εἰς τὴν κοπρηγίαν, καὶ λιμναζέ-
τωσαν ἡμῶν τοὺς κλήρους πάντας ἵ[ν]α τὰ πρόβατα ἐκεῖ κοιμηθῆι,
καὶ το[ὺ]ς ἐ[λαι]ῶνας τὸ δεύτερον
15 [ὕ]δω[ρ] λου[σ]άτωσαν, καὶ διάβα εἰς
Διον[υ]σιά[δα] καὶ γνῶθι εἰ πεπότισ-
ται ὁ [ἐ]λαιὼν δυσὶ ὕδασι καὶ δεδι-
[κ]ράν[ισται, εἰ] δὲ τι μὴ ποτισθήτωι
καὶ εν[.]τε . [.] . . ἀσφαλῶς δικρανισ-
20 [θ]ῆ μ[. .].κ . α . [.] αὐτοὺς διαπέσηι, καὶ
[δ]οὺς . [. . . κα]ὶ Ψέλλον τοὺ(ς) σιτολόγους
[.] . υχ [. . καὶ] Χαιρᾶν τὸν γρ(αμματέα) τῶν
[γε]ωρ[γῶν καὶ] Ἡρακλᾶν (δραχμὰς) ꝱ καὶ τόκους,

Lucius Bellenus Gemellus to his own Epagathos greeting. When you receive my letter, please have the manure heaped up in order that you may make the store place which you mention, and dig a deep trench around the oilpress outside in order that access to the winepress may not be easy, and remove the manure to the manure pile, and let them flood all our fields in order that the sheep may be folded there, and let them irrigate the oliveyards for the second time, and go over to Dionysias and find out whether the oliveyard has been watered twice and dug; and if not, let it be watered . . . and give to . . . and Psellos, the sitologoi (keepers of the public granaries) . . . and Chairas, the scribe of the cultivators, and to Heraklas ninety drachmas and interest, and to Chairas, the former tax collector, 24 drachmas, and Didas . . . the price of the barley, 240 drachmas and interest, and to Heron, the former president (?), two years interest, 120 drachmas. And let the carpenters set up the doors; I am sending the measurements to you. Make the hinges (?) of the oilpress double, and the ones of the stores single.

καὶ Χα[ιρᾶ]ν [τὸ]ν ποτε πράκτορα (δραχμὰς) κδ,
25 καὶ Διδᾶν [.]δουν τιμ(ὴν) κριθ(ῆς) (δραχμὰς) Σμ καὶ
τόκ(ους),
καὶ ''Ηρωνα τόν ποτε ἡγούμ(ενον) τόκ(ους) (ἐτῶν) β
(δραχμὰς) ρκ. καὶ τὰς Θύρας ἐπιστησάτωσαν
οἱ τέκτονες· πέμπω δέ σοι τὰ σχοι-
νία. τὰς δὲ ὠλένας τοῦ ἐλαιουργίου
30 δ[ι]πλᾶς ποίησον, τὰς δὲ τῶν κα-
ταβολα[ί]ω(ν) ἁ[π]λᾶς.   ἔρρωσο.
(ἔτους) ιδ Αὐτοκράτορος Καίσαρος Δομιτιανοῦ
[Σ]εβασ[τοῦ Γερμ]ανικοῦ, μηνὸς Γερμανικοῦ ιδ.
μὴ οὖν [ἄ]λλως ποιήσῃς.

Verso: ἀπόδος 'Επαγαθῷ ἀπὸ Λουκίου Βελλήνου Γεμέλλου.

Good-bye. (Year) 14 of the Emperor Caesar Domitianus Augustus Germanicus, the month of Germanicus 14. Therefore, do not act otherwise.

Outside address: Deliver to Epagathos from Lucius Bellenus Gemellus.

---

21 The editors note that if δούς is a correct reading, then Ψέλλον, and the other people's names in the accusative, should be in the dative.
22f. γρ(αμματέα) τῶν [γε]ωρ[γῶν]: see the introductory comments to PFay 18a, where it is suggested that the scribe of the cultivators was concerned with advancing the seed corn which was to be sowed by the cultivators of state (crown) land.

96 GEMELLUS TO EPAGATHOS
PFay 112

99 CE

Gemellus writes another letter to Epagathos, once again about agricultural details. In this instance, he is extremely dissatisfied with Epagathos' negligence. He objects to the high-handed way in which Epagathos treated a surveyor, and his failure to harvest all the grain on a piece of land at Apias.

Λούκιος Βελλῆνος Γέμελλος 'Επαγαθῶι
τῶι ἰδίωι χα(ίρειν). εὖ πυήσις διῶξαι τοὺς σκα-
φήτρους τῶν ἐλαιῶνον καὶ τοὺς ὑποσχ[ει]σμοὺς
καὶ διβολήτρους τῶν ἐλαιῶνον, καὶ [τὰ] ἀνα-
5 παύματα ὑπόσχεισον καὶ διβόλησον, [ἐ]πιτί-
νας τὸν ζευγηλάτην εἶνα ἑκάσ[της] ἡμέρας τὼ ἔργον ἀποδῦ, καὶ μὴ τῦς κε̣ι[.]ασι
ἀριθμὸν ταυρικὸν κόλλα. τῶν ὄγμ[ον] τῆς
'Απιάδος ἕως σήμερον οὐ ἐθέρ[ι]σας ἀλλ᾽ ἡμέ-
10 ληκας αὐτοῦ καὶ μέχρι τούτου τῷ ἥμυ-
συ αὐτοῦ ἐθέρισας, ἐπέχον τῷ δακ-
τυλιστῇ Ζωίλωι καὶ εἶνα αὐτὸν μὴ δυσω-
πήσῃς· ἀθέρισ(τον) αὐτὸν ἕως σήμερον ἄφι-
κας· διὼ μένφομαί σαι μεγάλως. ἐπίγνω-
15 θι εἰ ἐσκάφη ὦ τῆς Διονυσιάδος ἐλαιών·
εἰ μὴ δίωξον αὐτοῦ τῶν σκάφητρων
ἐν δυσὶ ἡμέρα⟨ι⟩ς. συνφέρι γὰρ εν . ικκον
αὐτὸν [σ]καφῆναι. μὴ σπουδασέτωσαν
ἄλω ανταλομμινα καὶ τὴν Σένθεως
20 ἕως γράψω. τὰς ἄλως οὐ πάσας θλάσον

Lucius Bellenus Gemellus to his own Epagathos greeting. Please urge on the hoeing of the olive groves, as well as the breaking up and the harrowing of the olive groves, and break up and harrow the fallow fields. Press the teamster (of oxen) in order that he accomplish his assigned work each day, and do not allow a number of bulls to unite (pasture together?). Up to today you have not harvested the strip of land at Apias, but have put it off and until now have harvested only half of it. Heed the surveyor, Zoilos, and do not regard him with aversion. Up to today you have left it (the field) unharvested; wherefore, I blame you a great deal. Find out whether the olive grove at Dionysias was hoed; if not, urge on the hoeing of it within two days. For it is advantagous that it be hoed. Do not let them be too hasty with the . . . threshing floor, nor the one at Senthis until I write. Do not overload all the threshing floors for the present. Make sure that you do not act otherwise. Good-

ἐπὶ τοῦ παρόντος. μὴ οὖν ἄλλως πυήσῃς.

ἔρρωσο. ἀσπάζου ῞Ηρωνα καὶ ᾿Ορσενοῦφιν
καὶ τοὺς ἐν ὕκῳ πάντες. (ἔτους) β Αὐτοκράτορος
Καίσαρος Νερούα Τραιανοῦ Σεβαστοῦ Γερμανικοῦ,
25 Παχὸν κς.

bye. Salute Heron and Orsenouphis and all those at home. (Year) 2 of the Emperor Caesar Nerva Trajanus Augustus Germanicus, Pachon 26.

Verso: some traces of an address

7 Read ἀποδοῖ.

7–8 The meaning of κόλλα is dependent upon that of the fragmented word at the end of line 7. The editors, Grenfell, Hunt and Hogarth, suggest that κέρασι is possible, but hardly fills the space and does not yield a satisfactory reading.

8 Read ταυρικῶν . . . τὸν ὄγμ[ον].

14 Read μέμφομαί σε.

16 Read τὸν σκάφητρον.

19 ἄλω ανταλομμινα: some activity of the threshing floor appears to be indicated by the second word here, but the original editors were unable to resolve its meaning.

23 Read ἐν οἴκῳ πάντας: despite his earlier accusation of negligence in the letter, Gemellus closes the letter by greeting family members of Epagathos. The high esteem with which Epagathos was customarily regarded is always evident in the opening address (as here), where Gemellus refers to him as "his own Epagathos." Moreover, Gemellus once announces that he is about to take a trip "to the city" and adds: "If I go away I will send to you to greet you" (PFay 116.20–21). At another time he inquires whether Epagathos has recovered from a fever (PFay 248) and, when writing Sabinus, he sends greetings to Epagathos (PFay 119.25).

97 GEMELLUS TO SABINUS
PFay 113   100 CE
PFay 114   100 CE

The following two texts are treated as one entry because they are almost identical in subject and phraseology, and were written within a few days of each other. In both, Gemellus instructs Sabinus to send Pindaros, an estate (field?) guard, from the Dionysias estate in order to assist a friend in thinning out his olive grove. The second letter clarifies his reason for requesting Pindaros (lines 15–17), "in order that those trees to be cut out may be cut out skillfully."

Pindaros was something of a specialist in the thinning and care of olive groves. Apparently, Sabinus replied to the first letter by explaining why he had kept Pindaros at Dionysias, and he complained about the prospects for cleaning grain at the coming harvest. Nonetheless, Gemellus repeats his request in an insistent and peremptory tone: "On receipt of my letter, please send Pindaros." And he continues, "do not talk foolishly about your threshing."

The message of both letters concludes with a request that fish be sent for a festal occasion, the "four-hundred-day" festival of the "little one" in the first and the birthday of Gemella in the latter. The little one is probably Gemella's small son and the four-hundred-day celebration was apparently a feast four hundred days after birth. This application of "little one" to a toddler suggests, by analogy, that Pompeius, "the young one," in letter 90 was also a child, a grandson, and not the grown son, Pompeius.

Letter A

Λούκιος Βελλῆνος Γέμελλος
Σαβίνωι τῶι οιειῶι χαίρειν.
πάντη πάντος πέμσις Πίν-
δαρον τὸν πεδιοφύλακα τῆς
5 Διονυσ[ιά]δος εἰ τὸν πατέρα αὐτοῦ,
ἐπὶ Ἑρμόναξ ἐρώτησέ με εἴνα
ἐφίδη τὸν [ἐ]λαιῶνα αὐτοῦ τὸν
ἐν Κερκεσούχυς ἐπὶ πυκνός
ἐστιν τῦς φυτῦς, καὶ ἐξ αὐτὸν
10 ἐκκόψαι θέλι.φυτά. εὖ οὖν πυήσας ἐξαυτῆς πέμσις αὐτὸν
ἐξαυτῆς· καὶ τῆι ιη εἰ ιθ τῇ
πόλι πέμσις εἰκθύας (δραχμῶν) ιβ
ἐπὶ τὰ τετρακοσ{σ}τὰ τοῦ μικροῦ
15 [..........ο]ιειοῦ Γεμέλλης

Lucius Bellenus Gemellus to his son, Sabinus, greeting. By all means, send Pindaros, the estate guard at Dionysias, or his father, since Hermonax has asked me that he (be allowed to) assist with his olive grove at Kerkesouchos, since it is overgrown with trees, and he wants to cut out some of them. Therefore, please send him immediately. And on the eighteenth or nineteenth send twelve drachmas' worth of fish to the city for the little one's four-hundred-day festival. . . .

---

2 Read υἱῷ.
3 Read πάντη πάντως, πέμψεις (also in lines 11 and 13).
5 Read ἤ.
6 Read Ἑρμῶναξ.
8 Read Κερκεσούχοις.
9 Read τοῖς φυτοῖς . . . αὐτῶν.
10 Read ποιήσας.
12 Read ἢ ιθ.
13 Read πόλει, ἰχθύας.
15 Read υἱοῦ.

Letter B

Λούκιος Βελλῆνος Γέμελλος
Σαβίνωι τῶι οιειῶι χαίρειν.
εὖ οὖν πυήσας κομισάμε-
νός μου τὴν ἐπιστολὴν
5 πέμσις μυ Πίνδαρον
εἰς τὴν πόλιν τὸν πεδι-
οφύλακα τῆς Διονυσιάδο(ς),
ἐπὶ ἐρώτησέ με Ἑρμό-
ναξ εἴνα αὐτὸν λά-
10 βῃ εἰς Κερκεσοῦχα
καταμαθῖν τὸν
ἐλαιῶνα αὐτοῦ ἐπὶ
πυκνός ἐστιν καὶ
θέλι ἐξ αὐτὸν ἐκκό-
15 ψαι φυτά, εἴνα ἐνπί-
ρος κοπῇ τὰ μέλλον-
τα ἐκκόπτεσθαι· καὶ
τὴν εἰκθὺιν πέμσις
τῆι κδ εἰ κε εἰς τὰ
20 γενέσια Γεμέλλης.
μὴ ο(ὖ)ν ληρήσῃς τὸν
ἐκτιναγμόν σου.
ἔρρωσο. (ἔτους) δ Αὐτοκράτορος
Καίσαρος Νερούα
25 Τραιαν[οῦ] Σεβαστοῦ
Γερμανικοῦ, Χύακ
ιη.

Lucius Bellenus Gemellus to his son, Sabinus, greeting. Upon receipt of my letter, please send Pindaros, the estate guard at Dionysias, to me at the city, since Hermonax has asked me to let him take him to Kerkesouchos to inspect his olive grove, since it is overgrown and he wants to cut out some trees, and in order that those to be cut out may be cut skillfully. And send the fish on the twenty-fourth or twenty-fifth for the birthday of Gemella. Therefore, do not talk foolishly about your threshing. Good-bye. (Year) 4 of the Emperor Caesar Nerva Trajanus Augustus Germanicus, Choiach 18.

---

2 Read υἱῷ.
3 Read ποιήσας.
5 Read πέμψεις.
9 Read ἵνα.
11 Read καταμαθεῖν.
14 Read θέλει.
15 Read ἐμπείρως.
18 Read ἰχθὺν πέμψεις.
19 Read ἤ.
26 Read Χοίαχ.

The number of misspelled and unknown words, along with various breaks, make this letter to Sabinus obscure in places. The middle of line 16 to the middle of 22 is so ambiguous that it is untranslated.

The letter shows that if the strategos was unable to perform his duties, through absence or other cause, a deputy was appointed by the prefect. The royal scribe appears to have a first claim to the office, and usually appears as the διαδεχόμενος τὴν στρατηγίαν, but actual confirmation rested with the prefect.

We noted above that Gemellus had learned the lesson of keeping in touch with the higher officials of the Arsinoite nome. His advice here regarding the royal scribe, who was recently appointed deputy strategos, illustrates his method: "If it seems good to you, send an artab of olives and some fish, for we have need of him" (lines 6–8).

The closing health formula, ἐρρῶσθαί σαι εὔχομαι (line 27), is not often found before the third century but, as the editors suggested, its occasional use at a much earlier period renders it an uncertain criterion of the date of letters.

Λούκιος Βελλῆνος Γέμελλος
Σεβίνωι τῶι υεἶωι χαίρειν καὶ διὰ παντὸς εὖ ⟨ἔ⟩χειν. γείνοσκαι Ἐλουρᾶν τὸν
βασιλεικὸν διαδέχεσθαι τὴν στρατη-
5 γείαν Ἐράσου ἐκ ἐπιστολὴν τοῦ κρα-
τείστου ἡγεμόνος. αἰάν συ δόξῃ πέμ-
σαι αὐτῷ ἐλᾶς ⟨ἀρτάβην⟩ α καὶ εἰκθύδιν ἐπὶ
χρίαν αὐτοῦ ἔχωμον. πέμσις ἡμῖν
εἰς ὐκον ατυμανια καὶ ἐλᾶν, ἐπὶ οὐ
10 ἔχουσι ἐλᾶν νέαν εἰς ὐκον. τοὺς θιώτας πέμσις ἐπὶ Ἔρασο[ς] τὰ Ἁρποχράτια
ὧδε τάχα ιδ πυ[ήσ]ι, καὶ τὰ βάκα-
να πέμ[σ]ον αὐ[τ]ῷ. πάντα τὰ κτήνη γεμίζι βάκανον καὶ πέμσομον
15 αὐτῶι βακάνου. [....]α πέντε καὶ εἰ-
ς ὐκον τῷ αὐτόν. γείνοσκαι εἰλη-
φαίναι.. [.]σσιον τῷ τρισελλον Ἐρά-
σου ⟨δραχμῶν⟩ τ, καὶ [...].[...]ν αὐτοῦ πεπύηται.
διὸ γράφο συ εἴν[α.] . [.]ης τοὺς ἵππους
20 οὓς λαβὸν ἀλλάσσου εἴν' αὐτοὺς
λαμβάνῃ. ἐκτίναξον τὸ διειρον εἴνα
ἀμέριμνος ἦς. ᾧ ἔγραφός μυ
μὴ ἡσυχάσαι τῷ κτιστῷ περι-
τὸν γέγραπτα[ι, κα]ὶ γράφις μυ λεί⟨α⟩ν
25 ὅτι εὐχαρι[σ]τῶ τῇ κόμῃ ὅτε
τέσσαρες [στ]α[τ]ῆρας καθ' ὑμὸν
γεγραφήκασι. ἐρρῶσθαί σαι εὔχομαι
εἰς τὸν ἀεὶ χρόνον. ⟨ἔτους⟩ ια Τραιανοῦ
Καίσαρος το[ῦ κ]υρίου, [Τ]ῦβι ιθ.

Verso: Χ ἀπόδ(ος) Σαβίνωι [τῷ] ο̣ι̣ε̣ι̣ῷ π(αρὰ) Λουκίου
Βελλήνου Γεμέλλου.

Lucius Bellenus Gemellus to his son, Sabinus, greeting and continual good health. Be aware that Elouras the royal scribe has been appointed deputy to the strategos, Erasus, by means of a letter from his excellency the prefect. If it seems good to you, send an artab of olives and some fish, since we have need of him. Send us . . . (?) for the house and olives, since they do not have fresh olives at the house. Send the loaves (?), since Erasus is going to celebrate the festival of Harpokrates as early as the fourteenth, and send the cabbages to him. Load all the animals with cabbage and we will send five . . . of cabbage to him and send the same amount to the house. . . . What you wrote to me, (advising me) about not being neglectful with the building, has been written more than enough, and you write too often to me that "I am thanking the village," when they have written four staters against you. I pray that you may have perpetual good health. (Year) 11 of Trajanus Caesar the lord, Tybi 19.

Outside address: Deliver to my son, Sabinus, from Lucius Bellenus Gemellus.

---

3 Read γείνωσκε (also in line 16).
5 Read ἐξ ἐπιστολῆς.
7 Read ἰχθύδιον.
8 Read ἔχομεν.
9 Read εἰς οἶκον (also in lines 10 and 16).
10 θιώτας: some form of food, perhaps loaves or cakes, since they had to be made.
12 βάκανον is thought to mean cabbage seed, but here it refers to the vegetable itself.
14 Read γέμιζε.
20 Read λαβών.
22 Read ἔγραφές μοι.

23 Read περιττόν.
30 The crosses mark the place for tying up the letter when folded (see Wilcken, *Chrestomathie*, p. 566).

Crosses also appear on the original of letter 103a, though not indicated. See also letters 99, 101, 104a–b, 107, 112, 115a.

99 HARPOKRATIŌN TO SABINUS
PFay 123

110–11 CE

It was noted above (introduction to letters 95–99) that both this letter and PFay 122 should be dated 110 CE or shortly thereafter, rather than 100, as the original editors suggested, since Sabinus functions with the authority of Gemellus in these two texts.

Here, Harpokration, Sabinus' brother, asks Sabinus for his decision on a proposed action. Harpokration states that a Jew, Teuphilos (Theophilos), who had been compelled to lease (cultivate) state owned land, wanted to be released from the obligation in order to go to Sabinus. Evidently, Teuphilos thought that Sabinus could procure his release from this compulsory labor (*leiturgeia*), but the correspondence itself does not indicate how he might accomplish such action.

Without explaining any details, Harpokration also notifies Sabinus that he has been delayed in coming down, because of being badly treated (beaten?) by someone.

῾Αρποκρατίων Βελλήνωι
Σαβείνωι τῶι ἀ-
δελφῶι χα(ίρειν). καὶ ἐκ-
θές σοι ἔγραψα διὰ
5 Μάρδωνος τοῦ σοῦ γ-
νῶναί σε θέλων ὅ-
τι διὰ τὸ ἐπηρεᾶσθαι
οὐκ ἠδυνήθην κατελ-
θεῖν, καὶ ὡς ἔχωι
10 ὧδε ἡμέρας ὀλίγας
ἐὰν δοκῇ σοι πέμψαι
τὸ ἀποχοον Ἰσᾶτος καὶ
παραλάβωμεν τὸ ἐλάδιο-
ν λυπὸν ἐὰν δόξῃ σοι.
15 ἐλήλυθεν γὰρ Τεύφι-
λος Ἰουδαῖος λέγων
[ὅ]τι ἤχθην ἰς γεωργίαν
καὶ βούλομαι πρὸς Σαβεῖ-
νον ἀπελθεῖ[ν]. οὔτε γὰρ εἴ-
20 ρηχε ἡμ[ῖ]ν ἀγόμενος
ἵνα ἀπολυθῇ, ἀλλὰ αἰ-
φνιδί[[.]]ως εἴρηχεν ἡμῖν
σήμερον. γνώσομαι γὰρ
εἰ ἀληθῶς λέγι.
25 ἔρρωσσο. ἀσπάζου
τοὺς ἀδελφοὺς Λύκον
κα[ὶ......]ν.
[Με]χειρ ιβ.

Verso: ἀπ[ό]δος ✕ Βελλήνῳ
Σαβείνωι

Harpokration to his brother, Sabinus, greeting. I wrote to you also yesterday through your man Mardon, wanting you to know that I was unable to come down, because of having been dealt with wantonly and, since I am remaining here a few days, send the measured out oil (?) of Isas, if it is agreeable with you, and let us take the remainder of the oil from him if you agree. Teuphilos the Jew has come, saying, "I have been pressed in as a cultivator and I want to go away to Sabinus." He did not say anything about being released at the time he was impressed, but suddenly he has told me today. I will find out whether he is telling the truth. Good-bye. Salute my brothers, Lykos and.... Mecheir 12.

Outside address: Deliver to Bellenus Sabinus.

3f. ἐκθές: χθές is usually lengthened to ἐκθές in the papyri.
12 το ἀποχοον: probably το ἀπόχυμα, not ἀποχήν (receipt?), as suggested by the editors.
14 Read λοιπόν.
15f. Read Θεόφιλος.
17 Read εἰς.
24 Read λέγει.

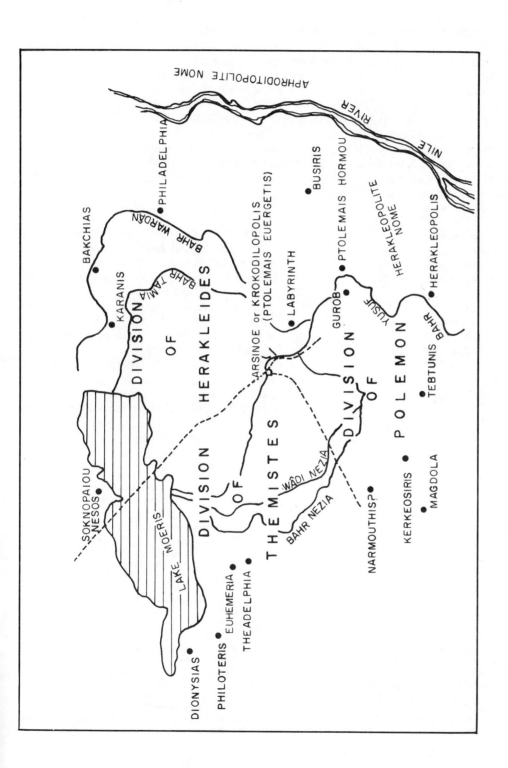

Fayum and Arsinoite
nome during the
Graeco-Roman
period.

100 ANTONIUS TO APULEIUS AND VALERIAS
PMich III 201

This nearly illiterate letter was written by Antonius (spelled Antonis) to Apuleius and Valerias, who were probably his brother and sister-in-law, about various articles of clothing. In the last half of the letter, Antonius invites a certain Atolessia and someone from the household of Apuleius and Valerias to pay a visit. Antonius concludes the message by conveying a reproach from Thermouthas, who is probably his wife, because the addressees have not been corresponding with her.

In addition to the numerous spelling errors, the letter has various other oddities. For example, the clause in the letter opening which begins with the phrase, "above all . . ." (πρὸ μὲν πάντων), proceeds in an unformulaic way with the sentiment: ". . . I extend greetings to you by letter." In line 7, the negative clause of purpose is expressed backwards as μη νά, rather than as ἵνα μή. Moreover, the letter concludes without a farewell, even though it is a family letter and has a complete date.

Ἀντῶνις Ἀποληείῳ καὶ Οὐαλε-
ριᾶτι ἀμφωταίροις χαίριν καὶ διὰ π-
αντὸς οἰγένιν. πρὸ μὲν πάντων σαι
ἀσπάσαιθε δι[ὰ ἐπι]στωλῆς. καλῶ-
5 ς ὂν ποιήσαται μελήσαιτε ἡμῖν περὶ τῶν ἀλ[ο]υρῶν τῶν δού-
ω, μὴ νά ἄλλος ἐκξενίκη αὐτὰ
καὶ τὰ εἰμάτι[α] τὰ σουβρίκια καὶ
τὼ παλλιώλιν αὐτῶν. καὶ ἐρω-
10 τήσαται Ἀπίνα περὶ τῶν φαιν-
ωλῶν, καὶ ἐρωτήσαται αὐτῶν ὅ-
τι πόσον δαπανήσουσιν ὕφανδρα.
καὶ καταβάτ[ω] Ἀτωλησσία ἡ Ἰσ-
ωτᾶ. γράψω ἐπιστωλήν. καταβά-
15 τω εἷς ἐκξ ἡμῶν. ἀσπάζεται ἡμᾶς
Θερμουθᾶς πολλὰ πολλὰ καὶ μέμ-
φαιταί σαι πολλὰ ὅτι οὐ πείμπις αὐτῇ ἐπιστωλὴν καὶ τὴν ἀντιφώνησιν.
ἔτ(ους) β̄ Αὐτοκράτορος Νέρουης Τραειανοῦ Σαιβαστοῦ
20 Γερμανικ[οῦ], Μεχὲρ ῑζ̄. καὶ τὼ πάλλι Δά-
φνης πέμψαται αὐτῇ.

Verso: ἀπόδος Ἀπολ[ηείῳ]
ἀπόδ[ο]ς Οὐαλερ(ιᾶτι).

1 Read Ἀντώνιος.
2 Read ἀμφοτέροις, χαίρειν.
3 Read ὑγιαίνειν. Read σε.
4 Read ἀσπάσατε(?): the writer may have had in mind the customary ἀσπάζεσθαί σε εὔχομαι.
5 Read οὖν, ποιήσετε, μελήσετε.
6 ἀλ[ο]υρῶν: the editors suggest that this mutilated word must have contained some reference to clothing. He thought the most likely solution was to take ἀλουρῶν as ἀλουργῶν, purple garments (robes). Read δύο.

Antonius to both Apuleius and Valerius greeting and continual good health. Above all I extend greetings to you by letter. Please be concerned for us about the two purple robes (?), lest someone else carry them off, and the clothing, the hoods and their mantle. And ask Apion about the cloaks, and ask him: "How much will the expenditures of weaving cost?" And send down Atolessia the daughter of Isotas. I will write a letter. And send down one of your people. Thermouthas sends you very many greetings and she reproaches you a great deal because you do not send a letter and a reply to her. (Year) 2 of the Emperor Nerva Trajanus Augustus Germanicus, Mecheir 17. And send Daphne's mantle to her.

Outside address: Deliver to Apuleius; deliver to Valerius.

7 Read ἵνα μή, ἐξενείκη.
8 Regarding σουβρικομαφόρτιον and σουβρικοπάλλιον in the papyri, see Reil, Beiträge zur Kenntnis, p. 120. Σουβρίκιον can probably be equated with subricula. For sublica, an upper garment, see Nettleship, Contributions, p. 590.
9 Read τὸ παλλιόλιον.
9–10 Read ἐρωτήσατε (also in line 11); Ἀπίνα is probably an error for Ἀπίωνα.
11 Read αὐτόν.
12 Read ὕφαντρα.
14 Read ἐπιστολήν (also in line 18).
15 Read ἐξ, ὑμῶν, ὑμᾶς.
16 Read μέμφεται.
17 Read σε, ὅτι, πέμπεις.
19 Read Τραιανοῦ, Σεβαστοῦ.
20 Read μεχείρ, τὸ πάλλιον.
21 Read πέμψατε; αὐτῇ probably refers to Thermouthas.

The following seven letters (103 and 104 each contain two letters) are either from soldiers, primarily young ones (letters 102, 103a, 104a–b), or, in one instance, to a soldier (letter 101). Winter analyzed six letters written from and to soldiers, two of which are included here (letters 104a–b), and described them as a kind of special category of family letters (see Winter, "In the Service of Rome" pp. 237–56). In addition to the customary epistolary conventions that one finds in family letters (e.g., assurances of well-being, the wish/prayer for the recipient's welfare, greetings to and from third parties, and the appeal for letters), in the case of raw recruits one finds assurances of, and thankfulness for, safe arrival or escape from some hazard (see letters 102, 103a, 104b), the nervous eagerness with which news of one's assignment is awaited—and conveyed (letters 103a, 104a–b), and the awareness, if only dimly realized, of the powerful presence of Rome.

101 APOLLONOUS TO TERENTIANUS
PMich VIII 464   16 (?) March 99 CE

Apollonous addresses Terentianus, a soldier, as her brother, but the manner in which she assures him about the management of his farm and the affairs of the household in his absence indicates that she is also his wife. Youtie and Pearl, the editors, note that the letter is written in a practiced hand. It is characteristic of the writer, who is probably Apollonous herself, to use καί almost everytime she takes up a new subject.

Ἀπολλωνοῦς Τερεντιανῶι τῶι
    ἀδελφῶι χαίρειν
καὶ πρ[ὸ] παντ[ὸ]ς ὑγένειν. γινώσκιν
σε θέλω ὅτι ἐπὶ προέγραψά σοι περὶ
5 [τῶν ὑ]παρχ[ό]ντων μοι λοιπὸν οὖν
[.]ατρ.[.]..[.....].απι...ι ὅτι τὰ
[ἐκ]φό[ρ]ια [καὶ τὰ σπ] ἑρματα πάντα ἐκ-
[β]ήσονται ὅ[λως. καὶ μ]ὴ λυποῦ περὶ τῶν
[τ]έκνων· κ[αλ]ῶ[ς] διάκινται καὶ εἰς
10 [δ]εσκάλην [π]αρεδρεύουσι. [κ]αὶ περὶ
τῶν σῶν [ἐ]δαφῶν κεκούφικα τὸν
ἀδελφόν σου δύο ἀρτάβας ἀπὸ τῶν
ἐκφορίων. λυπὸν οὖν ἀπ[ολα]μβάνο-
με παρ' αὐτοῦ πυροῦ ἀρτάβας ὀκτὼ καὶ
15 λαχανοσσπέρμου ἀρτάβας ἕξ. καὶ μὴ
λυποῦ περὶ ἡμῶν καὶ ἐπιμέλου σαυτοῦ.
μετέλαβον παρὰ Θερμουθᾶ[τ]ος ὅτι
εὐπόρησε[ς] σεαυτῷ ζεῦγος βαλτίων.
καὶ ἐχάρησα πολλά. καὶ περὶ τῶν ἐλαι-
20 ώνων εὐκαρποῦσι τὰ ἕως σήμερον.
καὶ θεῶν θελόντων ἐὰν δυνησ-

Apollonous to Terentianus her brother greeting and before all good health. I want you to know that since I wrote to you before about my circumstances, now . . . that the total amount of the rent and the seed will turn out okay. And do not worry yourself about the children: they are well and are attending to (occupied with) a teacher. And about your field, I have reduced your brother's rent by two artabs. Now I receive eight artabs of grain and six artabs of vegetable seed from him. I learned from Thermouthatas that you acquired a pair of belts for yourself, and I was very gratified. And about the olive groves, they are bearing well so far. And the gods willing, if possible, come to us. And I wish you to be well, and your children and all your people greet you. Good-bye. (Year) 2 of the Emperor Caesar Nerva Trajanus Augustus Germanicus, Phamenoth 20. . . .

Outside address: Deliver to Julius Terentianus, soldier.

θῆ παραβαλῖν πρὸς ἡμᾶς. καὶ ἐρῶσθαί
σε βούλομε, καὶ ἀσπάζοντέ ⟨σέ⟩ σου
τὰ παιδί[α] καὶ πάντες τοὺς σούς.   ἔρρωσο.
25 (ἔτους) β [Αὐ]τοκρά[τ]ορος Καίσαρος Νέ[ρ]ουσα
     Τραιανοῦ Σεβαστοῦ Γερμανικοῦ [Φα]μ[ε]νὼθ κ̄.
     Three lines, largeley illegible, in the left margin.

Verso: ἀπόδος Ἰουλίωι Τερεντιαν[ὼι] Χ στρατιώτηι.

3	Read ὑγιαίνειν, γινώσκειν.	18	Βαλτίων: from the Latin *balteus* (*balteum*); see PMich VIII 474.8–9.
4	Read ἐπεί.	21–22	δυνησθῆ: the editors suggest this is a compromise between δυνηθῇ and δυνασθῇ; see PMich VIII 518, note to line 5.
5	λοιπὸν οὖν: regarding this phrase and its meaning, see Ghedini, *Lettere cristiane*, p. 36, n. 2.		
7	ἐκφόρια: "rent in kind" (φόρος="rent in money").	22	Read παραβαλεῖν. Read ἐρρῶσθαι.
9	Read διάκεινται.	23	Read βούλομαι, ἀσπάζονται.
10	δέσκαλος=διδάσκαλος: see the editors' note to line 10.	24	τοὺς σούς: accusative for nominative.
13	Read λοιπόν: the word is spelled correctly in line 5.	27	Julius Terentianus: the editors suggest that this is probably the same family that is represented at Karanis in 173 CE by Gaius Julius Terentianus (PMich IV 224, 3476).
13–14	Read ἀπολαμβάνομαι.		
15	Read λαχανοσπέρμου.	Left margin	The three lines of largely illegible writing were probably a postscript.

102 THEONAS TO TETHEUS
POxy XII 1481

early II CE

Theonas, a young soldier in camp, writes to his mother, reassuring her about his health and acknowledging receipt of various presents from home. He expresses thanks (probably to the gods) but, because the letter breaks off at this point, we do not know whether thankfulness was expressed because of escape from a recent hazard, because of a recent gain, or for some other reason. Since it is a family letter, it is probably justified to assume that various salutations and a health wish would have been expressed at the close of the letter.

Θεωνᾶς Τεθεῦτι τῆι μητρὶ καὶ κυρίᾳ πλεῖστα χαί(ρειν).
γεινώσκειν σ[ε] θέλω ὅτι διὰ τοσούτου χρόνου οὐκ ἀ-
πέσταλκά σοι ἐπιστόλιον διότι ἐν παρεμβολῇ ἤμι καὶ
οὐ δι' ἀσθένε[ι]αν, ὥστε μὴ λοιποῦ. λείαν δ' ἐλοιπήθην
5 ἀκούσας ὅτι ἤκουσας· οὐ γὰρ δεινῶς ἠσθένησα. μέμ-
φομαι δὲ τὸν εἴπαντα σοι. μὴ ὀχλοῦ δὲ πέμπειν τι ἡ-
μῖν. ἐκομισάμεθα δὲ τὰ θαλλία παρὰ τοῦ {τοῦ} Ἡρακλεί-
δου. Διονυτᾶς δὲ ὁ ἀδελφός μου ἤνεγκέ μοι τὸν θαλ-
λὸν κα[ὶ τὴν] ἐπιστολήν [σου] ἐ[κο]μισά[μ]ην. εὐχαριστῶ
10 [τοῖς θεοῖς 13 letters] πάντοτε, ἐπικ.ε..τα
     [22 letters] νται δηλῶ ουπ ... αυ-   ....

Theonas to his mother and lady, Tetheus, very many greetings. I want you to know that the reason I have not sent you a letter for such a long time is because I am in camp and not on account of illness; so do not worry yourself (about me). I was very grieved when I learned that you had heard (about me), for I did not fall seriously ill. And I blame the one who told you. Do not trouble yourself to send me anything. I received the presents from Herakleides. My brother, Dionytas, brought the present to me and I received your letter. I give thanks to (the gods) ... continually, ...

In the left margin at right angles:
μὴ ἐπιβαροῦ πέμπειν τι ἡμῖν τω[

Verso: ἀπὸ Θεωνᾶτος [Τεθεῦτι...

Postscript: Do not burden yourself to send anything to me...

Outside address: From Theonas to (Tetheus...).

---

3 Read εἰμί.
4 Read λυποῦ... ἐλυπήθην.
7 θαλλία: examples of the use of *thallos* ("present") in the papyri are collected in PRyl II 166, note to line 18.
10 [τοῖς θεοῖς]: or [τῷ κυρίῳ Σαράπιδι]: see letter 103a.6.

103 CORRESPONDENCE FROM APION
SelPap I 112(=BGU II 423)   II CE
BGU II 632   II CE

In the first letter below, which has been frequently discussed and translated (e.g., Deissmann, *Ancient East,* pp. 179ff.; Milligan, *Selections,* pp. 90ff.), Apion is a young recruit from Egypt, who has just been shipped with his regiment to Italy. He writes to notify his father, Epimachos, that he has arrived safely after a stormy passage (see the notice of safe arrival also in letter 104b). He mentions that he has received travel allowance, that he is optimistic about advancement because of his father's fine training, that his military name is Antonius Maximus, and that he has forwarded a portrait of himself to the family. The remainder of the letter is taken up with various expressions of well-wishing, greetings and similar sentiments, which are so common in family letters. The outside address indicates that the letter was first sent to the headquarters of the writer's regiment in Egypt, from which it would be later forwarded, as opportunity offered, to Epimachos at Philadelphia.

In the second letter, written some years later, Apion uses only his soldier-name, Antonius Maximus, and a number of other changes have taken place as well. Evidently, both his lord father, Epimachos, and his sister Sabina's daughter have died. Sabina and her husband Copres now have a little boy named Maximus in honor of his soldier-uncle. Since the first letter, Apion himself has taken a wife and he has two daughters with her, named Elpis and Fortunata, and a small son, also named Maximus after his soldier-father. Apion seems to have written to his sister as often as possible and he has stayed in contact with his home place in Philadelphia, both by this means and through old friends. In the present instance, Apion writes in response to the news that Sabina is well, news which was sent to him by his friend Antonius.

Letter A

᾿Απίων ᾿Επιμάχῳ τῶι πατρὶ καὶ
κυρίῳ πλεῖστα χαίρειν. πρὸ μὲν πάντων εὔχομαί σε ὑγιαίνειν καὶ διὰ παντὸς
ἐρωμένον εὐτυχεῖν μετὰ τῆς ἀδελφῆς
5 μου καὶ τῆς θυγατρὸς αὐτῆς καὶ τοῦ ἀδελφοῦ
μου. εὐχαριστῶ τῷ κυρίῳ Σεράπιδι,

Apion to his father and lord, Epimachos, very many greetings. Before all else I pray that you are well and that you may prosper in continual health, together with my sister and her daughter and my brother. I give thanks to the lord Serapis because, when I was endangered at sea, he rescued me

ὅτι μου κινδυνεύσαντος εἰς θάλασσαν
ἔσωσε εὐθέως· ὅτε εἰσῆλθον εἰς Μη-
σήνους, ἔλαβα βιάτικον παρὰ Καίσαρος
10 χρυσοῦς τρεῖς καὶ καλῶς μοί ἐστιν·
ἐρωτῶ σε οὖν, κύριέ μου πατήρ,
γράψον μοι ἐπιστόλιον πρῶτον
μὲν περὶ τῆς σωτηρίας σου, δεύτερον περὶ τῆς τῶν ἀδελφῶν μου,
15 τρ[ί]τον, ἵνα σου προσκυνήσω τὴν
χέραν, ὅτι με ἐπαίδευσας καλῶς,
καὶ ἐκ τούτου ἐλπίζω ταχὺ προκο(μί-)
σαι τῶν θε[ῶ]ν θελόντων· ἄσπασαι
Καπίτων[α π]ολλὰ καὶ το[ὺ]ς ἀδελφούς
20 [μ]ου καὶ Σε[ρηνί]λλαν καὶ το[ὺ]ς φίλους μο[υ].
ἔπεμψά σο[ι εἰ]κόνιν μ[ου] διὰ Εὐκτή-
μονος· ἔσ[τ]ι [δέ] μου ὄνομα Ἀντῶνις Μάξιμος.   ἐρρῶσθαί σε εὔχομαι.
κεντυρί(α) Ἀθηνονίκη.

25 Postscript on left margin:
ἀσπάζεταί σε Σερῆνος ὁ τοῦ Ἀγαθοῦ [Δα]ίμονος
[καὶ . . . . .]ς ὁ τοῦ [. . .]
ρος καὶ Τούρβων ὁ τοῦ Γαλλωνίου καὶ Δ . [. . .]νᾶς ὁ
τ[οῦ . . .,. . .]σεν [. . .]
[. . . .] . [. . .] . [   ]

Verso: ε[ἰς] Φ[ιλ]αδελφίαν Ἐπιμάχῳ ἀπὸ Ἀπίωνος υἱοῦ.
ἀπόδος εἰς χώρτην πρίμαν Ἀπαμηνῶν
Ἰο[υλι]α[ν]οῦ ἀντ[ι-]]
λιβλαρίῳ ἀπὸ Ἀπίωνος ὥστε Ἐπιμάχῳ πατρὶ αὐτοῦ.

immediately. When I arrived at Misenum, I received three gold pieces from Caesar for traveling expenses and I am well. Therefore, I request you, my lord father, write me a letter, (telling me) first about your welfare, secondly about the welfare of my brother and sister, in order that, thirdly, I may make obeisance before your handwriting, because you trained me well, and I hope by this means to advance quickly, the gods willing. Salute Kapiton very much and my brother and sister and Serenilla and my friends. I sent my portrait to you through Euktemonos. My name is Antonius Maximus. I pray that you are well. Company Athenonike.

Postscript: Serenos, the son of Agathodaimon, salutes you and . . ., and Toubon, the son of Gallonios, and . . .

Outside address: To Philadelphia, to Epimachos from his son, Apion.

Additional address: Deliver at the camp of the first cohort of the Apameni to Julianus, vice-secretary, (this letter) from Apion to be forwarded to his father, Epimachos.

---

4 Read ἐρρωμένον.
9 βιάτικον is the Latin *viaticum* of the Roman soldier (see PKarGoods 30 [191–92 CE]).
14 τῶν ἀδελφῶν μου: various editors translate this as ". . . of my brother and sister" (rather than "brothers"), apparently because a singular brother and sister were cited in lines 4–5. Ἀδελφούς in line 19 is also translated as "sister."
14 Read χεῖρα.
17 Read προκόψαι.
22 "My (military) name is . . .": foreigners received a new Latin name when they entered Roman military service (see Gemellus, introduction to letters 95–99).

Letter B

Ἀν[τώνι]ος Μάξιμος Σαβίνῃ
τῇ ἀ[δ]ελφῇ πλεῖστα χαίρειν.
πρὸ μὲν πάντων εὔχομαί
σε ὑγιαίνειν, καὶ ʼγω γὰρ αὐτὸς
5 ὑγιαίν[ω]. μνίαν σου ποιούμενος παρὰ τοῖς [ἐν]θάδε θεοῖς
ἐκομισάμην [ἐ]ν ἐπι[σ]τόλιον
παρὰ Ἀντωνε[ί]νου τοῦ συν-
πολ[ε]ίτου ἡμῶν. καὶ ἐπιγνούς

Antonius Maximus to his sister, Sabina, very many greetings. Before all else I pray that you are well, for I myself am well. Making mention of you before the gods here, I received a letter from Antonius our fellow citizen. And when I learned that you were well, I rejoiced exceedingly. And I do not hesitate to write to you about my welfare and that of my family at every opportunity. Greet Maximus much and Kopres, my lord. My wife

10 σε ἐρρωμένην λίαν ἐχάρην.
  καὶ ᾽γω διὰ πᾶσαν ἀφορμὴν
  ο{ὐ}χ ὀκνῶ σοι γράψαι περὶ
  τῆ[ς] σωτηρίας μου καὶ τῶν
  ἐμῶν. ἄσπασαι Μάξιμον
15 πολλὰ καὶ Κοπρὴν τὸν κύριν
  μ[ου. ἀ]σπάζεταί σε ἡ σύμβι-
  ός [μου Α]ὐφιδία καὶ [Μ]άξιμος
  [ὁ υἱός μ]ου, [οὗ] ἐστι[ν] τὰ γενέ-
  [σια ᾽Ε]πειπ τριακὰς καθ᾽ ῞Ελ-
20 [ληνα]ς, καὶ ᾽Ελπὶς καὶ Φορτου-
  [νᾶτα]. ἄσπ[α]σαι τὸν κύριον
  six mutilated lines, probably containing additional
  salutations
28 [ἐρρῶσθαί σε εὔχο]μαι.

Verso: [Σαβίνῃ] ἀ[δε]λφ[ῇ] ἀπ[ὸ] ᾽Αντ[ω]νίου Μαξίμ[ο]υ
  ἀδελφ[οῦ].

(companion), Aufidia, greets you and so does my son, Maximus, whose birthday is the thirtieth of Epeiph according to Greek reckoning, as well as Elpis and Fortunata. Salute my lord. . . . I pray that you may be well.

Outside address: To his sister, Sabina, from her brother Antonius Maximus.

---

2 "his sister": the sister was named in the first letter (letter 103a), and since her daughter is not named in this second letter she has probably died in the meantime. Since the father, Epimachos, is not named in this second letter, he too has probably died.

15 Read κύριον (spelled correctly in line 21).

18–22 The restoration of these lines is from Deissmann (*Ancient East,* pp. 184ff.).

19 Epeip is the Egyptian month Epeiph.

104

APOLLINARIOS' LETTERS TO HIS MOTHER
PMich VIII 490 II CE
PMich VIII 491 II CE

These two letters from a young Graeco-Egyptian recruit to his mother were found in a large house in Karanis (see the detailed description of the house by Boak and Peterson, *Karanis,* pp. 9–20; see pp. 5 and 171 in this volume). This correspondence supplements the letter of young Apion (who came from the neighboring village of Philadelphia; see letter 103a) in revealing additional details about the process of induction into the Roman fleet. Since the handwriting of Apollinarios' letters differs markedly, he probably used professional scribes in both cases.

In the first letter, Apollinarios informs his mother that he had already dispatched a letter at Cyrene by means of a man who was journeying to Karanis. He is now writing a second letter (letter 104a below), on Pachon 25, upon arriving at Portus (Ostia). At this point, he has not yet gone to Rome to receive his assignment.

We learn from the second letter below that Apollinarios did reach Rome later that same day and that he was assigned to the fleet at Misenum (lines 5–6), but he is still without information about his century, which he would learn only on reaching Misenum. After urging his mother not to worry in this second piece of correspondence, Apollinarios concludes his message with the extensive greetings that are characteristic of letters from recruits (see Apion's first letter, letter 103a) and generally characteristic of this historical period.

Letter A

᾽Απολινᾶρις Ταησίῳ τῇ μητρὶ
  πολλὰ χαίρειν.

Apollinarios to his mother, Taesion, many greetings. Before anything else I wish that you are well,

πρὸ παντὸς ἔρρωσό μοι ὑγιαίνουσα
τὸ προσκύνημά σου ποιῶν παρὰ πᾶ-
5 σι τοῖς θεοῖς. καὶ ἀπὸ Κυρήνης εὑρὼν
τὸν πρὸς σὲ ἐρχόμενον ἀνάνκην ἔσχον σοι
δηλῶσαι περὶ τῆς σωτηρίας μου· καὶ σύ μοι
ταχύτερον δήλωσον περὶ τῆς ἀπροσκοπίας
σου καὶ τῆς τῶν ἀδελφῶν μου. καὶ νῦν ἀπὸ
10 Πόρτου σοι δηλῶ, οὔπω γὰρ ἀνέβην ἰς Ῥώμην
καὶ διετάγην. ἐπὰν διαταγῶ καὶ γνῶ ἰς ποίαν
ἴμι εὐθέως σοι δηλῶ, καὶ σὺ δὲ μὴ ὄκνι γράφιν περὶ τῆς σωτηρίας σου καὶ τῆς τῶν ἀδελφῶν μου. ἐὰν δὲ μὴ εὕρῃς τὸν ἐρχόμενον
15 πρὸς ἐμὲ γράψον Σωκράτῃ καὶ αὐτός μοι
διαπέμπεται. ἀσπάζομαι πολλὰ τὰ ἀδέλφια
καὶ Ἀπολιναρὶν καὶ τὰ τέκνα αὐτοῦ καὶ Καλαλᾶ⟨ν⟩
καὶ τὰ τέκνα αὐτοῦ καὶ πάντες τούς σε φιλοῦντες.
ἀσπάζεταί σε Ἀσκληπιάδης.
20   ἔρρωσό μοι ὑγιαίνουσα.
    ἰς Πόρτον παρεγενάμην Παχὼν κε̅.

2nd hand: γείνωσκε ὅτι ἰς Μεισηνοὺς διετάγην, ὕστερον γὰρ ἐπέ-
γνων.

Verso
1st hand: ἀπόδος ἰς Καρανίδα   ✕   Ταησίῳ ἀπὸ Ἀπολιναρίου
υἱοῦ.

✕

making obeisance on your behalf to all the gods. And when I found someone who was journeying to you from Cyrene, I thought it a necessity to inform you about my welfare; you must inform me at once, in turn, about your safety and that of my brothers. And now I am writing to you from Portus, for I have not yet gone up to Rome and been assigned. When I am assigned and know where I will be, I will tell you immediately; and, for your part, do not hesitate to write about your welfare and that of my brothers. If you do not find someone coming to me, write to Socrates and he will transmit it to me. I greet (salute) my brothers much, and Apollinarios and his children, and Kalalas and his children, and all your friends. Asklepiades salutes you. I pray that you are well. I arrived in Portus on Pachon 25.

Postscript in a second hand: Know that I have been assigned to Misenum, for I found out later (i.e., after the letter was written).

Outside address: Deliver to Karanis, to Taesion, from her son Apollinarios.

---

1 Ἀπολιναρις for Ἀπολινάριος=Ἀπολλινάριος (see line 2 Ταησίῳ: letter 104b has Ταησι. Youtie and Winter, the editors, call attention to similar variations in the papyri, e.g., *Thermouthion=Thermouthis* (see PMich III 191–92), *Dionysios=Dionytas* (PPrinc II 65), *Paomios=Paomis* (Collart, "Une nouvelle *Tabella Defixionis d'Egypte*," p. 254), *Theon=Theonas* (POslo II 47).

3 ἔρρωσο κτλ.: the imperative form of the opening wish is unusual, since it belongs at the end of the letter (the same formula closes the letter in line 20).

4 ποιῶν: one might take ποιῶν as an error for ποιοῦντι, in agreement with μοι, but it seems more likely that the scribe has combined (confused) conventions and is proceeding as if he had written the customary εὔχομαί σε ὑγιαίνειν (rather than ἔρρωσό μοι ὑγιαίνουσα).

6 Read ἀνάγκην.

8 ἀπροσκοπίας: the adjective is attested, but not the noun (See *LSJ*, Supplement, s.v. ἀπροσκοπία. This is the only example.)

10 Read εἰς (also in lines 11, 21, 22, 24).

12 Read εἶμι, ὄκνει.

12–13 Read γράφειν.

15 Read Σωκράτει. αὐτός: regarding its use for the third person pronoun, see Mayser, *Grammatik*, 2.1.64f.

17 *Kalalas*: written *Karalas* in letter 104b. The editor notes that a person of this name was living at Karanis in 172–73 CE (see PMich IV 224).

18 Read πάντες, φιλοῦντες. See PMich VIII 477, note to lines 40–41, regarding the interpretation of this formula.

24–25 Asterisk-like crosses mark the place for tying up the letter when folded. See letter 98, note to line 30.

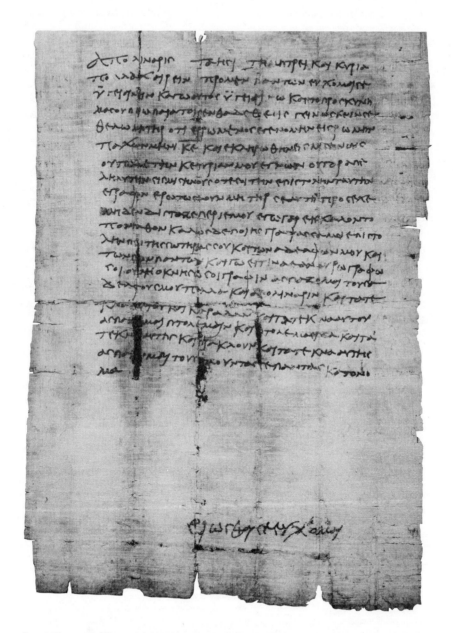

Letter from a soldier to his mother (letter 104a). Written by a Greek scribe with a pen. Contrast with the illustrations on pp. 1 and 45 written with a brush. Photograph reproduced with the permission of the Department of Rare Books and Special Collections, The University of Michigan Library.

Letter B

Ἀπολινᾶρις Ταῆσι τῇ μητρεὶ καὶ κυρίᾳ
πολλὰ χαίρειν. πρὸ μὲν πάντων εὔχομαί σε
ὑγειαίνειν, κἀγὼ αὐτὸς ὑγειαίνω καὶ τὸ προσκύνημά σου ποιῶ παρὰ τοῖς ἐνθάδε θεοῖς. γεινώσκειν σε
5   θέλω, μῆτηρ, ὅτι ἐρρωμένος ἐγενόμην εἰς Ῥώμην
Παχὼν μηνὶ κε καὶ ἐκληρώθην εἰς Μισηνούς.
οὔπω δὲ τὴν κε⟨ν⟩τυρίαν μου ἔγνων· οὐ γὰρ ἀπε-
ληλύτειν εἰς Μισηνοὺς ὅτε σοι τὴν ἐπιστολὴν ταύτην
ἔγραφον. ἐρωτῶ σε, οὖν, μῆτηρ, σεαυτῇ πρόσεχε,
10 μηδὲν δίσταζε περὶ ἐμοῦ· ἐγὼ γὰρ εἰς καλὸν τόπον ἦλθον. καλῶς δὲ ποιήσ⟨εις⟩ γράψασ⟨σ⟩ά μοι ἐπιστολὴν πε[ρ]ὶ τῆς σωτηρίας σου καὶ τῶν ἀδελφῶν μου καὶ
τῶν σῶν πάντων. καὶ ᾽γὼ εἴ τινα ἐὰν εὕρω γράφω
σοι· οὐ μὴ ὀκνήσω σοι γράφιν. ἀσπάζομαι τοὺς ἀ-
15 δελφούς μου πολλὰ καὶ Ἀπολινᾶριν καὶ τὰ τέκνα αὐτοῦ καὶ Καραλᾶν καὶ τὰ τέκνα αὐτοῦ.
ἀσπάζ[ο]μαι Πτολεμαῖν καὶ Πτολεμαείδα καὶ τὰ
τέκν[α] αὐτῆς καὶ Ἡρακλοῦν καὶ τὰ τέκνα αὐτῆς.
ἀσπάζομαι τοὺς φιλοῦντάς σε πάντας κατ᾽ ὄνο-
20 μα.
        ἐρρῶσθαί σε εὔχομαι.

Verso: ἀπόδ(ος) εἰς Καρανίδα   Ταῆσι ἀπὸ Ἀπολιναρίου νειοῦ
        Μισηνάτου.

Apollinarios to his mother and lady, Taesis, many greetings. Before all else I pray that you are well; I myself am well and make obeisance on your behalf to the gods here. I want you to know, mother, that I arrived in Rome safely on the twenty-fifth of the month Pachon and was assigned to Misenum. But I do not know my century yet, for I had not gone to Misenum when I wrote this letter to you. I request you, therefore, mother, attend to yourself; do not worry about me, for I came to a fine place. Please write me a letter about your welfare and that of my brothers and of all your people. And, for my part, if I ever find someone (to carry the letter), I will write to you; I certainly will not hesitate to write to you. I greet (salute) my brothers much, and Apollinarios and his children, and Karalas and his children. I greet Ptolemy, and Ptolemais and her children. I greet all your friends, each by name. I pray that you are well.

Outside address: Deliver to Karanis, to Taesis, from her son, Apollinarios, of Misenum.

---

1   Read Ταήσει, μητρί.
3   Read ὑγιαίνειν.
7   κεντυρίαν: compare this with Apion's assignment to "company (*kenturia*) Athenoike" at Misenum (letter 103a.24). The editors suggest that the century was identical with the ship and the assignment of a recruit to a century was made after he arrived at the naval base (see also Starr, *Roman Imperial Navy*, pp. 57–61).
7–8   Read ἀπεληλύθειν.
10–11   καλὸν τόπον: the editors suggest that the phrase refers to Apollinarios' "place" as a member of the fleet at Misenum, rather than to being at Rome. Apion was also satisfied in his assignment to the Misene fleet: καλῶς μοί ἐστιν (letter 103a.10).

13   εἴ τινα ἐάν=εἴ τινα ἄν=ἐάν τινα.
13–14   Compare with 103b.11–12: καὶ ᾽γω διὰ πᾶσαν ἀφορμὴν οὐχ ὀκνῶ σοι γράψαι.
14   Read γράφειν.
15   Read Ἀπολινάριον (see 104a, note to line 1).
17   Read Πτολεμαῖον, Πτολεμαΐδα.
19   τοὺς φιλοῦντάς σε πάντας, i.e., "all your friends": this is the interpretation of the editors of PMich VIII 477.40–41 (see a shortened form in PMich VIII 490.18=104a.18), who follow the interpretation of the phrase by *LSJ* (s.v. φιλέω, I, 1). The literal meaning is only emphasized, it seems, when used in a Christian context: ἀσπάζονταί σε οἱ μετ᾽ ἐμοῦ πάντες. ἄσπασαι τοὺς φιλοῦντας ἡμᾶς ἐν πίστει (Titus 3:15).
22   Read Ταήσει, υἱοῦ.

105 JULIUS APOLLINARIOS TO JULIUS SABINUS
PMich VIII 466   26 March 107 CE

This soldier, who had recently joined the Roman legion at Bostra, complains that his father has not been corresponding with him and, in particular, that his father has failed to inform him about his health. Julius Apollinarios wrote a letter to his mother a few weeks earlier (=PMich VIII 465), not included here, and the same kinds of family concern and sentiment came to expression: concern about his mother's health, a report on his favored status over the common soldier who performed hard labor (the phrase λίθους κοπτόντων, "cutting stones," appears in both), and his homesickness. He greets a large number of people in both letters.

The mention of Claudius Severus (lines 25–26) in the present letter is significant, since he was the first governor of the province of Arabia after A. Cornelius Palma conquered the district in 106 CE. Unlike the other letters from soldiers in this section, this one reveals something of the hard labor of an ordinary soldier in a frontier province. The soldiers referred to in this letter worked the stone quarries in the newly organized province of Arabia. Apollinarios may have mentioned in lines 20–21 (fragmented) what use was being made of the quarried stones, e.g., they may have been used to construct roads, cisterns, aquaducts, fortifications, etc. Since he wrote proudly about his position as an officer in both letters (in PMich 465 he referred to himself as a *principalis*, here as a *librarius Legionis*), his acquisition of rank must have been relatively recent.

'Ι[ο]ύλιος 'Απ[ολιναριος 'Ιο]υλίω Σαβείνωι τῶι
    γλυκυ[τάτω πα]τρὶ πλεῖστα χαίρειν.
πρὸ τῶν ὅλ[ων εὔχομ]αί σε ἐρρῶσθαι, ὅ μοι εὐκτόν
ἐστιν, [ὅτι σέβομ]αί σε μετὰ τοὺς θεούς. τοῦ-
5 το δὲ μ[οι ἠνώχ]λησεν ὅτι πλειστάκις
μου γρ[άψαντος διὰ] Σατουρνίνου τοῦ ση-
μεαφ[όρο]υ, ὁμ[ο]ίως διὰ 'Ιου[λ]ιανοῦ τοῦ τοῦ
Λονγείν[ο]υ [[καὶ διὰ Δίου]], καὶ οὔπω μοι ἀντέ-
γραψες περὶ τῆς σωτηρίας σου. ἀλλ᾽ ὅμως
10 ἐρω[τηθ]εὶς ἀναγκαίως σχέθητι πρὸ πάντων [γρά]ψαι μοι περὶ τῆς σωτηρίας [ὑ]μῶν.
πολ[λάκις δὲ] μου ἐρωτήσαντος Λονγεῖν[ο]ν
τ[ὸ]ν κομείζοντά σοι τὸ ἐπιστόλιον εἵνα
β[α]στάξη σοί τι, καὶ ἠρνήσατο λέγων οὐ δύ-
15 ν[ασ]θαι αὐτὸ λαμβάνειν. γι]νώσκιν δέ σε
θ[έλω ὅτι σφυρίδα μετεβάλ]ετο Δομίτιος
ὁ ἀρμι[κούστωρ ἐν ἧ ±5]ς σοι ἐνῆν.
γίνετα[ι δέ καλῶς μοι. μετὰ τὸ·] τὸν Σάραπιν
εὐτυχῶ[ς ἐνθάδε με εὐοδῶσαι ἄ]λλων ἀλ-
20 [λ .].. [±7   ] . ε . . . .
[. . . . .] . . . [. .] . . [.]ν [ὅ]λης τῆς
[ἡμέρ]ας λίθους κοπτ[ό]ντων καὶ
[ἄλλα π]οιούντων, ἐγὼ μέχρι σή-
[μερον] οὐθὲν τούτων ἔπαθον, ἀλλὰ
25 [καὶ ἐρω]τήσαντὸς μου Κλαύδιον
Σε[ουῆ]ρ[ο]ν τὸν ὑπατικὸν εἵνα με
λιβράριον ἑαυτοῦ ποιήσῃ, εἰπόντος

Julius Apollinarios to his dearest father, Julius Sabinus, very many greetings. Before all else I pray that you are well, which is what I have wished for, because I revere you next to the gods. But this has troubled me, that though I often wrote through Saturninus the *signifer*, likewise through Julius the son of Longinus [[and through Dios]], even yet you have not answered me about your health. Notwithstanding, now that you have been asked, consider it a necessity above all to write to me about your welfare. Several times I asked Longinus, who carries the letter to you, in order to take something to you, and he refused, claiming that he was unable to take anything; but I want you to know that Domitios the *armi/custos* took along a basket in which] there was a . . . for you. Things are [going well for me. After] Sarapis [brought me here] safely, while others . . . the whole day were cutting building stones and doing [other things], up to today I suffered none of these indignities; but, in fact, when I asked Claudius Severus the *consularis* that he make me a secretary of his own (staff), he said "a vacancy (place) does not exist but, in the meantime, I will make you a secretary of the legion with hopes of advancement." Therefore, with this assignment, I went from the *consularis* of the legion to the *cornicularius*. Consequently, if you love me,

δὲ [α]ὐτοῦ ὅτι τόπος οὐ σχολάζ[ι], ἐν
τοσούτῳ δὲ λιβράριόν σε λεγεῶνος
30 ποιήσω ἐφ' ἐλπίδων, κλήρῳ οὖν
ἐγενόμην ἀπὸ τοῦ ὑπατικοῦ τῆς
λεγεῶνος πρὸς τὸν κορνικουλάριον.
ἐὰν οὖν με φιλῇς εὐθέως ἐργασίαν δώ-
σις γράψαι μοι περὶ τῆς σωτηρίας σου καὶ
35 ἐὰν μοι μεληθῇς πέμψαι λίνα διὰ
Σεμπρωνίου· ἀπὸ Πηλουσίου γὰρ καθ ἡ-
μέραν ἔρχονται πρὸς ἡμᾶς ἔμποροι.
ἐργασίαν δὲ δώσω εὐθέως ἐὰν ἄρ-
ξηται ὁ ἡγεμὼν διδόναι κομμεᾶτον
40 εὐθέως ἐλθῖν πρὸς ὑμᾶς. ἀσπάζεταί
σε Οὐολύσσιο[ς] Πρόκλος Λονγεῖνος Πάκκιος
Οὐαλέριος Σεμπρώνι[ο]ς Οὐαλέριος Ἑρμα . . . .

Continued on left margin:

Ἰούλιος Πρίσκος Ἀπολλινάριος . . . . ίων [καὶ ο]ἱ
κοντ[ουβε]ρ[ν]ά̣ριοι πάντες. ἀσπάζου Ἰουλίαν τὴν
κυρίαν
μου ἀδελφήν, ὁμοίως Σαραπιάδα καὶ τ[ὴ]ν μητέραν, τὴν
μάμαν ΣαμΒάθιον, Θερμοῦθιν καὶ τὰ
45 τέκνα αὐτῆς, τὸν πατέρα Πακκίου καὶ πάντας τοὺς
κολλήγάς σου κατ' ὄνομα καὶ τοὺς ἐν οἴκωι.
ἐρρῶσθαί σε εὔχομαι. ἔτους ῑ Τραιανοῦ τοῦ κυρίου
ΦαμενὼΘ λ̄.

Continued in the right margin:

εὐχαριστῶ Οὐολυσσίῳ καὶ Λονγείνῳ τῷ Βαρβάρῳ.
Μεταδώσις τοῖς παρὰ Ἀφροδᾶτος τοῦ τοῦ
ἀρτυματοπώλο[υ]
ὅτι ἐστράτευσάν ⟨με⟩ ἰς χώ[ρ]την εἰς Βόστραν. κάθηται
[π]ρὸ η̄ ἡμερῶν Πέτρας καὶ τ⟨ ⟩

Verso: Two broken and faded lines, in which only the word
στρατ[ιώτου] is still legible.

---

4   σέβομαί σε μετὰ τοὺς θεούς: the writer of PMich
     III 209.12-13 has even less reserve, when prais-
     ing a brother: οὐ μόνον ὡς ἀδελφόν σε ἔχω ἀλλὰ
     καὶ ὡς πατέρα καὶ κύριον καὶ θεόν (see PMich
     VIII 502.10-11; SelPap I 121.27-28). See the
     editors' comments on PMich VIII 466.4 regard-
     ing the easy apotheosis to which Alexandrians
     were prone and the other examples that he cites
     there.
6-7 σημεαφόρου=Latin signifer.
8   Read λογγίνου (see lines 12, 41, 47). καὶ διὰ
     Δίου: the dotted letters are very faded and doubt-
     ful. According to the editors, horizontal strokes
     were drawn through the entire passage.
8-9 Read ἀντέγραψας.

---

you will make an effort immediately to write to me about your welfare and, if you are concerned about me, to send me linen garments through Sempronios, for merchants come daily to us from Pelusium. And I shall make an effort, just as soon as the commander begins to grant furloughs, to come to you immediately. Volusius Proclus greets (salutes) you, so too Longinus Paccius, Valerius Sempronios, Valerius Herma . . . , (Closing greetings continued on left margin:) Julius Priscus, Apollinarios . . . ion, and all their companions. Greet Julia my lady sister, similarly Sarapias and my mother, my grandmother Sambathion, Thermouthis and her children, the father of Paccius, and all your colleagues each by name and those in the house. I pray that you may be well. (Year) 10 of Trajan, our lord, Phamenoth 30.

Postscript continued in the right margin: I give thanks to Volusius and Longinus Barbaros. You will tell the people (the firm) of Aphrodas, the son of the condiment dealer, that they enrolled me in the cohort at Bostra. It lies eight days' journey from Petra and . . .

---

13   Read κομίζοντα, ἵνα (also in line 26).
15   Read γινώσκειν.
17   ἀρμικούστωρ: Latin armicustos=armorum custos?
     See the editors' comments on this word (PMich
     466.17). ἐνῆν: the meaning of the compound
     here is illustrated by PTebt II 414.19-20: τὸ
     σπυρίδιν μετὰ τῶν ἐνόντων (see PBrem 61.7-8).
27   λιβράριον ἑαυτοῦ, i.e., librarius legati.
28   Read σχολάζει.
29   λιβράριον . . . λεγεῶνος, i.e., librarius legionis.
30   ἐφ' ἐλπίδων=ἐπ' ἐλπίδων, a Greek translation of
     Latin military terminology.
31   ὑπατικοῦ: Latin consularis (commander of the
     legion).
32   κορνικουλάριον: Latin cornicularium.
39   κομμεᾶτον=Latin commeatum.
40   Read ἐλθεῖν.
43   κοντουβερνάριοι=Latin contubernales.
44   Read μητέρα. (The mother's name was Tasou-
     charion. See PMich 465.1-2.)
48   ἐστράτευσάν ⟨με⟩ ἰς χώρτην: read εἰς; χώρτη=
     Latin cohors; the use of στρατεύω with the mean-
     ing, "take or receive into the army, enroll," is a
     late usage (see LSJ, s.v. στρατεύω, II). "It lies
     eight days' journey": the editors note that the
     total distance from Petra to Bostra was about 212
     Roman miles, or 26.5 miles per day for eight days
     (see his additional comments, PMich 466, note to
     line 48).

A number of documents in PAmh II concern the affairs of Sarapion and his family. The total archive is even larger, however, since it was widely scattered by the antiquities market to two museums and five libraries in Europe and the United States. It runs to some 150 papyrus documents. Regarding the Amherst group, there are five letters between family members, in addition to the contracts of lease or applications for lease and accounts of farm receipts and expenditures. Four of these five Amherst letters are included here (number 106 has two letters). Almost all of the archive, including the personal correspondence, deals with the management of family farm properties. Both in this respect, as well as in the badness of the Greek and the occurrence of curious new words, the archive resembles the correspondence of Gemellus and his family (see the introduction to letters 95–99). Dated papyri in the archive were written in the reign of Hadrian and, consequently, it seems reasonable to assign the letters, all of which were undated (at least in PAmh II), to the first half of the second century.

N. Lewis notes that ca. 100 CE, when Sarapion (the son of Eutychides) was about forty, he took up residence in Hermopolis with his wife, Selene, their four sons and daughter, and the children's nurse. The farm property in the vicinity consisted of vineyards and pastures, as well as grain fields. Their flocks of sheep and goats numbered over a thousand head at one point. In addition to all this, the family cultivated many additonal fields nearby which they leased from others. Lewis suggests that they cultivated and harvested twenty to thirty times what an ordinary farmer would cultivate. Moreover, Selene owned land, probably through inheritance, in the toparchy to the north. The family leased that land out to local cultivators there because of the great distance of the property from Hermopolis (see Lewis, *Life in Egypt,* pp. 66–67, 131–32).

Three of the sons, Eutychides, Anoubion, and Heliodoros, are mentioned explicitly in the letters included here. The manner in which Sarapion greets his father and mother, along with Heliodoros, Anoubion and Anoubion's family, all in the same letter, suggests that, with the exception of Sarapion himself, they all lived in the same house or nearby. By contrast, Eutychides, like Gemellus' steward Epagathos, seems to have managed family property at some remove. Unfortunately, he seems to have lacked self-confidence and worried about decisions to the point of often becoming ineffective (e.g., see letters 106b, 107). Lewis describes him as a "hopeless neurotic" (*Life in Egypt,* p. 67).

Schwartz has edited the family records of Sarapion in considerable detail in his book, *Les archives de Sarapion et des ses fils.*

106

TWO LETTERS FROM SARAPION

PAmh II 131   early II CE

PAmh II 132   early II CE

Both of the letters below were sent from Sarapion: the first to "his sister Selene," who was also his wife; the second to his son Eutychides. The first is fairly well written and is probably the work of a professional scribe, apart from line 24 which was added by Sarapion himself. The second, which is shorter and written in large letters, is no doubt Sarapion's own handwriting.

Letter A

Σαραπίων Σελήνηι τῆι
      ἀδελφῆι χαίρειν.
ἕως ἂν ἐπιγνῶ τὸ ἀσφαλὲς τοῦ πράγματος περὶ οὗ κατέπλευσα ἐπιμενῶ,
5   ἐλπίζω δὲ θεῶν θελόντων ἐκ τῶν
λαλουμένων διαφεύξεσθαι καὶ μετὰ τὴν πεντεκαιδεκάτην ἀναπλεύ-
σειν. μελησάτω σοι ὅπως ἀγορασθῇ
τὰ κενώματα καὶ ὅπως τὰ παιδία
10 περὶ τὴν ἰδιοσπορίαν ἡμῶν καὶ τοὺς
γεωργοὺς ἐπιμελῶς ἀναστραφῶσιν,
μάλιστα δὲ περὶ τοὺς ἐνυφαντωνι ὅ-
πως μὴ δίκας λέγωμεν. οὕτως δὲ
ἠμελήσατε ἡμῶν ὡς ἀνειρημέ-
15 νων τὸ ἀναβολικὸν καὶ ἐχόντων ἐκ
τούτου εἰς ἡμᾶς δαπανῆσαι. ἐχρη-
σάμεθα οὖν παρὰ φίλων, ἐκ γὰρ ὧν
ἔπεμψας δραχμῶν διακοσίων διὰ
Ἡλιοδώρου ἀνηλώθησαν εἰς τέλη
20 καὶ ναῦλα ἀναπλοῦ καὶ καταπλοῦ (δραχμαὶ) νδ.
ἐπέμψαμεν δ᾽ ὑμῖν ἐπιστολὰς πολ-
λὰς καὶ διὰ τοῦ δούλου δὲ Σαραπίωνος
καὶ διὰ τοῦ υἱοῦ τοῦ βασιλικοῦ.

2nd hand: ἔρρωσο, Σελήνη ἀδελφή.

Verso
1st hand: Σελήνηι ἀδελφῆι ἀπὸ Σαραπίωνος.

Sarapion to his sister, Selene, greeting. Until I learn that the matter about which I sailed down is settled, I will remain, but I hope, the gods willing, to get away from talking (testifying?) and, after the fifteenth, to sail up. Make sure that the empty jars are bought and that the servants occupy themselves with the sowing of our private land and with the cultivators, and especially that they be concerned about the woven things, lest we have to speak about restitution (penalty, amends). You were negligent toward me, (assuming) as though I had received the deferred payment and could pay my expenses out of that. Consequently, I borrowed (money) from friends; for out of the two hundred drachmas that you sent through Heliodoros, fifty-four drachmas were spent for taxes and for the boat fare to and back. I sent you many letters both through the slave of Sarapion and by means of the son of the crown scribe. Good-bye, sister Selene.

Outside address: To my sister Selene from Sarapion.

---

12   The editors, Grenfell and Hunt, note that if the present reading is kept, ἐνυφαντωνι must be taken as two words, ἐν ὑφαντῶνι. They also suggest, however, that a safer course is to suppose that τοὺς ἐνυφαντάς or, more likely, τῶν ἐνυφαντῶν was intended (see letter 107.14: περὶ δὲ ὑφαντῶν).

14   Read ἀνῃρημένων.

Letter B

Σαραπίων Εὐτυχ(ίδῃ) τῶι υίῶι
χαίρειν. περισ(σ)ῶς μοι ἔ-
γραψας περὶ τοῦ μισθοῦ
τῶν ἐργατῶν, σὺ γὰρ διὰ σαυ-
5   τοῦ ἶ. ἐπίγνωθι οὖν τὸ
ἀσφαλὲς τί Πολεῖς δι-

Sarapion to his son, Eutychides, greeting. You wrote to me unnecessarily about the wages of the laborers, for you yourself are in charge. Therefore, find out—to be safe—how much Polis pays his workers and you pay the same. Let Horion the priest give you the money for the laborers. Tomor-

δοῖ τοῖς αὐτοῦ καὶ σὺ δός.
δότω σοι δὲ Ὠρίων ὁ ἱερεὺς
ἀργύριον χάριν τῶν ἐργατῶν. αὔριον δέ σοι
10 Ἀχιλλᾶν πέμψω ἵνα
καὶ σὺ εἰς Ἑρμούπολ(ιν) ἔλθῃς.
ἔρρωσο.

Verso: Εὐτυχ(ίδῃ) υἱῶι.

row I will send Achillas to you in order that you too may come to Hermopolis. Good-bye.

Outside address: To my son Eutychides.

2 The final ς of περισ(σ)ως is over the line.
5 Read εἶ.
7 ς of τοις is over the line.
9 χαριν των εργατων is over the line.
10 Read πέμψω.

107 EUTYCHIDES TO SARAPION
PAmh II 133

early II CE

This is a somewhat confusing letter from Eutychides to his father about farm matters. The letter relays several pieces of information but seems to be concerned primarily with farm tenants who had refused initially to work the land for the former amount of rent. As his father had instructed him to do, Eutychides had persuaded the tenants, by some means, to accept the former terms.

The immediately preceding letter (letter 106b) also concerns field work. Sarapion's comments there indicate that Eutychides lacked initiative and relied too much on his father's advice.

Εὐτυχίδης Σαραπίωνι τῶι πατρὶ χαίρειν.
πρὸ τῶν ὅλων ἀσπάζομαί σε καὶ εὐχαριστῶ σοι ὅτι ἐδήλωσάς μοι {σ}τὴν ὑγεί-
αν σου. περὶ τῆς κρειθ(ῆς) τῆς ἐνθάλλου εὐθύ-
5 μει, πέπρακα γάρ. περὶ τῶν κεραμίων
σου γράφω σοι ἵν᾽ εἰδῇς ὅτι οὐκ ἀμελοῦμεν,
ἠγορά[κ]αμέν σοι εὐώδη κεράμια ἑκα-
τόν. τὰ χλωρὰ τῆ(ς) πωεως οἰκονομήσα-
μεν, παραγενάμενοι γὰρ ἐκεῖ ἀντι. ἐνή-
10 καν ἡμεῖν δαπάνην οὐκ ὀλίγην, καὶ ὡς
ἐδὶ βρ.....[.]ν καὶ μετὰ πολλῶν κόπων
ἀνηκάσαμεν αὐτῶν ἀντασχέσθαι τῆς
τούτων ἐνεργίας ἐπὶ τῷ προτέρῳ ἐκ-
φορίου ὡς ἔγραψας ἐπὶ τῇ ἐντολῇ. περὶ
15 δὲ ὑφαντῶν πρὶν ἢ γράψῃ μοι δι᾽ ἡμερῶν ἐκεῖ πέμπω. περὶ τῶν χλωρῶν
οὔπω οὐδέν. παρακαλῶ σε γράψαι μοι
περὶ τῆς ὑγιείας σου. οὐ προχωρῖ ὁ πυ-
ρὸς εἰ μὴ ἐκ δραχμῶν ἑπτά.
20 ἔρρωσο καὶ παρακληθεὶς
συνεχῶς ἡμεῖν γράφε περὶ τῆ(ς) σωτηρίας σου.

Verso: Σαραπίωνι ✕ τῷ πατρί.

Eutychides to his father, Sarapion, greeting. Before all else I salute you and thank you that you informed me about your health. Do not be anxious about the sprouting (young) barley, for I have taken care of it. Regarding your jars I am writing to you in order that you may know that I am not being neglectful; I have bought you a hundred sweet smelling jars. I arranged about the green fodder . . . ; for when they arrived there . . . they involved me in no little expense, . . . and after much trouble I compelled them to stay at (?) their work at the former rent, as you wrote in your instructions. Regarding the woven things, I will send them several days before you proceed to write to me (?). Regarding the green fodder, still nothing (to report). I entreat you to write to me about your health. The grain does not advance (in price) beyond seven drachmas. Good-bye and please write to me frequently about your welfare.

Outside address: Sarapion to his father.

4 Read κριθῆς.
12 The first α of αντασχεσθαι is corrected from ε.
 Read ἠναγκάσαμεν αὐτοὺς ἀντισχέσθαι.
13 Read ἐκφορίῳ.
19 "seven drachmas": namely, seven drachmas per artab.

Eutychides was apparently summoned downriver to appear before the magistrates about some matter. He writes to his brother Anoubion, instructing him about various details and informing him about his own situation and about when he may sail up home. Sarapion and Selene, who are greeted in the letter opening, are the father and mother of the two brothers.

Εὐτυχίδη(ς) Ἀνουβ[ίω]νι τῷ ἀδελ[φ]ῶι
χαίρειν. ἀσπάζομαί σε πρὸ πά[ν-
των καὶ Σαραπίωνα καὶ Σελήνην
καὶ Εὐδαιμονίδα. ἔπιτα ἐρωτῶ
5 σε μὴ ἀμελεῖν μου ἐν ἀπου-
σίᾳ τοιαύτῃ ἀλλὰ τὴ(ν) φροντίδα
πάντων ποιεῖν ὡς ἰδίων σου.
ἀπ[ο]λήμψῃ [πα]ρὰ Ἑρμοφίλου
κεράμου μυριάδας δύο εἰς θραγη(ν)
10 ἐὰν γένηται ἡμᾶς μὴ ὑπογύως
ἀναπλεῖν μέντοιγε ὁ κύριος
τῇ γ̄ προέγραψεν ἡμᾶς με-
τὰ τῶν Κουσσιτῶν εἰς ῑϛ ἢ
     ἐν ποτέρῳ ἀκουθησόμεθα
καὶ [[προς εργ]] ἂν αὐτῷ δόξῃ. τί
15 δὲ ἡμεῖν συνέβη μετὰ τῶν
ἀρχόντων ἴσως ἐγνώκατε ἢ
κνώσ{σ}εσθε. περὶ τῶν κεραμίω(ν)
τῇ(ς) θαλλοῦ μελησάτω σοι ὅπως
ἐκξωδιασθῇ α[.] . ι̣[.] . . εση μετρη( )
20 ὁ σεῖτος τοῖς Πάλλαντος Κρίωνι.
ἄσπασαι Ἡλιόδ[ω]ρο(ν) καὶ Ἐξακῶντ(α),
ἄσπασαι Ἀπολ(λώνιον) τὸν ἡπ̣ητὴ(ν) καὶ Πλου-
τίωνα.
     ἐρρῶσθαί σε εὔχ(ομαι) μετὰ
25 τῶν τέκν[ω(ν)]. Τῦβ(ι) ε̄.

Verso: Ἀνουβ(ίωνι) ἀπὸ Εὐτυχ(ίδου) ἀδελφο(ῦ).

Eutychides to his brother, Anoubion, greeting. Before all else I salute you, and Sarapion and Selene and Eudaimonis. Next, I entreat you not to forget me in my absence, but to take care of everything as though it were your own. You will receive from Hermophilos twenty thousand . . . if it happens that I am unable to sail up suddenly. However, the lord (?) wrote me already on the third, (instructing me) that I be sure (?) to sail up with the people of Cusae on the sixteenth or when he should choose. . . . What happened to me with respect to the magistrates you have probably already heard or will learn. Regarding the jars for the festival, take care that they are paid. . . . (Make sure?) the corn (is measured out?) to the sons of Pallas (and?) Krion. Greet (salute) Heliodoros and Exakon. Greet Apollonios the cobbler, and Ploution. I pray for your health with that of your children. Tybi 5.

Outside address: To Anoubion from Eutychides his brother.

4   The κ of καί is corrected.
11 ἀναπλεῖν appears to be used both with γένηται and προέγραψεν.
16 The γ of εγνωκατε is corrected from κ.
17 Read γνώσεσθε.
18 θαλλοῦ: the literal meaning of thallos is young shoot or branch, especially of the olive. A secondary meaning is "gift." Probably an actual olive branch was given as a gift to a landlord by one whose bid for a lease was accepted (see LSJ, s.v. θαλλός, III). The idea of an annual gift, and particularly of one given at a festival, also came to be associated with the word. It is the latter meaning that the word has in the present text. See PAmh II 93.11–12, where payments for thallos, festival gifts ("festivities"), are made at the festival of Isis and the harvest festival (see also the notes on PAmh II 90.9f.; BGU 538.33). In these examples, thallos is equivalent to thalis (festivities), just as, conversely, thalia is sometimes used with the meaning of thallos ("gift").
19 Read ἐξοδιασθῇ.
20 Read σῖτος. τοῖς Πάλλαντος Κρίωνι: καί seems to have been omitted.
21. η of ηλιοδωρον is corrected from ε.

PMich VIII 467–81 consists, for the most part, of letters sent by a certain Claudius Terentianus to his father, Claudius Tiberianus. Though the family archive was discovered under the stairway of a house in Karanis (in the northeastern part of the Fayum, a few miles west of Bakchias and Philadelphia), all of the correspondence seems to have been written in or near Alexandria. None of the papyri bears a date, but the handwriting can be attributed to the first quarter of the second century CE. Various details in the correspondence indicate that the letters span a number of years within that period.

In addition to the letters from Terentianus to his father, there are three addressed to Tiberianus by other members of his circle. PMich VIII 473 (probably 474 as well, though the opening address is missing) is sent by his sister Tabetheus; 475 (=letter 109) by Papirius Apollinarius, who addresses Tiberianus as brother. One letter, from Tiberianus himself, was written at Alexandria and addressed to Longinus Priscus, who is treated with great deference. Since this text is not a letter draft (i.e., it was actually sent), it is not clear why it was found with the addressor, Tiberianus, rather than his recipient. Finally, 481 was written by Terentianus to his sister Tasoucharion (=letter 112).

The editors of these texts point to a noteworthy characteristic of the correspondence: letters 467–74 are written in Latin (all except 472 are from Terentianus to Tiberianus). Latin letters are late in the papyri and, because of the military vocation of both Tiberianus and his son, Terentianus, these provide an insight into the common use of Latin in army circles in Roman Egypt. In addition, the correspondence reveals something of Latin epistolary style at this time in Egypt. The editors note in this connection that the opening formulas, except for the use of *salutem*, closely follow Greek epistolary style in Egypt: "They do not conform to Seneca's statement: *Mos antiquis fuit usque ad meam servatus aetatem, primis epistulae verbis adicere: 'si vales bene est, ego valeo.'*" (Cf. Gummere, *The Epistles of Seneca* 15.1: "The old Romans had a custom which survived even into my lifetime. They would add to the opening words of a letter: 'If you are well, it is well; I also am well.'" Comments by Winter and Youtie in PMich VIII, p. 18.) The editors suggest further that the adaptation to Greek models extends beyond the prescript to the remainder of the letter where numerous expressions are borrowed from Greek epistolary style.

The Latin letters are earlier than those written in Greek. In PMich VIII 469, for example, which is in Latin, Tiberianus is still active in military service and is addressed with his title of *speculator*, an office which, like *frumentarius* ($\gamma\rho\alpha\mu$-$\mu\alpha\tau\eta\phi\acute{o}\rho o\varsigma$ in Greek; see PMich VIII 472, note to line 16), was concerned with the transmission of military post (in 472 he still has the same duties). By the time the Greek letters were written, he was a veteran, settled down at Karanis (see PMich VIII 475 in particular, where he is actually addressed as a veteran on the verso). Similarly, Terentianus tells the story of his enlistment in the Alexandrian fleet in 467 (in Latin), and in 468 (in Latin), while he is still in the fleet, he expresses the desire to be transferred to a cohort. The hope is realized by the time he writes 476 (in Greek), in which he describes himself as a legionary.

In addition to Tiberianus and his son, Terentianus, we have already mentioned the sister of Tiberianus, Tabetheus, who sent PMich VIII 473 and probably 474.

She asks Tiberianus in 473 to settle the legal claims which arose when her son, Saturnilus, murdered a servant. The son killed the servant in a rage, apparently after he discovered that the servant was appropriating family possessions for himself (see the editors' notes on 473).

Tabetheus seems, at least at one time, to have lived near or with Tiberianus (see PMich VIII 479). The writer of 474, who is probably Tabetheus, speaks of Tiberianus' daughter, Segathis, and son, Isidorus, who are present with her. She says that Segathis sent Isidorus to Tiberianus with belts. Though Papiris Apollinaris addresses Tiberianus as brother (475=letter 109), the tone of his letter suggests that the designation in his case is not used literally but as a term of equality. A number of other people are greeted in the closing of the letters. All live in close proximity to Tiberianus (Zotike in 475 and 477, Kephalon in 475, Kursilla in 476, Aphrodisia and Isityche in 467 and 468), but the correspondence does not reveal their exact relationship with Tiberianus. The wife of Tiberianus, and the mother of the family, is not identified explicitly.

Just like the letters from soldiers discussed above (letters 101–5), the present correspondence is concerned almost wholly with family life and business affairs. Though Terentianus appears to have participated in a number of significant military operations, he does not provide us with any essential details about these events. Both PMich VIII 477 and 478 indicate that he was involved, and probably wounded, in quelling a riot in Alexandria, but we do not learn anything about the cause of that riot. On the other hand, we can record the progress of certain details of his personal life. We referred above to the development of his military service, namely, his progress from being a recruit in the fleet to becoming a member of the cohort. Moreover, we can detect certain changes in his family life. In PMich VIII 476 (=letter 110) he asks his father if he may bring a woman into his house. Presumably, he was asking his father for the right to marry a woman (see letter 110, note to line 14). By the time Terentianus writes to his sister Tasoucharion (letter 112), he has a wife and children. The closing greetings of 479 (=letter 111.19f.: "All my househod greets you.") also indicates that Terentianus had persuaded his father to let him marry and set up his own household.

109 PAPIRIUS APOLLINARIUS TO TIBERIANUS
PMich VIII 475   early II CE

Papirius Apollinarius writes to Tiberianus, inquiring about a recent sale and asking when the will of a recently deceased person would be opened. Tiberianus was by this time already a veteran and settled down sufficiently at Karanis to answer such questions about the Fayum as those asked by Papirius Apollinarius. Though Tiberianus is addressed as "brother," the somewhat curt tone of the correspondence suggests a less intimate relationship. We are probably justified in regarding brother, in this case, as a term of familiarity and equality. Elsewhere in the archive, Papirius Apollinarius is mentioned in connection with Terentianus, the son of Tiberianus (PMich VIII 477). During the period of his service in the legion, Terentianus appealed to Papirius for advice regarding the registration of a document at Alexandria.

Zotike, Kephalon and Ptolemy are greeted by Papirius in the letter closing. They apparently lived near Tiberianus, but we know nothing about their relationship to Tiberianus from the remainder of the archive. Nor do we know anything about the people with Papirius who extend greetings to Tiberianus.

Παπεῖρις Ἀπολλινάρι[ος]
    Κλανδ[ί]ῳ Τιβεριανῷ
τῷ τε[ι]μιωτάτῳ χαίρε[ι]ν.
πρὸ παντὸς εὔχομαί σε
5 ὑ[γ]ιαίνε[ι]ν, ὑγια[ί]νω δ[ὲ] καὶ ᾽γ[ώ].
τ[ὸ] πρ[ο]σκύνημά σ[ο]ν ποιῶ
καθ᾽ ἑκάστην ἡμέραν παρὰ
τῷ κυρίῳ Σαράπιδι. ἔγραψάς
μοι λέγων ὅτι Γάιος πέπρα-
10 κέ τι. ἐρωτῶ σε οὖν, ἄδελφε,
ἵνα μάθῃς τί πέπρακεν, καὶ
ἀντίγραψόν μοι. καὶ περὶ
Σέξτου ἤκουσα ὅτι ἀπεγένε-
το. γνῶθι οὖν τίς αὐτοῦ
15 κληρονόμος ἐστὶ καὶ πότε
ἡ διαθήκη αὐτοῦ ἀνύγεται.
[ἀ]σπάζου Ζωτικὴν καὶ Κε-
[φά]λωνα καὶ τοὺς αὐτοῦ πάντες
[καὶ] Πτολεμαῖον. ἀσπάζεται
20 [ὑ]μᾶς Παπειρία καὶ Ἑρμῆς
[καὶ] Μένουθος καὶ Σεραπιάς.

Verso: Κλανδίῳ Τιβεριανῷ οὐετρανῷ π(αρὰ) Πα[πειρίου
    ᾽Απολλιναρίου]

Papirius Apollinarius to his most esteemed Claudius Tiberianus, greeting. Before anything else I pray that you are well; I myself am also well. I make obeisance on your behalf daily before the lord Sarapis. You wrote me, saying that Gaios has sold something. Therefore, I ask you, brother, that you find out what he has sold, and write an answer to me. And about Sextus, I heard that he departed life. Consequently, learn who his heir is and when his will is to be opened. Greet (salute) Zotike and Kephalon and all his household and Ptolemy. Papiria greets you, as well as Hermes and Menouthos and Serapias.

Outside address: To Claudius Tiberianus, veteran, from Papirius Apollinarius.

1 Read Παπίριος, Latin *Papirius*; see Meinersmann, *Wörter und Namen*, p. 91.
2 Read τιμιωτάτῳ.
6–8 The mere presence of the Sarapis-*proskynema* formula probably suffices to place the writer of a letter at Alexandria (see PMich VIII 476, note to lines 4–5).
16 Read ἀνοίγεται. The editor of PMich 475 suggests that the will would have been opened in the presence of the strategos (see Mitteis, *Grundzüge*, p. 241).
18 Read πάντας.
20 Παπειρία=Latin *Papiria*; see n. 1.

110 TERENTIANUS TO TIBERIANUS
PMich VIII 476   early II CE

Terentianus writes to his father, primarily to get his consent to bring a woman into his house. Evidently, Terentianus anticipated strong opposition, as the overloaded phrases in this section of the letter (see lines 10–19, especially 13–15) and the affirmations of filial obedience indicate. Though no legal details of Terentianus' proposal are discussed, it seems he was contemplating marital union (see the note to line 14 below).

The time at which the letter was written (at night) and the general similarity of the handwriting with PMich 478 and 479—also from Terentianus—suggest that Terentianus himself was the scribe. The editor notes that the mention of a Caesareum in line 23 is of some interest, but that the context does not reveal its location.

Κλαύδιος Τερ[εν]τιανὸ[ς] Κλαυδίῳ Τιβερ[ι]ανῷ τῷ κυρίῳ
[κ]αὶ πατρὶ πλ[εῖστα]
χαίρειν.
πρὸ μὲν πάντων εὔχομαί σε ὑγιαίνειν καὶ εὐτυχεῖν μοι, ὅ
μοι εὐκταῖόν ἐστιν,
ὑγιαίνω δὲ καὶ αὐτὸς ἐγὼ ποιούμενός σου τὸ προσκύνημα
καθ᾽ ἑκάστην ἡμέραν
5   παρὰ τῷ κυρίῳ Σεράπιδι καὶ τοῖς συννάοις θεοῖς.
γεινώσκειν σε θέλω, πατήρ,
κεκομί{κα]σ[θ]αι με παρὰ ᾽Αχιλλᾶτος καλάθιον. ὁμοίως καὶ
ἄλλο καλάθιόν μο[ι]
ἐδόθη ὑπὸ [τοῦ] στρατιώτου, ἐν ᾧ εὗρον ἄρτους μεγάλους
δύο καὶ φοινίκια καρ[[. .]]-
νοτά, καὶ παρὰ τοῦ πατρὸς ᾽Ιουλίου σφυριδάλλιον καὶ τὰ
ταλάριά μου καὶ
θήκην μαχαιρίου. ἔπεμψέ μοι φάσιν περὶ γυναικὸς,
γνώμην μου λαμ-
10   βάνων ἐωνεῖτό μοι. πάλαι ἂν πρὸ διετίας ἐσχήκειν εἰς τὴν
οἰκίαν
μ[ο]υ ἀλλὰ ο[ὐ]κ ἐπέτρεψα [ἐ]μαυτῷ οὐδὲ ἐπιτρέπω δίχα
σου λαβεῖν
τ[ι]να καὶ τοὔνπαλιν οὐκ ἔχεις ἀπ᾽ ἐμοῦ ἀκ[οῦ]σαι περὶ
τοῦ πράγμα-
[το]ς τούτ[ου]. εἴ π[ο]ύ ἐστιν ἣν ἐὰν δοκῇ μ[ο]ι κατενέγκαι ἡ
δυναμένη
μᾶλλο[ν ὑ]πὲρ ἐμοῦ σοι εὐνοεῖν καὶ φροντίζειν σου πλείω
ἐμοῦ, δια-
15   τ[ε]λεῖτα[ι] ἐμέ [σο]ι εὐχαρ[ι]στεῖν ἤ σὺ ἐμὲ μέμψασθαι.
διὰ τοῦτο ἕως
σήμερον γυνὴ οὐκ εἰσῆλθέ μου εἰς τὴν οἰκίαν εἰ μὴ ἦν σὺ
δοκι-
μάσῃς. [σὺ] δὲ οἶδες σατῷ πάλιν ὅτι ἐκπλέξας σου τὰ
μετέωρα ἔχω
. . . . . . α[. σ]ὺ μένεις τὸν χρόνον σου τῆς ζωῆς ἀκείνητός
μου γυ-
[ναι]κὸς ἀποτάσσομαι. εἰ δὲ οὔ, ἣν ἂν δοκιμάσῃς ταύτην
κἀγὼ θέ-
20   [λω]. νυκτ[ό]ς σοι ἔγραψα [τ]ὴν ἐπιστολὴν ταύτην εὑρὼν
εὐκαιρίαν,
οὐ δὲ δεδυνημένος σοι πέμψαι. καλῶς ποιήσεις ἀντι-
[γρ]άψ̣α̣ς μοι περὶ τῆς σωτηρίας σου καὶ τῆς ἐπιστολῆς
τὴν ἀν-
[τι]φώ[νησ]ιν. ἄσπασαι πάντες τοὺς ἐκ τοῦ Καισαρείου
κατ᾽ ὄνομα.
ἄσπασ[αι] Δίδυμον τὸν νομικὸν πανοικί. ἐρεῖς δὲ
Λονγείνῳ
25   ὅτι ἐλπ[ίζω] π̣ά̣λ̣ι̣ν ἀναβῆναι. ἐν δὲ εὐχαριστῶ τοῖς θεοῖς
ὅτι

Claudius Terentianus to his lord and father, Claudius Tiberianus, very many greetings. Before all else I pray that you are well and prospering, which is my desire. I myself am also well, making obeisance on your behalf daily before the lord Sarapis and the allied gods (literally: "the gods who share his temple"). I want you to know, father, that I have received a basket (*kalathion*) from Achillas. Similarly, another basket was given to me by the soldier, in which I found two large loaves of bread and dates, and from the father of Julius a small basket (*sphyridallion*) and my small baskets (*talaria*) and a sword-sheath. He sent word to me about a woman; on receipt of my consent, he would try to buy one for me. Already two years ago I wanted to take a woman into my house, but I did not allow myself nor am I now permitting myself to take someone apart from your approval, and you will not hear otherwise from me about this matter. If it is the case somehow that the woman I bring down should be one who, for my sake, would be more kindly disposed to you and to have more consideration for you than for me, it works out that I do you a favor rather than that I am a cause of blame by you. For this reason, lacking your approval, until today no woman has entered my house. You yourself know, for another thing, that I have driven away your difficulties (causes of consternation); [and if (?)] you remain immovable for the rest of your life I will renounce (the right to) my woman. If not, whatever woman you approve is the one that I also want. I wrote this letter at night, having found the opportunity, but I have not been able to send it. Please write me in reply about your welfare and in answer to this letter. Greet (salute) all those from the Caesareum, each by name. Greet Didymos, the notary, along with his whole household. You will tell Longinus that I hope to come up again. I give thanks to the gods for one thing, that I gave you more than the eight drachmas. If I had not, the same thing would have resulted. And if you go up to the Arsinoite nome, go by Kursilla and get the five logs of timber and bring them down when you come and whatever else you can carry down to us for the winter. Epitynchanon greets you. Greet all our friends, each by name.

πλείον[ας] δέδωκά σο[ι] τῶν ὀκτὼ δραχμῶν. εἰ μή, τὸ αὐτὸ
ἦν.

καὶ ἐὰν [ἀ]ναβῇς εἰς Ἀρσινοείτην ὕπαγε παρὰ
Κουρσίλλαν καὶ δέ-

ξαι τοὺς πέντε κορμοὺς τῶν ξύλων καὶ κατενέγκεις αὐτὰ
ἐρχόμ[ε]νος καὶ ἂν ἄλλα δυνασθῇς κατενέγκαι ἡμεῖν εἰς
τὸν

30   χειμῶναν. ἀσπάζεταί σε Ἐπιτυγχάνων.

Continued in the left margin:

ἄσπασαι πάντες τοὺς φιλοῦντες [ἡμᾶς] κατ᾽ ὄνομα.

Verso: ἀπόδ(ος) Κλαυδίῳ Τιβεριαν[ῷ] . [. .] . [. . .] . . . ωι
[π]α[ρὰ] Κλαυδίο[υ Τερε]ντιανοῦ υἱοῦ λε-
(γιῶνος) στρα(τιώτου).

Outside address: Deliver to Claudius Tiberianus
. . . from his son, Claudius Terentianus, a soldier
of the legion.

4–5   Sarapis and the συνναοι θεοί ("allied/fellow gods") are mentioned in a similar way in BGU VII 1680.2–3 (III CE) and in WChr 100 (see Wilcken, *Grundzüge*, pp. 122f.). See also letter 109, note to lines 6–8.

5   Σεράπιδι: according to Wilcken, the form of the name was Sarapis in the Ptolemaic period and only became Serapis in the Roman period (UPZ I, p. 86).

7–8   Read καρνωτά.
σφυριδάλλιον: regarding this late diminutive of σφυρίς, see W. Petersen, *Greek Diminutives in -ION*, pp. 254f.

12   Read τοὔμπαλιν.

14   σοι εὐνοεῖν: the editors note that in PSI I 64 this construction means a woman undertakes to live with a man as his wedded wife (καὶ εὐνοεῖν σοι). If the same meaning is applicable here, Terentianus is contemplating marriage.

15   Read σε.

17   Read οἶδας σεαυτῷ.

18–19   Read ζωῆς, ἀκίνητος.

23   Read πάντας.

23   Καισαρείου: the editors rightly note that the context does not supply the location of this Caesareum and add that it could not be the one at Alexandria, since Terentianus was writing from that city, nor probably the one at Arsinoe, since Tiberianus was not in the Arsinoite nome when the letter was written (see line 27).

24   ἐρεῖς: according to the editors, this was a standard expression at this time. See PLund II 2.13, 3.12–13; BGU II 597.24–26; PBad II 35.11; POxy VI 932.3. For μεταδώσεις in the same function, see PMich VIII 466.47. Read Λογγείνῳ (Latin *Longinus*).

25   ἐλπίζω κτλ.: see this same convention in PMich VIII 481.14–15.

29   Read ἡμῖν.

30   Read χειμῶνα.

31   Read πάντας τοὺς φιλοῦντας.

111   TERENTIANUS TO TIBERIANUS
PMich VIII 479

early II CE

Terentianus expresses dissatisfaction with his father because, after departing from Terentianus in a state of ill health, Tiberianus had not written to Terentianus about his welfare since arriving home. The other major occasion of the letter is Terentianus' directions for the delivery of a letter from the dioiketes to the strategos through Tabetheus, the sister of Tiberianus. The dioiketes is, in this instance, the chief of the διοίκησις, the fiscal office which was directly subordinate to the prefect of Egypt and which had its headquarters in Alexandria (see Wilcken, *Grundzüge*, p. 156). According to Youtie and Winter, the editors of this text, the message to the strategos was sent through Terentianus in response to a petition from him. The fact that the dioiketes expected a reply from the strategos indicates that he was seeking information from him which had a bearing on the subject of Terentianus' petition. The reference to this dioiketes (in Alexandria), as well as the dual reference to "sailing up" river (lines 5 and 15), suggests that Terentianus was writing from Alexandria.

Κλαύδιος Τερεντιανὸς Κλαυδίῳ Τιβεριανῷ
τῷ πατρὶ καὶ κ[υρί]ῳ πλεῖστα χ[α]ίρειν.
τρὸ μὲν πάντων εὔχομαί σε ὑγιαίνειν
καὶ εὐτυχεῖν, ὅ μοι εὐκταῖόν ἐστιν. θαυμά-
5 ζω πῶς ἀναπλεύσας οὐκ ἀντέγραψάς
μοι περὶ τῆς σωτηρίας σου, ἀλλὰ ἔως σή-
μερ[ο]ν ἀγωνιῶ διότι νωθρενόμε-
νος ἀπ᾽ ἐμοῦ ἐξῆλθες. καλῶς οὖν ποιήσεις
ταχύτερόν μοι ἀντιγράψαι περὶ τῆς σωτη-
10 ρίας σου. ἀναδώσις Ταβαθεῦτι τὴν ἐπιστολὴν τὴν τοῦ διοικητοῦ πρὸς τὸν στρατηγόν. πᾶν δὲ ποι(η)σάτω ἀναδοῦναι αὐτὴν ταχύτερον τῷ στρατηγῷ ἵνα πρὸς τὰ
γραφέντα αὐτῷ καὶ αὐτὸς ταχέως ἀντι-
15 γ[ρ]άψῃ. ἔμελλον κἀγὼ ἀναπλεῦσαι ἀλ-
[[αλ]]λὰ [ο]ὔπω τὰ μετέωρά μου ἐξέπλεξα
ἕως σή[με]ρον. καὶ ἐὰν γνοῖς περὶ Νεμεσι-
ανοῦ ποῦ διατρείβι ἀντίγραψόν μοι ἐπεὶ
ἀγωνιῶμεν καὶ περὶ αὐτοῦ. ἀσπάζονταί
20 σε οἱ ἐμοί. ἄσπα[σ]αι πάντες τοὺς φιλοῦν-
τές σε κατ᾽ ὄνομα.

2nd hand: ἐρρῶ[σθα]ί σε
[εὔ]χομ[α]ι.

Verso: Κλαυδ[ί]ῳ Τιβερια[νῷ] τῷ τειμιωτάτῳ π(αρὰ)
Κλα[υδίου]ἱ
[Τερεντιαν[οῦ].

Claudius Terentianus to his father and lord, Claudius Tiberianus, very many greetings. Before all else I pray that you are well and are prospering, which is my desire. I am surprised that after you sailed up-country you did not write to me about your health, but until today I have been worried because you were indisposed (ill) when you left me. Therefore, please write a reply to me about your welfare. You will deliver to Tabetheus the letter of the dioiketes to the strategos. And let her make every effort to give it to the strategos immediately, in order that he may write an answer quickly to what has been written to him. I intended also to sail up but until today I have not yet disposed of my difficulties. And if you know about Nemesianus, where he is staying, write me a reply, since we are worried about him too. All my household greets (salutes) you. Greet all your friends, each by name. I pray that you are well.

Outside address: To his most esteemed Claudius Tiberianus from Claudius Terentianus.

---

10 Read ἀναδώσεις.
12 ποι(η)σάτω: regarding this spelling, see PMich III 202.8 (see Mayser, *Grammatik* 1.1.87; Moulton, *Grammar* 2:73).
17 γνοῖς: according to the editor, a variant form of the subjunctive γνῷς (see also PMich VIII 510, note to line 24; see Youtie, "Parerga Papyrologia," p. 116, n. 55).
18 Read διατρίβει.
20-21 Read πάντας τοὺς φιλοῦντας.
24 Read τιμιωτάτῳ.

7-8 ἀγωνιῶ διότι νωθρευόμενος κτλ.: this sentiment in the letter opening is also found in BGU II 449.4–5; PGiss 17.5–6 (=SelPap I 115.5–6); PBrem 61.13–16. A more elaborate expression of this sentiment is found in PSI IV 333.1–2.

---

112 TERENTIANUS TO TASOUCHARION
PMich VIII 481

early II CE

Terentianus, who is probably in Alexandria, informs his sister that a basket has been sent along with the letter and he instructs her to notify him by letter about the basket's contents. This request for information about the receipt or condition of various kinds of "parcel" post is common in papyrus letters and was probably occasioned, for the most part, by the haphazard nature of private delivery through makeshift messengers. Terentianus also notifies Tasoucharion about another basket which had been sent through Valerius, a goldsmith, and he instructs her, upon receipt of that basket, both to write about her health and to tell him what she would like for him to get for her, since he intends to sail up river shortly. He mentions a few other matters, primarily details in preparation for the upcoming visit of Terentianus and his family. We can assume that some years have elapsed since Terentianus asked Tiberianus for the right to bring a woman into his house because, in the present letter, he has a wife and children.

T[ε]ρεν[τιανὸς T]ασο[υχαρίῳ]
τῇ ὑαή[λφῇ π]λεῖστα χαίρειν.
πρὸ μὲν [πάντ]ων εὔχ[ο]μαί σε
ὑγιαίνε[ιν μετ]ὰ τῶν σῶν πάν-
5 των. κόμισαι παρὰ τ[ο]ῦ ἀποδι-
δόντος σοι τὸ ἐπιστόλιον καλάθιον ἐν ᾧ ὃ ἐὰν εὑρίσκεις
αὐτὸ ἀντιγράψις μοι. καὶ διὰ
Οὐαλερίου τ[ο]ῦ χρυσοχ[ο]ῦ ἄλ-
10 λο σοι ἀπέσ[τα]λκα. καλῶς οὖν
ποιήσ[ι]ς κο[μ]ισαμένη ἀντιγράψαι μοι κ[αὶ] πε[ρὶ] τῆς σωτηρίας [ὑ]μῶν καὶ οὗ [ἐ]ὰν χρείαν ἔχῃς. κἀγ[ὼ] γὰρ ἐλπίζω τα-
15 χ[έ]ως πρὸς ὑμᾶς ἀν[ε]λθεῖ[ν]. πᾶν
ποί(η)σο[ν] φρ[ο]ντίσα[ι] ἡμε[ῖ]ν κεράμια δύω τὰ μ[έ]γιστα ὀ[λυ-]
ρῶν κ[α]ὶ ἀρτάβην ἐλαίου ῥαφα-
νίνου. ἔπεμ[ψ]ά σοι ὀριγάνιν
20 τὸ συνπαρὰ τῷ ἐλαίῳ. καὶ εἰ
ἔλαβ[ες] παρὰ Πτολεμαίου
ἃ ἔγραψα . . [.] . δη . οι γράψον
μοι . [. . . . . . .] τὰς δύο ἀρτάβας . [. . . . . . .] . . αν καὶ ἔχῃ
25 ἵνα [. . . . . . .]ἐνθάδε ἀναβάς.
ἀσπ[άζεταί σ]ε τὰ τέ[κν]α ἡμῶν
[. . . . .]α . [. . . . . .] καὶ
[. . . . .] . . [. . . . .]

Continued in the right margin:
[. . . .] . ἄσπασαι Π . . . . . .[. .κράτην σὺν ὅλῳ τοῦ οἴκου
30 [αὐτο]ῦ καὶ Πτολεμαῖον τὸν τοῦ Ἀρίου σὺν γυναιξὶ καὶ τοῖς
[τέκν]οις. ἄσπασαι Πτολεμαῖον καὶ Τιβερῖνον καὶ Τειπ . . .
[   ] . . ικει[. .] ἀσπ[αρά]γου πέμψαι νέο[ν]
[. . . .]ιν διὰ Μέλανος, ὅτι ἐρωτῶμέν σε, πατήρ, πέμψ[ο]ν
[. . . .]ιν [ἕν]. ἀσπάζονταί σε οἱ ἐν τῇ συνοικίᾳ πάντες
35 [. . . . .]ι κατ᾽ ὄν]ομα. ἔπεμψά σοι χάρτην ἵνα ἔχῃς μοι

Terentianus to his sister, Tasoucharion, very many greetings. Before all else I pray that you are well together with your whole family. Receive from the one who brings this letter to you a basket and write back to me what you find in it. And I sent another one to you through Valerius the goldsmith. Therefore, upon receipt of it, please write to me, both about your health and about whatever you may need. For I myself hope to come up to you soon. Make every effort to secure two jars of the largest size of *olyra* and an artab of radish oil. I sent the marjoram to you that goes with (i.e., for flavoring) the oil. And if you received from Ptolemy what I wrote . . . write to me . . . [lines 23–25 are fragmentary]. Our children greet (salute) you. . . . Greet P. . . . with his whole household and Ptolemy, the son of Arius, together with their wives and children. Greet Ptolemy and Tiberinus and T. . . . to send a fresh bundle (?) of asparagus through Melas, and because we ask it of you, father, send one bundle (?). All the members of the household greet you, each by name. I sent papyrus to you in order that you would be able to write to me about your health. I pray that you may always be well.

Outside address: Deliver to Tasoucharion from Terentianus.

1 The names are restored from the outside address (line 37).
8 Read ἀντιγράψεις.
9 χρυσοχοῦ: the space is not enough for χρυσοχόου.
11 Read ποιήσεις.
16 Read ἡμῖν.
16–18 κεράμια δύω . . . ἀρτάβην: Youtie and Winter, the editors, note that the measures have been interchanged. The artab is regularly a dry measure and the *keramion* is normally a liquid measure.
17–18 On olyra as emmer rather than spelt, as a type of

[γρά]φειν περὶ τῆς ὑγίας ὑμῶν. ἐρρῶσθαί σε εὔχομαι εἰς
αἰῶν[α].

Verso: ἀπόδ(ος) Τασουχαρίω Χ π(αρὰ) Τερεντιανοῦ.

grain, see N. Jasny, *Wheats of Classical Antiquity* pp. 119–24.

18–19 "radish oil": see the editors' note, where it is suggested that the oil, obtained from the seeds of the radish, had a disagreeable smell and that Pliny had stated that the radish was esteemed in Egypt on account of the large amount of oil extracted from it.

19 Read ὀριγάνιον (diminutive of ὀρίγανον).

29 τοῦ οἴκου: genitive for dative.

33 πατήρ: though the letter is written to his sister, Terentianus addresses his father in lines 32–34 (see PMich VIII 514.35–37, in which closing greetings are interrupted to address a third person).

The Egyptian year was essentially solar and consisted originally of twelve thirty-day months and five intercalary days. Though the Egyptian year was one-fourth of a day shorter than the natural year, the Egyptian calendar was stabilized by adding a sixth intercalary day every fourth year in the reign of Augustus. Egyptian months corresponded thereafter with the Roman calendar according to the chart below.

Macedonian months were originally lunar, so their relationship to Egyptian months was ambiguous in the early Ptolemaic period. However, before the end of the second century CE they were assimilated to Egyptian months according to the following chart.

Egyptian	Macedonian	Roman
Thoth 1	Dios 1	August 29 (or after leap-year, 30)
Phaophi 1	Apellaios 1	September 28 (29)
Hathyr 1	Audnaios 1	October 28 (29)
Choiach 1	Peritios 1	November 27 (28)
Tybi 1	Dystros 1	December 27 (28)
Mecheir 1	Xandikos 1	January 26 (27)
Phamenoth 1	Artemisios 1	February 25 (26)
Pharmouthi 1	Daisios 1	March 26 (27)
Pachon 1	Panemos 1	April 26 (27)
Payni 1	Loios 1	May 26 (27)
Epeiph 1	Gorpiaios 1	June 25 (26)
Mesore 1	Hyperberetaios 1	July 25 (26)
Intercalary 1	Intercalary 1	August 24 (25)

Adapted from A. S. Hunt and C. C. Edgar, *Select Papyri* 1, pp. xv–xvi.

SEMPRONIUS TO SATURNILA AND MAXIMUS
SelPap I 121 (=RevEg 1919, p. 204)

Sempronius writes two letters to his family on the same sheet of papyrus: the first is addressed to his mother and the second to his brother, with whom the mother lives. It is clear from the second letter, which admonishes the brother for treating the mother shabbily, that the mother herself was illiterate and that Maximus was the actual recipient of both letters. This is confirmed by the outside address, which is directed only to the brother. An interesting aspect of the opening health wish in the first letter is the prayer that the writer's family may be kept free from enchantment, often translated more specifically as "unharmed by the evil eye." This sentiment occurs with increasing frequency in the later Roman period (see letter 94.8f.).

Σεμπρώνιος Σατουρνίλᾳ τῇ μητρεὶ
καὶ κυρίᾳ πλεῖστα χαίρειν.
πρὸ τῶν ὅλων ἐρρῶσθέ σε εὔχομαι μετὰ καὶ τῶν
ἀβασκάντων μου ἀδελφῶν, ἅμα δὲ καὶ τὸ προσκύ-
5   νημα ὑμῶν ποιοῦμε ἡμερησίως παρὰ τῷ κυρί-
ῳ Σεράπιδι. τοσαύτας ὑμεῖν ἐπιστολὰς διεπεμψάμην κοὐδεμείαν μοι ἀντεγράψαται, τοσούτων
καταπλευσάντων. ἐρωτηθεῖσ⟨α⟩, ἡ κυρία μου, ἀνόκνως
μοι γράφειν περὶ τῆς σωτηρίας ὑμῶν ἵνα κἀγὼ ἀμε-
10   ριμνότερα διάγω· τοῦτο μοι γὰρ εὐκτέον ἐστὶν διὰ παντός. ἀσπάζομαι Μάξιμον καὶ τὴν σύμβιον αὐτοῦ καὶ Σα-
τουρνῖλον καὶ Γέμελλον καὶ Ἑλένην καὶ τοὺς αὐτῆς.
    μετάδος
αὐτῇ ὅτι ἐκομεισάμην Σεμπρωνίου ἐπειστολὴν
ἀπὸ Καππ οδοκίας. ἀσπάζομαι Ἰούλιον καὶ τοὺς αὐ-
15   τοῦ κατ᾽ ὄνομα καὶ Σκυθικὸν καὶ Θερμοῦθιν καὶ τὰ
πεδία αὐτῆς. ἀσπάζετε ὑμᾶς Γέμελλος.
ἔρρωσό μοι, ἡ κυρία μου, διὰ παντός.

Σεμπρώνιος Μαξίμωι τῷ ἀδελφῷ
πλ[ε]ῖστα χαίρειν. πρὸ τῶν ὅλων ἐρῶσθέ
20   σε εὔχομαι. μετέλαβον ὅτι βαρέως δουλεύ{ου}ετε
τὴν κυρίαν ἡμῶν μητέραν. ἐρωτηθείς, ἀδελφε γλυ-
κύταται, ἐν μηδενεὶ αὐτὴν λύπει· εἰ δέ τεις τῶν ἀ-
δελφῶν ἀντιλέγει αὐτῇ, σὺ ὀφείλεις αὐτοὺς κολαφί-
ζει[ν]· ἤδη γὰρ πατὴρ ὀφίλεις καλεῖσθαι. ἐπείσταμε
25   ὅτι χωρὶς τῶν γραμμάτων μου δυνατὸς εἶ αὐτῇ
ἀρέσε, ἀλλὰ μὴ βαρέως ἔχε μου τὰ γράμματα νουθε-
τοῦν[τ]ά σε· ὀφίλομεν γὰρ σέβεσθε τὴν τεκοῦσαν ὡς
θε[όν,] μάλειστα τοιαύτην οὖσαν ἀγαθήν. ταῦτά σοι ἔ-
γραψα, ἀδελφε, ἐπειστάμενος τὴν γλυκασίαν τῶν
30   κυ[ρί]ων γονέων. καλῶς π[ο]ιήσις γράψας μοι περὶ τῆς
σ[ωτ]ηρίας ὑμ[ῶ]ν. ἔρρωσό μοι, ἀδελφε.

Verso: ἀπόδ(ος) Μαξίμωι ἀπὸ Σεμπρωνίου
      ἀδελφοῦ.

Sempronius to his mother and lady, Saturnila, very many greetings. Before all else I pray that you are well together with my brothers, kept free from enchantment, and at the same time I make obeisance on your behalf daily before the lord Serapis. So many letters have I sent to you and not one have you written in return, even when many have sailed down! Please, my lady, write to me without hesitation about your health in order that I may live with less concern: for this (your welfare) is my continual prayer. I greet (salute) Maximus and his wife and Saturnilus and Gemellus and Helena and her family. Tell her that I received a letter of Sempronius from Cappadocia. I greet Julius and his family each by name and Skythikos and Thermouthis and her children. Gemellus greets you. May you always be well, my lady.

Sempronius to his brother, Maximus, very many greetings. Before all else I pray that you are well. I was informed that you serve our lady mother grudgingly. Please, sweetest brother, grieve her in nothing; and if one of our brothers speaks against her, you ought to slap them. For you ought already to be called (named) father. I know that without my writing you are able to please her, but do not take my letter rebuking you grudgingly; for we ought to revere the one who bore us as a goddess, especially this one who is so good. I wrote this to you, brother, knowing how sweet our revered parents are. Please write to me about your health. May you be well, brother.

Outside address: Deliver to Maximus from his brother.

3   Read ἐρρῶσθαι (also in line 19).
5   Read ποιοῦμαι.
7   Read ἀντεγράψατε.
8   ἀνόκνως=ἀόκνως; see POxy 743.39 (I BCE) and
     PFay 130.4 (III CE).
10 Read εὐκταῖον?

14   Read Καππαδοκίας.
16   Read παιδία, ἀσπάζεται.
21–22 Read γλυκύτατε.
22   Read τις.
24   Read ἐπίσταμαι.
26   Read ἀρέσαι.
27   Read σέβεσθαι.

114   LETTER FROM A PENITENT SON
SelPap I 120 (=BGU III 846)

II CE

This letter from a penitent son is, according to Deissmann (*Ancient East*, p. 188), "a remarkably good illustration of the parable of the Prodigal Son (Luke 15.11ff.)." He classifies it as a letter of contrition and compares it with a specimen letter of contrition (*Ancient East*, pp. 191f.), found in Proclus' handbook of epistolary types (*De forma epistolari*=letter 12 in Hercher, *Epistolographi Graeci*, p. 9).

ἡ ἐπιστολή. οἶδα σφαλεὶς κακῶς
σε διαθέμονος. διὸ μεταγνοὺς τὴν
ἐπὶ τῶ σφάλματι συγγνώμην αἰτῶ.
μεταδοῦναι δέ μοι μὴ κατοκνήσης διὰ
τὸν κύριον. δίκαιον γάρ ἐστι συγ-
γινώσκειν πταίουσι τοῖς φίλοις, ὅτε
μάλιστα καὶ ἀξιοῦσι συγγνώμης
τυχεῖν.

The letter. I know that I err in treating you badly. Wherefore, having repented, I beg pardon for the error. But for the Lord's sake do not delay to forgive me. For it is just to pardon friends who stumble, and especially when they desire to obtain pardon.

Ἀντῶνις Λόνγος Νειλοῦτι
[τ]ῇ μητρὶ π[λ]ῖστα χαίρειν. καὶ δι-
ὰ πάντω[ν] εὔχομαί σαι ὑγειαίνειν. τὸ προσκύνημά σου [ποι]ῶ κατ' αἰκάστην ἡμαίραν παρὰ τῷ
5   κυρίῳ [Σερ]άπειδει. γεινώσκειν σαι θέλω, ὅ-
τι οὐχ [ἤλπι]ιζον, ὅτι ἀναβένις εἰς τὴν μητρό-
πολιν. χ[ά]ρειν τοῦτο οὐδ' ἐγὸ εἰσῆ⟨λ⟩θα εἰς τὴν πόλιν. αἰδ[υ]σ οπο[ύ]μην δὲ ἐλθεῖν εἰς Καρανίδαν
ὅτι σαπρῶς παιριπατῶ. αἴγραψά σοι, ὅτι γυμνός
10 εἰμει. παρακα[λ]ῶ σαι, μήτηρ, δ[ι]αλάγητί μοι. λοιπὸν οἶδα τί [ἐγὼ?] αἰμαυτῶ παρέσχημαι. παιπαί{δ}-
δευμαι καθ' ὃν δῖ τρόπον. οἶδα, ὅτι ἡμάρτηκα.
ἤκουσα παρὰ το[ῦ . . .] . υμου τὸν εὑρόντα σαι
ἐν τῷ Ἀρσαινοείτῃ καὶ ἀκαιρέως πάντα σοι δι-
15 ήγηται. οὐκ οἶδες, ὅτι θέλω πηρὸς γενέσται,
εἰ γνοῦναι, ὅπως ἀνθρόπω [ἔ]τ[ι] ὀφείλω ὀβολόν;
[. . . . . .]ο[. . . . .]σὺ αὐτὴ ἐλθέ.
[. . . . .]χανκ [. . .]ον ἤγουσα, ὅτι . .

Antonius Longus to his mother, Nilous, very many greetings. I pray continually that you are well; I make obeisance on your behalf each day before the lord Serapis. I want you to know that I was not expecting you to go up to the metropolis; on this account I myself did not come to the city. And I was ashamed to come to Karanis, because I go about in filth. I wrote to you that I am naked. I entreat you, mother, be reconciled to me. Now (well), I know what I have done to myself. I have been duly taught a lesson. I know that I have sinned. I heard from . . . who found you in the Arsinoite nome and he reported everything accurately to you. Do you not know that I prefer to be maimed than to be conscious that I still own an obol to a man? . . . come yourself! . . . I have heard that . . . I entreat you . . . I entreat you . . . I myself desire . . . do not act otherwise . . .

[. . . . .] . λησαι [. .] παρακαλῶ σαι

20 [. . . . .] . . . α[.] . αἰγὼ σχεδν

[. . . . .] ω παρακαλῶ σαι

[. . . . .]ωνου θέλω αἰγὼ

[. . . . .]σει . . . . . . οὐκ ε.

[. . . . .] . . . . ἄλλως ποι[.]

Here the papyrus breaks off.

Verso: Νειλοῦτι] μητρεὶ ἀπ᾽ Ἀντωνίω Λόνγου
νείοῦ.

Outside address: To Nilous his mother from Antonius Longus her son.

1 Antonis is short for Antonius (see letter 103a.22).
3 Read σε, here and elsewhere in the letter (σαι= σε).
4 Read καθ᾽ ἑκάστην ἡμέραν.
6 Read ἀναβαίνεις.
6f. "the metropolis," i.e., Arsinoe, the capital of the nome.
7 Read τούτου ἐγώ.
8 Read ἐδυσωπούμην.
9 Read περιπατῶ, ἔγραψα.
11 Read ἐμαυτῶ, πεπαίδευμαι.
13 Read τοῦ εὑρόντος.
14 Read Ἀρσινοίτῃ, ἀκεραίως.
15–16 Read γενέσθαι ἢ γνῶναι.
25 Read Ἀντωνίου.

115 CORRESPONDENCE TO APOLLINARIUS
PMich VIII 498   II CE
PMich VIII 499   II CE

The two letters included in this entry were addressed to Apollinarius by his brothers, Gemellus (letter 115a) and Sabinianus (letter 115b). They are only two of some half dozen letters which are addressed to Apollinarius in PMich VIII (see 496–500, 502) and there seems to be one by Apollinarius himself in the same collection (PMich VIII 501). The manner in which his brothers address him suggests that he was probably an older brother, whom they revered. He is described as a veteran on the verso of letter 115a.

In 115a, Gemellus thanks his brother warmly for the support which he and a friend had rendered in their recommendation on his behalf. The language used in reference to the recommendation is reminiscent of that found in actual letters of introduction. In the second letter, Sabinianus also expresses gratitude to Apollinarius for help which he had rendered. In this instance, Apollinarius had aided their sister. Sabinianus alleges, for his part, that he has been a responsible correspondent, but that the carelessness of his letter carriers has resulted in a breakdown in communication. The real point of the letter, however, is neither the expression of gratitude nor the statement of faithful correspondence but the entreaty in lines 14–16. Sabinianus entreats his brother to encourage their sister to accept Sabinianus as her legal guardian.

In addition to Gemellus and Sabinianus, a certain Rullius addresses Apollinarius as brother in PMich 500. Rullius' use of "brother" is evidently a mark of affection, however, since Gemellus refers to this same Rullius as a "very good friend" of Apollinarius (see 115a.8–10; also see PMich VIII 485.9, 496.2 and 521.1 for other examples of the figurative use of this expression).

Letter A

Γέμελλ[ο]s Ἀπολιναρίωι
τῶι τιμιωτάτωι [ἀ]δελ-
φῶι χαί[ρει]ν.

Gemellus to his most esteemed brother, Apollinarius, greeting. Very many thanks to you, brother, because of having been concerned about me; your

χάρις σοι πλείστη, ἄδελ-
5 φε, μεριμνήσαντί με·
ἡ σύστασίς σου πολύ με
ὠφέλησε. καὶ πρότε-
ρον μεμελήκι τῷ ἀγα-
θωτάτῳ σου φίλῳ ῾Ρουλ-
10 λίῳ εἰδότι ἣν ἔχις ἰς
ἐμὲ εὔνοιαν τὴν ἀπου-
σίαν σου ἀναπληρῶσαι·
πρὸς τὸν Αἰμιλλιανὸν
ἀνόκνως καὶ σπουδαί-
15 ως συνέστακέ ⟨με⟩ ὡς συν-
γενῆν σου ὃν ἥδιστα ἔσ-
χε. καὶ ἐρωτῶ, ἄδελφε,
ἀνθομολογῆσαί σε τῷ
῾Ρούφῳ ἐὰν αὐτῷ γράφῃς.
20 ἔπεμψά σοι τὰ ἐπιστό-
λια Αἰμιλλιανοῦ καὶ ῾Ρού-
φου καὶ Χαρίτωνος. γράφε
μοι περὶ τῆς σωτηρίας σου
καὶ ὧν θέλις. ἄσπασαι τοὺ[ς]
25 σοὺς πάντας μεθ᾽ ὧν καὶ
ἔρρωσσο, ἄδελφε.

Verso: ᾽Ιουλίῳ ᾽Απολιναρίωι ✕ οὐετρανῶι ἀπὸ Γεμέλλου.

recommendation helped me a great deal. And before that your very good friend Rullius was concerned. Knowing the good will that you have for me and to make up for your absence, he introduced me to Aemilianus zealously and without hesitation as your kinsman, whom he held to be most dear. And I ask, brother, that you give thanks in return to Rufus if you write to him. I sent the letters of Aemilianus and Rufus and Chariton. Write to me about your health and about what you want. Greet (salute) all your household, together with whom I pray that you may be well, brother.

Outside address: To Julius Apollinarius, veteran, from Gemellus.

6 σύστασις, i.e., "*letter* of recommendation." See Keyes, "Letter of Introduction," pp. 28–44, especially p. 39, and Kim, *Familiar Letter of Recommendation,* pp. 82–87.

8 μεμελήκι for ἐμεμελήκει. Regarding the omission of the augment in the pluperfect, see Moulton, *Grammar* 2:190: "In the pluperfect the augment is usually dropped."

10 Read ἔχεις εἰς.

13 The editors of this text note that the usual construction with συνίστημι, "recommend," is the dative but that πρός with the accusative has also been used with this verb.

14 ἀνόκνως: the more customary form is ἀόκνως but, as evidenced by frequent usage in the letters of this collection, ἀνόκνως is common in the papyri.

15–16 Read συγγενῆ.

16–17 ὃν ἥδιστα ἔσχε: regarding this idiom, see POxy IX 1218.12, XIV 1758.20.

24 Read θέλεις.

26 Read ἔρρωσο.

Letter B

Σαβεινιανὸς ᾽Απολιναρίωι
τῷ ἀδελφῷ καὶ κυρ[ί]ῳ πλεῖστα
χαίρειν.
καθ᾽ ⟨ἑκάστ⟩ην ἡμέραν καὶ αὐτὸς ὑπὲρ τῆς
5 σωτηρίας ⟨σου⟩ εὐχὰς ποιοῦμαι παρὰ τοῖς
ἐνθάδε θεοῖς ὑπὲρ τοῦ ζώσζεσθαί
σε ἰς μακροὺς χρόνους. πλεῖον ἢ μᾶλλον παρέχεις καὶ παρέ[σ]χες τῇ ἀδελφῇ,
ὅθεν ἀνθομολογοῦμ[α]ι πάσην χάριν
10 σοι παρὰ πᾶσιν θεοῖς, ἐμαρτυρήθη γάρ
μοι καὶ ὑπὸ τῆς ἀδελφῆς καὶ τῆς μητρός.
πολλάκι σοι ἔγραψα, κα[ὶ] ἡ τῶν παρακο-

Sabinianus to his brother and lord, Apollinarius, very many greetings. Daily I myself make prayers regarding your welfare before the local gods that you may be preserved for a long time. You supply and have supplied more than enough to our sister, on which account I extend hearty thanks to you, in turn, before all the gods, for it (your generosity) has been attested to me both by our sister and our mother. I wrote to you often, and the negligence of those who carry (the letters) has accused us falsely as negligent. So that she may accept me completely as her guardian, I entreat you to attend to

μισ⟨ζ⟩όντων ἀμέλεια διέβαλεν ἡμᾶς
ὡς ἀμελεῖς. ὡς πάντος ἐμοὶ κύριον
15 λαμβάνῃ, παρακαλῶ προσέχειν τῇ⟨ν⟩
ἀδελφῇ ἐν οἷς ἐάν σου δεηθῇ. ἀσπάσ-
ζομαι Ἀβάσκαντον τὸν χρησιμώτατον
καὶ τοὺς σοὺς πάντας κατ᾽ ὄνομα.
ἐρρῶσθαί σε εὔχομαι
20 πανοικεί.
Μεχεὶρ ῑη̄.

Verso: Ἰουλίῳ Ἀπολιναρίωι ἀπὸ Σαβεινιανοῦ ἀδελ[φο]ῦ
Ἀπολ[ι]ν̣α̣ρ̣ί̣ο̣υ̣ τοῦ....

our sister in whatever she should ask of you. I greet (salute) the most worthy Abascantus and all your household, each by name. I pray that you may be well, together with your entire household. Mecheir 18.

Outside address: To Julius Apollinarius from Sabinianus, the brother of Apollinarius...

6 ζώσζεσθαι=σώζεσθαι; see lines 12–13 (read παρακομιζόντων) and 16–17 (read ἀσπάζομαι): in all these cases, σζ=ζ. See Mayser, *Grammatik* 1.1.177.
7 Read εἰς.
7–8 πλεῖον ἢ μᾶλλον: the editors suggest that this phrase is unparalleled; normal expressions are πολὺ μᾶλλον and πολλῷ μᾶλλον. They also suggest that with μᾶλλον one should supply, e.g., τοῦ δέοντος; see *LSJ*, s.v. μάλα, II.
9 Read πᾶσαν.
14 Read πάντως. ἐμοί: the dative for the accusative. κύριον: certain kinds of legal transactions were prohibited to a woman not assisted by a "guardian" (see Taubenschlag, *Law of Greco-Roman Egypt*, pp. 128–33).
21 This date is 12–13 February.

116 EIRĒNE TO TAONNOPHRIS AND PHILO
POxy I 115

II CE

Taonnophris and Philo, a wife and husband living at Oxyrhynchos, have recently lost a son and Eirene, who is a friend of the family, expresses her sympathy to the couple. Having lost a husband or son herself (see lines 4f., where she refers to the death of a certain Didymas), she is better able to sympathize with their grief than others might be. She consoles the couple by stating that she and her family have fulfilled the customary duties required by the situation. She closes the correspondence by admitting that nothing can actually console a person in such a crisis and that the couple will need to comfort each other as well as possible.

Commenting on this letter, Deissmann (*Ancient East,* pp. 176–78) suggests that though Eirene's sympathy is genuine, similar words of consolation were common to the age and that the letter of consolation existed as a specific epistolary type. For example, he notes that both Demetrius of Phalerum and Proclus cited model letters of consolation in their collection of epistolary types. Regarding the closing words of resignation in particular, one may compare the saying which Wilcken noted was frequent in epitaphs, "No one is immortal," and the closing statement in Demetrius' model letter: ἐννοηθεὶς δὲ ὅτι τὰ τοιαῦτα πᾶσίν ἐστιν ὑποκείμενα..., "bearing in mind that such dispensations are laid upon us all" (see letter 5 in Demetrius; see Hercher, *Epistolographi Graeci,* p. 2). The same type of situation is envisioned in the apostle Paul's advice to the Thessalonians, though he alleges that the Christian should be more hopeful than other people in such a crisis (see 1 Thess 4:13–18). The full text of Proclus' model letter may be adduced for the purpose of comparison with Eirene's letter (see letter 21 in Hercher, *Epistolographi Graeci,* p. 10).

ἡ ἐπιστολή. λίαν ἡμᾶς ἡ ἀπο-
βίωσις τοῦ μακαρίου τοῦ δεῖνος,
ἐλύπησε καὶ πενθεῖν καὶ δακρύειν
ἠνάγκασε· τοιούτου φίλου γὰρ σπου-
δαίου καὶ παναρέτου ἐστερήθημεν.
δόξα οὖν καὶ αἴνεσις τῶι ἐν σοφίᾳ, καὶ
ἀκαταλήπτῳ δυνάμει καὶ προνοίᾳ
κυβερνῶντι θεῷ τὰς διεξόδους τῷ
θανάτῳ καὶ τὴν ψυχὴν ἡνίκα συμφέρει
παραλαμβάνοντι.

Εἰρήνη Ταοννώφρει καὶ Φίλωνι
    εὐψυχεῖν.
οὕτως ἐλυπήθην καὶ ἔκλαυσα ἐπὶ τῶι
εὐμοίρωι ὡς ἐπὶ Διδυμᾶτος
5   ἔκλαυσα, καὶ πάντα ὅσα ἦν κα-
φήκοντα ἐποίησα καὶ πάντες
οἱ ἐμοί, Ἐπαφρόδειτος καὶ Θερμού-
φιον καὶ Φίλιον καὶ Ἀπολλώνιος
καὶ Πλαντᾶς. ἀλλ’ ὅμως οὐδὲν
10 δύναταί τις πρὸς τὰ τοιαῦτα.
παρηγορεῖτε οὖν ἑαυτούς.
    εὖ πράττετε. Ἁθὺρ ā.

Verso: Ταοννώφρει καὶ Φίλωνι.

The letter. The death of S. O., the blessed one (i.e., "the dearly departed"), has grieved us exceedingly and has occasioned both our mourning and weeping; for we have been bereaved of such an earnest and entirely virtuous friend. Therefore, glory and praise be given to God, who in wisdom and incomprehensible power and providence governs the issues of death and, when it is expedient, receives the souls unto himself.

Eirene to Taonnophris and Philo, be of good courage. I was as grieved and wept for the departed one as much as I wept for Didymas. And everything that was fitting I have done, as well as my entire household, Epaphrodeitos and Thermouthion and Philion and Apollonius and Plantas. But, notwithstanding, one is unable to do anything against such things. Therefore, comfort one another. May you fare well. Hathyr 1.

Outside address: To Taonnorphris and Philo.

---

2   εὐψυχεῖν: this salutation is used in place of the customary *chairein* because of the nature of the letter. The same verb is common, in the form *eupsuchei* ("farewell!"), in inscriptions on tombs (see *LSJ*, s.v. εὐψύχεω, II). The verb is also found in BGU 1097.15 (I CE) and Paul's letter to the Philippians (2:19). Eirene writes the usual formula in POxy 116.
5   "everything that was fitting," i.e., all the customary religious rites and prayers. We do not know, specifically, what Eirene means.

11 "Therefore, comfort one another": Paul's exhortation in 1 Thess 4:18 (see also 1 Thess 5:11 and Heb 3:13), "Wherefore, comfort one another with these words," sounds reminiscent, but this may not mean he is drawing on an actual epistolary formula.
13 "To Taonnophris and Philo": Deissmann suggests that since the wife's name is in first position in both the initial salutation and on the verso Eirene was a friend of the mother in particular.

117   TO STEPHANOS FROM HEPHAISTIŌN
SelPap I 138 (=POxy VII 1065)   III CE

In this note, Hephaistion warns Stephanos with some urgency that if Stephanos does not come to his aid immediately he will destroy the gods. The gods to which he refers are evidently representations of the deities which were kept in the household. A similar sentiment is expressed in SelPap I 114.11f. (II CE). Despite the threatening tone of the letter, the recipient's name is written before that of the sender. This is unusual in private letters. Perhaps Hephaistion is a servant of Stephanos.

Στεφάνῳ παρὰ Ἡφαιστίωνος.
λαβὼν τὰ γράμματα τοῦ υἱοῦ
μου Θέωνος ἐξαυτῆς πάντα ὑπερ-
θέμενος ἐλθέ μοι εἰς τὸ ἐποίκιον
5 διὰ τὰ συμβάντα μοι. ἐὰν δὲ
ὀλιγωρήσῃς, ὥσπερ [ο]ἱ θεοὶ οὐκ ἐ-
φίσαντό μ[ο]υ, οὕτως κἀγὼ
θεῶ[ν] οὐ φί[σ]ομαι.
[ἔρρωσ]ο.

To Stephanos from Hephaistion. When you receive the letter of my son Theon, put everything aside and come to me immediately at the homestead on account of what has happened to me. If you make light of the matter, just as the gods did not spare me, so too will I not spare the gods. Good-bye.

2 "When you receive the letter . . .": regarding this convention, see SelPap I 109, 126, 135, 140, 155, and 156.

Opposite: Ostracon
Writing on a broken potsherd (ostracon). See the description of kinds of documents written on pieces of broken pottery on p. 213. Photograph courtesy of the Kelsey Museum of Archaeology, The University of Michigan.

GREEK LETTER WRITING

II

1. GENERAL OBSERVATIONS

The earliest Greek letter preserved in its original form is from the fourth century BCE. Copies of letters attributed to contemporaneous and even earlier figures, e.g., Philip of Macedon, Plato, and Alexander the Great,[1] are mostly now regarded as schoolboy exercises or forgeries of some sort. We have a number of authentic Greek letters only a little later, however, from the first half of the third century BCE, and letters continue in great number into the late Roman and Byzantine periods.

The largest single body of primary correspondence is the papyrus letters, at least a few thousand in number, preserved in Egypt by an arid climate. Most of this correspondence has been classified by scholars as documentary or, to use a more popular designation, non-literary. Unfortunately, the latter designation suggests that the correspondence was poorly written by the barely literate. This is not always the case. Though many are poorly written pieces of private correspondence, many others are written by Ptolemaic and Roman chancery secretaries and government officials, including edicts in letter form by Ptolemaic kings and Roman emperors. Though not so extensive, there are a number of Hellenistic royal letters that were inscribed on stone after delivery. These letters are diplomatic in nature and largely concerned with benefactions from Hellenistic kings to their dependencies during the last three centuries BCE.[2] Still another large body of correspondence is preserved from the Graeco-Roman period by Josephus and other ancient historians, who quoted royal and diplomatic letters. The originals for these letters are not extant. Some of the quoted letters may be fabrications; others surely depend on some actual epistolary situation. Moreover, there are several hundred literary letters that have survived through literary transmission, including the correspondence of Cicero, Seneca, Horace, Pliny, and the great Christian letter writers of late antiquity.

2. LETTER WRITING AND EPISTOLARY THEORY

The bulk of this analysis treats the practice of letter writing as it is reflected in the documentary letter tradition preserved on papyrus from Graeco-Roman Egypt. The diplomatic inscriptions and the literary letter tradition are simply too extensive to receive comparable consideration in this volume. Notwithstanding, a more objective analysis of the papy-rus letters will be facilitated if they are framed at the start with a discussion of the ancient scholarly letter theory and of letter writing in the schools. It is anticipated, by this means, that certain similarities and dissimilarities between the papyrus letters and the literary letter tradition will become more apparent, and also that we will be better able to delineate distinctive characteristics or tendencies in the documentary letter tradition itself.

It will prove useful, in this connection, to refer to three modern studies which examine the ancient epistolary theorists. Two of the studies are monograph-length and are written by Heikki Koskenniemi (*Studien zur Idee*) and Klaus Thraede (*Grundzüge*) who concentrate on the study of documentary papyrus letters and literary letters respectively. Both authors also include an analysis of the scholarly letter theory. The third work, "Ancient Epistolary Theorists," is an extensive collection of comments by ancient epistolary theorists, edited by A. J. Malherbe, who also interprets the ancient scholarly letter theory and comments on letter writing in the schools.

(a) Letter Writing in the Schools

Though we do not have copies of the elementary manuals which would have been used in the schools to teach basic letter writing skills, the number of epistolary conventions in the papyrus letters, which retain their formulaic identity over several centuries, is sufficient evidence of a rudimentary instruction in letter writing. Following an elementary education in the grammar and form of letters, it seems students were instructed at more advanced levels in subtleties of epistolary style and perhaps at an even more advanced stage, students were taught epistolary theory by rhetoricians.

The bilingual Bologna Papyrus, PBon 5 (III–IV CE), which contains eleven examples in Latin and Greek of various kinds of letters, without accompanying explanation, may be the exercises of a student who worked with an intermediate level handbook of epistolary style. The collection of twenty-one epistolary types, entitled *Typoi Epistolikoi* (III BCE–III CE) and falsely attributed to Demetrius of Phalerum (Pseudo Demetrius), seems to be intended for roughly the same level of instruction, but Malherbe thinks that it was designed for professional letter writers, not instruction in the schools. The other major handbook on letter writing, entitled *Epistolimaioi Characteres* (IV–VI CE) and ascribed in one manuscript tradition to Libanius and in another to Proclus (Pseudo Libanius), is both more extensive (it enumerates

---

[1] See Rudolf Hercher, *Epistolographi Graeci*.

[2] See C. B. Welles, *Royal Correspondence,* a collection of seventy-five of these letters.

forty-one epistolary types) and theoretical but, like the Pseudo Demetrius handbook, it also appears to have been designed for professional scribes.[3]

To return to the subject of training in the schools, students engaged in the exercise of *prosopoeia* at an advanced level of training. This was the act of representing (imitating) someone, often a famous person, in sentiments and activities suitable to that person, e.g., see the *progymnasmata* (exercises in composition) of Theon, a first-century contemporary of Quintilian.[4] The purpose of the exercise was apparently to encourage flexibility and sophistication in style or mood, not in the technique of letter writing itself. Even though it was essentially rhetorical in intent, *prosopoeia* is probably the primary source of the so-called "forged" letters ascribed to famous ancient people.

(b) Handbooks, the Schools and Epistolary Theory

It is difficult to assess the relation of the handbooks of Pseudo Demetrius and Pseudo Libanius, which were apparently intended for the professional scribes, to letter writing as it was taught in the schools. It is equally difficult to ascertain the relation of these manuals to more theoretical discussions of epistolary theory. One thing is certain. There was never a full integration of the practice and the theory. Ordinary letter writing, occasioned by practical necessities, influenced the theory but did not dominate it. Eventually, epistolary theory seems to have influenced the practice. This is evident in the aforementioned handbooks. While continuing to reflect customary practice, subtleties of epistolary style are discussed in connection with the practice and a certain amount of rhetorical skill is presupposed.

Indeed, Koskenniemi is probably correct in his interpretation that these handbooks do not illustrate twenty-one or forty-one actual letter types. What they illustrate are a selection of styles appropriate to different circumstances and the tone in which letters may be written.[5] Many of these motifs occur in papyrus letters, to be sure, but the ordinary letter writer would not have thought of them as specific categories and certainly not as letter types.

To express the matter in reverse, epistolary theory was never able to assimilate or to control the practice of letter writing. The ancient epistolary theorists acknowledged this

difference between the ideal and the practice. Thus, so far as the ideal is concerned, Thraede amply illustrates that Greek and Latin rhetoricians regarded the letter, when fully actualizing its potential, as a cultivated expression of friendship whereby the writer's very personality was made present to the recipient.[6] But Cicero distinguishes this type of correspondence, which communicates the mood of the writer, from ordinary letters occasioned by necessity: "That there are many kinds of letters you are well aware; there is one kind, however, about which there can be no mistake, for indeed letter writing was invented just in order that we might inform those at a distance if there were anything which it was important for them or for ourselves that they should know. A letter of this kind you will of course not expect from me...."[7]

Apparently, a similar distinction between the letter as a cultivated form of communication and ordinary letter writing was in the mind of Pseudo Demetrius when he said: "While (letters) ought to be written as skillfully as possible, they are in fact composed indifferently by those who undertake such services for men in public office."[8]

(c) The Theory and Practice of Letter Writing

Despite something of an ongoing tension with the practice of letter writing, epistolary theory was nonetheless related to it in a root sense, both at its inception and subsequently. Let us look at the connection between practical necessity and the ideal of the letter in connection with a statement found in the earliest extant treatise on epistolary theory, a work from the second to the first centuries BCE. It is entitled *On Style* and, like one of the two aforementioned handbooks, it was also attributed to Demetrius. Regarding the "plain style" of letters, Pseudo Demetrius states that Artemon, the editor of Aristotle's letters, likened letter writing to one-half of a spoken conversation and, correspondingly, that he advocated writing a letter in the same manner as a conversation.[9] Demetrius himself suggests that a letter should be a little more studied than a conversation, since it is committed to writing and that, in a way, it is sent as a gift.[10] By means of the first part of this statement, which is attributed to Artemon, Demetrius acknowledged that a letter, like spoken conversation, was subject to misunderstanding and that, unlike spoken dialogue, the recipient of a letter

---

[3] Malherbe, "Ancient Epistolary Theorists," pp. 7–9, 14f.

[4] See Hock and O'Neil, eds., "The Chreia Discussion" in *The Chreia in Ancient Rhetoric*, pp. 61–112. The most relevant sections are 276–97 (pp. 98–101).

[5] *Studien zur Idee*, p. 62.

[6] See the comments on the letter as a "conversation" and as a medium of the sender's "presence" (*parousia*) in Klaus Thraede, *Grundzüge*, pp. 17ff. and 125ff. See the comments in Cicero *Letters* 2.4.1, 16.16.2; Demetrius *On Style*, sec. 227; Seneca *Epistles* 40.1, 75.1; see too the

references in Malherbe, "Ancient Epistolary Theorists," pp.15–17.

[7] Cicero *Letters* 2.4.1.

[8] Demetrius *Typoi Epistolikoi*, introductory comments on Epistolary Types. See the Greek text with English translation in A. J. Malherbe, "Ancient Epistolary Theorists," pp. 28f.

[9] *On Style*, sec. 223.

[10] *On Style*, sec. 224.

could not ask for immediate clarification. Consequently, though naturalness, along with brevity, was regarded as an important presupposition of letter writing, clarity was even more essential.[11] In keeping with the naturalness of the conversation, the subject matter of a letter should not be written with the affected style of an orator nor in the technical language of a treatise.[12]

The latter part of Demetrius' statement above, the idea that the letter is sent as a gift, derives from the presupposition that the letter, like conversation, is a familiar type of dialogue between friends. This suggests that the private or personal letter was regarded as the most original kind of correspondence. In any case, the refined or cultivated letter of friendship was, for Greek and Roman epistolary theorists, the most authentic and highly esteemed form of correspondence. It hardly needs to be stated that clarity would be a corollary of one's consideration for the recipient.

Recognizing that the letter should be a worthy substitute for one's conversation, the theorists advise that one speak to the absent party as though he were actually present and, in order to properly convey one's presence, the language of the letter should communicate the writer's personality and reflect his mood. In particular, Demetrius suggests that the letter, like spoken dialogue, should abound in glimpses of character, because character is more clearly exhibited in the letter than in any other form of composition.[13] Similarly, Seneca stated that he wanted his letters to be just like the conversation he would speak if he were actually sitting or walking in one's company, and that he wrote nothing strained or artificial in his letters.[14] In likening the letter to actual conversation, Julius Victor advised one to use expressions which recognize the recipient's presence, such as "you too?" and "just as you say!" and "I see you smile. . . ."[15]

Frequent comments by the theorists to the effect that the letter should be conceived as a conversation and should properly convey one's presence to the absent party led Nils Dahl to conclude that the Greeks originated the idea of the "Familiar Letter" as the most authentic form of correspondence.[16] Greeks—or, more appropriately stated, Greek and Latin rhetoricians—may well have originated the idea that the letter of friendship was the most authentic kind of letter (they certainly encouraged the practice of writing cultivated pieces of friendly correspondence), but they did not originate

the practice itself. Paul Dion has identified a number of Ancient Near Eastern letters between family members which, though not so self-consciously literate as the rhetoricians' letters of friendship, are characterized by analogous epistolary sentiments and were written for the enhancement of the correspondents' personal relationship, not out of specific need. So far as the Aramaic and Greek family letters from Egypt are concerned, he suggests that their style shows that they were influenced by the native Egyptian epistolary tradition.[17] Extant family letters from Egypt are so common in the Roman period, and certain themes are expressed so formulaically, that Koskenniemi identifies them as an epistolary type.[18] It appears, then, that the cultivated letter of friendship had its roots in the common letter tradition which, in this instance, was probably influenced by the native Egyptian tradition.

(d) The Origin of Written Correspondence

Occasionally, the theorists refer to letters of diplomacy. Demetrius recommends, for example, that letters written to states or royalty must be composed in a slightly elevated style but that the heightening should not become so extensive as to result in a treatise.[19] Though the diplomatic letter is not included in the twenty-one entries in the Pseudo Demetrius handbook, the diplomatic style (*presbeutike*) is listed as one of the identifying names to which letters are subject in the Pseudo Libanius handbook.[20] Julius Victor distinguished two major classes of correspondence, the negotial (official?) and personal.[21] Characteristic of the negotial type are its weighty statements, clarity of diction, and succinct expression. Though these references are not extensive, it is nonetheless clear that, for the theorists, the distinctive intention of the diplomatic letter called for a more precise and elevated style than ordinary letter writing.

One might conclude that the theorists' scant references to diplomatic letter writing style indicates that the diplomatic letter, like the cultivated letter of friendship, developed out of the common and personal letter. Luther Stirewalt has argued just the reverse, however, by reviewing the evidence which shows that official communiques were the earliest form of written correspondence both in the ancient Near East and in Greece. Under Persian influence, according to his survey, the Greeks began using written correspondence

---

[11] *On Style*, sec. 226; see Julius Victor, "De Epistolis," in Giomini and Celentano, eds., *Ars Rhetorica*, pp. 105f.; Pseudo Libanius, sec. 48–49 (see the English translation in "Ancient Epistolary Theorists," p. 69).

[12] *On Style*, secs. 225, 230–32.

[13] *On Style*, sec. 227; see Cicero *Letters* 2.4.1, 16.16.2.

[14] Gummere, *The Epistles of Seneca*, 75.1f.; see Pseudo Libanius *Epistolimaioi Characteres*, sec. 2.

[15] Giomini and Celentano, eds., *Ars Rhetorica*, pp. 105f.

[16] "Letter," pp. 539.

[17] Dion, "Aramaic 'Family Letter,'" pp. 69–71.

[18] *Studien zur Idee*, pp. 110ff.

[19] *On Style*, sec. 234.

[20] *Epistolimaioi Characteres*, sec. 76.

[21] Giomini and Celentano, eds., *Ars Rhetorica*, pp.105f.

in place of official oral communications.[22] Statements by Herodotus show that he was impressed by the use of official letter writing in the East.[23] Thucydides and Xenophon also refer to official letter writing, often quoting portions of such texts.[24] The practice of writing official messages grew and this is reflected in the orations of Demosthenes, who cites numerous letters from Philip of Macedon.[25] Indeed, Philip was the first to establish the office of epistolographer in Greece and his use of the office was imitated both by his son, Alexander, and by Alexander's successors.[26]

Stirewalt further supports his thesis that letter writing originated in official correspondence in a survey of the Greek words for letter writing. The two principal Greek words for letter are ἐπιστολή and γράμματα. Much less frequent are the terms βυβλίον (βιβλίον) and δέλτος (δελτίον). While both γράμματα and ἐπιστολή came to be used interchangeably for a letter, the term γράμματα could refer to anything written, including the letter. Ἐπιστολή (plural: ἐπιστολαί), on the other hand, referred specifically in earlier usage to an oral injunction and the verb form, ἐπιστέλλειν, had the meaning, "give an (oral) order." When the verb acquired the additional meaning, "to write a letter," it retained the meaning of injunction and, consequently, was used in reference to a written order or request, especially in connection with military and diplomatic correspondence. Though the noun ἐπιστολή (ἐπιστολαί) was extended eventually to include all kinds of letters, Stirewalt suggests that something of the original idea of injunction—which could be adapted to include request, exhortation, admonition, or instruction—continued to exert an influence on the Greek idea of letter writing. Thus, whereas βυβλίον and δέλτος were borrowed eastern words which connoted two types of writing material, "papyrus" and "tablet" respectively, and whereas γράμματα was a neutral designation for almost anything written, ἐπιστολή conveyed the specific idea of injunction, whether oral or written.[27] In short, Greek letter writing evolved out of the written injunctions of a military and diplomatic nature, even though personal letter writing became so common that, in time, it came to exert an influence on the language of diplomatic correspondence.[28]

(e) Adaptation of the Letter to Wider Purposes

Despite the theorists' admonition against writing in an affected manner, and their advice against writing about subjects which are artificial to a conversation (e.g., the exposition of a technical subject), treatises in letter form increased steadily in late antiquity. In fact, the theorists' admonitions were probably prompted by the growing popularity of such "letter essays." It is not too difficult to understand why the letter form was adapted to these wider purposes, however, and in certain cases the adaptation was almost natural.

The democratization of knowledge in the Hellenistic period contributed to the publication of popular essays, and certain types of instruction at the time made the transition even easier. For example, popular "street philosophy" used *diatribe* as a means of instruction, quoting phrases of an imaginary opponent in order to refute them in a series of questions and answers. Though not as dialogical in nature as the diatribe, the oral discourse (the oration, described in philosophical terms as *homilia* or *disputatio*) was sufficiently akin to the oral character of the letter that both the oration and the diatribe were adapted to the written medium of the letter by late classical writers as a means of addressing a wider audience. Consequently, though the epistolary theorists cited above considered this kind of practice an abomination, other rhetoricians made the transition rather easily.

(f) Summary

Letter writing was invented because of the writer's need to inform (or to be informed by) those at a distance about something they (or the writer) should know. In the earliest stage of writing, the messages appear to have been official injunctions of a military or diplomatic nature. The necessities of ordinary life, aided by the relatively inexpensive and available writing material of papyrus in the Hellenistic period, increased the writing of letters between private citizens who were separated spatially. Though most extant papyrus letters address some specific need, there are a number which were written for the more general purpose of maintaining family or friendly ties. Epistolary theorists regarded this function of letter writing, especially when it was expressed in a culti-

---

22 Stirewalt, "Uses of Letter-Writing," pp. 2f. Stirewalt uses the designation "official" for a broader spectrum of letters than I do. In the Introduction to this book, I apply "official" specifically to administrative correspondence and use the designation "diplomatic" for many letters Stirewalt calls official. Clarity is needed in the differentiation of official letter types.

23 See *Herodotus* 8.98.

24 See *Thucydides* 7.11.1; *Xenophon: Hellenica* 1.1.23; 1.7.4; *Agesilaus* 8.3; and *Cyropaedia* 7.6.17.

25 For example, see *Demosthenes: Orations* 12.1ff. See also 23.160-62.

26 Stirewalt, "Uses of Letter-Writing," pp. 3f.

27 Stirewalt, "Index of Terms," pp. 1–11. Stirewalt cites various references from Aeschylus, Sophocles and Herodotus in support of the original use of ἐπιστολή to mean oral injunction (e.g., see *Herodotus* 4.10, 6.50). He suggests that the use of ἐπιστολή for a written document occurs as early as Thucydides (e.g., *Thucydides* 7.11).

28 See C. Bradford Welles, *Royal Correspondence*, pp. xlii–xliii.

vated manner, as the most authentic form of correspondence.

Since the letter arose as a substitute for an oral message, the theorists reasoned that correspondence should be conversational in style. Moreover, it should be natural and straightforward, but not so brief as to be ambiguous, because the recipient could not ask for clarification in a written conversation as he could in an oral conversation. Even though letters ought to be detailed enough to be comprehensible, they ought not to be verbose and, according to the theorists, it falls outside their purpose as situational pieces of communication for letters to be used as expositions of technical subjects.

The documentary letters that provide the focus of this study are mostly of that kind which Cicero said he would "not" write to his friends, namely, letters occasioned by the necessity to communicate or to receive some specific information. The primary exceptions to this usage are the "family letters" which, like the cultivated friendship correspondence of Cicero, were written to enhance familiar ties.

A more detailed comparison of the documentary letter tradition with the epistolary styles identified in the handbooks will be made in the following analysis. The general structure of the letter, along with the identification of epistolary types, will also be taken up in connection with the analysis of the documentary letter tradition preserved on papyrus.

3. The Greek Documentary Letter Tradition Preserved on Papyrus

A few words are required regarding the broader social setting of the Greek documentary letter tradition before turning to the linguistic study of letter writing. Though some of this information appears in the introduction to this volume, certain parts bear repeating now.

Most extant papyrus letters of the Hellenistic and Roman era were written and delivered in Egypt. Some were sent from outside the country but even in these cases the correspondence was largely concerned with affairs in Egypt. The earliest extant letters, in large number, date from the reign of Ptolemy II Philadelphos (ca. 270 BCE). The paucity of data from the first Ptolemy, Soter, may be accounted for in part by the fact that the machinery of government had not developed sufficiently to send the later mass of administrative correspondence, and because Soter was a warrior king who was more concerned with external conquest than with developing the internal possibilities of Egypt. But the climate of the delta in which Soter's administration was largely confined also accounts for the small number of extant documents; climatic conditions facilitated the preservation of documents

from Philadelphos and his successors, but were antagonistic during the reign of Soter.

Almost all the papyri, both from the rule of Philadelphos and from his successors, were discovered in the drier communities upriver from Alexandria and the delta. To insure the loyalty of his soldiers, and to wed them to the soil of Egypt, Philadelphos initiated the practice of granting land allotments to his soldiers, varying in size according to their rank. He accomplished his purpose without disturbing the existing agricultural plots owned or worked by native Egyptians by initiating a vast land reclamation in the area of the Fayum. Through the construction of an elaborate irrigation system, thousands of acres were cleared of brushwood and made arable. By this means he both increased the productivity of the country and retained the service of his soldiers. Much of the correspondence from his reign was discovered in or near the newly created communities that he created in the Fayum. The papyri survived because the communities bordered on a dry desert climate.

By contrast, though Soter may also have busied letter writers with his affairs of state the evidence is almost all lost because his operation was largely confined to the damper conditions of the delta or to places outside Egypt whose climates were also detrimental to the preservation of papyri.

Regarding the manner in which letter writing was influenced by the political situation, it is evident that the programatic management of Egypt from the latter half of Philadelphos' reign onward encouraged the broad spectrum of administrative correspondence at a number of levels, which is so characteristic of Ptolemaic Egypt. The elaborate checks and balances which Philadelphos initiated to ensure stability also contributed to the variety of other kinds of official and legal correspondence, such as letters of petition or complaint that were addressed to the king (the prefect, in Roman times) and to lower officials by petitioners who were trying to receive redress for an assortment of grievances. Moreover, despite the blanketing bureaucracy, a considerable number of people were able to engage in private business and corresponded with each other about such interests. In the case of the famous Zenon archive (see letters 5–26 of the above letter collection), it is evident that, at a kind of intermediate level, private and state business sometimes overlapped.

On the basis of this general background to the subject, we can now turn to a more specific analysis of letter writing. It will prove advantageous, in this connection, to look at a few actual letters. This will enable the reader more easily and concretely to understand the formulaic conventions, the letter types, and epistolary structure and function.

(a) Specific Epistolary Types

1) *Letters of introduction and recommendation.* The first example we will use to illustrate the common letter tradition

is a letter of introduction, referred to as ἡ ἐπιστολὴ συστατική by ancient epistolary theorists (letter 11).[29] I quote only the English translation here. Identifiable divisions within the body are indicated by double slash marks.

Opening
Sostratos to Zenon greeting.

Body
I do not think you are ignorant regarding Aischylos, that he is no stranger to us. He has now sailed up river to your company in order to be introduced to Kleonikos. // Therefore, please make a sincere effort to introduce him to Kleonikos; and if he does not come upon the latter in your company, get letters of introduction to him (i.e., Kleonikos) from his friends. // By doing this you will do us a favor; for I am interested in him. You also must write to us regarding whatever we could do to favor you.

Closing
Good-bye. (Year) 28, Peritos 20.

Letters of introduction and recommendation were recognized as a specific type by ancient epistolographers, and at least two modern scholars, Clinton Keyes and Chan-Hie Kim, have described their stylistic and formal features. The following elements are characteristic of the letter's opening and closing.

The form for the opening address/greeting, like that for most non-literary papyrus letters, is: "A (=sender) to B (=recipient) χαίρειν (greeting)." The closing formula is ἔρρωσο (farewell), followed by the date. Though the opening and closing may include a health wish, it is not expressed in our letter and, even when present in letters of recommendation, it is neither elaborate nor lengthy.

In the body of the letter, the introductory phrase identifies the person being recommended (the letter carrier) and/or his relation to the sender, i.e., "I do not think that you are ignorant regarding Aischylos, that he is no stranger to us. He has now sailed up river to your company in order to be introduced to Kleonikos." This convention is followed, in turn, by the sender's recommendation (request) on the letter bearer's behalf: "Therefore, please make a sincere effort to introduce him to Kleonikos; and if he does not come upon the latter in your company, get letters of introduction to him (i.e., Kleonikos) from his friends." Finally, the letter writer states that

the recipient will favor him by aiding the letter carrier, the person recommended, and he promises to repay the favor: "By doing this you will do us a favor; for I am interested in him. You also must write to us regarding whatever we could do to favor you."

This distinctive threefold cluster of conventions remains constant in the body of letters of recommendation through several centuries, varying only in the phrasing used to express the conventions. The opening and closing, while equally constant, are not so distinctive. They are typical of the majority of letters written between friends and peers. So far as I can tell, the only thing that seems to differentiate the opening and closing of letters of introduction from other friendly or familiar letters is the omission or brevity of the wish of health. In that respect, they appear to be more business-like and less familiar.

In summary, since the correspondence itself assumes that writer and recipient had enough status to benefit the person recommended, we deduce that in this type of epistolary situation the correspondents were social equals of relatively high social status. It is equally clear that this type of correspondence was personal (not official) and friendly in nature.

2) *Letters of petition.* The next example that we use for illustration is a letter of petition (PEnteux 32 [220 BCE]). This letter is not included in the collection, but letters 20, 37, 50 and 86 are all the same type of letter. Once again, only the English translation is quoted and isolable parts of the body are marked off by double slash marks.

Opening
To king Ptolemy, greeting, from Philista, daughter of Lysias, resident in Trikomia.

Body
I am wronged by Petechon. For as I was bathing in the baths of the aforesaid village, on Tybi 7 of the year 1, and had stepped out to soap myself he, being bathman in the women's rotunda and having brought in the jugs of hot water, emptied one over me and scalded my belly and my left thigh down to the knee, so that my life was in danger. On finding him, I gave him into the custody of Nechthosiris, the chief policeman of the village, in the presence of Simon the epistates. // I beg you therefore, O king, if it pleases you, as a suppliant who has sought your protection, not to suffer me, who am a working woman to be treated so lawlessly, but to order Diophanes the strategos to instruct Simon the epistates and Nechthosiris the policeman to bring Petechon before

---

[29] See also letters 77, 78, 79. A man thanks his brother for a recommendation in letter ll5a.

him that Diophanes may inquire into the case, // hoping that, having sought your protection, O king, the common benefactor, I may obtain justice.

Closing
Farewell (εὐτύχει).
Docket of instruction in a second hand: To Simon. Send the accused.

The singular function of the petition, like the letter of introduction, is to request something of the addressee. Since the essential function for the two letters is the same, the bodies of the letters have an analogous three-part structure. As in the letter of recommendation, the occasion of the request is announced, in the introduction to the body, providing an explanation of the request. The content of this initial statement in the body varies, of course, from that of recommendation. In this case, the petitioner introduces the message by stating that she has been wronged by someone. In other examples, the petitioner may refer more obliquely to the circumstances of the situation (e.g., by referring to the day, time of day, etc., of the infraction), which necessitate the petition. Following this "background" statement, and analogous once more to letters of recommendation, the petitioner states the request itself. The petitioner entreats the king (or, in many examples, a lower official) to rectify the situation, employing such verbs of request as δέομαι (above), ἀξιῶ, ἱκετεύω, and παρακαλῶ. Finally—and analogous to letters of introduction in which the writer expresses appreciation to the recipient for attending to the request—the body concludes with the petitioner's statement that she will be benefited and justice will be accomplished by the king's favorable response to her request.

In short, the internal structure of the petition parallels that of the recommendation. In both, the sender introduces the body by reciting the circumstance(s) (the "background") of the request. And following the request in both situations, the sender acknowledges that he or she will benefit from the recipient's favorable response.

Because of the petitioner's lack of status in the epistolary situation, she obviously cannot offer to return the favor requested in the manner of letters of introduction. Consequently, despite the essential similarity of function of the two letters, and a correlative structure by means of which the sender tries to persuade the recipient to do something for her, the relative status of the correspondents is quite different in the two cases. Whereas the petitioner writes in the position of inferior, the author of the letter of recommendation writes as an equal.

The petitioner's inferior status is reflected formally in the letter's opening. Writing out of deference to the recipient, she places the addressee's name before her own in the address, in the form, "To B χαίρειν A," i.e., A (nominative case) sends greetings to B (dative). All petitions to the king and queen of Egypt and occasionally to other high officials have this same form, which is limited chronologically to the Ptolemaic period.

An alternative form of the petitionary address that omits the greeting was used during both the Greek and Roman period to address all other officials. It has the form: "To B from A (genitive case)." Just as petitioners always wrote the recipient's name before their own in the opening address, so too they always wrote εὐτύχει (διευτύχει in the Roman era) as the closing convention.

In general, the nature of the petitioner's relation to the addressee in the epistolary situation—an inferior writing to a superior about some grievance and requesting redress—was a deterrant to expressions of familiarity. Thus, one never finds either an opening or concluding wish of health, nor prayers of supplication on the recipient's behalf, nor greetings extended to a third party.

"Applications" for rental or purchase, along with certain other legal documents in letter form (birth and death notices, census registrations, etc.), like petitions, regularly display the recipient's name before the sender's in the address (in the form of address which omits the greeting). These documents do not always have a closing formula but if one is included it, like the closing formula in petitions, is εὐτύχει.

There are several hundred petitions and other legal documents (e.g., applications) addressed to state officials in which the sender's inferiority is openly acknowledged by means of the opening address. The sender's inferior status is only rarely signaled in any other kind of correspondence, however, so that most Graeco-Roman papyrus letters have "A to B χαίρειν" as their opening address/greeting. From the second century BCE onward, this convention often combines syntactically with the wish for health, i.e., "A to B greeting and good health." Correspondingly, apart from petitions and like documents, the typical word of farewell is ἔρρωσο, regardless of the relation between the correspondents.

There are a few examples in the present collection in which the opening or closing of the letter does not fit the usual classification, however, and the kind of circumstance(s) that could produce such an exception is worth noting. Letter 10, for example, is a request that is expressed in the language of a petition or complaint and, correspondingly, the letter closing has the petitionary farewell, εὐτύχει. Nonetheless, the sender's name is written before the recipient's in the opening address. At least two factors may be relevant to the situation. The addrssor is obviously a woman of some standing who, in ordinary circumstances, would be a social peer of the recipient, Zenon, and therefore her name is written prior to his. But her son's mistreatment in the employ of Zenon's chief, Apollonios, who was the chief financial   195 minister of Ptolemy II, necessitated the request. Since the request could only have been granted by Apollonios himself, she had to rely upon Zenon's personal intervention with Apollonios on her behalf. It may be for this reason, out of deference to Zenon's personal influence with Apollonios, that she closed the letter with the more formal εὐτύχει, even though he was not himself a state official but the private secretary of Apollonios.

An analogous situation prompted the odd combination of epistolary conventions in letter 13. Like letter 10, the letter begins with the ordinary address/greeting, "A to B greeting." In addition, the sender includes an extensive wish of health, a sign of the correspondents' familiarity and equality. Nonetheless, the sender closes the letter with the formal petitionary word of farewell, εὐτύχει, used also by the sender of letter 10. The unusual combination of an informal or familiar letter opening and formal, petitionary closing arose in this instance because the sender, a certain cavalry commander named Alexandros, desired Zenon's support in getting overdue wages from Apollonios, the minister of finance. Thus, though Alexandros was Zenon's peer, as indicated by the opening health wish and the informal address, he was depending on Zenon's intervention on his behalf and, for this reason, he closes the letter with εὐτύχει rather than the familiar ἔρρωσο.[30]

On occasion, the sender writes the recipient's name first in the opening address, in the manner of the petition, even though he is writing an informal letter. Letter 117 is an example of this oddity. Both in letter 117 and in most other similar letters, the sender is an employee of the recipient and usually a native Egyptian. The form of the opening address is an acknowledgment of the sender's inferiority.[31]

3) *Family letters.* The third example from the documentary letter tradition, letter 104b of the collection, is one which belongs to the type classified as "family letters" by Koskenniemi.[32] More particularly, it belongs to a kind of sub species which J. G. Winter identified as "letters from soldiers."[33] The stylistic features which Koskenniemi identifies in connection with family letters,[34] and which also apply to soldiers' letters, are quite rare in the Ptolemaic period but common during the Roman rule of Egypt. Once again our letter is cited in English and this time, since the character of the opening and closing is distinctive in family letters, we identify conventions at the beginning and end of the letter (rather than in the body) by means of double slash marks.

Opening

Apollinarios to his mother and lady, Taesis, many greetings. // Before all else I pray that you are well; I myself am well // and make obeisance (*proskynema*) on your behalf to the gods here.

Body

I want you to know, mother, that I arrived in Rome safely on the twenty-fifth of the month Pachon and was assigned to Misenum. But I do not know my century yet, for I had not gone to Misenum when I wrote this letter to you. I request you, therefore, mother, attend to yourself; do not worry about me, for I came to a fine place. Please write me a letter about your welfare and that of my brothers and of all your people. And, for my part, if I ever find someone (to carry the letter), I will write to you; I certainly will not hesitate to write to you.

Closing

I greet (salute) my brothers much, and Apollinarios and his children, and Karalas and his children. I greet Ptolemy, and Ptolemais and her children. I greet all your friends, each by name. // I pray that you are well.

We may make a number of observations on family letters as a group. They all identify the recipient in the opening address, as here, with some familial modifier, e.g., brother, father and mother, sister. The designation "lady" or "lord" is often applied respectively, to the sender's mother and father. Recipients who are characterized as "sister" in the opening address are often the sender's wife. "Sister," then, may be used as a term of endearment. On the other hand, the designation should sometimes be understood literally, since marriage between brother and sister was common in Egypt. It is also common in family letters, as here, to expand the opening address/greeting with the qualification of "much" (πλεῖστα) or "many" (πολλά) greetings. Similarly, almost all family letters express the wish for health in the opening or closing of the letter or in both places.

We find an additional formula in many family letters, which Koskenniemi calls the προσκύνημα formula.[35] This phrase, as in the present letter, indicates that the sender is making supplication to the god(s) on behalf of the recipient. Koskenniemi suggests that the convention arose in Egyptian religious circles in connection with a specific god, especially

---

[30] Letters 26 and 42, for reasons similar to those for letters 10 and 13, also combine the customary, familiar letter opening with the formal, petitionary farewell.

[31] Perhaps letter 20 is another example of this practice, since the letter seems to be written in the form of a petition as much because the sender is a native who is in Zenon's employ as because the situation called for a petition.

[32] *Studien zur Idee*, pp. 110ff.

[33] "In the Service of Rome," pp. 237–56; see the introductory comments to letters 101–5.

[34] See Koskenniemi, *Studien zur Idee*, pp. 104–14. The stylistic features of family letters are identified above, immediately following the letter that is quoted.

[35] *Studien zur Idee*, p. 113.

Sarapis, and that it was taken up into the Greek letter tradition by the time of the Roman era.[36] Most often, as here, it combines syntactically with the health wish and extends its sentiment by including the religious dimension.

Concerning the letter closing, we often find extensive salutations extended to or from third parties. It is also common, as already suggested, to find a closing health wish and, in the Roman era, it replaces the earlier truncated form which served as the "farewell."

Subjects which come to expression in the body of family letters are joy over reception of a letter and complaint about the recipient's failure to write (e.g., letter 105), which usually implies a desire for family news in general and interest in information about the recipient's welfare in particular. Quite similar, though not expressed so negatively, are those requests for information regarding the recipient's welfare (e.g., letters 103a, 104a–b). The other side of the request for information is the sender's announcement of specific facts which show how well he is doing (e.g., letters 101–2). The sender also encourages the recipient or other absent family members to visit (e.g., letter 101).

In short, almost everything which is discussed in the body of family letters is an extension of the correspondents' interest in each other's welfare. Koskenniemi states, consequently, that family letters fail to take advantage of the full potential of the letter. Namely, there is no isolable message or body apart from the correspondents' interest in each other's welfare.[37]

4) *Memoranda*. There is one other epistolary type to which the writers of the non-literary letter tradition refer, the memorandum ($\dot{v}\pi\acute{o}\mu\nu\eta\mu\alpha$). Several of these letters are sent by inferiors in the epistolary situation and use language reminiscent of the petition (e.g., PHib II 240; PColZen I 44, II 86; PMert I 100). Consequently, Paul Collomp suggested that whereas petitions addressed to the king were called $\dot{\varepsilon}\nu\tau\varepsilon\acute{v}\xi\varepsilon\iota\varsigma$ in the Ptolemaic period, the $\dot{v}\pi\acute{o}\mu\nu\eta\mu\alpha$ was a form of petition addressed to a lesser official.[38]

On the other hand, we also find correspondence between equals, or letters to superiors which are not petitions, described as $\dot{v}\pi\acute{o}\mu\nu\eta\mu\alpha$. In the case of correspondence between equals, sometimes the style or language of either the opening or closing conventions is formally akin to the petition, but often the letters are private letters of request in which the sender entreats the recipient to oblige him with certain kinds of personal favor. Letter 8 in the collection is this kind of letter. Though letter 9 is not itself described as $\dot{v}\pi\acute{o}\mu\nu\eta\mu\alpha$, in line 11 its author, Philotas, refers to a previous letter, sent to the same recipient as letter 9, as a memo-

randum. The people who sent letters 13 and 18 also appear to be social peers of the recipient, Zenon, and refer either to the document itself (13.3f.) or to a previous letter as a memorandum (18.2–4). In the last two examples, the senders describe their requests explicitly as "reminders." In these cases, then, the term memorandum retains something of its root meaning of "reminder." This nuance, "reminder," is not limited to letters between equals, however, since $\dot{v}\pi\acute{o}\mu\nu\acute{\eta}\mu$-$\alpha\tau\alpha$ are addressed occasionally to the king and his officials These letters are not petitions, but are intended to be reminders of future business (PSI IV 429 and 430) or about business dealt with in the past (PCairZen II 59218 and 59297).

In still other cases, instructions from a superior may be referred to as a memorandum (see letters 18.25f. and 36.17f., which describe instructions from superiors in this way). Rostovtzeff comments on this type of memorandum in his introductory remarks on PTebt III 703, which is a letter of instruction from the dioiketes to a subordinate.

The apparent latitude of meaning in letters which are styled $\dot{v}\pi\omega\mu\nu\acute{\eta}\mu\alpha\tau\alpha$ makes them a complicated epistolary type and I am presently unable to explain the apparent breadth of meaning which attaches to the letter type.

(b) Considerations in the Study of Epistolary Types
1) *Classifying Letters.* The isolable types of non-literary letters appear to be largely limited to those specified in the preceding section—letters of recommendation, petitions, family correspondence, and memoranda. Most other correspondence combines two or more of the purposes already identified in connection with those letters, along with specific sub-functions or nuances. In general, there are three broad purposes served by letters: to convey information, to make requests or give commands, and to enhance or maintain personal contact with the recipient ("to stay in touch"). The emotional mood of correspondence colors its purpose. The mood of a letter tends to be affected by the relative status of the sender to the recipient, e.g., inferior to superior, equal to equal, superior to inferior. We saw in the preceding section, for example, how a request in the letter of recommendation, in which the correspondents are equals, differs in mood and style from a petitioner's entreaty. Julius Victor described how status relations affected correspondence when he stated that a letter to a superior should not be droll (formal, reserved and respectful?) and that correspondence to an inferior should not be haughty.[39] His comments reveal the tendency that was operative in writing either to one's superior or to an inferior. In the same context, he advises that correspondence between equals should not be

---

[36] *Studien zur Idee,* pp. 139–45.
[37] See Koskenniemi, *Studien zur Idee,* pp. 110f.; Dion, "Aramaic 'Family Letter,'" pp. 59–73.
[38] Collomp, *Recherches,* p. 18.
[39] Giomini and Celentano, eds., *Ars Rhetorica,* pp. 105f.

cold. These comments are sufficient to indicate that multiple factors—content and broad epistolary purpose, emotional tone, and the social status of the correspondents—need to be recognized in the classification of letters.

So far as content is concerned, one should not attempt to determine the intention of a letter on the basis of one or two epistolary formulas within the body. For example, the addressor may introduce the message with a disclosure formula (i.e., "I want you to know that . . .") and, later, request something from the recipient. It may be that the sender has combined two independent epistolary functions, information and request. On the other hand, the initial disclosure may serve merely as background information to justify the request. Consequently, one needs to examine the logical relationship of conventions to each other and to determine the thrust of the correspondence on the basis of the larger contours or pattern of phrases. Martin Buss recently argued that such considerations were important to the study of the letter as a genre[40] and William Doty advocated essentially the same viewpoint several years ago.[41]

2) *Analyzing formulas and conventions.* In light of the foregoing, it seems advisable to analyze formulaic conventions of the non-literary letter tradition according to position within the letter and to determine the purpose that formulas serve in their respective positions in relation to other conventions. It will prove unfeasible, in practice, to trace the actual concatenation or cluster of formulas in each letter of our collection. But that kind of analysis would not be especially fruitful anyway. The more important exercise is to learn something about the undergirding structure(s) of letters, by examining the kinds of formulas which tend to appear exclusively or primarily as opening and closing conventions, on the one hand, and by studying those that are used, on the other hand, within the body. By this means we can better understand the role of the respective letter elements (opening, body, and closing) on the basis of the conventions that are used to express those elements. Then, one may plot the particular nuance or implementation which a letter writer gives to the opening, body, or closing on any given occasion.

(c) Epistolary Functions and Letter Elements

There is a correlation between the aforementioned epistolary functions (maintenance of contact, communication of information, and requests or commands) and the three parts of the letter. Thus, the general nature of the relationship between sender and recipient is conveyed by the opening and closing so that, in the case of family letters and friendly correspondence, the maintenance or enhancement of relationship comes to expression through various conventions which open or conclude the letter. On the other hand, the specific occasions which prompt the message of the letter, and which are associated with the disclosure of information and the request or command reqarding something, come to expression in the body of the letter.

Owing to the correlation of epistolary tasks and the respective letter parts, conventions will be presented according to the broad epistolary function they serve and, correlatively, according to the place in the letter where they occur. Opening and closing formulas will be examined in tandem, since they serve the same broad purpose (the maintenance of relationship), and collectively, they will provide an index to the various dimensions of this purpose. Then, stock phrases in the letter bodies will be surveyed to determine the kinds of specific need that occasioned the letters.

1) *Letter openings and closings.* F. X. J. Exler analyzed opening and closing epistolary phrases extensively in his 1923 study, *The Form of the Ancient Greek Letter.* After deciding that Greek papyrus letters fell into four broad classes, he set out the opening and closing phrases characteristic of each category. His four classes were: familiar letters (correspondence between relatives and friends), business letters (all commercial and legal documents drawn up in epistolary form, including contracts, leases, acknowledgments of receipt of rent, etc.), petitions and applications (letters requesting redress), and official letters (letters written or received by officials, i.e., administrative and state correspondence).[42] In addition to identifying the phrases that introduce and conclude the letter, Exler examined the initial and final phrases in the body of the letter. Most of the phrases which he classified as initial and final phrases of the body occur in familiar letters and could be described as health wishes or address formulas. Since they, like the formulas which introduce and conclude the letter, serve the same broad purpose of enhancing the correspondents' relationship, it is more accurate to regard them as opening and closing conventions than as phrases in the body.

a. *Opening and closing formulas.* The customary opening address/salutation (*praescriptio*), as suggested above in the analysis of the sample letter of recommendation, is "A (sender) to B (recipient) greeting." The typical word of farewell in letters which begin with this initial phrase is ἔρρωσο. The principal variant of the opening formula, and the form which was illustrated by means of the letter of petition above, is that in which the recipient's name is written first, either with or without the salutation. The principal word of farewell in letters which write the recipient's name first is εὐτύχει.

Apart from petitions, applications, and similar legal docu-

---

[40] "Principles for Morphological Criticism," pp. 74ff.
[41] "Classification of Epistolary Literature," pp. 197f.

[42] *Ancient Greek Letter,* p. 23.

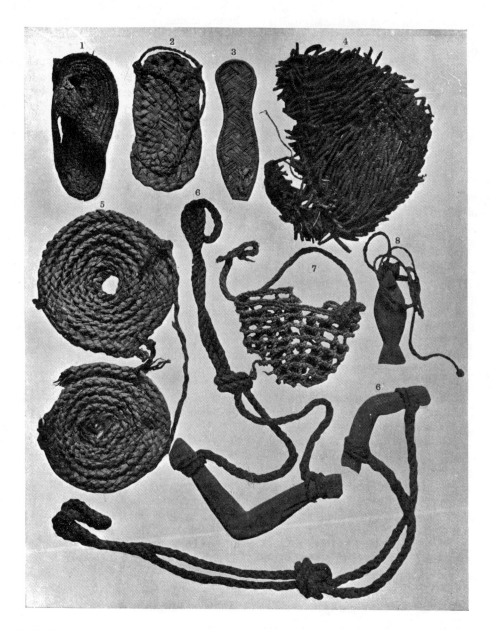

1.	Sandal (rope)	4.	Fringed cap (?)	7.	Muzzle for camel or ox
2.	Sandal (rush)	5.	Ox-blinkers (?)	8.	Float (?)
3.	Sandal (papyrus)	6.	*Shaduf* ropes		

Photograph reproduced with the permission of the Committee of the Egypt Exploration Society.

ments, almost all papyrus letters have "A to B greeting" as their initial formula and ἔρρωσο as the word of farewell. From the second century BCE onward the opening salutation of this initial formula often combined syntactically with the wish for health, e.g., "Dionysios to Ptolemy greeting and health" (letter 38). Similarly, by the first century CE, the closing formula often combined with the wish (prayer) for health so that, by the third century CE, it was expressed more often as an explicit wish for health than as a simple word of farewell.

Letters between family members and friends (Exler's "familiar letters") often indicate the familial relation of the correspondents by the addition of appropriate words to the address and/or the salutation.[43] Family designations in the address, and especially honorific descriptions like "lady" or "lord," "dearest," and "my own," are more characteristic of letters from Roman Egypt than of the Ptolemaic period. Indeed, the frequency of such designations in correspondence from Roman Egypt suggests a development in Greek epistolary style under the influence of Latin letter writing practices.

Julius Victor suggested that the openings and conclusions of letters should reflect the degree of friendship the correspondents shared and they should be written according to customary practice.[44] Pseudo Libanius, by contrast, reacted negatively to the excessive sentiment conveyed by such terms in his day and advocated return to the simpler letter opening formulas of ancient times. Consequently, he said the formula should include only the following: "So-and-so to so-and-so, greeting."[45]

The qualifying designations in the initial address/greeting of legal texts that appear in letter form (e.g., agreements of sale, loans, contracts; see letters 30 and 33) differ considerably from those in familiar correspondence. As we could anticipate, familial descriptions of the recipient are absent and, because of the legal character of the correspondence, the sender's patronymic, guardian (in the case of women), occupation, and city (village) of residence are specified. Documents of this type usually specify the date, either at the beginning or end, but often omit the farewell.

Correspondence between state administrative officials, like letters between relatives and friends, could include terms of familiarity and cordiality in the opening address/ salutation if the correspondents happened to be friends, relatives, or equals. More frequent than the use of these terms, however, was the specification of the officials' titles in the address.[46]

b. *Expressions of health and greeting.* We already noted that by the second century BCE the opening address/salutation could be combined with the wish for health. Correspondingly, by the early Roman period, the word of farewell was often stated explicitly as a prayer for health rather than as the earlier, truncated "farewell." The health wish was often more extensive, however, in both the Greek and Roman period, and was often expressed independently of the opening and closing formulas.

The standard health wish in a letter opening consisted of two parts, an expression of concern (a wish or prayer) about the recipient's welfare, and an assurance of the sender's own well being. Though the essential idea remained constant during the six centuries examined (III BCE–III CE), each century or two developed its characteristic phrases, and the individual variety of expression within each period is significant. The Greek formula differs in this respect from the more uniform *formulis valetudinis* in Latin letters.

In an earlier, random sampling of 660 letters from Graeco-Roman Egypt, I found that about one in six letters had the wish (prayer) for health in the letter opening. The percentage is considerably more in the present collection because, on the one hand, it contains fewer legal documents and petitions/applications (neither of which category includes the wish for health) and because, on the other hand, more familiar letters are included, which tend to express the health wish.

The following recognizable stages in the development of the health wish may be traced.

The health wish in the letter opening was expressed as a separate formula, distinct from the initial address/salutation, in the third century BCE and into the first half of the second century BCE.[47] By the mid-second century BCE, and into the late first or early second centuries CE, letter writers began to combine the health wish with the address/salutation in the form: . . . χαίρειν καὶ ἔρρῶσθαι (or ὑγιαίνειν), i.e., ". . . greeting and health."[48] The qualifying phrase, διὰ παντός, was added to this latter form of the convention from the reign of Augustus up to the second century CE. The new phrase means, ". . . greeting and *continual* good health."[49] But, during the second and third centuries CE, writers separated the convention once more from the salutation and the qualifying

---

43 Regarding the various designations by means of which the addressee could be identified, and the manner in which the initial greeting could be elaborated, see John L. White, "Epistolary formulas," p. 291.

44 *Ars Rhetorica*, pp. 105f.

45 *Epistolimaioi Characteres*, sec. 51.

46 Exx.: letters 46–47, 50, 61, 76–77, 88.

47 Exx.: letters 6.1f., 26f.; 13.1f.; 14.1f.; 15.1; 16.1–3; 18.1f.; 22.1f.; 24.1f.; 26.1–3; 28.2–5; 34.2–6; 35.2–5; 36.1–7; 39.2f.; 40.1f.; 41.1f.

48 Exx.: letters 38.1f.; 45.1f.; 53.2; 54.2f.; 56.2f.; 66.1f.; 69.1f.; 78.2.

49 Exx.: letters 63.1; 64.2f.; 65.3f.; 74.2f.; 77.3f.; 81.3f.; 90.2f.; 92.2; 93.2f.; 98.2f.; 100.2f.; 101.2f.

phrase, πρὸ μὲν πάντων (variants: πρὸ παντός; πρὸ τῶν ὅλων), became common. This phrase means "*above all* I pray that you are well."[50] During this same period, the convention was commonly written as a prayer, expressed especially as obeisance/supplication before the god(s) on the recipient's behalf, e.g., "... and I make supplication (προσκύνημα) for you daily before the Lord Serapis." Koskenniemi calls this the προσκύνημα phrase, because of the word used for obeisance/supplication.[51]

The individuality with which the health wish was sometimes expressed suggests that the letter writer could personalize the convention in a manner appropriate to the occasion. The sentiments which extend, or function as a substitute for, the health wish provide further evidence of the deliberateness with which the convention could be expressed. For example, the letter writer could replace either the wish for the recipient's health or the assurance of his or her own welfare, if the situation called for it. To be specific, after conveying good wishes regarding the recipient's welfare in letter 14, the sender notifies Zenon, the recipient, that he himself has fallen into a grave illness and, for that reason, would like to receive special consideration from Zenon.[52] Analogously, if the sender has learned that the recipient has been ill, or a family member has died, the wish for health may be replaced with a statement of concern, anxiety, or grief.[53] Or, the sender may offer encouragement in the face of adversity (letter 43) and death (letter 116).

Another relatively common motif in the letter opening is the exclamation of joy at receipt of a letter, expressed by means of the convention, "I rejoiced greatly (λίαν/μεγάλην ἐχάρην) at receipt of your letter." In such cases, the sender's joy was occasioned not merely because of the maintenance of contact but because of news about the recipient's welfare. Consequently, the expression of joy in the letter opening is, or usually is, a variant or surrogate statement of the sender's concern about the recipient's welfare.[54] Similarly, the writer might express regret or grief at receipt of bad news.[55]

In contrast to the sympathetic or positive disposition toward the recipient conveyed by these two conventions, the writer sometimes expressed aggravation and incredulity at the recipient's negligence, especially the failure to write, either with the formula, θαυμάζω πῶς (ὅτι) ..., or by referring to the number of letters the recipient had failed to

answer.[56] The sender often wrote just to allay such fears, by informing an absent husband, father, or brother that the children were well or that business affairs at home were fine (letter 101; see letter 107). The receipt of news that the recipient was well could occasion thanks to the gods (see letters 34 and 35). Or the sender might offer thanks to the god(s) because of his own rescue from danger, as an oblique means of informing the recipient of the satisfactory nature of the sender's present condition (see letter 103a).

Several years ago, I suggested that both the expression of joy and of incredulity or dissatisfaction were conventional means of introducing the body of the letter. But more recently, Nils Dahl convinced me that such phrases, like the opening and closing greetings, the wish for health, and related expressions, tend to maintain contact between correspondents, which is more characteristic of the opening and closing of the letter.

The wish for health was expressed less often in the letter closing than in the opening, especially during the Ptolemaic period. Perhaps during the first 150–200 years of the Ptolemaic rule, the word of farewell continued to retain something of its original meaning, so that there was little need for an additional health wish. In any case, when the convention began to appear as a fuller, explicit, wish for health, it functioned in a manner comparable to the opening wish for health, except that reference to the sender's own welfare was omitted. In the third century BCE, and well into the second century BCE, there was a tendency to state that the writer would be "favored" if the recipient concerned himself with his bodily health, e.g., "Therefore, you would do me a favor by taking care of yourself ("body") to stay well" (letter 28.37–39; see letters 34.31f., 55.19–22; see also UPZ I 64.13f.). This use of the expression of thanks, in the sense of "doing a favor" for the letter writer, is common in or near the close of the letter. However, it was slightly more common to talk about being favored in the manner illustrated in the above letter of recommendation, or following other kinds of requests in the body, than in connection with the health wish.

Whether the closing health wish included the expression of favor or not, the writer usually enjoined the recipient to take care of his "body" (physical health?) in the earlier Ptolemaic period. But in the later Ptolemaic period and on into

---

[50] Exx.: letters 103a.2–6; 104a.3–5; 104b.2–6; 105.3f.; 109.4–8; 110.3–5; 111.3f.; 112.2–5; 113.3–6, 19f.; 115b.4–7.

[51] *Studien zur Idee*, pp. 139–45.

[52] See letter 92 in which, after wishing the recipient good health, the sender states that her own situation is a bad one. In letter 100, after wishing good health, the sender asks the recipient to be concerned about certain personal clothing items of the sender's family. In 18, the sender

requests the recipient to keep him in mind.

[53] See SelPap I 89: "I suffered anxiety when I heard of your long protracted illness, but am delighted to hear that you are convalescent and already on the point of recovery."

[54] Exx.: letters 28.10f.; 93.3–6; 103b.9f.

[55] Exx.: letters 87.6–9; 102.4f.; 116.3–9.

[56] Exx.: letters 28; 105; 111; 113.

the early Roman era, the second person reflexive pronoun replaced the word "body," i.e., "Take care of *yourself* to stay well."[57] Also, from the late second century BCE until at least midway through the first century CE, the closing health wish was often introduced with the phrase, τὰ δ' ἄλλα, which means, "for the rest," i.e., "For the rest, take care of yourself [or, "*Favor* me by taking care of yourself"], to stay well."[58]

By the latter half of the first century CE, and through the third century CE, the health convention was expressed as a prayer, which combined syntactically with the word of farewell to produce the form, ἐρρῶσθαί σε εὔχομαι (βούλομαι), "I pray (wish) that you are well."[59]

Though sentiments could extend or replace the closing wish for health, I am not able to identify as many patterns as in the letter opening. One kind of identifiable addition or alternative is the sender's request for information regarding the recipient's welfare.[60] Another isolable convention that occurs with some frequency is the sender's request that the recipient come home or make a visit, or the sender states that he himself hopes to visit the recipient.[61]

One may recall how, in connection with the discussion of ancient epistolary theory, the letter was regarded as a substitute for the correspondents' actual conversation and presence. But at best, the letter remained only a substitute, and consequently, we can understand how a visit became the ideal means of enhancing the correspondents' relationship with each other. In the case of familiar letters, almost all requested or projected visits appear to be mutually beneficial to the correspondents, and thus such conventions properly contribute to the general purpose of the letter opening and closing by furthering the correspondents' personal relationship.

On the other hand, the request or demand for the recipient's presence or the sender's own anticipated visit sometimes conveyed a threatening nuance.[62] In these cases, the letter was usually concerned with some alleged irresponsibility of the recipient in business or administrative affairs. The projected necessity of either the recipient's visit to the

sender or of the sender's visit to the recipient served to frighten the recipient into responsible and immediate action. Since the primary purpose of this type of threat was to improve business, and not the correspondents' friendship, this use of the convention served the purpose of the body and not the closing of the letter. The aforementioned request for information near the end of the letter, like the projected visit, could function as a letter body formula as well as a letter closing convention; in addition to requesting that the recipient convey news about his or her welfare, the sender might request or demand information related to the business addressed in the letter.

Before proceeding to the analysis of formulas in the body of the letter, we need to identify one remaining type of convention in the letter closing, namely, the closing greetings. Letter writers began with some frequency, from the reign of Augustus onward, to extend greetings to or from a third party (or parties) in the letter closing. The large majority of these closing greetings used the verb ἀσπάζεσθαι, sometimes expressed in two or three forms: e.g., "Greet (ἄσπασαι) all those from the Caesareum, each by name"; "greet (ἄσπασαι) Didymos, the notary, along with his whole household . . ."; "Epitynchanon greets (ἀσπάζεται) you"; "greet (ἄσπασαι) all our friends, each by name."[63]

2) *Epistolary theorists and the letter body.* We observed above, in the discussion of ancient epistolary theory, that the epistolary types identified by Pseudo Demetrius and Pseudo Libanius are not so much sample letter types as a spectrum of styles appropriate to the moods occasioned by the needs of letter writing. Or, as Pseudo Demetrius suggests in the introductory comments to his epistolary types, they represent the types of persuasion which may be employed in letter writing. These handbook types are more relevant to the body of the letter than to letter openings and closings.

About half of Pseudo Demetrius' twenty-one sample letter descriptions are more appropriate to the literary letter tradition than to the documentary papyrus letter tradition. On the other hand, the descriptions amount, in a few cases, to full-

---

[57] Customarily, the injunction to concern was expressed with the verb ἐπιμέλομαι; the participial form of the verb during the earlier Ptolemaic period and the imperative form during the later Ptolemaic and early Roman periods. See this verb in the closing health wish in letters 28, 34–35, 49, 55, 60, 63–65, 67, 69, 71, 73, 77–78. The final or purposive clause that completed the verb of injunction during the Ptolemaic and early Roman period was ἵνα ὑγιαίνεις, i.e., take care of yourself "in order to stay well." See the letters cited in connection with the verb of injunction.

[58] Exx.: letters 45.26; 55.19f.; 65.12f.; 73.17; 78.9f.; other exx.: PTebt I 55.6–10 (late II BCE); POslo II 47.14f. (1 CE); BGU IV 1208.48–50 (Age of Augustus); POxy XVII

2148.18 (27 CE); X 1292.18f. (30 CE); PPrinc III 161.12 (35 CE).

[59] Exx.: letters 90.18ff.; 98.27f.; 101.22f.; 103a.23; 103b.28; 104a.20; 104b.21; 105.46; 107.20–22; 108.24f.; 111.22f.; 112.35f; 115.19f.

[60] E.g., see letters 41.6f.; 105.33; 107.17f., 21f.; 110.21–23; 112.35f.; 113.8–11.

[61] Exx.: letters 22.23f.; 34.28–31; 35.20–23; 55.16–18; 56.7–14; 57.21–23; 60.14f.; 85.11, 14f.; 91.11f.; 92.9ff.; 97a.10–12; 100.14f.; 101.21f.; 105.38–40; 110.24f.; 112.14f.

[62] Exx.: letters 27.5f.; 31.4f.; 32.5f.; 59.23–25; 76.7–9.

[63] Letter 110.23f., 30f.; other examples of the greeting convention: letters 67.24f.; 83.11f.; 84.10f.; 94.6–10; 96.22f.; 99.25–27; 100.15–18; 101.23f.; 103a.18–20; 103b.14–21;

blown papyrus letter types. In other cases, they seem to fit specific epistolary formulas. Intermediate between these two extremes, we find descriptions that are appropriate to the major focus or primary message of certain letters.

The twenty-one epistolary styles identified by Pseudo Demetrius are as follows:

the friendly	(φιλικός)
commendatory	(συστατικός)
blaming	(μεμπτικός)
reproachful	(ὀνειδιστικός)
consoling	(παραμυθητικός)
censorious	(ἐπιτιμητικός)
admonishing	(νουθετητικός)
threatening	(ἀπειλητικός)
vituperative	(ψεκτικός)
praising	(ἐπαινετικός)
advisory	(συμβουλευτικός)
supplicatory	(ἀξιωματικός)
inquiring	(ἐρωτηματικός)
responding	(ἀποφαντικός)
allegorical	(ἀλληγορικός)
accounting	(αἰτιολογικός)
accusing	(κατηγορικός)
apologetic	(ἀπολογητικός)
congratulatory	(συγχαρητικός)
ironic	(εἰρωνικός)
thankful	(ἀπευχαριστικός)

The admonishing, vituperative, praising, advising, allegorical, accusing, apologetic, congratulatory and ironic styles are both too specialized in function and too rhetorical in expression—at least as these styles are described by Pseudo Demetrius—to qualify as specific papyrus letter types. If one is somewhat less technical in defining these styles, however, they can apply to sentiments that come to expression in the documentary letter tradition (e.g., Apollonios sends a brief note of approval and praise to Zenon in letter 21; though not formal or legal apologies, letter writers attempt to defend themselves against actual or possible accusations in letters 14, 15 and 18).

Three sample letter types appear to correspond to the three isolable papyrus letter types illustrated and explained earlier, namely, the friendly (or family), commendatory, and

supplicatory (petitionary) letters. However, Pseudo Demetrius' description of the supplicatory type suggests that he may have something more extensive than the letter of petition in mind.

One other type of correspondence identified by Pseudo Demetrius, the letter of consolation (condolence), may qualify as an identifiable papyrus letter type. I say "may" qualify because there are only a handful of extant examples (e.g., see letter 116 and PSI XII 1248 [235 CE]). See the discussion of conventional language in letters of consolation in the comments on letter 116 of this collection.

The eight remaining letter styles are broadly reminiscent of the themes and tone of many letters, though it is difficult to differentiate some of the categories which Pseudo Demetrius identifies. For example, blaming, reproachful, censorious, and threatening expressions all occur, but it would be very difficult to differentiate them as separate epistolary functions or types of expression. The inquiring, responding and thankful styles are easily recognizable, but they could hardly qualify, except perhaps in rare cases, as specific epistolary types.

It is neither feasible nor advantageous to review the forty-one epistolary types identified by Pseudo Libanius in the manner that the epistolary styles in the handbook of Pseudo Demetrius have been examined. The work is probably later than the last stage of our letter collection and, consequently, its value for understanding letter writing in the Ptolemaic/early Roman period is questionable at best. Many of the styles identified by Pseudo Demetrius reappear in Pseudo Libanius, but almost half of them do not. Like the letters from Pseudo Demetrius' handbook, the sample letter styles from Pseudo Libanius' handbook appear to be a mixture of literary and non-literary types. One epistolary style which Pseudo Libanius identifies, the mixed (μικτή) type, is worth noting because many papyrus letters tend to combine such epistolary functions as friendship, disclosure of information, and request.

3) *Conventions in the letter body.* Having made these preliminary comments on epistolary style and the letter body, we may proceed to identify various conventions in the body of Greek non-literary letters. Since this analysis traces formulaic conventions according to position within the letter, we will differentiate formulas as introductory, transitional, or concluding. A summary of the stages identified in

104a.16–19; 104b.14–20; 105.40–46; 108.21–23; 109.17–21; 111.19–21; 112.29–35; 113.11–16; 115a.24f.; 115b.16–18. Though much less common, προσαγορεύειν and ἐπισκόπεισθαι appear to be used, like ἀσπάζεσθαι, as verbs of greeting in the letter closing, e.g., letter 90.24–27. In addition to the meaning, "Send regards to so-and-so" (i.e., "greet so-and-so"), ἐπισκόπεισθαι conveys the meaning,

"look after," in the sense of "take care of," when the imperative form of the verb is used in the letter closing. This form of the verb functions like the health wish, in enjoining the recipient(s) to take care of someone. Exx.: 43.12–14; 71.43f.; other exx.: PTebt I 58.62f. (111 BCE); PTebt III, pt.1 768.23–28 (116 BCE); POxy II 294.31f. (22 CE); II 293.16f. (27 CE).

connection with letters of recommendation and petition will illustrate the sequence of formulas in the body. We begin with formulas concluding the body because, in letters of petition and often in other letters with requests, they tend to be more stereotyped than phrases that introduce the body.

a. *Formulas for concluding the letter body.* When the letter writer expressed a closing health wish in the early Ptolemaic period, he often wrote that he would be "favored" if the recipient took care of his health. But the "favor" more often referred to the recipient's willingness to attend to some other kind of request, usually specified earlier in the letter, than to his welfare. When it was used in this way, it functioned as a stock means of concluding the body rather than as an item in the letter closing. The "classical" use of the formula, perhaps, was in letters of recommendation.

Letters of recommendation contain a three-part body: (1) the writer introduced the body of the letter by recommending the letter carrier to the recipient, specifying the carrier's relation to the writer; (2) the writer requested the recipient to assist the recommended person; and (3) the writer concluded the body by expressing appreciation to the recipient, by stating that he would be "favored" by the assistance and/or by offering to repay the favor should the recipient write for something which he wanted. Though the expression of appreciation is characteristic of letters of recommendation, it is common elsewhere in letters of request, serving as a polite or subtle means of persuading the recipient to grant the request.[64]

The threefold sequence of formulas in the body of letters of petition is quite analogous to that in letters of recommendation. The petitioner's recitation of the circumstances which necessitate the request, like the introduction of the recommended person, serves as the "background" to the request itself. And following the second part of the body, the request, the petitioner concludes by acknowledging that she will be benefited by the recipient's fulfilment of the request. It is justifiable to conclude, in fact, that this threefold structure is characteristic of letters of request and, to an appreciable extent, of all requests in letters.

The "background" section introduces the body by explaining the circumstances of the request. The request, in turn, is logically connected to the background by a conjunction which means "therefore" (e.g., $o\mathring{v}\nu$ and $\delta\iota\acute{o}$). Finally, the letter writer encourages the recipient to attend to the request by stating either that he will be benefited by a positive response and that justice will be accomplished (in petitions)

or, in correspondence between equals, that he will be favored by fulfilment of the request.

In letters where request is only one of the functions in the body, the "background" is often omitted as a formal element. It is functionally present, however, in $\emph{ἵνα}$, $\emph{ὅπως}$ and $\gamma\acute{α}\rho$ clauses which follow the request and provide an explanation of it.

The most common means of making requests is to employ some form of the polite convention, $\kappa\alpha\lambda\hat{ω}\varsigma$ $\mathring{α}\nu$ $o\mathring{v}\nu$ $\pi o\iota\acute{η}\sigma\alpha\iota\varsigma$, which means "therefore, you would do well to . . . ," or, simply phrased, "Please. . . ."[65] This phrase occurs hundreds of times, usually with a conjunction meaning "therefore," and almost always as a transitional statement in the body, following some introductory explanation of the request which it expresses.

In addition to making requests, epistolary formulas are used in the letter body to give or seek information. Consequently, a spate of disclosure phrases, often employing a verb with the meaning, "to know," are employed by the sender. The following are used as means of concluding the body, either to disclose or seek information.

Informational Formulas

1. Formula disclosing information

$\gamma\acute{ε}\gamma\rho\alpha\phi\alpha$ $o\mathring{v}\nu$ $\emph{ὅπως}$ $\emph{εἰδῇς}$.
"Therefore I wrote to you in order that you may know."

2. Formulas requesting information

$\gamma\rho\acute{α}\psi o\nu$ $(\mathring{ε}\pi\acute{ι}\sigma\tau\epsilon\iota\lambda o\nu)$ $\emph{ἡμῖν}$ $(\mu o\iota)$ $\emph{ἵνα}$ $(\emph{ὅπως})$ $\emph{εἰδῶμεν}$.
"Write in order that we (I) may know."
$\delta\iota\alpha\sigma\acute{α}\phi\eta\sigma\acute{o}\nu$ $\mu o\iota$ $(\emph{ἡμῖν})$ $\pi\epsilon\rho\acute{ι}$ . . .
"Inform me (make quite clear/show plainly) about . . ."
$\mathring{α}\nu\tau\acute{ι}\gamma\rho\alpha\psi\acute{o}\nu$ $(\mathring{α}\nu\tau\iota\phi\acute{ω}\nu\eta\sigma\acute{o}\nu)$ $\mu o\iota$ . . .
"Write back (reply) to me . . ."

Though the first example is most common in the third to second centuries BCE, it continues throughout the six centuries of this study, if one includes certain abbreviations and substitutions of vocabulary.[66] Common abridged forms of the formula are "therefore I wrote to you" or "in order that you may know."

The first formula for requesting information above seems to span the period examined. But the full phrase occurs less

---

[64] Exx.: letters 6.9f., 36–38; 9.11f.; 11.4–6; 13.9f.; 14.3f.; 39.8f., 12f.; 45.25f.; 52.15–17; 54.8–11; 66.17–22; 71.38–41; 73.16f.; 77.9–12; 79.9f.; 81.23–26; 115a.22–24.

[65] Exx.: letters 6.6, 22, 34f., 43, 47; 11.2f.; 18.2, 29; 22.21f.; 24.4f.; 25.3; 34.29; 36.11; 40.3; 43.6f.; 52.9; 57.11f.; 66.4f.; 84.3ff.; 85.5f.; 94.4–6; 95.3ff.; 96.2ff.; 97a.10f.; 97b.3; 100.4f.; 104b.11; 110.21–23; 113.30f.

[66] Exx.: letters 7.8; 9.10f.; 12.13f.; 16.5f.; 17.7f.; 19.7f.; 40.4; 46.4f.; 47.21–23. See also letters 53.13f.; 58.17–20; 64.15f.; 113.28–30.

often than one or the other of the two parts, i.e., either "write to me (us) about (your health, some kind of requested information, etc.) . . ." or "that I (we) may know."[67] When the sender instructs the recipient to write about his welfare, the convention serves a letter closing function. "Inform me about . . ." is common only in the Greek period.[68] "Write back to me . . ." appears to span a large part of the Graeco-Roman rule of Egypt.[69]

The information phrases close the body, either by explicitly stating the sender's primary reason for writing or by requesting information which necessitates correspondence from the recipient. We may anticipate other conventions which conclude the body by reviewing the other purposes that this part of the letter serves.

We noted earlier that certain phrases used in the letter closing may also be employed, with a slightly different nuance, to conclude the body. Three conventions that may function in this dual capacity are the announcement of or request for a visit, the sender's statement that he will be "favored" if the recipient attends to something, and the sender's request for information. In family letters, the sender requests the recipient to send information about her health, the "favor" which the addressor seeks is that the recipient take care of herself, and the visit will further enhance family bonds. If concern about personal ties is regarded as an epistolary message (body), then these phrases function like body-concluding formulas. They build a bridge to further communication in a manner analogous to the above formulas, which request information as a way of concluding the body. Like the use of the "favor" phrase in letters of recommendation (or the appreciation phrase, following the request in petitions) the body-concluding formulas "nail down" the request by encouraging the recipient to grant it. But, in the case of family letters, the request that the sender wishes to have granted is an ongoing relationship with the recipient through correspondence or a visit.

Many letters do not conclude the body in any identifiable manner. Nonetheless, a sufficient number of identifiable conventions gravitate toward the end of the body that we may attribute a discrete purpose to them. In general, these conventions appear in the part of the letter where the purpose of the communication is completed. When the indicative form of the disclosure formula is expressed (i.e., "I wrote in order that you know."), the intent of the communication is indicated. The finalizing import is probably more evident, however, in those formulas in which the letter writer tries to per-

suade or coerce the recipient into attending to something previously requested in the body or, if necessity dictates, by urging the recipient to send desired information. The persuasion varies according to the nature of the correspondents' relationship.

Statements Used to Persuade, Coerce, or Threaten

1. Expressions indicating thanks, confidence, and a willingness to repay favors

τοῦτο γὰρ (δέ) ποιήσας εὐχαριστήσαις ἡμῖν (μοι)
or: ἔσῃ μοι κεχαρισμένος . . .
   "For by doing this, we (I) will be favored . . ."
οἶδα γὰρ ὅτι . . .
or: εἰδὼς ὅτι . . .
   "For I know that . . ."
   or: "Knowing that . . ."
καὶ σὲ δὲ γράφε (γράψον/ἐπίστελλε/σήμανον/ διασάφησον, etc.) πρὸς ἡμᾶς (ἡμῖν μοι) περὶ (ὑπέρ) ὧν ἂν βούλῃ (ὧν ἐὰν θέλῃς αἴρῃ, etc.)
   ". . . and you too must write to us about whatever you want."

2. Expressions urging responsible behavior

μὴ οὖν (ἐὰν δέ) ἀμελήσῃς . . .
   "Therefore, do not (and if you) neglect to . . ."
ἐπιμέλειαν δὲ ποίησαι (ἔχε, etc.) ὅπως
or: ἐπιμελοῦ δέ . . .
   "Make it your concern to . . ."
   or: "Take care that . . ."
μελησάτω σοι ὅπως . . .
   "Take care that . . ."
φρόντισον οὖν ἵνα (ὡς) . . .
   "Therefore, take care (thought) that . . ."
μὴ οὖν (or: καὶ μὴ εἰ δ᾽) ἄλλως ποιήσῃς . . .
   "Therefore, do not (and if you) act otherwise . . ."
γινώσκων ὅτι ἐάν . . .//γίνωσκε (ἐπίστασο) σαφῶς (ἀκριβῶς) ὅτι . . .
   "Knowing that if . . ."//"Understand clearly that . . ."

3. Expressions indicating the necessity of an urgent response

ὡς ἂν (ἅμα) οὖν λάβῃς/λάβετε (ἀναγνῶτε) τὴν ἐπιστολήν . . .
   "Therefore, as soon as you receive (read) my letter . . ."

---

[67] Exx.: letters 2.15f.; 4.6f.; 5.6; 18.8f.; 82.22f.; 104a.14–16; 115a.22f.

[68] Exx.: letters 39.10ff.; 41.6f. An equivalent function is rendered by the imperative form of the verb δηλόω under

Roman rule, e.g., see SelPap I 125.24f. (II CE); PFlor III 338.15f. (III CE).

[69] Exx.: letters 67.17–20; 69.14–17; 109.10–12; 110.21–23; 111.17–19.

ἔτι οὖν καὶ νῦν . . .
"Therefore, even now . . ."

The first block of conventions consists of congenial expressions, usually exchanged between equals. The first example is commonly used after a request.[70] as a means of acknowledging that the recipient will favor the sender by granting the request. Or, the sender sometimes states, by means of the same or similar language, that he or she will be favored, if the recipient takes care of himself.[71] This formula, the second phrase in the first group, is not as common as the other phrases in the group.[72] The third convention is often related to the first, namely, after stating that he will be favored if the recipient grants a request, the sender encourages the recipient to write about whatever he may want in return.[73] Sometimes, after requesting something of the recipient, the sender expresses confidence in the recipient's willingness or ability to grant the request (the perfect form of the verb, meaning "to know," is used for this purpose).

All of the expressions urging responsible behavior suggest, in a more explicit manner than the first block of conventions, that the recipient is being coerced or persuaded to attend to some duty or request which was earlier specified in the letter. Whereas the preceding group of formulas are characteristic of friendly correspondence between equals, the phrases under this second heading tend to occur more often in letters from superiors and in administrative correspondence. They do not always stand in final position in the body, but they almost always depend upon earlier instructions or requests in the body, and consequently, they gravitate toward the end of the message rather than the beginning.

The first three entries use either a verb or a noun which actually connotes responsibility.[74] The fourth entry, like the first three, suggests that the recipient should put forth some effort in attending to what the sender has specified.[75] Both the fifth and sixth conventions tend to convey a negative, and often, a threatening, connotation.[76] The phrases under this second heading are sometimes accompanied by a conditional clause, e.g., "And if you should neglect . . . ," or, "If you should act otherwise. . . ." In almost all of these cases, as well as other occurrences of the condition in or near the close of the body, the conditional clause conveys a threatening nuance.

Both of the constructions under the third heading indicate that the recipient should respond immediately to the sender. The first convention is written in a form that is found during the rule of the Ptolemies and up to the rule of Augustus. The corresponding phrase in the first through third centuries CE, which does not occur in the present letter collection is: κομισσμενός (λαβών) μου τὴν ἐπιστολήν (τὰ γράμματα) . . . , i.e., "upon receipt of my letter . . ."[77] The second phrase is less a convention than a nuance, which can occur with a variety of different instructions. The sender indicates, by means of the phrase, that the instructions or request had been asked at least once before and, consequently, that it is already overdue.[78]

Statements of Reassurance, Concern, and Other Conventions

1. Expressions of prohibition, employing the subjunctives

   ἀγωνιάω or δοκέω.
   "Therefore, I entreat you not to be anxious (. . . not to worry)."
   or: "Do no think that I have neglected to . . ."

2. Expressions of concern about the recipient using ἀγωνιάω.

3. Concluding transitions

   τὰ δὲ λοιπά (λοιπὸν οὖν) . . .
   "For the rest . . ."
   (Therefore, finally . . .)

---

70 For further explanation, see p. 194 in this volume.

71 Exx. of convention following request: letters 6.9f.; 9.11f.; 39.8f., 12f.; 52.15–17; 67.17–22; 77.9f.; 79.9f. Exx. concerned with recipient's health: letters 24.3f.; 28.37–39; 34.31f.; 35.22f.; 39.13f.

72 Exx.: letters 13.7–9; 18.5; 74.10–13. See POxy IV 745.7–9 (ca. 1 CE); PWarr 14.8f. (II CE); PFlor III 338.17f. (III CE).

73 Exx.: letters 6.13f.; 9.12; 11.5f.; 14.3; 39.8; 45.25f.; 54.8–10; 67.21f.; 71.38–40; 73.16f.; 77.10–12; 81.23–26; 115a.22–24.

74 Exx. of ἀμελέω: letters 59.23–25; 70.14; 76.8f.; 80.10–13; 106a.13f.; see PWarr 14.40f. (II CE); exx. of ἐπιμέλομαι/ ἐπιμέλεια: 2.20f.; 14.3; 24.9; 82.17–20; see 18.4; exx. of μελῶ: 108.17–20; see 106a.8.

75 Exx.: letters 5.4f.; 44.6f.; 51.16–20. For related phrases with the meaning "try to . . . ," see letters 23.6; 24.8; with the meaning "see that . . .": 48.5–7; with the meaning "make an effort to . . .": 18.4f.; 83.6–9.

76 Exx. of the "do not act otherwise" phrase: letters 29.8f.; 32.5f.; 69.11f.; 73.14f.; 83.9; 95.34; 96.21; see 47.9; exx. of the "understand clearly . . ."/ "knowing that . . ." phrases: 1.6f.; 27.5f.; 38.33–36; see 76.5–9.

77 Exx. of the two types: 4.5f.; 31.4f.; 45.9f.; see 63.4–6; other exx.: PHib I 45.3ff. (257 BCE); PTebt III, pt.I, 713.4ff. (II BCE); PFay 114.3ff. (100 CE); BGU VII 1676.11ff. (II CE); POxy VII 1065.2ff. (III CE).

78 Exx.: 18.9f.; 31.3f; 43.6f.; 68.8ff.; see 72.3f. near beginning of body.

4. Expressions indicating a willingness to help the recipient

καὶ σὺ δὲ ἐάν τινος χρείαν ἔχῃς . . . γράφε ἡμῖν.

"Moreover, if you ever have need of anything . . . write to us."

The first convention in this group serves as a means whereby the sender may encourage the recipient not to be concerned, either about some aspect of the sender's affairs (including health) or about some detail of the recipient's business, which he fears may suffer in his absence.[79] The second phrase indicates that the sender is concerned about some aspect of the recipient's affairs or about some personal interest which may be in jeopardy at the recipient's end.[80] Like the "favor" convention, these first two phrases sometimes convey the sentiment of a health wish. When this is the case, they function as letter closings. The third and fourth conventions qualify other phrases which conclude the body. The phrase, τὰ δὲ λοιπά, is translated, like τὰ δ᾽ ἄλλα, as "finally" or "for the rest." Unlike τὰ δ᾽ ἄλλα, which often introduces the closing wish for health, however, it introduces the last item of the body.[81] The fourth convention is usually a variation of the "offer to repay a favor" convention. Instead of writing "you, too, if ever you want anything . . . ," the sender states "you, too, if ever you *need* anything. . . ."[82] On occasion, after requesting something of the recipient, the sender will state more bluntly, ". . . for I have need of it."[83]

b. *Formulas for introducing the letter body.* Since the two primary purposes of the body are either to inform or to request something of the recipient, it is appropriate to examine the various respects in which these two functions are introduced.

Informational Formulas

1. Disclosure phrases

γίνωσκε (ἴσθι, μάθε) ὅτι (ὡς) . . .
"Know that . . ."
γινώσκειν σε θέλω ὅτι . . .
"I want you to know that . . ."

2. Notice of appended letter

ὑπογέγραφά σοι τῆς (τά) παρά . . . , ἐλθούσης μοι ἐπιστολῆς (γράμματα) τὸ ἀντίγραφον.

"I have appended below for you a copy of the letter which came from so-and-so."

3. Response to information received

ἐκομισάμην (ἐλάβομεν) τὸ παρὰ σοῦ ἐπιστόλιον (τὴν ἐπιστολήν), ἐν ὧι (ἐν ἧι) γράφεις . . .

"I received your letter in which you write . . . (or: When I received your letter . . .)."

4. Acknowledgment of or compliance with received information

καθάπερ (καθότι, ὡς) ἡμῖν (μοι) ἔγραψας (ἐπέσταλκας) . . .

"Just as you wrote (instructed) us (me) . . ."

Περί with the genitive

περὶ τῶν συμβόλων γεγράφαμεν Κρίτωνι καὶ Καλλικλεῖ, . . .

"Concerning the receipts, we have written to Kriton and Kallikles that . . ."[84]

The two disclosure phrases, the first two formulas above, appear to serve the same function. The shorter, imperative form is characteristic of the Ptolemaic period, whereas the longer, more polite, formula arose during Roman rule and largely supplanted the earlier, shorter form. The appearance of the longer convention seems to coincide with the disappearance of the "motivation for writing" phrase which was used in the Ptolemaic period to conclude the body (i.e., "I wrote to you in order that you know"). Consequently, the explicit explanation of the reason for writing appears to have largely shifted to the introductory part of the body during the Roman period.[85] The notice of an appended letter is the formulaic notification that a copy of someone's letter is enclosed or appended to the letter writer's own correspondence. Occasionally, two or more letters may be appended, especially in administrative instructions to subordinate officials.[86] In addition to these more formulaic means of intro-

---

[79] Exx.: letters 28.22f.; 72.13f.; other exx.: PMich I 18.3f. (257 BCE); POxy VIII 1154.6f. (I CE); BGU II 665, col. III, lines 11ff (I CE); POxy III 530.7f. (II CE); VI 930.11ff. (II/III CE); PTebt II 413.6f. (II/III CE); BGU II 380.19–25 (III CE); POxy X 1296.5–7 (III CE).

[80] Exx.: letters 38.30ff.; 41.6f.; 111.17–19; see PTebt III, pt.1, 763.11ff. (late III BCE).

[81] Exx.: letters 10.14f.; 49.13; 54.8–11; 81.13; 91.11; see PSI V 500.8f. (257 BCE).

[82] Exx.: letters 6.13–15; 23.4; 26.6f.; see SelPap I 89.16f. (256 BCE).

[83] Exx.: letters 8.20–22; 26.6f.; 89.6f.; 93.20f.; see 19.11f.; and, introducing the body, 25.1f.

[84] Letter 1.2–6. See letter 100.4ff.; POxy III 530.2ff. (II CE); PTebt II 423.2ff. (III CE).

[85] Examples of introductory disclosure phrases: letters 11.1f.; 22.2–4; 41.2f.; 42.14ff.; 45.2f.; 52.5f.; 59.2ff.; 72.3f.; 73.3ff.; 91.3–5; 98.3ff.; 101.3ff.; 102.2f.; 104b.4–6; 106a.3–8; 110.5f.; 114.5–8.

[86] For examples of the appended letter phrase see letters 12.2; 27.1f.; 36.7f.; 51.1.

ducing information, certain stock subjects of letter writing are often introduced in a less formulaic way. For example, since Egypt was an agricultural country, it was common to inform the recipient that grain, farm workers, tools, etc., had either been sent or received. Two verbs that were often used to indicate that something had been sent are πέμπω and ἀποστέλλω.[87] Such statements often come from subordinates and, not infrequently, in response to the recipient's instructions. Another common motif which introduces information is one or another reference to the act of letter writing, e.g., "We (I) wrote to . . ."[88] and "so-and-so wrote/informed/announced that. . . ."[89]

In the third category of informational phrases listed above, it is implied that the letter writer is responding to a letter or other information which he or she has received. The first entry acknowledges receipt of a letter or instructions.[90] Though not so extensive in formulaic language, we find other phrases with a similar meaning introducing the message, e.g., "You wrote me about (that). . . ."[91]

The next entry is not only an acknowledgment of received information but an explicit statement of compliance with that information, namely, "Just as you wrote (instructed) me, I have. . . ."[92] Whether in tandem with a stereotyped phrase, or in a non-formulaic clause, περί (ὑπέρ) with the genitive case often signals a reply to something which the recipient has written. On occasion, the letter writer uses the construction to refer to something which he himself had previously written. In either case, the construction may introduce the message of the letter.[93] Though common in this position, περί with the genitive is more often used subsequently in the body to respond to information. In this case, an appropriate conjunction is added, e.g., "Moreover (also), about the. . . ."

The following set of conventions introduce requests or commands. Only the more obvious means of anticipating requests are identified below as "background" statements. Even disclosure phrases may introduce information which explains the occasion or need of a request. Thus, as suggested previously, the use of an epistolary convention should be determined with reference to the broader context of the letter in which it occurs.

Requests, Instructions or "Background" Statements

1. Expressions conveying incredulity and dissatisfaction

θαυμάζω (ἀηδίζομαι) ὅτι (πῶς, ἕνεκα)

I am astounded (dissatisfied) that (how, on account of) . . .

Reference to multiple unanswered letters

τοσαύτας ὑμεῖν ἐπιστολὰς διεπεμψάμην κοὐδεμείαν μοι ἀντεγράψαται, τοσούτων καταπλευσάντων.

"So many letters have I sent to you and not one have you written in return, even when many have sailed down!"

ἐγὼ δὲ καὶ πρότερόν σοι ἐγεγράφειν περὶ τούτων.
or: ἐγράψαμέν σοι πρότερον περί . . .

"And, indeed, I had written to you about this before."
or: "We (I) wrote (sent) to you before about the . . ."

2. Expressions indicating urgency of response

ὡς ἂν (ἅμα, etc.) τάχιστα λάβηις (ἀναγνῶτε) τὴν ἐπιστολήν (τὰ γράμματα, τὴν ἐντολήν), λαβέ (ἀπόστειλον, etc.) . . .

"As soon as you receive (read) this letter (order), take (send, etc.) . . ."

3. Non-formulaic conventions setting out circumstances ("background") of requests/instructions

The genitive absolute and other participial constructions

παραγινομένου μου ἐγ Βουβάστου εἰς Μέμφιν ἐνετέλλετο Ἀπολλώνιος μάλιστα μὲν αὐτὸν διελθεῖν πρὸς σέ, . . .

"When I was coming from Boubastos to Memphis, Apollonios ordered that, if at all possible, I myself should go over to you, . . ."

Phrases introduced with ἐπεί (ἐπειδή)

ἐπεὶ διέγνωσται τὸν ἐπιμελητὴν παραγίνεσθαι ἅμ' ἡμέραι τῆι ιε εἰς Βερενικίδα . . .

"Since it is decided that the epimeletes will proceed as soon as it is daybreak on the fifteenth to Berenikis, . . ."

4. Requests or instructions introducing the body

Requests introduced with καλῶς ποιήσεις . . .
"You would do well to . . ." (or: "Please . . .")

Non-formulaic instructions introducing the body

παραγίνου τῆι η τοῦ Ἀθυρ κομίζων τόν τε λόγον τοῦ Φαῶφι καὶ τὰ περίοντα χρήματα, . . .

"Come up on the eighth of Hathyr bringing both the account of Phaophi and the remaining (outstanding) money, . . ."

---

87 Exx.: letters 2.2–4; 16.3–5; 17.9–11; 89.3–5; 94.3–6; other kinds of notice: "I have spent my travel allowance" (51.1f.) and "I have bought the olives for you" (90.3f.).
88 Exx.: letters 66.2f.; 82.3f; 99.3ff.
89 Exx.: letters 9.1f.; 45.2ff.; 58.4ff.; 64.4–9; 85.4f.
90 Exx.: letters 18.11f.; 34.7ff.; 35.5ff.; 45.15–17; 49.2–5; 64.3; 65.4ff.; 83.3f.; 93.3–6.
91 Exx.: letters 15.2f.; 68.3–5.
92 Exx.: letters 1.5f.; 17.1f.; 26.3f.; 81.5f.; 91.3–5.
93 Exx.: letters 1.2–6; 4.1–4; 9.1f.; 15.1–3; 20.1f.; 49.2–5; 62.2ff.; 68.3–5; 85.5f.; 91.3–5; 101.3ff.; 106b.2–5; 107.4f.

Rolls of papyrus as found in the threshold of a doorway between rooms D and E of House 5026 in Karanis, Egypt. Photograph courtesy of Kelsey Museum of Archaeology, The University of Michigan.

In addition to appearing in family letters as an extention of the health wish,[94] expressions of dissatisfaction appear in correspondence other than letters between family members and friends (see the first two entries above). In these cases, the dissatisfaction is occasioned by negligence in some type of business operation. These two uses of the conventions, either to extend the health wish or to introduce the body of the letter, serve comparable functions. When the sender expresses aggravation in the letter opening, either by stating that she is "astonished" at the recipient's failure to write or by referring to the number of unanswered letters, the aggravation serves as a background to the subsequent request for a letter. Similarly, when astonishment is expressed because of some negligence in business, the sender anticipates a request or order that the problem be rectified. In both cases, the expression of aggravation requires the recipient to try to alleviate the sender's dissatisfaction.

The personal relationship of the corresponding parties tends to come to expression in letter openings and closings. From the sender's perspective, for example, a temporary break in family ties is indicated by the recipient's failure to write and the failure is expressed, consequently, in the letter opening. Similarly, when astonishment is expressed in business correspondence, such as we described above, the dissatisfaction also tends to occur near the beginning or end of the letter, and the sender's disposition toward the recipient is revealed. However, in the latter case, we would be justified in interpreting the astonishment as occasioned by dissatisfaction with the recipient's business activities (an aspect of the body) rather than with negligence in maintaining friendly ties (an aspect of the letter opening). In any case, there is enough similarity of function in the two cases that the lines between opening, closing and body is somewhat more fluid than previously proposed, even when the aforementioned tendencies identified with the opening, closing and body are operative. Suffice it to say, when a negative or positive response to some action (or inactivity) of the recipient is expressed, it tends to be stated either near the beginning or the end of the letter and it conveys the sender's disposition toward the recipient.[95]

"And, indeed, I had written to you about this before" refers, like the multiple letters phrase, to the recipient's failure to reply. Unlike that convention, however, this convention almost always introduces the body and signals the letter writer's need for business information, not his interest in the recipient's welfare.[96]

The convention urging hasty response may also be used, with the addition of the conjunction "therefore" to conclude the body.[97] Though urgency or necessity of response may be introduced by other means in the letter collection, those other phrases do not occur with either the frequency or the formulaic vocabulary of this convention.[98]

Both of the conventions under the third heading above are common means of introducing the body and of anticipating a request. The first, which uses various participial constructions including the genitive absolute, is employed frequently in letters of petition to set out the circumstances that have occasioned the petition. Sometimes the participial constructions occur within conventions that employ stereotyped vocabulary.[99] The second convention, which introduces

---

[94] The two conventions of this type that were identified are the letter writer's statement that he or she is "astounded" ("surprised"?) by the recipient's failure to maintain contact and, similarly, the letter writer refers to the multiple letters which the recipient has failed to answer. For surprise at the recipient's failure to maintain contact, see letter 111.4ff. Regarding multiple unanswered letters, see letters 105.4ff.; 113.6ff.; see also BGU IV 1079.2f. (41 CE); PMich III 221.4ff. (296 CE); VIII 484.3ff. (II CE); POxy IX 1216.4ff. (II/III CE).

[95] Exx. of astonishment expressed in business correspondence: letters 18.8f.; cf. 18.11f. and 15.10f., in which the letter writer uses θαυμάζω to indicate that the recipient had been "astounded" by some action or proposal of the letter writer; see also PMert II 80.3–6 (II CE). Though it does not introduce the body, θαυμάζω in PRyl IV 573.7 (231 BCE) shows an official's dissatisfaction with a subordinate's negligence; see also POxy I 113.20f. (II CE), in which θαυμάζω πῶς expresses astonishment at the recipient's failure to comply with the sender's request. A comparable expression of dissatisfaction, διὸ μένφομαί σαι μεγάλως ("wherefore, I blame you greatly"), introduces body of PFay 111.3 (95–96 CE). The same phrase, though used later in the body, also conveys the sender's dissatisfaction with the recipient in letter 96.14. See it used to complain about the recipient's failure to write in letter 100.15–18. Exx. of θαυμάζω πῶς (ὅτι) or equivalent letter-opening phrases, occasioned by the recipient's failure to write or to come home: letters 34.12ff. (see 34.25–27); 111.4–8. See PMert II 80.3ff. (II CE); PMich III 209.6ff. (II/III CE); PCorn 52.5ff. (late III CE).

[96] Exx.: letters 4.1f.; 67.2–10. The same phrase is used a little later in the body of letter 80 (lines 7–9). Other exx.: PMich I 16.2f. (III BCE); 56.2ff. (III BCE); POxy II 293.3ff. (I CE); PPrinc III 161.2ff.(I CE); BGU II 530.8ff. (I CE); POxy XII 1408.2ff. (III CE).

[97] Exx. introducing the body: letters 23.1ff.; 32.2–5; 47.2–6; 53.3ff.; 92.2f.; 95.3ff.; 97b.3ff.; 117.2–5. See exx. concluding the body in the preceding analysis of conventions which close the body.

[98] See the phrase, "We have need of . . . ," in letter 25.1f. Urgency of response is encouraged, sometimes accompanied by a threatening tone, in letters 29.2–7; 31.1–3; 70.3–9; 80.3–7.

[99] Exx. of participial phrases introducing the body: letters 10.1ff.; 13.2f.; 19.1f.; 31.1–3; 34.7ff.; 35.5ff.; 46.2ff.;

phrases with ἐπεί (ἐπειδή), is also used with some frequency to introduce the body and to set out the circumstances of the request.[100] Like the immediately preceding convention, the ἐπεί clause may combine with other stock phrases.

So far, we have reviewed conventions that introduce the body by anticipating a request. The fourth and final category is concerned with how requests or instructions introduce the body directly. The first of the two conventions listed under this fourth heading is the formulaic phrase, καλῶς ποιήσεις. Ordinarily, this phrase does not appear in first position, as an introduction to the body, but subsequently within the body, following background information, where it includes the conjunction "therefore," i.e., "Therefore, you would do well to. . . ." There are a few examples in the present collection, however, of this polite request phrase introducing the body immediately, without the benefit of prior "background" information.[101] In these cases, an explanation for the request is usually provided subsequently within the letter. The second convention, non-formulaic instructions, employs the imperative of the verb at the beginning of the body to instruct or order the recipient to do something.[102] Like the polite form of the request (καλῶς ποιήσεις . . .), an explanation usually accompanies the command.

c. *Transitional conventions in the letter body.* In many cases, it would be artificial to talk about the "middle" which lies between the introductory and concluding phrases of the letter body, since a large number of papyrus letters are simply too brief to be described in this manner. Nonetheless, stock transitional phrases or grammatical connectors develop the initial subject or move to a new subject with enough frequency that a description of such conventions is warranted. For example, the conjunctions, οὖν, διό, and ὅθεν, are standard means of indicating the transition from the background to a statement of request. And, though it tends to be employed more often to encourage compliance with a request at the end of the message, the elaborate conjunction, ἔτι οὖν καὶ νῦν ("even now . . .," or "still . . ."), may also mark the transition from background to request. The phrase, καλῶς ποιήσεις, is a very common means of indicating a transition in the letter body,[103] and it usually includes the conjunction "therefore." Another common convention which, like the polite request phrase, is found both introducing the body and subsequently within the body is the prepositional phrase, περί (ὑπέρ) δέ, with the genitive. This phrase, it will be recalled, usually indicates that the letter writer is replying to some inquiry of the recipient, i.e., "Con-

cerning the. . . ." Like the polite request phrase, it is expressed more often at a later point in the body than at the very beginning.

The combination of conjunctions δὲ καί and ὁμοίως (ὡσαύτως) δὲ καί is a standard means of turning to a new subject in the letter body. The disclosure formula as well as certain other formulaic phrases of an informational nature may serve the same purpose when the appropriate conjunction is added, e.g., "Know *also* that . . ." and "I want you to know, *too*, that. . . ."

(d) Epistolary Clichés

In addition to the aforementioned conventions, identified in connection with the opening, closing or body, a case may be made for another group of stereotyped expressions in the letter: clichés. Though the distinction between formula and cliché is still tentative, Henry Steen's analysis was essentially correct in his long essay on epistolary clichés.[104] We may describe clichés at the start as ornamental trappings which, strictly speaking, are not essential to the expression of an epistolary function. Their role is to provide nuance, tone, or mood to an epistolary convention.

1) *Overview and critique of "Les clichés."* Though in general agreement with Steen's treatment and definition of clichés, I am not completely satisfied with his application to the papyrus letters. Consequently, it will be advantageous both to review Steen's essay and to indicate, in the process, the modifications that seem to be required. The comments and examples in this section are intended to be illustrative and feasible, not exhaustive and certain.

Whereas the study of Greek papyrus letters by Ziemann and Exler was concerned with the initial and final formulas of the letter, Steen turned his attention to epistolary phrases characteristic of the body. In particular, he identified expressions that either soften or intensify epistolary imperatives. He called such phrases clichés.[105]

Despite Steen's helpful description of clichés as ornamental phrases and his obvious contribution to the identification of epistolary request phrases, his interpretation of clichés appears to be questionable in two respects. First, he restricts the study of clichés too narrowly to only one of the two major epistolary functions of the letter body, the command/request. Just as the imperative or request was subject to ornamental addition, so too the informational function was sometimes qualified with clichés. Second, it seems unwarranted to assume, as Steen does, that all requests are derivative forms

---

56.3ff.; 73.3ff. See also 27.2ff., in which the participial construction is very near the beginning of the body.

[100] Exx.: letters 43.2ff.; 48.1ff.; 61.3ff.; 67.2ff.; 69.2ff.

[101] Exx.: letters 18.2; 24.4; 84.3–7; 96.2ff.; 100.4ff.

[102] Exx.: letters 29.3ff.; 75.4–8; 76.3ff.; 80.3ff.

[103] Exx.: letters 6.6, 22, 34f.; 43, 47; 11.2f.; 18.29; 22.21f.; 25.3ff.; 43.6f.; 52.9ff.; 66.4f.; 85.5ff.; 97a.10ff.; 97b.3ff.; 100.4ff.

[104] "Les Clichés," pp. 119–76.

[105] "Les Clichés," p. 123.

of the imperative. Steen's definition derives too narrowly from his understanding of the types of rhetoric practiced by the Greek orator. Namely, he notes that Attic orators had learned that, in order to persuade their audiences to adopt a certain course of action, they had to use periphrastic constructions, rather than simple commands.[106] However, Steen's idea that either the command or a softened form of request were viable alternatives is often not applicable to the epistolary situation. For example, because of the lack of social status, the imperative was not a viable possibility for the petitioner. For this reason, stock request phrases in letters of petition should be classified as formulas, not clichés. On the other hand, when the petitioner qualified the petition with the deferential phrase, "if it seems good to you," he was using an ornamentation or nuance that *is* appropriately termed cliché, even though such phrases are common in petitions.

2) *Classification of clichés.* In spite of Steen's apparent assumption that request phrases in general are clichés, his actual examples illustrate ornamental phrases within requests that could be justly classified as clichés. As previously suggested, Steen classified clichés according to two basic categories, those that "soften" and those that "intensify" the imperative. These may, in turn, be subdivided.

Softening expressions are of two types: (a) qualifying/modifying expressions, and (b) expressions of urbanity. The qualifying/modifying expressions may be further divided into those which: (a.1) use the ethical dative with the health wish in the letter closing, e.g., $\ddot{\epsilon}\rho\rho\omega\sigma\acute{o}$ $\mu o\iota$, $\dot{\alpha}\delta\epsilon\lambda\phi\acute{\epsilon}$ and $\dot{\epsilon}\pi\iota\mu\acute{\epsilon}\lambda o\upsilon$ $\sigma\epsilon\alpha\upsilon\tau\hat{\eta}s$ $\ddot{\iota}\nu\alpha$ $\mu o\iota$ $\dot{\upsilon}\gamma\iota\alpha\acute{\iota}\nu\eta s$;[107] (a.2) use conditional phrases to soften the imperative, e.g., "if it seems good to you" ($\epsilon\ddot{\iota}$ $\sigma o\iota$ $\delta o\kappa\epsilon\hat{\iota}$; $\dot{\epsilon}\grave{\alpha}\nu$ $\phi\alpha\acute{\iota}\nu\eta\tau\alpha\iota$), "if it is possible," "if you have the leisure," etc.;[108] and (a.3) use verbs meaning "to tell," "to order," "to write," qualified with adverbs such as $\dot{\eta}\delta\acute{\epsilon}\omega s$, $\pi\rho o\theta\acute{\upsilon}\mu\omega s$, $\phi\iota\lambda\iota\kappa\hat{\omega}s$, and $\dot{\alpha}\nu\acute{o}\kappa\nu\omega s$, by means of which the letter writer encourages the recipient to freely express his requests.[109] This third type of expression, by means of which the writer expresses his willingness to oblige the recipient, is usually located near the close of the letter. For example, the aforementioned offer of the letter writer to repay a requested favor, which appears at the end of the body, employs such adverbs. Steen's other class of softening phrases, expressions of urbanity, are employed to make requests in petitions, i.e.,

phrases introduced with the verbs, $\delta\acute{\epsilon}o\mu\alpha\iota$, $\dot{\iota}\kappa\epsilon\tau\epsilon\acute{\upsilon}\omega$, $\dot{\alpha}\xi\iota\acute{o}\omega$ and $\pi\alpha\rho\alpha\kappa\alpha\lambda\hat{\omega}$.[110] As I said before, it would be more appropriate to describe these petitionary phrases as formulas than as clichés. A comparable and more ordinary phrase for softening requests is $\kappa\alpha\lambda\hat{\omega}s$ $\ddot{\alpha}\nu$ $\pi o\iota\acute{\eta}\sigma\alpha\iota s$ ($\pi o\iota\acute{\eta}\sigma\epsilon\iota s$) . . . , i.e., "You will (would) do well to. . . ." This qualifying phrase, identified above as a common means of marking the transition from background to request in the body, strikes me as more ornamental (cliché-like) than the use of petitionary verb clauses.[111]

Steen's second major body of clichés are those which "intensify" the imperative. In certain cases, these clichés allowed the writer to intensify his instructions because of his superior status. On other occasions, the intensification was positive and friendly. In both situations, the strengthening was accomplished by one of two means: by the addition of adverbial expressions of intensity or through intensifying the verb. For example, the adverbial phrase, $\pi\rho\grave{o}$ $\mu\grave{\epsilon}\nu$ $\pi\acute{\alpha}\nu\tau\omega\nu$, was often used in the Roman period to strengthen the opening wish for health.[112]

3) *Illustration of clichés.* The following examples from the letter collection further illustrate Steen's classification of clichés. Among the more common conditional phrases that soften a request is one which means "if it pleases you"/"if it seems good to you."[113] Another conditional phrase that occurs with some frequency is $\dot{\epsilon}\grave{\alpha}\nu$ $\delta\acute{\upsilon}\nu\eta$, which means "if you are able."[114] Though not expressed as a condition, the superlative adverb $\mu\acute{\alpha}\lambda\iota\sigma\tau\alpha$ was used in the early Ptolemaic period with the comparable meaning, "if at all possible."[115] Also similar in nuance, but classified by Steen as an intensification of the imperative, was the use of a phrase which means "by all means" ($\dot{\epsilon}\kappa$ $\pi\alpha\nu\tau\grave{o}s$ $\tau\rho\acute{o}\pi o\upsilon$; $\pi\acute{\alpha}\nu\tau\omega s$; etc.).[116]

Though various other qualifying or intensifying phrases could probably be illustrated by means of the collection, we will limit our remaining examples to those which either invoke or make reference to the gods. The writer's hope, desire, or intention is often expressed with the qualification, "the gods willing" or "with the gods' leave."[117] This kind of phrase is often expressed in connection with the writer's anticipated visit to the recipient. Comparable phrases in the collection are the expressions, "the gods would know best" (letter 15.4), "the outcome is up to the gods" (letter 28.31f.), and "so far as a man (i.e., human) can tell" (letter 15.4). On

---

[106] "Les Clichés," pp. 123f.

[107] "Les Clichés," pp. 125f.

[108] "Les Clichés," pp. 126–28.

[109] "Les Clichés," pp. 128–30.

[110] "Les Clichés," pp. 131–38.

[111] For examples of the $\kappa\alpha\lambda\hat{\omega}s$ $\ddot{\alpha}\nu$ $\pi o\iota\acute{\eta}\sigma\alpha\iota s$ phrase, see "Les Clichés," pp. 138–52.

[112] For adverbial expressions of intensity, see "Les Clichés,"

pp, 153–58; for intensification of the verb, see pp. 158–68.

[113] Exx.: letters 20.4; 22.19; 67.17; 78.7f.; 98.6f.; 99.11, 14.

[114] Exx.: letters 70.10; 81.13; 101.21.

[115] Exx.: letters 8.16; 19.2, 5; 27.11.

[116] Exx.: letters 82.9, 20; 83.7; 97a.3.

[117] Exx. of $\theta\epsilon\hat{\omega}\nu$ $\theta\epsilon\lambda\acute{o}\nu\tau\omega\nu$: letters 101.21; 103a.18; 106a.5; ex. of $\sigma\grave{\upsilon}\nu$ $\theta\epsilon o\hat{\iota}s$: 15.7.

two occasions, the letter writer intensifies his dissatisfaction with the recipient by means of an oath.[118]

4. WRITING MATERIALS, POSTAL SERVICE, AND SCRIBES IN ANTIQUITY

A description of the documentary or non-literary letter tradition would hardly be complete without some treatment of writing materials, scribes, and the delivery of letters.

(a) Writing Materials

Letters were written on a number of materials in antiquity. Before the Persian and Graeco-Roman periods, correspondence in Mesopotamia and certain other ancient Near Eastern areas was written on clay tablets in the Cuneiform script with a square-ended reed. Papyrus was the most widely used writing material during the Persian and Graeco-Roman periods and it was used even earlier in Egypt.

It was also common during these two later periods to write on broken pieces of pottery since they were so accessible and because their porous surfaces could be written on easily with brush or reed pen. Though pieces of pottery or, as they are technically named, *ostraca*, were used extensively in Graeco-Roman Egypt for tax receipts, school exercises, various kinds of lists, and magical spells, their surfaces were too small for most correspondence. Consequently, when letters were written on ostraca, whether they were written in Hebrew, Aramaic or Greek, the physical limitation of the writing surface resulted in shorter messages or notes and greater abbreviation and omission of opening and closing conventions.

Like potsherds, wooden tablets were an inexpensive and widely used writing surface during the Graeco-Roman period. Also like potsherds, physical characteristics limited their use in letter writing. They were used to draft offhand notes to nearby people, but were impractical writing surfaces for longer messages that had to travel great distances. Wood was used in one of two ways: (1) the wood was written on directly and whitened to show up the writing, or (2) melted wax was poured onto tablets, which had raised edges. The wax was inscribed with a stylus, the other end of which was used by the recipient to erase the message in order to reuse the tablet for the reply. For school exercises, tablets were joined together by means of strings that were passed through holes in the raised edges.

Less common writing materials than those which have been mentioned were stone, used for inscriptions, and leather. When the benefactions or edicts of Hellenistic rulers were considered worthy of permanent record or if they contained information which needed to be viewed publicly, they were inscribed on stone after delivery.[119] Parchment and vellum (skins), like stone, were also used for more important correspondence and documents but not for ordinary letters. In Egypt, they were seldom used even for more important texts prior to the second century CE.

Since all the letters in this collection were written on papyrus, a more detailed description of its production and use is relevant here.

Papyrus was grown especially in marshes in the Nile Delta. Egyptians had discovered how to make "paper" from the papyrus plant by 3,000 BCE, and it was apparently possible to harvest the plant throughout the year. There is good evidence that in the Graeco-Roman era, the harvest and sale of papyrus was a state operated monopoly.[120] As far as we can tell, papyrus was grown commercially only in Egypt and "paper" was exported to the rest of the Mediterranean world until the early Middle Ages, when the use of rag paper was introduced with the Arab conquest.[121]

Paper was made from the papyrus plant by the following means. After stripping off the bark, the interior pith was cut into thin strips, placed side by side with a little overlap, and a second layer of strips was placed upon the first at right angles. The two layers were hammered together, perhaps without the use of any adhesive other than the papyrus plant's own sap, and the paper was then polished for use. A number of sheets, each called a *kollema*, were pasted together in a roll. The horizontal fibers of the single *kollemata* were generally on the inside of the roll, which is called the *recto*. The sheets whose fibers ran vertically were the outside of the roll, the *verso*. The only exception to this means of joining the horizontal to the vertical fibers was the outermost sheet of papyrus on the roll, called the *protokollon*, on which the inside fibers ran vertically (at a right angle to the rest of the roll) in order to protect the interior fibers of the roll.

The recto, or inside of the roll, was customarily used for writing and, whenever the purchaser needed to draft a letter, he would cut off as much as he required from the roll. Though it is unusual for a document to be continued on the verso, a new document was often written on the verso, after the recto had been used previously for another document.

---

[118] Letters 38.30; 42.2f. See Henry A. Steen, "Les Clichés," pp. 157f.

[119] See the collection by C. B. Welles of seventy-five of these diplomatic inscriptions (*Royal Correspondence*).

[120] E.g., see PTebt III, pt.1, 709, a letter in which the police

and other village officials of Tali are informed of the name of the subcontractor for the sale of papyrus at their village, and they are instructed to assist him in case any infringement of the monopoly is detected.

[121] See N. Lewis, *Life in Egypt*, pp. 128f.

213

Delivery instructions (envelope information) were written on the backside (verso) after the letter had been written on the front side (recto) and had been folded or rolled and tied for delivery.

Prior to Graeco-Roman times, a common implement used for writing on papyrus was a reed that was split to act as a brush. During the Graeco-Roman rule of Egypt, reeds were cut to a point and split like a quill-pen.[122] Ink was a black carbon (charcoal), kept in a dried cake that the scribe touched with his moistened pen. Native Egyptians, accustomed to writing Demotic rather than Greek, wrote in broad strokes and continued, at least in some cases, to use a brush instead of a pen during Graeco-Roman times.[123]

(b) Postal Service

1) *Government postal service.* The first organized postal system with an elaborate network of highways and relay stations was established by the Persians or perhaps by their recent precursors, the Assyrians. The Persian postal service dates to the sixth century BCE, when Cyrus set up a pony express system with relay stations at intervals that could be covered by a running horse in one day. The courier could obtain a fresh horse at each station and, if necessary, a night relay could be added. In addition to carrying official communiques, often of a military nature, the system was also used to transport the king and his officials. Upkeep of the 1,700 mile relay chain was borne, and services provided, by the people through whose territory it passed.[124]

Herodotus' admiration for the Persian relay service was so glowing that it is retained and applied to the modern post: "Neither rain nor snow nor heat nor gloom of night stays these couriers from the swift completion of their appointed rounds."[125] The Greek general, Xenophon, spoke with equal praise when he said the Persian courier covered his course more swiftly than cranes could fly the route.[126] The courier's rapid course is a metaphor for the shortness of life in the biblical book of Job (9:25). And, in Esther, the Persian system is described in connection with the swift dispatch of the counter order which rescued the Jews from their persecutors: "The writing was in the name of King Ahasuerus and sealed with the king's ring, and letters were sent by mounted couriers riding on swift horses that were used in the king's service, bred from the royal stud" (8:10).

Unlike Persia, classical Greece had no organized postal system. Individual cities maintained messengers and ships for diplomatic and military correspondence. In the east, however, the Persian post served as a model for Alexander the Great and his successors. The actual network was reorganized by Antigonus I and continued under the Seleucids and Romans. Alexander's successors in Egypt, the Ptolemies, adopted the idea of the transport system for officials but made improvements in mail delivery. They established two primary mail routes and systems. One, which ran north and south and followed the Nile, was an express post that employed mounted couriers in a relay chain. The second, which relied on foot messengers for mail and a camel service for parcels, was slower and ran cross-country. A Nile boat system also seems to have transported parcels during the reign of the Ptolemies.[127]

The best organized postal system in antiquity was the Roman *cursus publicus* established by the first emperor, Augustus. Initially, Augustus had organized a relay system of foot messengers in Italy and the west. But apparently because of the postal system he found in the east, the whole system was changed. He introduced relay stations which provided horses for mounted couriers so that a single messenger could cover the whole distance. Later, couriers thundered down highways in chariots and all other travelers had to give up the right of way.

Though developed in a manner analogous to that employed by the Persians and the Hellenistic monarchies of Alexander's successors, the excellent condition and the extensive network of the highway system, as well as the distance markers and the spacing of stations and inns, made the Roman system even more efficient than its precursors. Indeed, the word "post" is derived from the Latin *positus*, which means "fixed" or "placed" and refers to the fixed posts or stations in the relay system.[128]

A major function of the *cursus publicus* was to carry military dispatches but, in a manner comparable to the Persian and Hellenistic systems, the organization was also used for troop movements and for the transport of officials, both of which took advantage of the services rendered at the relay stations and inns. Earlier, messages were carried by imperial *tabellarii* (freedmen or slaves employed as state couriers), but in important cases, trusted soldiers, especially the emperor's *speculatores*, were used. In the second century CE, the *frumentarii* took over the service and combined the delivery of

---

[122] This kind of pen, the κάλαμος, would have been used by the New Testament authors (see 3 John 13).

[123] See the introductory comments to letter 20.

[124] See W. L. Westermann, "On Inland Transportation," pp. 364–87; M. Rostovtzeff, "Angariae," pp. 249–58; "Postal Service," in *Oxford Classical Dictionary*, 2d ed., p. 325.

[125] *Herodotus* 8.98.

[126] Xenophon *Cyropaedia* 8.6.17–18.

[127] See F. Preisigke, "Die Ptolemaische Staatspost," pp. 241–77.

[128] The word "mail" originated several centuries later and referred originally to the leather bag which the postman carried. Eventually, the name was applied to the contents of the bag. See Laurin Zilliacus, *From Pillar to Post*, pp. 10, 13 and 19.

confidential mail with the work of a secret police. Tiberianus, of the "Tiberianus Archive" in this collection, had the military title of speculator and was involved in the delivery of military post.[129]

2) *Private postal service.* Throughout the period described above, from the time of Cyrus into the Roman empire, the postal system was created by rulers only to serve public or government ends, to carry military post and to serve the various levels of administrative correspondence or other state business. To be sure, officials often used public service to carry private correspondence, despite official fulminations. Sometimes they were even persuaded to use the service for other people's mail. But, strictly speaking, there was no state post for private citizens.

Tabellarii were employed as couriers by companies and important private citizens during the Roman period. To reduce costs, friends sometimes shared the services of such couriers. Wealthy Roman families used trusted slaves as their couriers, especially when confidential messages were dispatched. Wealthy Egyptian Greeks also used trusted letter carriers, either servants or employees. But the average letter writer, who was unable to avail himself either of the government post or of a trusted, personal courier, was dependent on traveling business men (e.g., those traveling in camel caravans) or friends and passing strangers who happened to be going in the same direction as the letter.[130]

There is considerable evidence in the present letter collection of the unreliability of this kind of postal service. In a number of letters, for example, the sender provides a description of slaves, animals, or parcel post sent to the recipient, which reads like a modern shipping list.[131] The importance of such "packing lists" is confirmed by those letters in which the addressor acknowledges receipt of parcel post and lists the goods that have arrived.[132] Fear of the carrier's theft or negligence, including one example of actual accusation, is indicated in the following examples: "I sent the breadbasket to you by means of Taurinos, the camel driver; regarding which, please send word to me that you received it" (letter 94.3–6); "Receive from the one who brings this letter to you a basket and write back to me what you find in it" (letter 112.5–8); "I wrote to you often, and the negligence of those who carry (the letters) has accused us falsely as negligent (letter 115b.12–14)."[133]

Negligence in the delivery of goods could also arise because of the poor judgment of one's own people, as correspondence from a certain Appianos indicates: "When one dispatches even the smallest load, he ought to send it with a letter stating what has been sent and by what carrier. And the goods which you dispatched were not so many as to require a man and a donkey to leave their work, only four baskets of rotten figs" (PFlor II 176.2ff. [256 CE]).

The following statement of a recent recruit, Apolinaris, illustrates the practical correlation of letter writing and the availability of someone who was traveling in the direction of the letter: "And when I found someone who was journeying to you from Cyrene, I thought it a necessity to inform you about my welfare. . . . If you do not find someone coming to me, write to Socrates and he will transmit it to me" (letter 104a.5–7, 14–16). The same writer acknowledges dependence upon a passing stranger in a second letter to his mother (letter 104b.13f.). This was the customary practice for the delivery of private letters. On the other hand, there is evidence that soldiers could avail themselves of state postal service for private correspondence. For example, the outside address of letter 103a indicates that another recruit, a certain Apion, who also had been recently shipped to Italy from Egypt, sent his letter by military post to his regiment in Alexandria, from which it would be forwarded to the writer's father in Philadelphia. It is not clear why our former recruit did not use this service.[134]

The three letters from the two aforementioned recruits are so similar in writing, style, and contents to other Graeco-Egyptian letters that the scribes who wrote them must have been trained in Egypt. Though it is possible that Apion wrote his own letter, it is obvious that Apolinaris dictated his correspondence to an *amanuensis* because there is a marked difference in the script of his two letters.

(c) Scribes and Messengers

The extensive amount of papyrus correspondence at all levels of Egyptian society suggests that illiteracy was not as great in the ancient world, even in the smaller towns and villages of Egypt, as we thought only a century ago. To be sure, we can not always tell whether the addressor was actually writing the correspondence, but the number of grammatical and spelling errors indicate that in many cases the addressor was also probably the scribe. For example, though Lucius Bellenus Gemellus was clearly a shrewd old farmer

---

[129] For more on speculator and frumentarius, see the introduction to letters 109–12.

[130] See J. G. Winter, *Life and Letters*, pp. 82f.

[131] See letters 16.3–14 and 17.3–5, 9–11. See also POxy I 116.2–20 (II CE).

[132] E.g., see letters 49.1ff.; 64.3ff.; 65.5ff.; 110.5–9.

[133] Similarly, if the suggested reading is correct in PMich VIII 500.11f. (II CE), the letter writer states that he has sent the letter in duplicate, each copy entrusted to a different traveler, in order to insure delivery. See also the notice of something sent, and the sender's apparent fear that it did not arrive, in POxy XII 1488.3ff. (II CE).

[134] Letter 13 was also sent because someone was traveling in the direction of the recipient. Even though the addressor,

and business man, grammatical and spelling atrocities abound in his letters (see letters 95–98). The likelihood that Gemellus wrote his own letters is strengthened by the shaky and nearly illegible writing of PFay 118, which was written when Gemellus was seventy-seven years old (the same year in which he died). Similar kinds of errors are characteristic of letters written by Apollonios, who was a younger brother of Ptolemy the recluse and who, for a while, was the older brother's scribe.[135]

Even if literacy was more common than we imagined previously, Naphtali Lewis is surely right in stating, at least in connection with smaller towns and villages, that the cultured few lived surrounded by the illiterate many.[136] The majority could hardly trace their signatures clumsily at the end of legal documents and letters. These people paid professional scribes to draft communications on their behalf. The practice passes undetected in private correspondence. But whenever scribes were employed to draft official letters or legal documents on a person's behalf, they were apparently required to indicate that they were writing for someone who was illiterate. Thus, after stating his own name, immediately preceding the farewell, the scribe would state that he had written the document on the addressor's behalf, because the addressor was illiterate.[137]

Lewis notes that people still bring letters to be answered, as well as contracts to be drawn up and signed, to scribes in the Near and Middle East. About the only major difference between the present and the past is that scribes now sit at a small portable table near a main thoroughfare, whereas in Graeco-Roman Egypt they sat cross-legged, writing in their laps. There, "in the street," as a number of Oxyrhynchos contracts state, most of the villagers' paperwork was done. Though the educational level of scribes varied, most leave the impression of being merely literate rather than highly educated. Their documents consist largely of stock phrases and clichés; not only the contracts but also private letters, many of which are little more than collections of greetings and good wishes, use standard conventions and clichés.[138]

The scribe was sometimes hired to deliver the letter as well as to write it. The messenger would have been somewhat more trustworthy in these cases—both as interpreter of the letter's contents and as letter carrier—than messengers who merely happened to be traveling toward the letter's destination. In the case of the messengers of the wealthy and

eminent, we may assume that couriers tended to be even more conversant with the letter's contents and capable of adding supplementary news by word of mouth. Chan-Hie Kim has examined twenty-five letters of invitation, for example, in which the customary opening address/greeting are omitted. They seem to have been carried by a messenger who saluted each guest orally, before reading the message of invitation that was left with each guest.[139]

In one of the letters of this collection, Simale concludes her correspondence by instructing Zenon to find out any additional information from the letter carrier: "The rest please learn from the man who brings you the letter. For he is no stranger to us" (letter 10.14f.).

(d) Addresses and Dockets of Receipt

After a letter was written, it was folded into a long, narrow strip, doubled and tied around the middle with a thread of papyrus fiber, then sealed with clay. The name of the person to whom the letter was addressed was written in large letters on this backside of the letter (formerly the outside or verso of the roll). A further direction could be added, whereby the recipient's village or city was named.

The original editor of letter 90 in our collection states that the delivery instructions of the letter, while imperfect, are among the longest that we have in private letters: "Deliver to her father Pompeius from Herennia . . . to the father of Onomastos(?) . . . deliver to the house of Nemesous." This editor suggests that since private letters were carried by friends or private messengers, they rarely mentioned the town or village of their destination, still more rarely the house to which they were to be delivered.[140] The editor, however, refers to various exceptions. Another example that contains more information than what he says was customary may be cited from our collection: "To Dionysios, who is also called Amois, son of Ptolemy and brother of Apollonios the village secretary of Tholthis, who is staying near Theon, the son of Ischyrion."[141]

The dispatch of administrative (state bureaucratic) correspondence was frequently accompanied by fuller envelope information. For example, in addition to specifying the name of the recipient and his village or city of residence, an abstract of the letter's contents was sometimes stated. A number of the Zenon archive letters which were addressed to Apollonios during the period when Zenon functioned as his

---

Alexandros, was a soldier with more status than our two young recruits, he sent a letter with Mys, who happened to be traveling to Zenon, with whom Alexandros wanted to correspond.

[135] See letters 41 and 42 and the introductory comments to letters 34–42.

[136] See Lewis, *Life in Egypt*, p. 82.

[137] See the "Illiteracy Formula" in Exler, *The Form*, pp. 124–27.

[138] Lewis, *Life in Egypt*, p. 82.

[139] "The Papyrus Invitation," pp. 391–402.

[140] See Winter, *Life and Letters*, pp. 82f.

[141] Verso of letter 67. See also the verso of letters 94; 103a; PTebt III 583; POxy III 529.

private secretary contain this full verso information. The abtract of contents may have facilitated the sorting and identification of correspondence.

In addition to the sender's instructions on the verso, the recipient would often docket the receipt of administrative correspondence by writing the date (and, in the case of Zenon, the place) of the letter's reception, the name of the sender, and the subject of the letter (see letters 3–5, 8–21, 24–25, 27–28). Like the sender's abstract of contents, this information may have facilitated filing and the easy retrieval of correspondence.

In the third century BCE, Zenon docketed receipt information on the verso, on the same side as the envelope information. Menches, a village secretary in the late second century BCE, docketed the receipt of correspondence on the top of the recto, immediately above the beginning of the letter (see letter 49). We can tell by the extensive abbreviation in Menche's dockets that administrative record keeping encouraged its own kind of shorthand. Zenon's filing technique was especially sophisticated. Because he varied the sequence of docket items from one chronological period to another, we are able to identify the period within which a letter was written and received, even when the date is fragmented.[142]

5. FIRST DRAFTS AND APPENDED (QUOTED) LETTERS

Letters were abbreviated or modified as a result of being quoted in, or appended to, another letter. A comparable phenomenon is the abbreviation which appears in first drafts. In his study of letter-opening formulas, Exler lists several examples which are abbreviated versions of the standard address forms, e.g., "A" and "To B." Though he lists these phrases as if they were independent, stock conventions, he admits that they are probably only abbreviated expressions of the standard forms.[143] It can be demonstrated in almost every case that these anomalous forms appear in first drafts or in letters quoted within another letter. Wilcken concurs when he states: "Da das praskript unvollstandig ist, so liegt eine Kopie vor."[144] Though it is not possible to identify patterns of abbreviation too specifically, it is clear that the opening and closing of the letter were most vulnerable to abbreviation/omission.

(a) Abbreviations and Omissions in First Drafts

Fortunately, in one case, we have the fair copy to compare with the rough draft and it shows that the abbreviated opening formula arose only because of being a first draft. Apart from minor grammatical corrections in letter 46, the message portion of letters 46 and 47.11–24 are identical. However, the initial address in 47.11 is a considerably truncated version of the address in 46.1f. The letters in number 6, five rough drafts by Zenon, are all concerned with the same message, which was sent to five different recipients. Note that in each case the opening formula is reduced to the recipient's name and that the greeting is omitted altogether (see lines 1, 16, 26, 40 and 45). However, the closing farewell is expressed in the first three letters and omitted only in the last two. A health wish is stated only in the letter opening of the first and third letters. It is not likely, even in the fair copies, that Zenon expressed the wish for health in the three remaining letters. It is noteworthy that by the time Zenon had written the fifth letter, he avoided the redundancy of rewriting the common part of the message by stating at the beginning of the body, "the same" (line 45).

(b) Abbreviations and Omissions in Appended Letters

Letters which were appended to, or quoted in, another letter were subject to some of the same abbreviations that we have noted in connection with first drafts. When state administrative instructions passed through the various bureaucratic levels, a "chain letter" frequently resulted; each respective official attached a copy of the order received at that point to his own forwarding note. Five or six attached letters would sometimes reach the last official in the chain. In these cases, the opening formula was often shortened in the appended letters to the form, "To B," and the word of farewell was omitted. An analogous abbreviation of the opening formula is found in the subscription ($\dot{\upsilon}\pi o\gamma\rho\acute{\alpha}\phi\eta$) appended to the bottoms of petitions, i.e., a note written by the king or another official instructing a subordinate to investigate the petitioner's complaint. Unfortunately, there are no examples of lengthy administrative chain letters in our collection (see letter 51, which has one appended administrative letter). We may illustrate the practice, however, by means of PTebt I 30 (115 BCE), a text which contains three appended letters and a subscription from state scribes (regarding their investigation of the petition enclosed in the correspondence), in addition to the covering letter. In the covering letter, both the opening and closing conventions are intact. In the first and second appended letters, the opening formula is retained but the farewell is omitted. The third enclosed letter, which is a petition and the cause of all the correspondence, appears to be quoted fully. In the scribal subscription, the farewell is omitted and the opening formula is abbreviated to the form, "From the secretaries."

In this collection, letters 12, 17, 27 and 51 each contain

---

[142] See John L. White, "A Note," pp. 129–31.
[143] Exler, *The Form*, pp. 66f.

[144] U. Wilcken, *Chrestomathie*, p. 252, n. 17.

one quoted letter and in each case the full text of the original letter appears to be enclosed. The only other example of appended correspondence is number 18, in which Panakestor encloses two pieces of correspondence in a letter to Zenon. The first appended letter is a note of disapproval from Apollonios, the common superior of Zenon and Panakestor, regarding Panakestor's management of certain agricultural matters. The second appended letter is a copy of Panakestor's response to the criticism of Apollonios. The opening formula is abbreviated in both appended letters—"A" in the first and "To B" in the second—and the word of farewell is omitted in both.[145]

6. CONCLUSION

The following remarks are offered in anticipation of the use of this analysis and letter collection for studying the early Christian letter tradition. We begin with summary reflections on ancient Greek letter writing and then discuss various respects in which the documentary letter tradition is relevant for understanding New Testament and Patristic letters.

We suggested above that Greek letter writing originated in diplomatic or military injunctions. Owing to the inexpensive cost of papyrus in Graeco-Roman Egypt, however, letters were written eventually by all levels of society. Though most letters were prompted by some specific need, a number have survived from Roman Egypt which were written for the more general purpose of maintaining family ties or personal friendship. Ancient Greek and Latin rhetoricians regarded the latter use of letter writing, especially when expressed in a cultivated manner, as the most authentic form of correspondence.

In general, ancient epistolary theorists regarded treatises in epistolary form (letter essays) as artificial and inconsistent with the conversational intent of letters. Nonetheless, the use of the letter to address broad constituencies on technical or philosophical subjects increased steadily in late antiquity. Moreover, when the letter was used as a written substitute for popular oral forms of "street philosophy," the letter was not really an artificial medium. Cynic-Stoic philosophy employed conversational forms of oral instruction like diatribe, which had a natural affinity with the conversational char-

acter of the letter. Rudolf Bultmann noted that the dialogical element in St. Paul's letters (especially in Romans) was related to the Cynic-Stoic diatribe.[146]

Certain scholars have suggested more broadly that the length and instructional nature of Paul's letters (and the New Testament letters in general) is more like the literary letter tradition than the documentary letters represented by this collection. For example, Klaus Berger recently argued against my use of documentary correspondence for studying New Testament letters by contending that ancient philophical letters of instruction are a more appropriate body of comparative correspondence for the New Testament letters.[147]

I agree with several of Berger's suggestions about the similarities between literary letters of instruction and the New Testament letters. But, as suggested in the introduction of this book, the most essential issue is not the determination of the most exact body of ancient correspondence to use in studying the early Christian letter tradition. The first issue, as Paul Schubert suggests, is to understand Christian letters as letters.[148] We should not go off looking for this or that parallel phrase in ancient letters which corresponds to what we find in the New Testament and Patristic letters. Our initial task is to discern the essential purposes that letters serve and to map out the epistolary contours customarily used to express such functions. For this purpose, we need to understand ancient Greek letter writing in general, and ordinary letters have a significant role to play in such comprehension.

The significance of this procedure may be illustrated by one of the more common and important epistolary motifs, the use of the letter as a substitute for the writer's actual presence. Because the New Testament and Patristic letters were written by people either in their capacity as apostles or in some other role as Christian leaders, they convey a conception of presence and authority comparable to the philosophers' letters of instruction to their students. However, this similarity is not entirely adequate to understand the epistolary use of presence as it applies to the Christian letter tradition. A general conception of epistolary presence, based on a broad spectrum of epistolary information, is relevant to the discussion of this question.

We suggested above that ancient Greek letters served three broad functions: the maintenance of contact, the communication of information, and the statement of request or

---

[145] There are no other examples of embedded letters in the collection. Though 113 is an example of two letters on the same piece of papyrus, the second of the two letters is not appended, nor are the two letters rough drafts. In the first of the the two letters, Sempronius writes to his mother and in the second he writes to a brother. It is clear from the second letter, in which the brother is chided for treating their mother shabbily, that the mother was illiterate and

that, even though the first letter was addressed to the mother, the sender expected both letters to be read only by the brother.

[146] *Der Stil der Paulinischen Predigt,* pp. 2–12, 64–71.

[147] "Hellenistische Gattungen im Neuen Testament," pp. 1327–40.

[148] "Form and Function of the Pauline Letters," pp. 372–77.

command. Moreover, we proposed a correlation between these reasons for writing and the tripartite structure of the letter. Namely, the keeping-in-touch aspect of letter writing (maintenance of contact), which reveals the general character of the correspondents' relationship toward each other, comes to expression primarily through conventions that open or conclude the letter. The more specific occasions which prompted the message of the letter, and which are to be identified with the two remaining epistolary functions, are expressed primarily through stock phrases of the letter's body.

It is clear, then, that the degree and type of friendship shared by the correspondents comes most naturally to expression in the opening and closing conventions of the letter. The writer's presence and disposition in writing is conveyed to the recipient(s) in these two parts of the letter's structure. In the case of St. Paul's letters, the religious nature of the epistolary setting is indicated by Paul's substitution of an opening grace blessing for the opening greeting and the expression of thanksgiving to God as a surrogate form of the conventional wish for health.[149] The specific character of Paul's authoritative presence is communicated by Paul's description of himself as "apostle" or an equivalent designation.[150]

So far, the expression of Paul's authoritative presence is analogous to what one finds in philosophical letters of instruction. However, when Paul addresses his churches with such important religious terms as "saints," "called," "sanctified," and "beloved," it is clear there is a more egalitarian aspect to Paul's sense of presence with his churches than in a teacher's letter to his students. The equality Paul shared with his congregations is also indicated at major transitional points in Paul's letters where he refers to his recipients as "brethren."[151] The broader epistolary tradition is probably no more helpful than the philosophical letters in providing exact parallels for the unexpected form of Paul's apostolic presence. But at least the components of his presence, authority and equality, are represented by the broader epistolary spectrum. And a knowledge of both aspects is important to the interpretation of Paul's expression of presence in his correspondence.

The broader epistolary tradition is also useful in illuminating another aspect of the sender's epistolary presence, the form of presence that belongs to the body of the letter. We noted in the above analysis that certain phrases in the letter's opening and closing could be employed with a different nuance to serve the business aspect of the letter. For example, we noted in connection with the keeping-in-touch aspect of letter writing that the writer sometimes indicated aggravation at the recipient's failure to answer letters. On occasion, however, the same formula could express the sender's dissatisfaction with the recipient's negligence in business. Similarly, we noted that the sender's statement near the close of the letter, that the sender would be "favored" if the recipient attended to something the sender wanted, was a convention that could convey either the sender's wish for the recipient's welfare (health wish) or as a body-concluding formula for "nailing down" a request that the sender had made earlier in the body.

Though these dual purpose formulas may be used either to maintain the correspondents' relationship or to further the business aspect of the correspondence, there is a similarity of function in the two uses. In both cases the sender communicates a form of presence and, generally speaking, conveys his disposition toward the recipient. We referred in the analysis to a spectrum of means whereby, at the close of the body, letter writers pleaded, cajoled, and threatened recipients to attend to some duty earlier specified in the letter. This, too, is a form of epistolary presence, one colored by the sender's attempt to persuade the recipient into a certain course of action.

We find this aspect of epistolary presence also at the close of the body of Paul's letters. It is apparent in Paul's appeal to one or another aspect of his apostolic presence that he used his apostolic authority to persuade recipients into adopting his prescribed course of action. Robert Funk observed in this connection that Paul often indicated his reason for writing, his intention to dispatch an apostolic courier to represent him in the situation envisioned by the letter and his desire or intention to make a personal visit to the church. According to Funk, all three aspects of Paul's apostolic presence (apostolic letter, apostolic messenger, and Paul's own visit) tended to converge in the closing section of the body.[152] Funk notes that in actual practice only two of the three aspects of Paul's apostolic presence come to expression in an individual letter. Either Paul calls attention to the apostolic character of his letter or he recommends the messenger who carries the letter, but he does not refer to both on the same occasion.

---

149 See Rom 1:1–14; 1 Cor 1:1–9; 2 Cor 1:1–7 (a blessing replaces the thanksgiving prayer); Gal 1:1–10 (Paul's strong statement of dissatisfaction replaces the thanksgiving prayer); Phil 1:1–11; 1 Thess 1:1–10 and Phlm 1:1–7.

150 See Rom 1:1–6; 1 Cor 1:1; 2 Cor 1:1; Gal 1:1; Phil 1:1; Phlm 1:1.

151 See Rom 1:13; 7:1, 4; 8:12; 10:1; 11:25; 12:1; 15:14–15, 30; 16:16; 1 Cor 1:10–11, 26; 2:1; 3:1; 4:6; 7:24, 29; 10:1; 11:2, 33; 12:1; 14:6, 20, 26, 39; 15:1, 50, 58; 16:15. The use of "brothers" is equally extensive in the remaining letters of Paul.

152 "The Apostolic *Parousia*," pp. 258–61.

The letter came to the fore and was referred to explicitly when, temporarily, Paul was unable to send an apostolic messenger to represent him. Contrariwise, when the messenger was available, and is identified in the letter, there was no need to refer to the letter itself.[153]

We could refer in a comparable manner to Paul's use of parenetic instruction as a form of apostolic presence in the section of the body which usually follows Paul's announcement of a visit.[154] But these examples are sufficient to indicate the general shape that a letter writer's presence could take within his correspondence with a certain constituency. Hopefully, the various nuances illustrated in connection with Paul's sense of epistolary presence show the value of a broad conception of epistolary function and structure.

No body of comparative data, even the extensive documentary letter tradition preserved on papyrus, is adequate to illustrate the creativity of a letter writer like St. Paul, who adapted episto conventions to convey a special kind of function. However, the peculiar character of his epistolary genius, as well as the genius of other great letter writers of antiquity, may be better ascertained and evaluated by means of a broad knowledge of letter writing in antiquity. Such knowledge ought, ideally, to include familiarity with the various branches of the literary letter tradition, Hellenistic letters of diplomacy, the varied dimensions of the documentary letter tradition, and any other major corpus of letters. A knowledge of these large epistolary divisions, allied with a knowledge of the major social and religious dimensions of early Christianity itself, should prepare us for analyzing the early Christian letter tradition in a meaningful and productive manner.

---

[153] "The Apostolic *Parousia*," pp. 258–61.

[154] For example, see my analysis of parenesis as an expression of Paul's apostolicity in "Saint Paul and the Apostolic Letter Tradition," pp. 438–42.

Aharoni, Yohanan and Michael Avi-Yonah. *The Macmillan Bible Atlas*. Rev. ed. New York: Macmillan Publishing Co., 1977.

Bell, Harold I. *Egypt From Alexander the Great to the Arab Conquest*. Oxford: Clarendon Press, 1948.

_____. "Hellenic Culture in Egypt." *Journal of Egyptian Archaeology* 8 (1922): 139–55.

_____. *Jews and Christians in Egypt: The Jewish Troubles in Alexandria and the Athanasian Controversy*. (=PLond VI). London: Oxford University Press, 1924.

Berger, Klaus. "Hellenistische Gattungen im Neuen Testament." Pp. 1031–1432 in *Aufstieg und Niedergang der römischen Welt* 25.2, edited by Hildegard Temporini and Wolfgang Haase. Berlin and New York: Walter de Gruyter, 1984.

Berneker, Erich Karl. *Zur Geschichte der Prozesseinleitung im Ptolemäischen Recht*. Inaug. diss., Munich. Ansbach: C. Brugel & Sohn, 1930.

_____. *Zur griechischen Rechtsgeschichte*. Darmstadt: Wissenschaftliche Buchgesellschaft, 1968.

Bevan, Edwyn. *A History of Egypt Under the Ptolemaic Dynasty*. London: Methuen & Co., 1927.

Boak, A. E. R. "The Anagraphai of the Grapheion of Tebtunis and Kerkesouchon Oros. Pap. Michigan 622." *Journal of Egyptian Archaeology* 9 (1923): 164–67.

Boak, A. E. R. and Enoch E. Peterson. *Karanis, Topographical and Architectural Report of Excavations during the Seasons 1924–28*. Ann Arbor: University of Michigan Press, 1931.

Bouché-LeClercq, Auguste. *Histoire des Lagides*. 4 vols. Paris: E. Leroux, 1903–1907.

_____. *Histoire des Seleucides, 323–64 avant J.-C.* 2 vols. Paris: E. Leroux, 1913–14.

Brownson, Carleton L. *Xenephon*, vol. 1: *Hellenica*, Books I–V. Loeb Classical Library. London: William Heinemann, 1918.

Bultmann, Rudolf. *Der Stil der paulinischen Predigt und die kynischstoische Diatribe. Forschungen zur Religion und Literatur des Alten und Neuen Testaments* 13. Göttingen: Vandenhoeck & Ruprecht, 1910.

Buss, Martin. "Principles for Morphological Criticism: with special reference to Letter Form." Pp. 71–86 in *Orientation by Disorientation: Studies in Literary Criticism*. Presented in honor of William A. Beardslee. Pittsburgh, PA: Pickwick Press, 1980.

Calderini, Aristide. "Ricerche sul regime della acque nell' Egitto greco-romano." *Aegyptus* 1 (1920): 37–62, 189–216.

Collart, M. Paul. "La Révolte de la Thébaïde en 88 avant J. C." Pp. 273–82 in *Recueil D'Etudes Egyptologiques dédiées à la Mémoire de Jean-François Champollion*. Paris: Librairie ancienne honoré Champion, 1922.

_____. "Une nouvelle *Tabella Defixionis* d'Égypte." *Revue de Philologie de Littérature et d'Histoire anciennes* 4 (1930): 248–56.

Collomp, Paul. *Recherches sur la chancellerie et la diplomatique des Lagides*. 1925. Reprint. Milano: Cisalpino Colliardica, 1977.

Crawford, Dorothy J. *Kerkeosiris. An Egyptian Village in the Ptolemaic Period*. Cambridge, MA: Cambridge University Press, 1971.

_____. "Ptolemy, Ptah and Apis in Hellenistic Memphis." Pp. 1–42 in *Studies on Ptolemaic Memphis*, edited by Dorothy J. Crawford, Jan Quaeqebeur and Willy Clarysse. *Studia Hellenistica* 24. Louvain, 1980.

Dahl, Nils A. "Letter." Pp. 538–40 in *Interpreter's Dictionary of the Bible*, supplementary volume, edited by Keith Crim. Nashville: Abingdon Press, 1976.

Deissmann, Adolf. *Bible Studies*. Translated by A. Grieve. Edinburgh: T. & T. Clark, 1901.

_____. *Light from the Ancient East*. 1922. Reprint of English translation of 4th German edition. Grand Rapids: Baker Book House, 1978.

Dion, Paul. "The Aramaic 'Family Letter' and Related Epistolary Forms in other Oriental Languages and in Hellenistic Greek." *Semeia* 22 (1982): 59–76.

Doty, W. G. "The Classification of Epistolary Literature." *Catholic Biblical Quarterly* 31 (1969): 183–99.

Edgar, C. C. "The Problem of Dating." Pp. 50–57 in *University of Michigan Papyri*, vol. 1: *Zenon Papyri in the Univesity of Michigan Collection*. Ann Arbor: University of Michigan Press, 1931.

Eitrem, S. and Leiv Amundsen. "Three Private Letters from the Oslo Collection." *Aegyptus* 31 (1951): 177–83.

Exler, Francis X. J. *The Form of the Ancient Greek Letter. A Study in Greek Epistolography*. Washington, D.C.: Catholic University of America, 1923.

Feldman, Louis H. *Josephus*, vol. 9: *Jewish Antiquities, Books XVIII–XX*. Loeb Classical Library. Cambridge, MA: University of America, 1923.

Forester, R., ed. *Libanii Opera*, vol. 9 (=Pseudo Libanius Handbook) Leipzig: B. G. Teubner, 1927.

Funk, Robert W. The Apostolic *Parousia*: Form and Significance." Pp. 249–68 in *Christian History and Interpretation: Studies Presented to John Knox*, edited by W. R. Farmer, C. F. D. Moule and R. R. Niebuhr. Cambridge, MA: Cambridge University Press, 1967.

Geer, Russel M. *Diodorus of Sicily*, vol 10, books 19.66–110 and 20. Loeb Classical Library. Cambridge, MA: Harvard University Press, 1963.

Ghedini, Guiseppe. *Lettere cristiane dai papiri greci del III e del IV secolo*. Milano: Supplementi ad *Aegyptus*, 1923.

Giomini, R. and M. S. Celentano, eds. *C. Julius Victor. Ars Rhetorica*. Leipzig: B. G. Teubner, 1980.

Godley, A. D. *Herodotus*, vol. 1, books I and II. Loeb Classical Library. Cambridge, MA: Harvard University Press, 1966.

_____. *Herodotus*, vol. 2, books III and IV. Loeb Classical Library. Rev. ed. Cambridge, MA: Harvard University Press, 1963.

_____. *Herodotus*, vol. 4, books VIII–IX. Loeb Classical Library. Rev. ed. Cambridge, MA: Harvard University Press, 1961.

Grenfell, B. P. "A New Papyrus concerning the Revolt of the Thebaid in B.C. 88." *Revue des études grecques* 32 (1919): 251–55.

_____, ed. *Revenue Laws of Ptolemy Philadelphus*. London: Oxford University Press, 1896.

Grenfell, B. P., A. S. Hunt, and D. G. Hogarth. *Fayum Towns and their Papyri*. London: Egypt Exploration Fund, 1900.

Grenfell, B. P., A. S. Hunt, and J. G. Smyly. "The Land of Kerkeosiris and its Holders." Appendix I, pp. 538–80 in *The Tebtunis Papyri*, vol. 1. London: University of California Publications, 1902.

Gueraud, O. ENTEYΞΕΙΣ. *Requetes et plaintes addressees au Roi d' Egypte au IIIe siecle avant J. C.* Cairo: Publications de la Societe royale egyptienne papyrologie, 1931.

Gummere, Richard M. *The Epistles of Seneca*. 2 vols. Rev. ed. Loeb Classical Library. Cambridge, MA: Harvard University Press, 1928, 1932.

Hercher, R. *Epistolographi Graeci*. 1873. Reprint of Paris edition. Amsterdam: A. M. Hakkert, 1965.

Hock, Ronald F. and Edward N. O'Neil. *The Chreia in Ancient Rhetoric*, vol. 1: *The Progymnasmata*. Atlanta: Scholars Press, 1986.

Hunt, A. S. and C. C. Edgar. *Select Papyri*, vol. 1: *Non-Literary Papyri Private Affairs*. Loeb Classical Library. Cambridge, MA: Harvard University Press, 1932.

_____. *Select Papyri*, vol. 2: *Non-Literary Papyri Public Documents*. Loeb Classical Library. Cambridge, MA: Harvard University Press, 1934.

Jasny, Naum. *The Wheats of Classical Antiquity*. Baltimore: The Johns Hopkins Press, 1944.

Jones, Horace L. *The Geography of Strabo*, vol. 8, book 17. Loeb Classical Library. Cambridge, MA: Harvard University Press, 1949.

Jones, W. H. S. *Pausanias. Description of Greece*, vol. 1, books I and II. Loeb Classical Library. London: William Heinemann, 1918.

Jouguet, Pierre. "Les Lagides et les indigènes égyptiens." *Revue belge de philologie et d'histoire* 2 (July 1923): 419–45.

_____. "Ptolémée X Soter et la révolte de la Thébaide." *Bulletin Correspondance Hellenique* 21 (1897): 141–47.

Keenan, James and John Shelton. "Introduction." Pp. 1–18 in *The Tebtunis Papyri*, vol. 4. London: Egypt Exploration Society, 1976.

Kenyon, F. G. "The Serapeum at Memphis." Pp. 1–43 in *Greek Papyri in the British Museum*, vol. 1 (PLond I). London: Oxford University Press, 1893.

_____. *Greek Papyri in the British Museum*, vol. 2, nos. 139–484 (PLond II). London: Oxford University Press, 1898.

Keyes, Clinton W. "The Greek Letter of Introduction." *American Journal of Philology* 56 (1935): 28–44.

Kim, Chan-Hie. *The Familiar Letter of Recommendation*. Missoula, MT: Scholars Press, 1972.

_____. "The Papyrus Invitation." *Journal of Biblical Literature* 94 (1975): 391–402.

Koskenniemi, Heikki. *Studien zur Idee und Phraseologie des griechischen Briefes bis 400 n. Chr.* Helsinki: Akateeminen Kirjakauppa, 1956.

Lewis, Naphtali. *Life in Egypt Under Roman Rule*. Oxford: Clarendon Press, 1983.

Liddell, H. G., R. Scott, and H. S. Jones. *A Greek-English Lexicon, With a Supplement*, edited by E. A. Barber. Oxford: Clarendon Press, 1968.

Lindsay, Jack. *Daily Life in Roman Egypt*. London: Frederick Muller, Ltd., 1963.

Malherbe, Abraham J. "Ancient Epistolary Theorists." *Ohio Journal of Religious Studies* 5,2 (1977): 3–77.

Marchant, E. C. *Xenophon. Scriptura Minora* (includes *Agesilaus*). Loeb Classical Library. Reprint. Cambridge, MA: Harvard University Press, 1962.

Mayser, E. *Grammatik der griechischen Papyri aus der Ptolemäerzeit mit Einschluss der gleichzeitigen Ostraca und der in Ägypten verfassten Inschriften*. 2 vols. in 6 parts. 2d ed. Berlin: Walter de Gruyter & Co., 1923–1970.

Meecham, Henry G. *Light from Ancient Letters*. London: George Allen & Unwin, Ltd., 1923.

Meinersmann, Bernhard. *Die lateinischen Wörter und Namen in den griechischen Papyri*. Leipzig: Dieterich, 1927.

Miller, Walter. *Xenophon*, vol. 2: *Cyropaedia*, books V–VIII. Loeb Classical Library. London: William Heinemann, 1914.

Milligan, G. *Selections from the Greek Papyri*. Cambridge, MA: Cambridge University Press, 1910.

Mitteis, Ludwig and Ulrich Wilcken. *Grundzüge und Chrestomathie der Papyruskunde*. Band 1, *Historischer Teil*, 1 Hälfte: *Grundzüge*; 2 Hälfte: *Chrestomathie* (U. Wilcken). Band 2, *Juristischer Teil*, 1 Hälfte: *Grundzüge*; 2 Hälfte: *Chrestomathie* (L. Mitteis). Leipzig: B. G. Teubner, 1912.

Moulton, J. H. *A Grammar of New Testament Greek*, vol 1: *Prolegomena*. 1919. Reprint. Edinburgh: T. & T. Clark, 1967–68.

_____. *A Grammar of New Testament Greek,* vol 2: *Accidence and Word-Formation*, edited with W. F. Howard. 1919. Reprint. Edinburgh: T. & T. Clark, 1967–68.

Mullins, Terence Y. "Petition as a Literary Form." *Novum Testamentum* 5 (1962): 46–54.

Musurillo, Herbert A. *The Acts of the Pagan Martyrs. Acta Alexandrinorum*. Oxford: Clarendon Press, 1954.

Nettleship, Henry. *Contributions to Latin Lexicography*. Oxford: Clarendon Press, 1889.

Oates, J. F., R. S. Bagnall, and W. Willis. *Checklist of Editions of Greek Papyri and Ostraca*. 2d ed. *Bulletin of the American Society of Papyrologists*, Supplement 1. Missoula, MT: Scholars Press, 1978.

Otto, Walter G. *Priester und Tempel im hellenistischen Ägypten*, vol. 1. Berlin: B. G. Teubner, 1905.

_____. *Priester und Tempel im hellenistischen Ägypten*, vol. 2. Leipzig and Berlin: B. G. Teubner, 1908.

Packman, Zola M. *The Taxes in Grain in Ptolemaic Egypt: Receipts from the Granary of Diospolis Magna, 164–88 B.C.* American Studies in Papyrology 4. New Haven and Toronto: The American Society of Papyrologists, 1968.

Parássoglou, George M. "Property Records of L. Pompeius, L. F.,

Tribu Pollia, Niger." *Bulletin of the American Society of Papyrologists* 7 (1970): 87–98.

Peterson, W. *Greek Diminutives in -ION*. Weimar: R. Wagner, 1910.

Pomeroy, Sarah B. *Women in Hellenistic Egypt. From Alexander to Cleopatra*. New York: Schocken Books, 1984.

Preisigke, Friedrich. *Namenbuch enthaltend alle griechischen, lateinischen, ägyptischen, hebraischen, arabischen und sonstigen semitischen und nichtsemitischen Menschennamen, soweit sie in griechischen Urkunden (Papyri, Ostraka, Inschriften, Mumienschildern usw.) Ägyptens sich vorfinden*. Heidelberg: Selbstverlag, 1922.

———. "Die Ptolemäische Staatspost." *Klio* 8 (1907): 241–77.

———. *Wörterbuch der griechischen Papyrusurkunden mit Einschluss der griechischen Inschriften ausschriften Ostraka Mummienschilder usw. aus Ägypten*. Berlin: Selbstverlag, 1925–31.

Reich, Nathaniel Julius. "New Documents from the Serapeum of Memphis." *Mizraim* 1 (1933): 9–129.

Reil, Karl Theodor. *Beiträge zur Kenntnis des Gewerbes im hellenistischen Ägypten*. Leipzig: R. Noske, 1913. Reprint. New York: Arno Press, 1979.

Roberts, W. Rhys. *Demetrius: On Style*. Rev. ed. Loeb Classical Library. Cambridge, MA: Harvard University Press, 1932.

———. *Rhetoric*. Pp. 593–675 in *The Works of Aristotle*, vol. 2. Chicago: Brittanica Great Books, William Benton, Publisher, 1952.

Rolfe, J. C. *Quintus Curtius*, vol. 1, books I–V. Loeb Classical Library. Cambridge, MA: Harvard University Press, 1962.

Rostovtzeff, M. "Angariae." *Klio* 6 (1906): 249–58.

———. "The Foundations of Social and Economic Life in Egypt in Hellenistic Times." *Journal of Egyptian Archaeology* 6 (1920): 161–78.

———. "Instructions of a Dioecetes to a Subordinate." Pp. 66–73 in *The Tebtunis Papyri*, vol. 3, part 1, edited by A. S. Hunt and J. Gilbart Smyly. London: Oxford University Press, 1933.

———. *A Large Estate in Egypt in the Third Century B.C.* Madison: University of Wisconsin Press, 1922.

———. *The Social and Economic History of the Hellenistic World*. 3 vols. Oxford: Clarendon Press, 1941.

Rübensohn, O., ed. *Aegyptische Urkunden aus königlichen Museen in Berlin: Griechische Urkunden*, Sonderheft. *Elephantine-Papyri*. Berlin: Weidmann, 1907.

Samuel, Alan E. "P.Tebt. 703 and the Oikonomos." Pp. 451–60 in *Estralto da Studi in Onore di Eduardo Volterra*, vol. 2. Milano: A. Giuffrè, 1969.

———. *Ptolemaic Chronology*. Münchener Beiträge zur Papyrusforschung und antiken Rechtsgeschichte 43. Munich: C. H. Beck, 1962.

Schnebel, Michael. "An Agricultural Ledger in P.Bad. 95." *Journal of Egyptian Archaeology* 14 (1928): 34–45.

———. *Die Landwirtsschaft im hellenistischen Ägypten*. Münchener Beiträge zur Papyrusforschung und antiken Rechtsgeschichte. Heft 7. Munich: C. H. Beck, 1925.

Schubert, Paul. "Form and Function of the Pauline Letters." *Journal of Religion* 19 (1939): 365–77.

Schwartz, Jacques. *Les archives de Sarapion et des ses fils*. Cairo: Institut français d'archéologie orientale, 1961.

Segré, Angelo. "Note sul documento greco-egizio del grapheion (ad PSI VIII 901–918)." *Aegyptus* 7 (1926): 97–107.

———. "The Status of the Jews in Ptolemaic and Roman Egypt." *Jewish Social Studies* 6 (1944): 375–400.

Semeka, Gregor. *Ptolemäisches Prozessrecht; studien zur ptolemäischer gerichtsverfassung und zum gerichtsverfahren*. Munich: O. Beck, 1913.

Skeat, T. C. *The Reigns of the Ptolemies*. Münchener Beiträge zur Papyrusforschung und antiken Rechtsgeschichte 39. Munich: C. H. Beck, 1954.

———. "The Reigns of the Ptolemies. With Tables for Converting Egyptian Dates to the Julian System." *Mizraim* 6 (1937): 7–40.

Smith, Charles Foster. *Thucydides*, vol 4: *History of the Peloponnesian War*. Books VII–VIII. Loeb Classical Library. London: William Heinemann, 1923.

Stambaugh, John E. *Sarapis Under the Early Ptolemies*. Leiden: E. J. Brill, 1972.

Starr, Chester G. *Roman Imperial Navy, 31 B.C.–A.D. 324*. New York: Barnes & Noble Books, 1960.

Steen, Henry A. "Les Clichés épistolaries dans les Lettres sur Papyrus Grecques." *Classica et Mediaevalia* 1,2 (1938): 119–76.

Stirewalt, M. L. "A Classified Index of Terms used in reference to Letter-Writing in Greek Literature." Unpublished essay, 1975.

———. "A Survey of the Uses of Letter-Writing in Hellenistic and Jewish Communities through the New Testament Period." Unpublished essay.

Stowers, Stanley Kent. *The Diatribe and paul's Letter to the Romans*. SBL Dissertation Series 57. Chico, CA: Scholars Press, 1981.

Swarney, Paul R. *The Ptolemaic and Roman Idios Logos*. Toronto: A. M. Hakkert, 1970.

Tait, John G. "The Strategi and Royal Scribes in the Roman Period." *Journal of Egyptian Archaeology* 8 (1922): 166–73.

Taubenschlag, Raphael. *The Law of Greco-Roman Egypt in the Light of the Papyri, 332 B.C.–640 A.D.* 2d ed. Milano: Cisalpino-Goliardico, 1972.

Tcherikover, Victor A. "'The Jewish Question' in Alexandria." Pp. 25–107 in *Corpus Papyrorum Judaicarum*, vol. 2, edited with Alexander Fuks. Cambridge, MA: Harvard University Press, 1960.

———. "Palestine Under the Ptolemies (A Contribution to the Study of the Zenon Papyri)." *Mizraim* 4–5 (1937): 9–90.

———. "Prolegomena." Pp. 1–111 in *Corpus Papyrorum Judaicarum*, vol. 1, edited in collaboration with Alexander Fuks. Cambridge, MA: Harvard University Press, 1957.

Thackeray, H. St. J. *Josephus*, vol. 1: *The Life. Against Apion*. Loeb Classical Library. Cambridge, MA: Harvard University Press, 1966.

Thraede, Klaus. *Grundzüge griechisch-romischer Brieftopik*. Munich: C. H. Beck, 1970.

Titchener, Margaret Seymour. "Guardianship of Women in Egypt during the Ptolemaic and Roman Eras." Pp. 20–28 in *University of Wisconsin Studies in Language and Literature* 15. Madison: University of Wisconsin Press, 1922.

Turner, E. G. *Greek Papyri. An Introduction*. Princeton, NJ: Princeton University Press, 1968.

Vince, J. H. *Demosthenes,* vol. 1: *Orations,* I–XVII, XX. Loeb Classical Library. Reprint. Cambridge, MA: Harvard University Press, 1970.

_____. *Demosthenes,* vol. 3: *Orations,* XXI–XXVI. Loeb Classical Library. Reprint. Cambridge, MA: Harvard University Press, 1964.

Weichert, Valentin. *Demetrii et Libanii qui ferunter TYPOI EPISTOLIKOI et EPISTOLIMAIO CHARAKTERES.* Leipzig: B. G. Teubner, 1916.

Welles, C. Bradford. *Diodorus of Sicily,* vol. 8, books 16.66–95 and 17. Loeb Classical Library. Cambridge, MA: Harvard University Press, 1963.

_____. "The Role of the Egyptians under the First Ptolemies." Pp. 505–10 in *Proceedings of the Twelfth International Congress of Papyrology.* Toronto: A. M. Hakkert, 1970.

_____. *Royal Correspondence in the Hellenistic Period.* New Haven: Yale University Press, 1934.

Westermann, W. L. "An Egyptian Farmer." Pp. 171–90 in *University of Wisconsin Studies in Language and Literature* 3. Madison: University of Wisconsin Press, 1919.

_____. "On Inland Transportation and Communication in Antiquity." *Political Science Quarterly* 43 (1928): 364–87.

_____. "The Ptolemies and the Welfare of their Subjects." *American Historical Review* 43 (1937–38): 270–87.

White, John L. "Epistolary Formulas and Cliches in Greek Papyrus Letters." *Society of Biblical Literature 1978 Seminar Papers* 2 (1978): 289–319.

_____. *The Form and Structure of the Official Petition.* Missoula, MT: Scholars Press, 1972.

_____. "A Note on Zenon's Letter-Filing." *Bulletin of the American Society of Papyrologists* 3 (1976): 129–31.

_____. "Saint Paul and the Apostolic Letter Tradition." *Catholic Biblical Quarterly* 45 (1983): 433–44.

Wilcken, Ulrich. "Papyrus-Urkunden. I.PAmh II." *Archiv für Papyrusforschung und verwandte Gebiete* 2 (1903): 123f.

_____. "Papyrus-Urkunden (PLond III und BGU IV)." *Archiv für Papyrusforschung und verwandte Gebiete* 4 (1908): 567f.

_____. "Papyrus-Urkunden (*Recueil Champollion* s. 273ff.)." *Archiv für Papyrusforschung und verwandte Gebiete* 7 (1924): 298.

_____. *Urkunden der Ptolemäerzeit,* vol 1: *Papyri aus Unterägypten.* Berlin-Leipzig, 1927.

_____. "Zu den κάτοχοι des Serapeums." *Archive für Papyrusforschung und verwandte Gebiete* 6 (1920): 184–212.

Williams, W. Glynn. *Cicero. The Letters to his Friends.* Loeb Classical Library. 2 vols. Rev. ed. Cambridge, MA: Harvard University Press, 1943, 1954.

Winter, J. G. "In the Service of Rome: Letters from the Michigan Collection of Papyri." *Classical Philology* 22 (1927): 237–56.

_____. *Life and Letters in the Papyri.* Ann Arbor: University of Michigan Press, 1933.

Witkowski, Stanislaus. *Epistulae privatae graecae quae in papyris aetatis Lagidarum servantur.* 2d ed. Leipzig: B. G. Teubner, 1911.

Wolff, H. J. *Das Justizwesen der Ptolemäer.* Münchener Beiträge zur Papyrusforschung und antiken Rechtsgeschichte 44. Munich: C. H. Beck, 1962.

_____. "The Political Background of the Plurality of Laws in Ptolemaic Egypt." Pp. 313–18 in *Proceedings of the Sixteenth International Congress of Papyrology.* Chico, CA: Scholars Press, 1981.

Youtie, Herbert Chayyim. "The *Kline* of Sarapis." *Harvard Theological Review* 41 (1948): 9–29.

_____. "Parerga Papyrologia." *Transactions of the American Philological Association* 78 (1947): 105–22.

Ziemann, F. *De Epistularum Graecarum Formulis Sollemnibus Quaestiones Selectae.* Berlin: Haas, 1912.

Zilliacus, Laurin. *From Pillar to Post. The Troubled History of the Mail.* London: William Heinemann, 1956.

Antigrapheus
("controller") an official in the early Ptolemaic period responsible for examining the records of the oikonomos, the chief financial officer of the nome (administrative district).

Archidikastes
("chief judge") a Roman official in Alexandria with legal jurisdiction in civil suits, one of whose functions was to legalize contractual agreements, and who probably assisted the prefect in his legal duties.

Basiliko-grammateus
("royal scribe") chief assistant in the early Ptolemaic period of the oikonomos (chief financial official at the nome level) and from the third century BCE the chief assistant of the nome (district) strategos.

Chrematists
a board of judges in the Ptolemaic period who held court periodically in various local districts of Egypt (a board of assizes); in Roman times it refers to a tribunal in Alexandria.

Dioiketes
the king's minister of finance in Ptolemaic times, who was responsible for taxation, supervision of agricultural production, and so forth; in Roman times a financial administrator of more restricted scope. The title was also given to subordinate officials in both the Ptolemaic and Roman periods.

Dokimastes
("controller") an official in the third century BCE responsible for examining the records of the trapedzites.

Epimeletes
generally "superintendent" but a title of various officials at various periods.

Epistates
in Ptolemaic documents usually the head of the village or head of the village police.

Epistolographos
("letter writer") chancery secretary of the Ptolemaic court at Alexandria.

Epistrategos
governor over one of the three large administrative divisions of Roman Egypt (Lower, Middle, or Upper Egypt) but not a military commander.

Exegetes
("explicator," or "advisor") one of the metropolitan (municipal) magistrates during Ptolemaic and Roman rule; in Roman times the title is also applied to an Alexandrian official with certain judicial duties.

Hypomnematographos
("memoranda writer") chancery secretary at Alexandria under the Ptolemies but in Roman times usually an Alexandrian magistrate who assisted the prefect in his judicial functions.

Idios Logos
("Privy purse administrator") an administrator appointed directly by the emperor who shared the chief financial duties of Egypt with the prefect.

Juridicus
("pronouncer of law") a judge in Roman times who seems to have assisted the prefect and who probably had certain independent judicial duties.

Komarch
an official exercising various administrative functions at the village level and subordinate in authority to the toparch.

Komogrammateus
("village scribe") administrative secretary at the village level.

Nomarch
an official exercising various administrative duties at the nome (district) level.

Oikonomos
("steward") in the third century BCE the chief financial official of each administrative nome (district); by the second century BCE much of his responsibility was taken over by the strategos.

Prefect
the governor of Egypt in Roman times who, with the Idios Logos took over the Ptolemaic responsibilities of the dioiketes.

Sitologos
an administrative official concerned with agriculture, who received deliveries of grain and who recorded the amounts delivered and measured out for planting.

Strategos
the governor of a nome (administrative district); during Ptole-

225

maic rule he retained some of the military authority associated with the title but had only civil authority under Roman rule.

Toparch

an official performing various duties within one of the divisions of a nome, subordinate to the nomarch of the nome (district).

Topogrammateus

an administrative secretary with duties within a topos (division) of a nome (district).

Trapedzites

in Ptolemaic times the chief officer of the government bank in each of the nomes (administrative districts).

Index of Personal Names

233